Melody is the essence of music.

Mozart

This book is dedicated to the music inside you, always waiting to be heard.

Pattern Play

Volume 1-A: Melody

First Edition and First Printing

ISBN 0-9753959-0-4

Design, Layout, and Photos (except page 82)	Forrest Kinney
Project Guide	Akiko Kinney
Creative Advisor	Alfred Rordame
Cover Painting and Drawing for *Beethoven*	Phil Jensen
Painting for *Too Late Blues*	Peggy Rita
CD Recording and Mastering	Scott Levitin, Steve Crockett
Piano Technician	Chris Trivelas
Copyeditor	Bonnie Mortell
Printing	CDS Publications

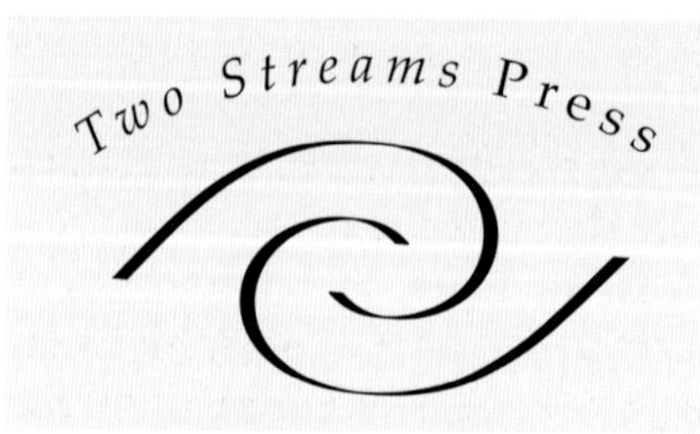

P.O. Box 1310
North Bend, WA 98045

Imagine!

Imagine you couldn't speak without reading aloud or reciting a book from memory. That without print, you were as mute as a stone. There would be no heart-to-heart conversations with friends, no long talks on the phone, no joking around. Whenever you wanted to say something to someone or even shout at a barking dog, you'd have to first read, rehearse, and recite the words of some famous author. How frustrating that would be! (And at times, simply ridiculous.) In such a situation, wouldn't you give almost anything to be able to spontaneously speak your own feelings, in your own words, in your own way?

If you are like most people who have learned to play the piano, this scenario is, unfortunately, not hard to imagine. You have been taught to read and recite the musical thoughts of others, but you probably can't speak or write your own feelings with the "words" of music. This book is for you if you feel the utter strangeness of this situation and are frustrated by it. This book is for you if you want to develop at the piano the same kinds of creative abilities you now have with words.

And Now, Here's a Different World

Imagine yourself sitting at your piano (or keyboard) in the near future, making new music effortlessly. The music expresses your mood and your mind in that very moment, and it is music that you have never heard before. This magic happens *every time* you sit at the piano.

You are able to create in any style, with any kind of chord, in any key, with any mode or scale. You can have deep musical conversations with your friends who play all kinds of other instruments. You can write musical essays using your favorite ideas, and make your own arrangements of popular melodies, just as the master composers did. You are able to do what you once only dreamed of. And best of all, imagine that you learned to do all this in a creative and enjoyable way, never having to perform mechanical exercises or study music theory in advance, always learning to create by actually *creating* at every step of the way.

In this scenario, making music is much more than a way of entertaining others. It is a way of realizing and expressing who we are. It becomes a celebration, revelation, meditation, consolation, diary, therapy, and hobby all rolled into one.

This can happen to you. Without a doubt! It has happened to me and to all my students who have had the desire to create their own music. The ability to spontaneously make new music is not reserved for a few rare geniuses. It is your right, as much as it is your right to speak new sentences each day. This may seem hard to believe now, but after a while, your new abilities at the piano will seem quite natural. Like me, you may even start to ask anyone who will listen, "Why doesn't everyone create music this way? This is what they mean when they say *playing* the piano!"

Contents

Introduction

If you want to start creating your own music right now, read the section *How To Play This Book* on pages 10 and 11 and then go directly to *World Piece* on page 17. The other pages are a general introduction to the *Pattern Play* way of making music and can be read later.

The section called *Doors to Infinity* describes what the *Pattern Play* books can offer you and why this series of books came to be. This section also explores why being a beginner at creating your own music (or practicing any art) is such a valuable state of being.

About the Pattern Play Books explains how these books work and how you can learn to create music as you learned to create with words. It gives an overview of all the books in the series, and explains the grand design and the guiding vision.

What Will I Need to Start? describes some mental attitudes that help ensure you will enjoy the surprising and uncertain process of creating what only you can create.

The last section, *Questions and Answers*, tries to answer the questions you might have as you begin this creative adventure.

Creating with Pentatonic Scales: Scales of the World

In the beginning, you create sounds and melodies using five-tone (Pentatonic) scales, mostly on black keys. Many people throughout the world create music with these scales. As you travel through these six pieces, you will be exploring the musical sounds of other countries. While doing so, you will be creating your own melodies, rhythms, and variations on the accompaniment patterns you are playing. Included in this section are ideas that will help you create more freely as you walk down the *Creator's Road*.

Creating with Major Scales: The Master Scale

In this section, you create melodies with the most popular scale in the Western world during the last three centuries—the Major Scale. Most familiar tunes and classical masterworks are made using the seven tones of this scale, with other tones sprinkled in for flavor. In this section, you can create with a number of musical patterns used by master creators such as Beethoven, Mozart, and Chopin.

Creating with Minor Scales: Moods and Emotions

In this section, you create with the second-most popular scale—the Minor Scale. Though it is known for its somber, introspective side, this scale has multiple personalities. It can be tough, brash, gentle, angry, cool, wistful, and much more. It sometimes alters its sixth and seventh notes to create different scales, allowing a much wider range of expression. In this section, you can explore some of this scale's many moods and emotions.

Creating with Blues Scales: The Scale for Modern Times

In this section, you create with the Minor Blues Scale. Since its birth in the songs of Africans living in America, this scale has spread far and wide, finding a home in many other styles of music because of its ability to express feelings that other scales simply cannot. This scale can be both cool and hot, sweet and sour, involved and detached, edgy and calm, all at the same time. This is a modern scale for modern times. Here, you can also learn to create with the much-neglected, good-natured Major Blues Scale.

Looking Ahead

The two pieces in this section introduce you to musical patterns explored in depth in later volumes of *Pattern Play*. These jazz pieces are more challenging than the others. If you find them too difficult, just listen to them on the CD to hear what your future may sound like. The last page in the book is the Index.

Doors to Infinity

Though this book appears to be a collection of short piano pieces, this is only a small part of the truth. These various pieces are really so many doors, all of them opening to reveal different kinds of music that can flow from your hands into the world.

Our creative abilities are infinite—roads dissolving into a distant horizon, two mirrors reflecting each other without end, skies filled with stars that live beyond time. The *Pattern Play* books offer a thousand pieces, each one allowing us to explore and celebrate another flavor of the unimaginable creative potential within us all.

As we learn to create our own music at the piano and explore our creative potentials, we discover many other valuable abilities along the way. We become able to spontaneously create music with other musicians. We can help others discover their unique music. We become better equipped to play, learn, and appreciate the works of the master composers. Above all, we develop the confidence to be who we truly are, creating our music and life according to our unique nature.

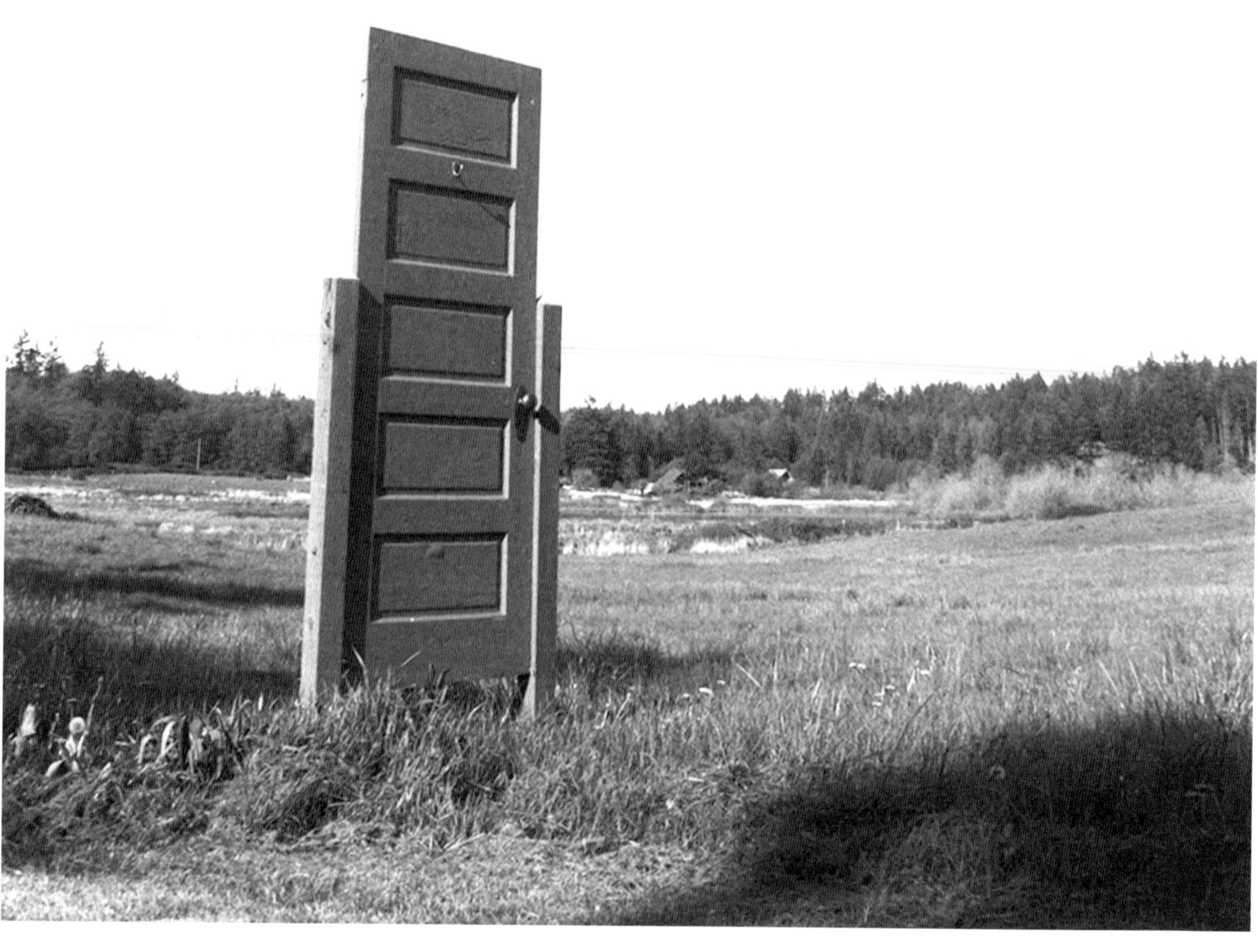

Something for Everyone

If you want to create your own music, what kind of music will that be? Jazz? These books have numerous doors that open into that world and allow you to create there. But there are *many* other doors to choose from!

You may want to create music that sounds like Chopin, Debussy, or some other classical composer. You may want to create pop music, new age, or folk. You may want to write your own songs with lyrics, and play them in a band. You may want to compose pieces for choirs, orchestras, or jazz bands. You may want to make your own arrangements of popular tunes, and be able to play them at public events. The various pieces in the *Pattern Play* books develop your ability to think and create as a composer and, by exploring many musical styles, take you in the direction of your own style. With these books, you will simultaneously gain an understanding of the patterns from which music is made and the creative potentials from which you are made.

The *Pattern Play* books have all kinds of pieces so you can find the ones that really interest you. The volumes are designed so that, even if you explore only three or four pieces in each main section, you will gain the essence of the book and will be able to move on to the next volume. This book is like a large table covered with foods from around the world, and you choose the ones that look the tastiest. Or it is like a store filled with many styles of shirts and shoes, and you choose those that fit you best. There's something here for everyone—every style, every level, every mood.

Some pieces may be too challenging for you to play at this time. This doesn't mean that you can't play them—each piece in this book can be played as a duet, either with your teacher, a musical friend, or perhaps even yourself on a recording. For example, many of my students have enjoyed the sound of the piece called *Endless Road*. However, the accompaniment of this piece is played with the right hand, and it is a challenge to create melodies with the left hand. So I usually play this piece with my students as a duet until they feel ready to do it on their own.

Being a Beginner

Though you have probably played piano long enough to be able to read music written by others, you may be a complete beginner when it comes to making your own music. This is a fine place to be! Though being a beginner has its awkward and frustrating moments, it's also where the most fun and excitement is. As a beginner, you get to experience the joy of creating music for the first time, and this usually brings a special and unrepeatable feeling of aliveness. It's no wonder young children often have a look of delight on their faces—their world is always fresh and surprising, happening for the first time. To be a beginner is to feel the excitement a traveler feels at the beginning of a long journey into foreign lands. This is why the poet Cesare Pavese could write, "The only joy is to begin."

The master of any art is a person who has acquired a wide range of skills but, most importantly, has never lost the excitement and fresh vision of a beginner. Such a person is forever willing to take on new challenges and learn new things. As you take the journey toward creating your own music, the challenge is always to keep this willingness to learn something new, no matter how skillful you become. The poet Rainer Maria Rilke once wrote that inspiration comes to us whenever we make the decision to "always start afresh: To be a beginner!" Each day, to open a new door, walk through, and start life all over again.

This is the real secret of the arts: Always be a beginner. —Shunryu Suzuki

About the *Pattern Play* Books

The *Pattern Play* books offer an enjoyable and natural way to learn how to compose, arrange (make your own versions of popular songs and pieces), and improvise (spontaneously create) music at the piano. Improvising is not only done in jazz styles! Perhaps the greatest improvisers in history were Bach, Beethoven, and Mozart—their ability to create "on the spot" is legendary.

This approach is most effective when used as a companion to the usual course of piano instruction. Then you will be able to play the amazing music of the masters, as well as create your own music.

How Does It Work?

In the *Pattern Play* way of making music, you learn to create melodies the same way you learned to make sentences. You will develop the same kind of creative powers with tones that you now have with words.

Each piece in this book introduces you to a new "word" of the musical language—I call this word a Pattern. Each Pattern is a short bit of music, stylish and easy to learn. You will sound good when playing it. After learning a short Pattern, you immediately begin to "speak" with it, creating your own musical sentences while being guided by suggestions. Over time, you create with hundreds of short Patterns and gain a large musical vocabulary capable of expressing anything you feel, alone or in conversations with other musicians. Simple Patterns grow into more complex musical Patterns naturally. At the same time, the common language of musical Patterns will grow into a more private language, able to express something uniquely your own.

Over time, just by playing Patterns and enjoying creating, you will learn to think like a composer, and become quite knowledgeable about music theory. After all, music theory is, in essence, the recognition of musical Patterns. You will become able to write musical essays (compose), tell familiar musical stories in your own, fresh way (arrange), and talk with tones (improvise). All this grows out of simply playing with Patterns. Musicians in many musical traditions all over the world learn to create music with just such an approach. It's natural, meaningful, and fun, all at the same time.

Overview of the Entire *Pattern Play* Series

This book is the first of many more to come. Together, these books form an encyclopedia of the Patterns that comprise the vast world of piano music. This is a *progressive* encyclopedia, first exploring more basic and common Patterns, and ending with complex and rare Patterns.

In this first book of the *Pattern Play* series,**Volume 1-A**, you learn to *improvise* (spontaneously create) your own melodies in diverse musical styles with the four most popular scales. This ability is the foundation for all that will follow. You will also learn to make your own variations on the given accompaniment patterns. In the companion volume to this book, **Volume 1-B**, *Melodies in All Keys,* you improvise melodies in many more styles in all the Major and Minor Keys, and begin to create your own accompaniment patterns out of intervals, the most basic elements of harmony.

While Volumes 1-A and 1-B are about creating your own melodies, Volumes 2-A and 2-B are about creating your own harmonies. In **Volume 2-A**, *Chords,* you learn how to create your own accompaniments with all the common chords in over thirty distinct ways and in a diverse array of musical styles. You also use this skills to *arrange*—that is, make your own piano pieces from popular melodies. In **Volume 2-B,** *Chords in All Keys,* you create and arrange with chords in all the Keys.

Overview of the Entire *Pattern Play* Series, continued

Once you have learned to create melodies with scales and accompaniments with chords, you are prepared to *compose* pieces. In *Pattern Play*, **Volume 3-A**, *Modes*, you learn to improvise and compose with all the materials you have learned so far, plus a variety of exotic scales known collectively as *modes*. As far as I'm concerned, modes are the best-kept secret in music because they are so amazingly expressive. In **Volume 3-B**, *Modes in All Keys*, you create with modes in all Key signatures, and create striking effects by moving between various modes in remote Keys. You begin to think and make decisions as a composer does, as well as expand your skills as an improviser and arranger.

In *Pattern Play*, **Volume Four**, *Seventh Chords in All Keys*, the exploration of harmony resumes. You learn to improvise, arrange, and compose with the various kinds of seventh chords in many diverse ways and styles, in all the Keys and modes.

Volume Five is an in-depth exploration of how to create with ninth, eleventh, and thirteenth chords—what I call "color chords." These are the harmonies used in much modern music, especially jazz. **Volume Six** returns to the exploration of melody, focusing on uncommon modes and scales, including some really strange and exotic ones. **Volume Seven** returns one last time to chords, and explores the ways that various notes within color chords can be altered. You will then be able to create your own music with the complex harmonies used in modern jazz and contemporary classical music.

In addition to these books, there will be one more which develops piano technique using the *Pattern Play* approach. Technique can be learned musically rather than mechanically. Creating is the key.

By the time you have finished playing Volume 2-A, you will know enough about music to create new music every day for the rest of your life. Each volume beyond 2-A adds a new dimension to your playing, another layer of understanding. This is a journey of many years, a journey of endless discovery. It is not a question of advancing quickly through the volumes and becoming accomplished, but of enjoying the discoveries made each day, watching the music and your creativity grow. It's also not a question of how many doors are opened, but of enjoying opening a new door each time we play, revealing another one behind it, and so on, with no end to the delight in making new discoveries.

My Vision

A vision guides me as I create the *Pattern Play* books. I imagine a world where people are encouraged to practice music (or any art) in such a way that they learn to be true to their unique selves and discover the music that they alone can create. I imagine confident, creative, and happy people, able to explore and express their gifts. I also see a world where people of all kinds can come together to speak the language of music freely with one another, either in private conversations or at great international festivals of music. I imagine people sharing music that is not rehearsed, but created together in that moment, always a revelation, forever fresh.

I am hoping that these books will spark a renaissance of spontaneously made music and restore a lost tradition. After all, every notable composer (except Wagner) from Bach until the dawn of the 20th century was a great improviser at the keyboard: Mozart, Beethoven, Chopin, Liszt, Brahms, and Debussy, to mention just a few of the biggest names. The music of these composers was profound because their connection to the piano was deep and strong, developed through years of spontaneous creating. My hope is that our musical language will once again become a profound, *living language* that is not only read but created fresh every day. Above all else, I am hoping that people everywhere will experience the amazing joy of creating what only they can create.

The only joy is to create! —Frederic Delius, composer

How To Play This Book

Authors create with words while painters create with paints. What do pianists create with? *Patterns* of tones. Each piece in this book offers at least one new Pattern to create with. There are just two steps to take in learning to create with all the Patterns in this book, and a few other things to keep in mind.

Step One Learn the Pattern and the Vacation by memory.

There are thirty-two pieces in this book, and each one has a measure or two (occasionally more) marked **Pattern.** Play this Pattern, and memorize it right away. If you don't read music yet, have your teacher read the Pattern and teach it to you. When you know a Pattern *by heart*, then there is room in your mind for creative ideas to come in and play. When we are busy thinking about *how to* play Patterns, we can't play, and it is only when we are *playing* with Patterns that we can feel the joy of being a creator.

Each piece has another measure or group of measures named **Vacation**. A Vacation is a Pattern that contrasts with the main Pattern, and can be played whenever you feel you want to take a break from playing the main Pattern. Learn the Vacation by memory too. Now you're ready to create music.

Step Two Create with the Pattern and the Vacation.

While playing the Pattern over and over with one hand, create melodies and sounds with the other. Generally, it's best to begin creating on just a few keys so you don't have to move your hand around. This makes it much easier to coordinate the two sides of the body. As you continue to create melodies, feel free to vary the way you play the accompaniment Patterns.

Important note: Every single repeat sign in this book means *repeat as many times as you like*. It doesn't mean *repeat once* as it does in other music books. So repeat a Pattern four times or four hundred times as you create with it. Play it over and over without shame. This is the natural way to learn and also—once we get over our learned resistance to it—the most enjoyable way to learn.

What about beginnings and endings?

A good way to begin a piece is to play the Pattern a few times by itself. This sets the mood and helps us settle into the music and our feelings. As for endings, when we are improvising, endings are to be discovered as we go along. We may lose interest in what we are doing and just stop. Our creation may die with a whisper, or it may end with a bold and triumphant exclamation point. Sometimes we may end with the Pattern, other times with the Vacation. The phone may ring and this may be the end of the piece. Each time we create with a Pattern, the piece and the ending can be different.

How can I make longer pieces?

Most music is made using two main sections (an *A* and a *B* section, or a verse and a chorus), which alternate any number of times. If we move between a Pattern and its Vacation many times, we can create a long piece using just these two short patterns. Many pieces in this book have more than one Pattern and one Vacation, allowing us to move between all of them to make more complex pieces.

Should I play all the pieces in the book?

Feel free to skip over pieces that are over your head or don't capture your interest. Perhaps come back to them later. Focus on the pieces you find exciting, mysterious, or beautiful. When we love playing a Pattern, it will be full of life, and grow into something unique. Unbelievable creativity comes whenever we feel an intense love for what we are doing.

In general, the pieces get harder as you move through a section, and the pieces in the back of each section are clearly for more advanced players. If you want to play these pieces, just make them into a duet and play with a pianist friend or with your teacher. Though you may skip many pieces, I suggest trying to play all of them in some way (solo or duet) at least for a little while. I also suggest reading through the text in all the pieces to learn the concepts. These ideas may be useful in the other pieces.

Should I work on just one piece at a time?

Most people seem to enjoy working on two, three, or even four pieces at any one time. Work on as many as you need in order to keep your imagination stimulated and your interest level high.

How long should I stay with one piece? Should I try to finish it?

I think of my favorite pieces in this book as friends. When do we "finish" a friendship? Friendships can last as long as we are interested in keeping them going. It's the same with these pieces. The Patterns can grow into new music as long as we are willing to grow along with them. Resist the urge to "finish" a piece by playing it in one final way. Allow these pieces to be different each time.

Some Patterns in this book may really grab you, and you may want to explore them for a long time. These are the ones that will grow into your own way of making music. When you find such a Pattern, explore all the suggestions given on the pages following the Pattern. These suggestions reveal a few of the endless possibilities of expression that wait within every Pattern.

These Patterns are, by nature, open-ended. They may never be "finished" because they can always be reshaped by the uniqueness of each moment. Whereas most music is *done*, these Patterns act as if they are made of curious water, forever unformed and unfinished, always molding themselves to the contour of the land over which they are flowing. The more we play these Patterns, the more they are shaped by our hands and our feelings, gradually becoming something entirely our own.

Is it okay to change the way I play the Patterns and Vacations?

Yes, yes, yes! This is the main difference between this book and most other music books. In other books, you are *not* supposed to change any of the notes. In this book, you are *supposed* to change all the notes eventually! Your own music is going to slowly grow out of these Patterns, so let the Patterns change into your own music. These Patterns are just words of a musical language growing inside you. As you learn more and more Patterns, you will find that you can mix them up and change them in endless ways to express how you feel each day. With this said, I think it is generally a good idea to learn the Patterns and Vacations as written *first*, before you change them.

Notes are lifeless and rigid, sitting in the same place on the same page year after year, until the books that hold them finally become dust or ash. But music is something alive! Music is made of tones that like to change in midair and disappear from our ears the moment we hear them. Musical tones make a river, while notes are like stones. The art is to let the tones of our own music gradually erode and change the shape of every note in this book.

What Will I Need to Start?

A Piano or...

An electronic piano, synthesizer, organ, accordion—any instrument with a keyboard attached. In this book, I write as if you were playing a piano, but any keyboard will do.

The Ability to Read Music, or a Music Teacher

To use this book, you will need to know how to read piano music at a basic level, or be working with a teacher who can show the Patterns to you. You don't have to be experienced at reading music because, most of the time, you will be playing the Patterns from memory while creating with them.

A Desire to Create Your Own Music

The secret to being a creator is to have a great passion for whatever we are doing. Mother Teresa once wrote, "We can do no great things—only small things with great love." If we have a great love for creating music, that's all we will ever need. Everything else follows from that.

Other than these three essentials, there is nothing else you need to be able to create. This includes talent, good hands, long hair, or coordination. However, you will be helped enormously if you adopt certain attitudes. We need to bring the following attitudes to our piano to be a happy creator.

No Judgments

Judgments may have a place at the end of a project, but not at the beginning. Just as we don't judge infants for making grammatical errors, we cannot fairly judge ourselves for our early efforts. Judgments pull seeds out of the ground, which if just left alone, would grow into trees with delicious fruits. Each time you touch a piano to create your own music, let all judgments be dissolved.

Trust

At first, you may wonder how you are ever going to find your own music. Trust that unique music is waiting inside you to be discovered, and this music will guide you in its direction every time you sit at the piano. As you continue to play, you will find that the piano, the moment, your feelings, and an inner knowing will all guide you to the music that only you can make. Until we see the proof of this process, we have to trust that it is unfolding. Chopin and Beethoven trusted their musical instincts, and this is how they left us with such unique music. No one but Beethoven could possibly know how to make Beethoven's music. Trust that your own music waits for you.

No Comparisons

The music of the master composers is so amazing that it is easy (and common) to feel small for wanting to create our own music, and then retreat into silence once again. Yet, this is a strange attitude. Do we quit speaking just because Shakespeare was so much better at it? Do we quit running, skiing, and riding bikes just because Olympic athletes do it so much better than we ever will? No, of course not! So why is it so different with music? To create happily, we can't compare ourselves with the master composers and worry about whether we are "good enough." We will be good enough whenever we care about what we do.

No Comparisons (continued)

The *Pattern Play* way of making music is more like talking, while the usual way of making music is like reading aloud. When we talk, we don't worry about sounding as good as our favorite authors. We speak to express something, to converse, to communicate, to discover, not to sound masterful. The experience of saying something is what is important, more than the way in which it is said. And that's the case with this way of making music. Even if the music itself is not "great," the experience of creating music may well be a great one.

The music you will be creating with this book will generally be more repetitive than the classical music or jazz you have played and heard. This is the nature of speech—it is more redundant than text. When we write down our ideas, they can be rewritten many times before they are finalized, so there is less rambling and repetition in essays and musical scores. The moral is that we can't compare our spontaneous creations with music that has been written—they are quite different. So be repetitive, especially in the beginning. The more you repeat Patterns, the more they will become a part of you.

Patience

In my many years of helping others to create, I've seen many problems come and go. These problems are almost all caused by impatience. People try to create with Patterns before they've really learned them well enough. Or they try to create complex music before they can. What's the rush? An artistic experience arises when we can *play* with a Pattern—if we are struggling with it or pushing it around, there is no art. Remember: It takes time to learn to speak any language, and the music of the piano is a complex language. Patience is the key. Things will eventually come our way, but often they just come slower than we had hoped!

A quick way to gain patience is to put aside expectations. If you have read music for a while, you probably are expecting that you should immediately sound like that when creating. Not so! Being able to read music is not the same thing as being able to "speak" it. It's an entirely different process, and may take some time to learn. So don't expect that just because you can read music, you should immediately be able to create your own music at the same level. That's not being fair to yourself.

Lots of Mistakes

Printed music has a curious and powerful effect on the mind. Because it is fixed and unchanging, it breeds the idea that this is the nature of music, and this discourages us from wanting to go through the messy process of learning to "speak." All the mistakes we make! As a result, the language of classical music has become something like Latin, a mother tongue to no one, a language that people read but no longer speak. It is becoming more and more like the print in which it has been captured—fixed in time, no longer growing and alive. Let's bring it back to life!

To learn to speak, we must make a million mistakes. Sorry! That's a requirement! With each mistake, we learn more. Mistakes are evidence that we are taking the necessary risks to learn our own way. Though we may find mistakes annoying, we may as well learn to love them.

A Willingness to Keep Growing

There will forever be a new Pattern to be found, a new melody to discover, a new way to play. A true creator never loses his or her curiosity, passion, and willingness to pursue new adventures. A true creator takes even the greatest difficulties and frustrations as challenges to grow. May you always have these companions on a creative journey that never ends.

Questions and Answers

With this book, will I learn how to create melodies?

Yes, but this book will not tell you exactly how to make melodies. Instead, it will give you the means to spontaneously discover your own, personal melodies. That's where the fun and meaning is. If we make melodies according to a formula, we can't discover the true joy of creating something unique. And so, this is an intuitive approach to making music rather than an analytical one.

How will I learn to be original by borrowing your ideas?

We usually think that originality means not borrowing ideas from others. But don't we borrow words from others to learn a language, and then speak our own ideas? So feel free to borrow musical Patterns to be able to create your own musical ideas. Patterns, like words, belong to us all.

Who should I say composed the music I create with these Patterns?

The Patterns in this book are just "pieces of pieces." You are the one who makes whole creations out of them. In many cases, you are the composer. I supplied the words and you made the sentences. In some cases, it might be more accurate to think of your creations as "co-creations" with me.

Can I play the Patterns with other musicians?

Yes! Definitely! It's often the best way to play them. Invite your musical friends over to play these Patterns with you. Some pieces in this book are on black keys. Though black keys are easier for pianists to play when learning to create melodies, it won't be as easy for your friends who play other instruments. You could tell them: "You flute players (trumpet, sax, whatever) only have to think about one note at a time, while piano players have to think about many at once! Though it's a strange Key for you, just play more slowly, holding tones longer." This argument will usually win them over.

Some instruments are *transposing* instruments. This means that when your friends play music written in the Key of C on some other instruments, the tones they play actually *sound* in another Key. For example, your friends may be reading and playing *c*, but the sound they make on their trumpet is *b flat*. To sound in the same Key as you, they have to *transpose* (change) to a different Key.

If your friends play a flute, oboe, violin, viola, cello, bass, harp, guitar, or trombone, these are C instruments. Your friends can read the same notes as you and sound in the same Key. However, if your friends play trumpet, tenor saxophone, soprano saxophone, or clarinet, these are B-Flat instruments. This means you hear them playing *b flat* when they are reading and playing *c*. To play in your Key, they have to play up a whole step. If you are in C Major, they have to play in D Major, and if you are in G-Flat, they have to play in A-Flat. If your friends play alto saxophone, this is an E-Flat instrument. Have them play in the Key three half steps below the Key you are playing in. If you are in C Major, they need to create in A Major. If you are in G-Flat Major, they will play in E-Flat Major.

Encourage others to play the piano with you, even if they have never done it before. If they resist, say, "Just make sounds using black keys." Use the word "sounds" rather than "melodies" or "music" because the thought of making "melodies" or "music" might scare a non-musician, whereas anyone can make "sounds." Encourage others to just explore without worrying about whether it sounds good or not. It usually will, creating a good time for all.

What about moving the Patterns to other Keys?

It's a great idea, if you know how. I limited this book to just four Keys, the ones that are easiest to create with in the beginning. (On the next page, I explain why I capitalize the word "Keys" in these books.) I encourage you to venture out into the other Keys you know. There is a companion book to this one,Volume 1-B, that has pieces in all the other Major and Minor Keys. It also explains how to move a Pattern from one Key to another. Once you know how to do this, then you can transpose any Pattern in this book into any other Key. This will not only develop your ears and mind, but it will give you lots of new ideas. Each Pattern sounds different when transposed to other Keys and feels different when played on different piano keys. These differences give you new inspirations.

Most instruments of the world—nearly all folk instruments—are tuned to just one Key. If you want to play an Irish penny whistle, for example, you need to buy a number of them to play in different Keys. The piano, as you know, can play in all Keys. This is wonderful, but it makes learning the piano much more challenging. I think it is wise to learn the piano as other musicians learn their instruments, by becoming quite familiar with one Key (scale) at a time. When a Key becomes "second nature," that's when we can become creative with it.

Should I try to remember my ideas?

As you play with the musical patterns in this book, you will discover musical ideas that you really like. Should you try to remember them? Should you try to play the piece the same the next day, or let it be new and different each day? I suggest that you don't make an effort to remember your ideas, at least not for now. Instead, try to create new music each time, discovering the music of each unique moment. When our minds are full of yesterday's music, there's no room for the music of today. Taking this approach will develop your creative powers more fully.

Now and then, you will have an especially striking idea. Perhaps this is an idea to record or write down and develop into a true composition, a musical essay. But generally speaking, writing musical essays should come later on, after you have learned how to speak music with ease. If you want to keep a record of your best ideas, you could start a musical diary. Buy a recorder, and begin recording the striking ideas that emerge from your daily creations. When you want to compose pieces later, you will have a large supply of good ideas on hand. That's how I created the music in these books.

How should I use the recording that comes with this book?

I debated about whether I should include a CD of improvisations with this book. In the end, I decided to do it because I wanted to suggest how much music could be made out of what may appear to be just short and simple Patterns. I wanted you to hear what these pieces could sound like and how Patterns could grow and change, especially if you don't have a teacher who can play these pieces for you. I also wanted you to have ideas to copy, because imitating is how we begin learning any art. Feel free to copy my ideas at first. This way, you will have some seeds to start growing your own garden.

The drawback of having a recording is that you may come to think the pieces "should" sound a certain way. Not so! Though these pieces are in distinct musical styles, they sound different each time I play them, and that is precisely why I enjoy them so much. Sometimes I will play a piece one way, and the next day I will play it at half the tempo and half the volume! I don't want my creations to set a standard because we all are to develop our own ever-changing style. I only hope my improvisations inspire you to develop your own creative potentials. I suggest playing the pieces before listening to the CD, so that you are not locked into my conceptions. Then listen to the CD to give you ideas, inspiration, and a sense of the different personalities of these pieces. Play the Patterns slower or faster than I play them, louder or softer, sweeter or more sour—however you like!

What if I'm not very good at coming up with ideas?

I wasn't good either at first, but now I hardly know what to do with all the new ideas that visit me each day. Give yourself a fair chance—two years or so! Just stay with it, and the ideas will come.

If you are having a hard time coming up with new melodic ideas, it usually means that you don't know the Pattern well enough yet. Once we learn a Pattern well, it likes company and will invite new melodies over to play. Other times, we are "blocked" simply because we try to do too much too soon. Simplify. Slow down. Ideas will come.

Many approaches to creating new melodies are sprinkled throughout this book. Here are two I didn't mention elsewhere: Say a short sentence aloud a few times, and then borrow the rhythm of the sentence to make a new melody. Another approach is to significantly change the tempo of the Pattern—this can often stimulate a new group of melodic ideas.

Why is the book notated this way?

You may wonder why I hardly ever write the two hands together in this book. This is to encourage you to learn and play the Patterns and Vacations by memory. It is when we know the Patterns "by heart" that something new and creative can happen.

Why say "right side" rather than "right hand"?

I often use the terms "right side" and "left side" where other people would say "right hand"and "left hand." Why? When we are creating our own music, we don't just create with our hands. Our whole body (and soul) plays the piano. When we are creating, we feel that both sides of our body are fully involved, feeling electric and alive. Awareness flows through every nerve. Saying "right side" rather than "right hand" is a way of reminding ourselves to ask, "Am I playing with my whole self or just from my knuckles down? Are my wrists flexible? Are my forearms tight?" Tightness blocks the flow of inspiration in the body. The more we play the piano in a relaxed, flowing way, the more inspired is the music that flows through us.

Why capitalize the words Major, Minor, and Keys?

To be more clear. In music, "major" and "minor" are overworked adjectives, used to distinguish different chords, scales, keys, and intervals. This can (and does) cause confusion. For example, it is common to think that we create in a Minor Key while playing a minor chord, but more often we are to create melodies in a Major Key while playing a minor chord. To help avoid these sorts of confusions, I use minor and major in the lower case when talking about intervals and chords (which I do a lot in the following volumes) and capitalize these words when talking about Keys. As for the word "key," I capitalize this word when used with Major and Minor because it is then becomes part of a unit, and this also distinguishes Keys from the actual keys of the piano.

What if I have other questions?

You can write to me at the address on page 2. Or, after December of 2004, you can send an e-mail to me at: *www.patternplay.com*. I may not be able to write back right away, but I'll respond eventually. I would enjoy hearing of your experiences with this book. I would especially appreciate any suggestions you might have on how to make my books more helpful to you. Enjoy creating!

Creating with Pentatonic Scales

Musicians throughout history have created music with scales that have five tones within each octave. Since *Penta* is the Greek word meaning "five" and *tonic* means "tone,"such scales are called *pentatonic* scales. Historians tell us that pentatonic scales occurred in nearly every ancient culture, whether in Africa, the South Seas, North America, China, or Scotland. They are still used today all over the world, and are especially common in Asia, Africa, and the folk music of European cultures.

By playing on black keys, you can create the two most common pentatonic scales—the Major Pentatonic and the Minor Pentatonic. In this section of the book, you can create with these two scales plus a strange and beautiful pentatonic scale from ancient Japan, played here on white keys.

Many people have the notion that black keys are hard to play. On the contrary! They are much easier than white keys when it comes to learning how to create melodies. This is because black keys always make melodic sounds when played together. They have acquired the undeserved reputation of being difficult because they are generally harder to *read*. However, they are really only harder to read when white and black keys are all mixed together—then it can be hard to keep track of what keys to play. In all but one of the pieces in this section of the book, black keys alone are used for creating. The five flats in the Key signature simply mean that you play all five notes of the scale on black keys. Since every note you see says, "play a black key," there's no confusion!

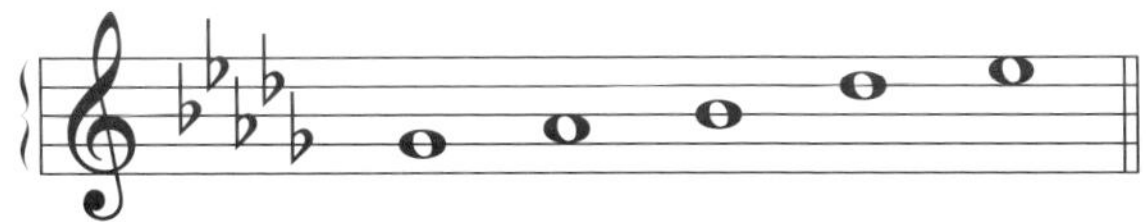

The Creator's Road

Between most of the pieces in this section, you will see pictures of road signs accompanied by short essays. These essays discuss issues that may arise as you start making your own music and begin walking down what I call *The Creator's Road.* If you are not interested in the topics they discuss, feel free to skip over them or come back to them later. Though these ideas can help your creative ideas flow, they are not essential to the flow of the book.

World Piece

Each piece in this book offers you new Patterns from which you can create your own music. This music may eventually take the form of compositions, improvisations, songs, or arrangements. Here, you begin creating melodies and rhythms using two of the most popular scales in the world. You will also be using the most popular accompaniment pattern in the world. I'm referring to the sound of a *fifth*. A fifth is made whenever you play a pair of keys written five lines and spaces apart. Fifths have a distinctive sound that is perfect for accompanying melodies.

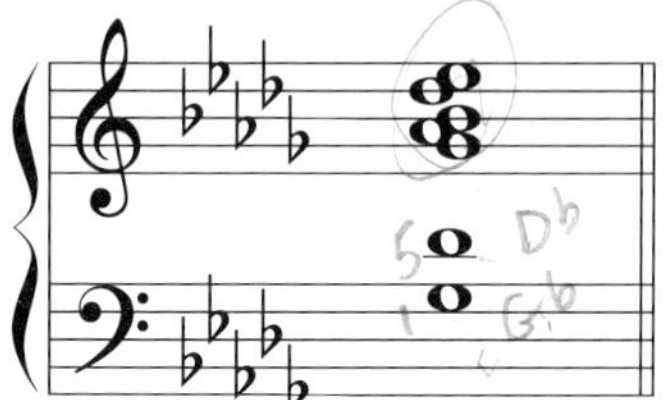

To begin: Press down the sustain pedal and play these notes, feeling the shapes your hands make. You are playing a *fifth* with your left hand and all the five notes of a *Major Pentatonic Scale* with your right hand. Your right hand is molded to what I call a "five-key Hand Shape." Now play any of these five keys individually to make simple melodies and sounds. Continue to play the fifth on your left side, repeating it as often as you like.

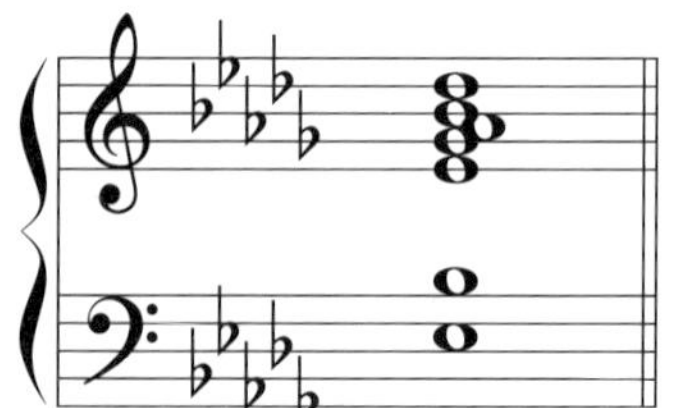

Now do the same thing with these new notes. Press down the pedal and feel these shapes. Your left hand is again playing a fifth while your right hand is playing the tones in a *Minor Pentatonic Scale*. Create melodies using this new five-key Hand Shape. As you will see (hear) in the pages to come, these simple scales are at the core of our musical tradition. Our most popular scales have grown out of them.

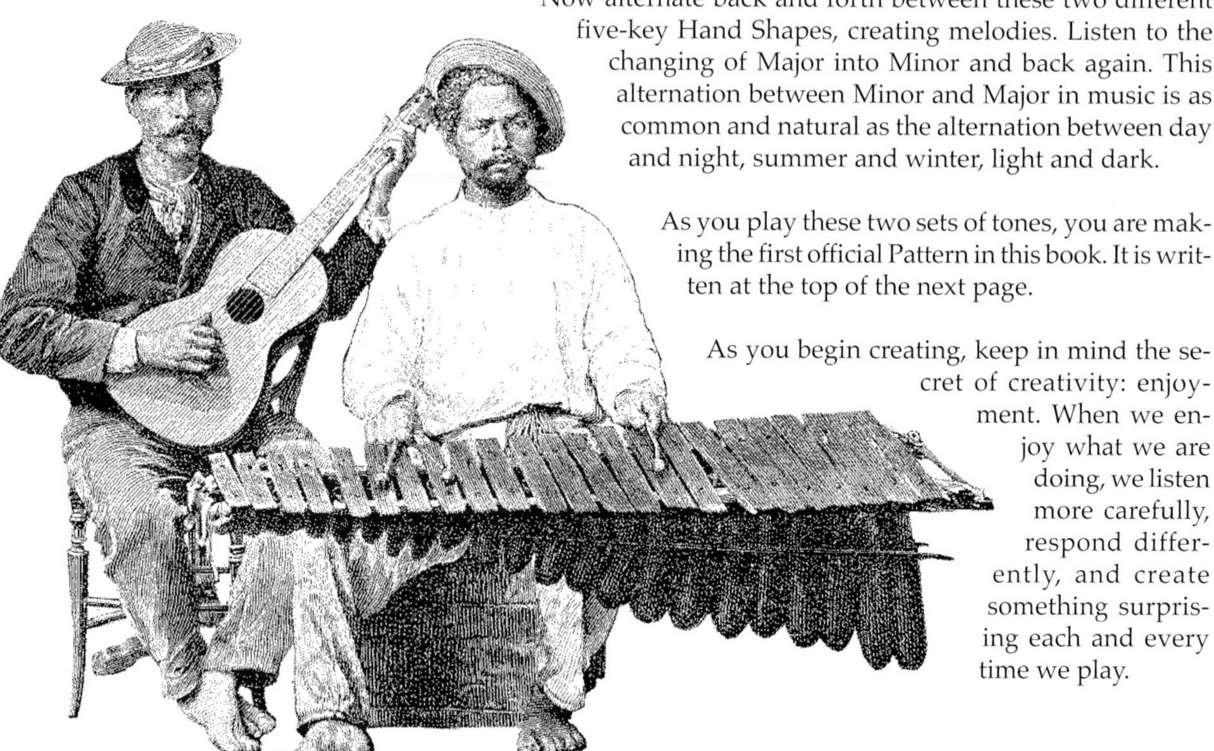

Now alternate back and forth between these two different five-key Hand Shapes, creating melodies. Listen to the changing of Major into Minor and back again. This alternation between Minor and Major in music is as common and natural as the alternation between day and night, summer and winter, light and dark.

As you play these two sets of tones, you are making the first official Pattern in this book. It is written at the top of the next page.

As you begin creating, keep in mind the secret of creativity: enjoyment. When we enjoy what we are doing, we listen more carefully, respond differently, and create something surprising each and every time we play.

Pattern

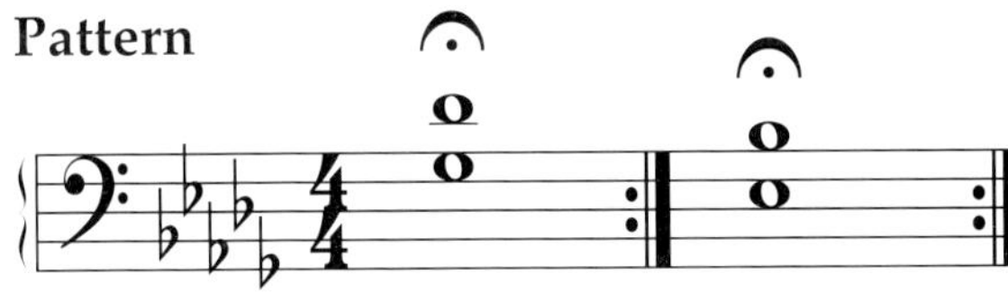

The *fermatas* mean to hold the notes as long as you like. Remember: *Every* repeat sign in this book means "repeat as many times as you like." You may also repeat the whole Pattern as many times as you like.

Vacation

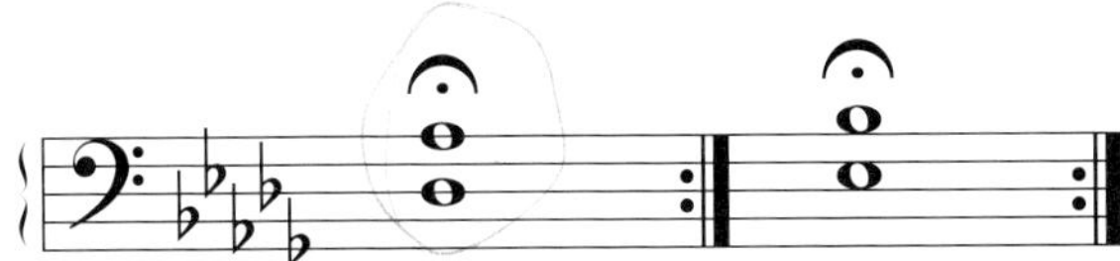

In this book, every Pattern has a Vacation. Vacations have sounds that contrast with the Pattern. After playing them, the Pattern will sound fresh again. Repeat the cycle of Pattern and Vacation as many times as you like, perhaps varying the way you play them.

Other Fifths to Try

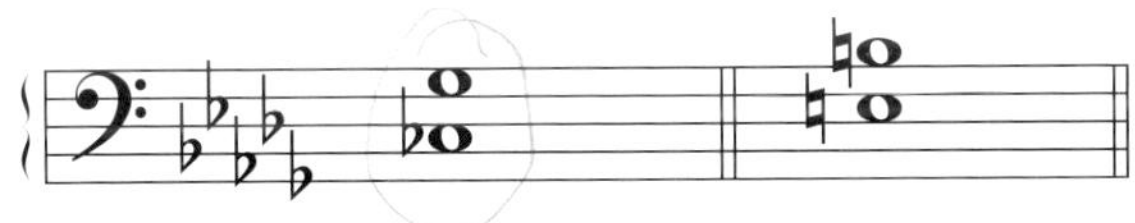

Though you may prefer to accompany with just black keys, here are two fifths that use white keys. These sound good with the Pentatonic scale even though they aren't a part of it. Make your own Vacations using these fifths and the black-key fifths shown above.

Ideas for Melody Making

- In addition to the five-key Hand Shapes for the right hand shown on the previous page, there are others that can be made on black keys. Find these, and then create melodies using all these Hand Shapes, moving all over the upper part of the keyboard. It's a good idea to keep your hand in a Hand Shape when creating melodies, even when you are pressing just one key. This is so you won't have to look and reach for keys all the time. This way, keys will be "on hand," right there when you need them. Your playing will flow.

- Give both your hands a new job. Play the accompaniment Pattern on your right side, and make melodies on the left. To do this, you could play the Pattern as written, or play it an octave higher than written. If you are a member of the human race, you will probably find this a bit awkward at first because your left side is not used to playing melodies. Try creating with the lowest black keys on the piano—now you have marked out the entire black-key domain.

- When making melodies, try playing pairs of keys at once, some close together and others far apart, listening to the different sounds they make. Try playing three keys at once, and even four and five.

- If your hand is big enough to do it comfortably, create with five-key Hand Shapes that skip over one black key. For example, you might play *g flat,* skip over *a flat,* and then play *b flat, d flat, e flat,* and *g flat.*

- In general, play with your eyes closed as much as possible.

Different Friendships Between Tones

Each different melody tone makes a different kind of friendship with the fifth in the accompaniment. Though at first these friendships might not sound very different, they will after a while. Just as a painter learns to see shades of color that other people cannot see, you will begin to hear differences between the tones that you couldn't hear yesterday. So, as you play, *listen* to the different relationship that each melody note has with the same accompaniment Pattern. From such listening, new ideas will come, and new melodies will be born.

Accompaniments Change Too

Until now, your right side has been doing most of the creating, making melodies by playing the individual keys of the five-key Hand Shapes. However, you can also be creative with your left hand. Play the fifths in different ways to make new accompaniment Patterns. On these two pages are twelve new accompaniment Patterns, all of which are Variations on the fifths in the original Pattern. All the Patterns in this book can eventually change like this to reflect your own unique tastes and desires. This is what is supposed to happen! It will occur naturally if you allow it.

Pattern Variation One

This Pattern is the same as Pattern One except the music now has a heartbeat, a pulse. Feel a steady beat, and hold each sound for four beats. Play the Vacation in the same way.

Pattern Variation Two

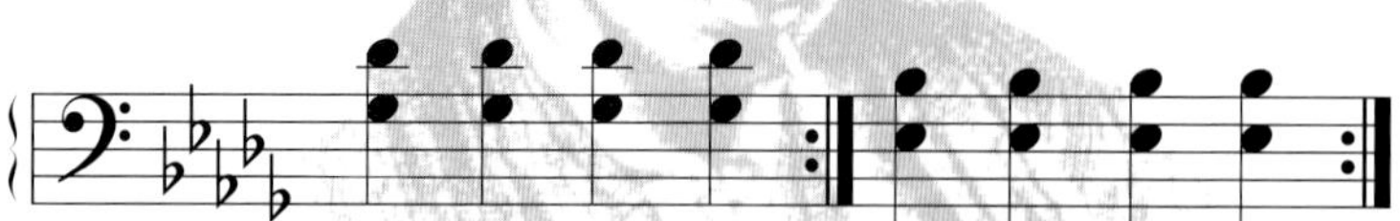

With Variation One, you could *feel* a beat but you couldn't *hear* it in the accompaniment. With this Pattern, you can now hear each of the four beats in each measure.

Pattern Variation Three

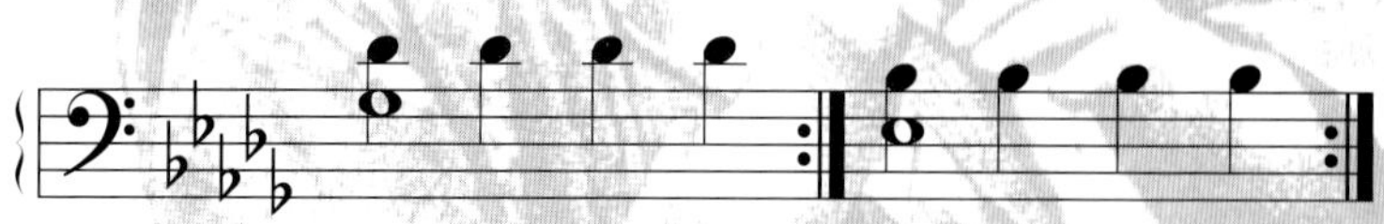

This is my favorite Variation on the Pattern because it has the rhythmic movement of Variation Two without the heaviness of the repeated fifth.

Pattern Variation Four

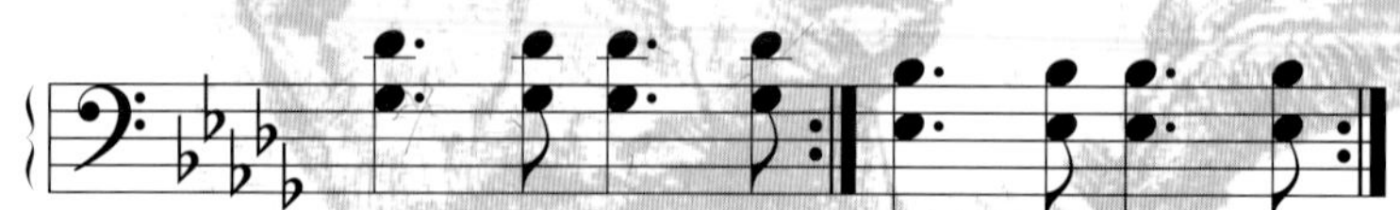

As you start adding melodies above this, create melodies in the same rhythm at first. You'll find you are able to create melodies much more easily.

Pattern Variation Five

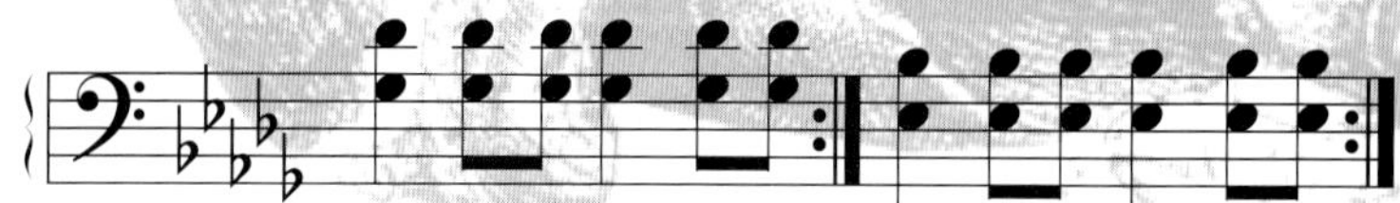

Like the previous Pattern, this one creates a satisfying rhythm by alternating regularly between slower notes and quicker notes.

Pattern Variation Six

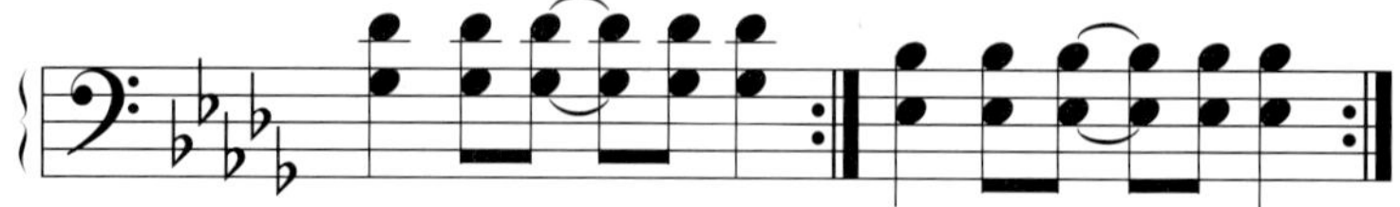

This Variation features a syncopated rhythm. Once again, create melodies in the same rhythm at first.

Mix and Match

You can move between these various Pattern Variations as you play. The piece you end up creating will be a large pattern of Patterns. Keeping the same underlying beat will hold everything together, and also make the rhythmic differences between the Variations more clear and interesting.

All these Variations can be played on your right side while you make melodies on your left. Try playing the Pattern an octave higher to make more room for the melodies. To make duets: One person plays the Patterns while adding *g flat* or *e flat* down in the bass while the other creates melodies.

Pattern Variation Seven

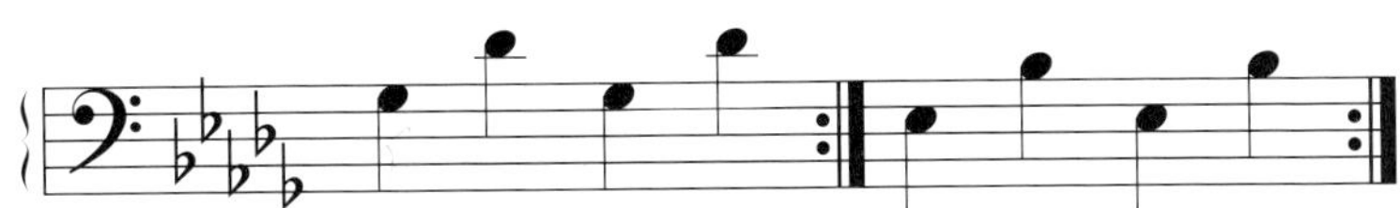

Why always play the notes of the fifth together? Play this Pattern at different speeds for different effects. Slow down, speed up.

Pattern Variation Eight

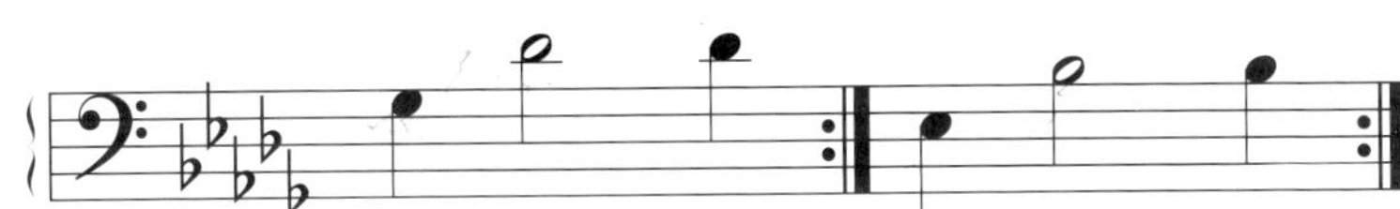

Try playing this Pattern as written, and then shift to *cut time.* (Play it twice as fast as written here.) Then it will feel like dance music.

Pattern Variation Nine

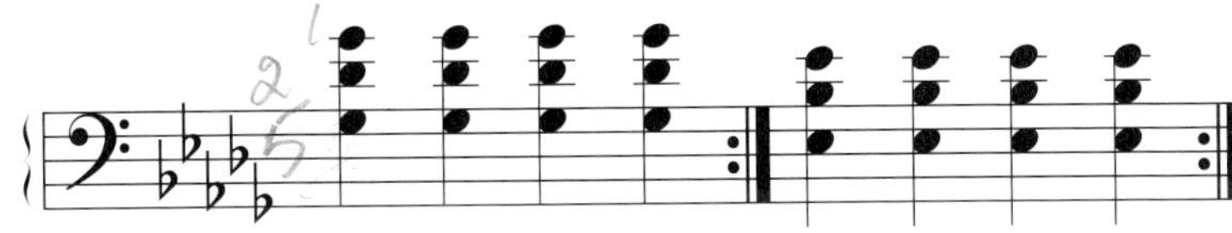

To create more Variations, add the key that is an octave above the lowest note of each fifth. If your hand won't reach, just play these notes one at a time, as shown below.

Pattern Variation Ten

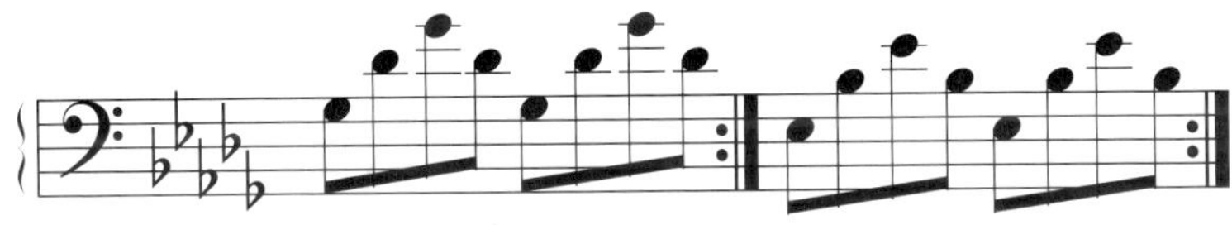

In this Variation, Variation Nine is broken up to create a new Pattern of flowing eighth notes. Try sustaining some of the notes to make your own rhythmic variations on this.

Pattern Variation Eleven

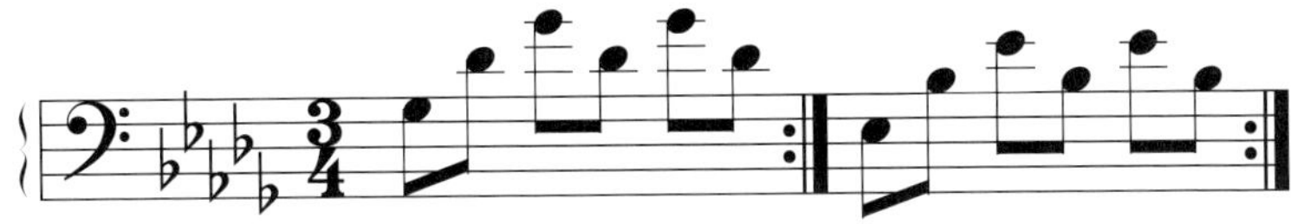

All the Variations so far have been in 4/4. Here's a Variation in 3/4, and below is a Variation in 6/8.

Pattern Variation Twelve

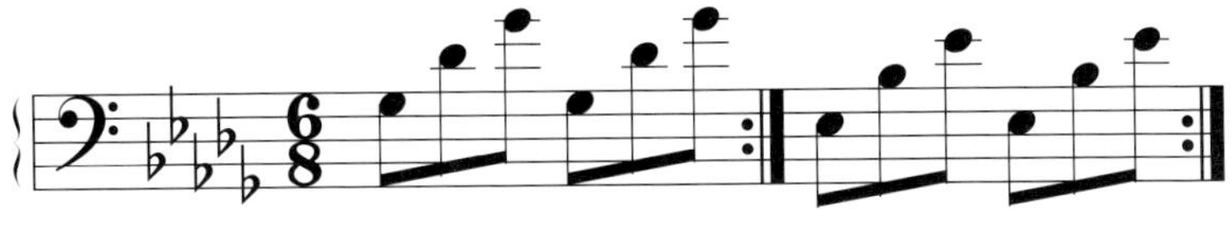

All these Variations can be played up or down an octave, louder or softer, faster or slower, energetically or lazily, and so on. Keep exploring. I'm out of room on this page.

Playing Different Rhythms at the Same Time

As your accompaniment Patterns become more complex, you will probably begin to ask questions that every pianist asks sooner or later: "How do I get the two sides of my body to play together? How can I play two different rhythms at the same time?" The greatest challenge for most pianists is to play one rhythm in one hand while playing a different rhythm in the other. Fortunately, there are ways.

When is it possible for two people of different cultures to live and play together? Isn't it when they feel something in common with one another? When I feel that you and I share similar pains and dreams, that we spin together on the same little blue planet in the vastness of space, then I feel a kindness toward you and a respect for your different ways of living.

It's the same with the two sides of our body. When they feel united by a common beat, they can work and play together. The more our two sides feel connected by a strong beat, the more they can play in their own way and not lose the feeling of togetherness.

Here's a way to strongly feel the beat that is unbeatable. (Now that's a strange sentence!) As you play the example below, feel both your arms moving up and down together, playing the common beat. To stay relaxed, let your wrists relax each time you lift your arms, and let your hands droop for an instant. After playing this example over and over, begin creating your own melodies using quarter notes and half notes. This will keep your two sides playing *together, right on the beat.*

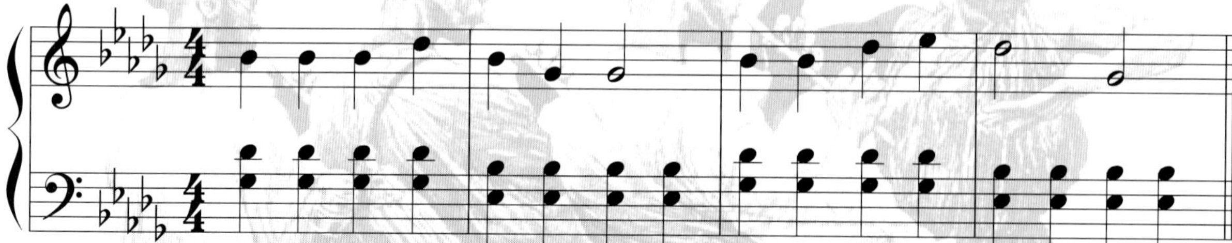

As you feel your arms moving together with your whole body, you will find that your arms *naturally* begin to move independently of one another. You will start to play in the spaces between the beats, as the melody below illustrates. You will naturally begin making your own melodies with eighth notes, still feeling the beat strongly.

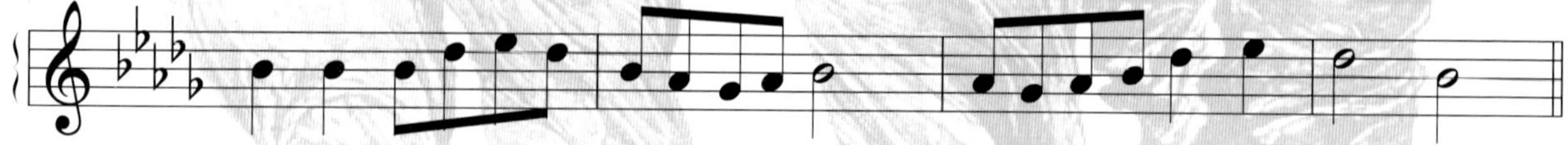

To create a *swing rhythm,* that smooth, lilting sound used in jazz and blues music: Play your favorite melody again, but this time, whenever you have a pair of eighth notes, play the first one twice as long as the second one. In other words, the first eighth note lasts for two thirds of the beat rather than half.

The Beat Shared By All

An African marimba band, a symphony orchestra playing Beethoven, a Balinese gamelan orchestra, a jazz combo—all these groups have many people playing different rhythms, but everyone is united by a common beat. The individual rhythms are unique and the overall sound is diverse and complex, but the beat is simple and shared by all.

Other Rhythms

After you can easily feel your right hand playing two notes per beat (eighth notes), why not try playing *three* notes for every beat played by your left hand? Such notes are called *triplets* because three notes are born in one beat. Triplets make a rolling, flowing sound. Create your own melodies using triplets such as the one below.

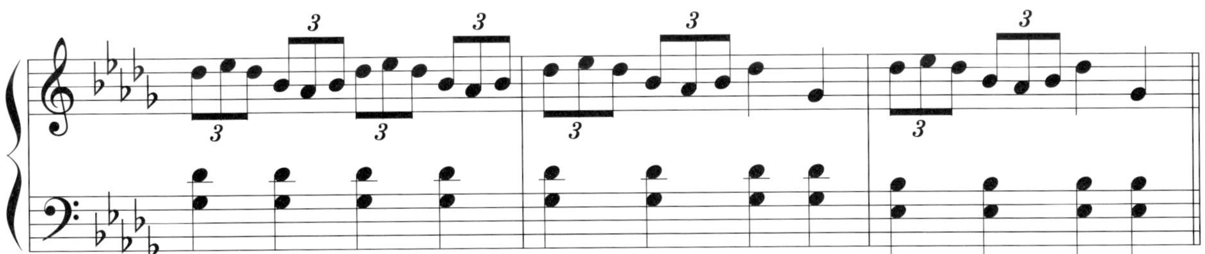

When you feel your hands playing the beat together quite securely, why not try creating with four notes in your right side to every one in the left? Here are some sixteenth-note rhythms I once heard played by a Peruvian harpist.

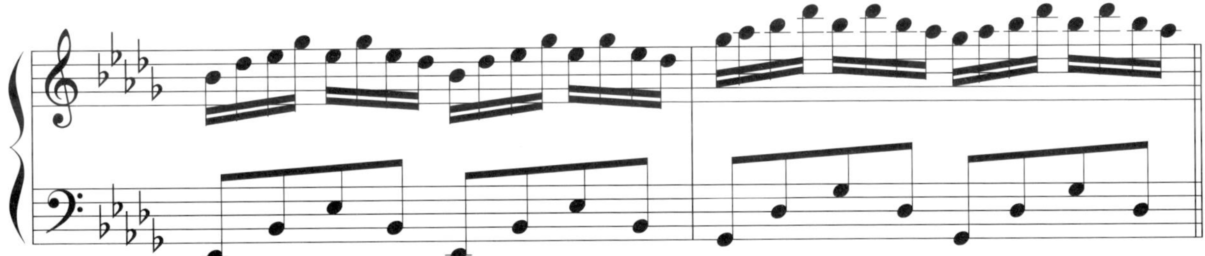

For experienced players: Once you create with sixteenth notes, you can play rhythms that mix both sixteenth and eighth notes in the same beat. Play these two melodies with the Pattern, and then make your own melodies using the same rhythms. Then make up your own rhythms.

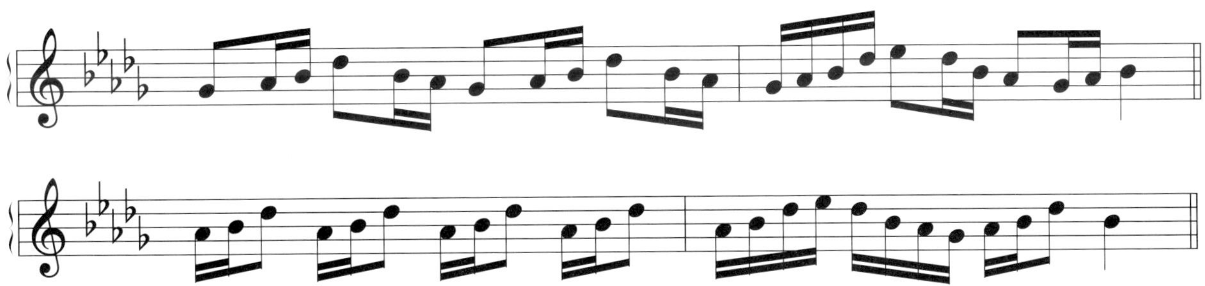

After some time, you will be able to move freely between these different rhythmic feelings. Here is a melody that moves between triplets in the first measure, eighth notes in the second, and triplets in the third. This may be much harder to play than it looks!

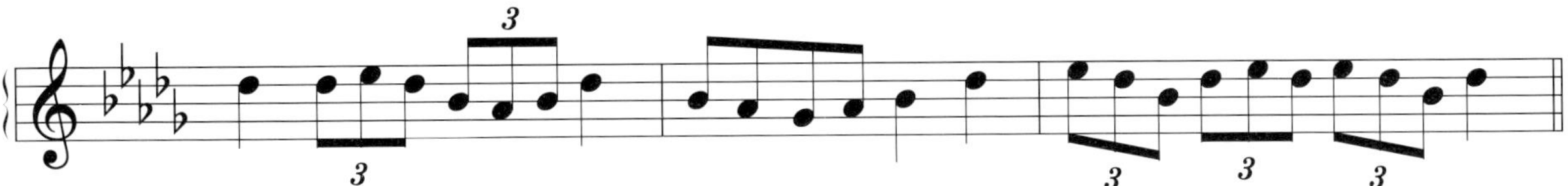

What Are the Rules Here?

There are surprisingly few "Wrong Way" signs on the *Creator's Road*. It may even seem like too few! If you are like most people, you will want some guidelines on how to make your own melodies. You will sometimes feel adrift in an endless sea of possibilities and ache for the dry, hard land of rules.

Sorry! When it comes to discovering your own music, the music that *only you* can make, there is guidance but there are few firm rules. You can't merely follow someone else's idea of what music should be (which is what a rule is), because you are now headed where none have gone before. Others can give you very useful techniques and perspectives, but ultimately no one can tell you exactly how to create the music that is yours alone. You are discovering your own way. Trust yourself.

With this said, on the next page are three guidelines to keep in mind when you are creating your own music.

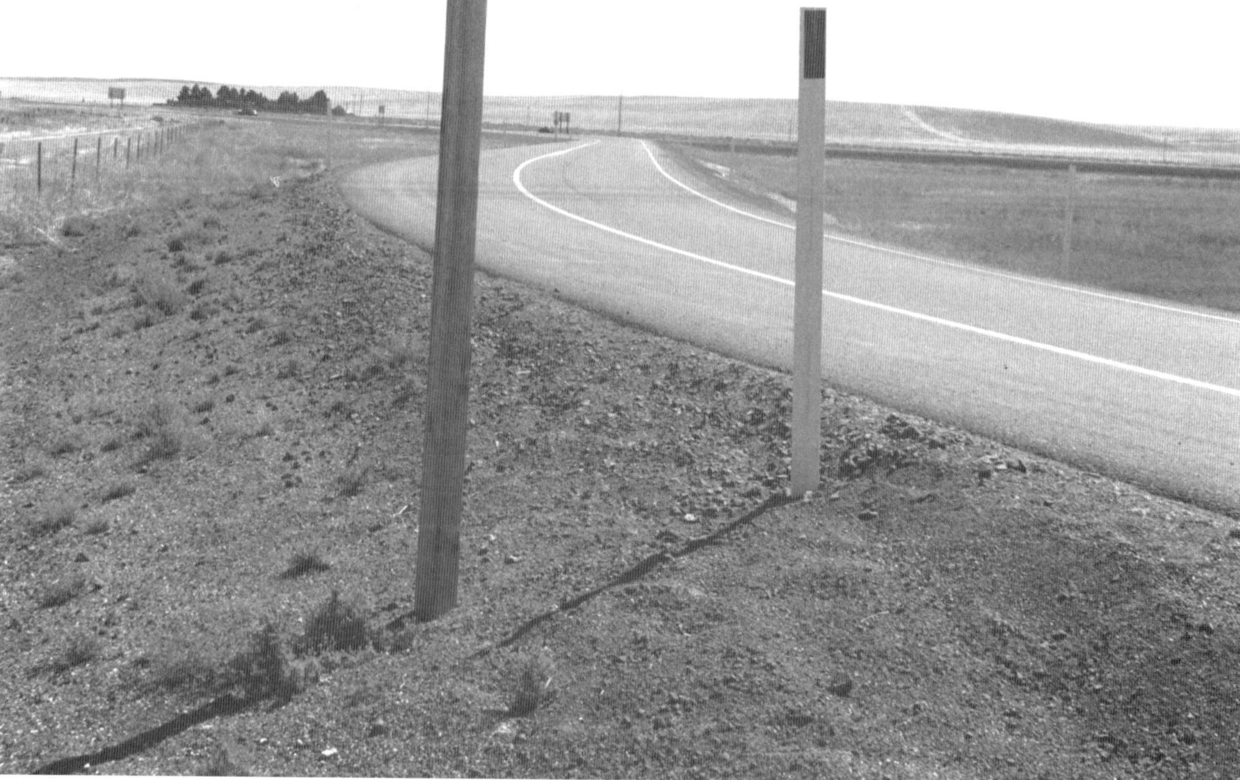

Let the music flow. Don't stop for mere mistakes.

The three most important qualities you can develop in your playing are: flow, more flow, and, of course, even more flow. When playing flows, creation grows. If flow is the most valuable thing, then the worst thing we can do is to stop the music. Stopping is the death of flowing. Stopping kills the poor music. So we must stop all that stopping, especially for mere mistakes.

This explains why it is so important for us to really know the Patterns well before we create with them. Otherwise, our playing will inevitably splutter, and never get up enough speed to lift off the ground and fly. The need for flow also explains why it is so important to keep our playing simple at first. If our minds are too far ahead of our hands, then our playing will keep crashing to the ground. "Keep it simple" is a good motto when it comes to creating.

Get into ruts. Then get out of them.

Did I say get *into* ruts? Yes. Everyone gets into ruts. To make a rule against getting into ruts would be like making a rule against sleeping. But once in a rut, we need to climb out of it! As long as we keep the desire to keep climbing out of ruts, our music (and our lives) will remain fresh and interesting.

There are many ways to de-rut a rut. The main thing is to recognize that we are in a rut and then learn new ideas that will get us out. If you (or your teacher) hear that you are playing with only eighth notes, then try playing something in triplets for a while. If you are playing at only one tempo, play faster or slower for a while. In the ice cream shop of life, why eat only vanilla?

A creator is always watching out for habits that may harden into ruts, and always exploring new possibilities and long-forgotten ones. To be in a rut is to be closed off to new possibilities. It's a temptation to sprawl on the sofa of easy, comfortable habits, and announce, "Don't disturb me because I have found my style." We have to resist that urge! "Style" is usually just a polite name for "rut." Let us try to be like Debussy or Picasso who were always exploring new ways of creating. They were always offering surprising discoveries to the world.

Does the music sound good to you?

Duke Ellington, the great jazz composer, once said, "If it sounds good, it *is* good." That's a fine rule of thumb (rule of ear?) to guide us. We have to learn to trust our own ears as we discover our own ways of making music. Of course, we can still listen openly to other people's advice because they have fresh ears when hearing our music, and often they have useful experiences to share. However, we need to listen most to what our own music has to say.

The poet T.S. Eliot once wrote about making poems, "There is no method except to be very intelligent." I would say, "When it comes to making music, there is no rule except to be honest." Does my music fit my feelings or am I making music according to someone else's idea of what it means to be "good"? Am I playing by habit or by inspiration? Am I merely trying to show off? When we are honest with how we are playing, our music will be beautiful, even if it may not always sound that way to others. The composer Arnold Schoenberg said it so well: "The beautiful in music is a byproduct of the composer's integrity." When we have integrity, we will also get beauty.

So ultimately, be honest with yourself is the only rule when it comes to creating. If we continue to look at ourselves honestly, then we will continue to grow out of our ruts, our mistakes, and our limits. Then our music making will always be deep, authentic, and beautiful.

China

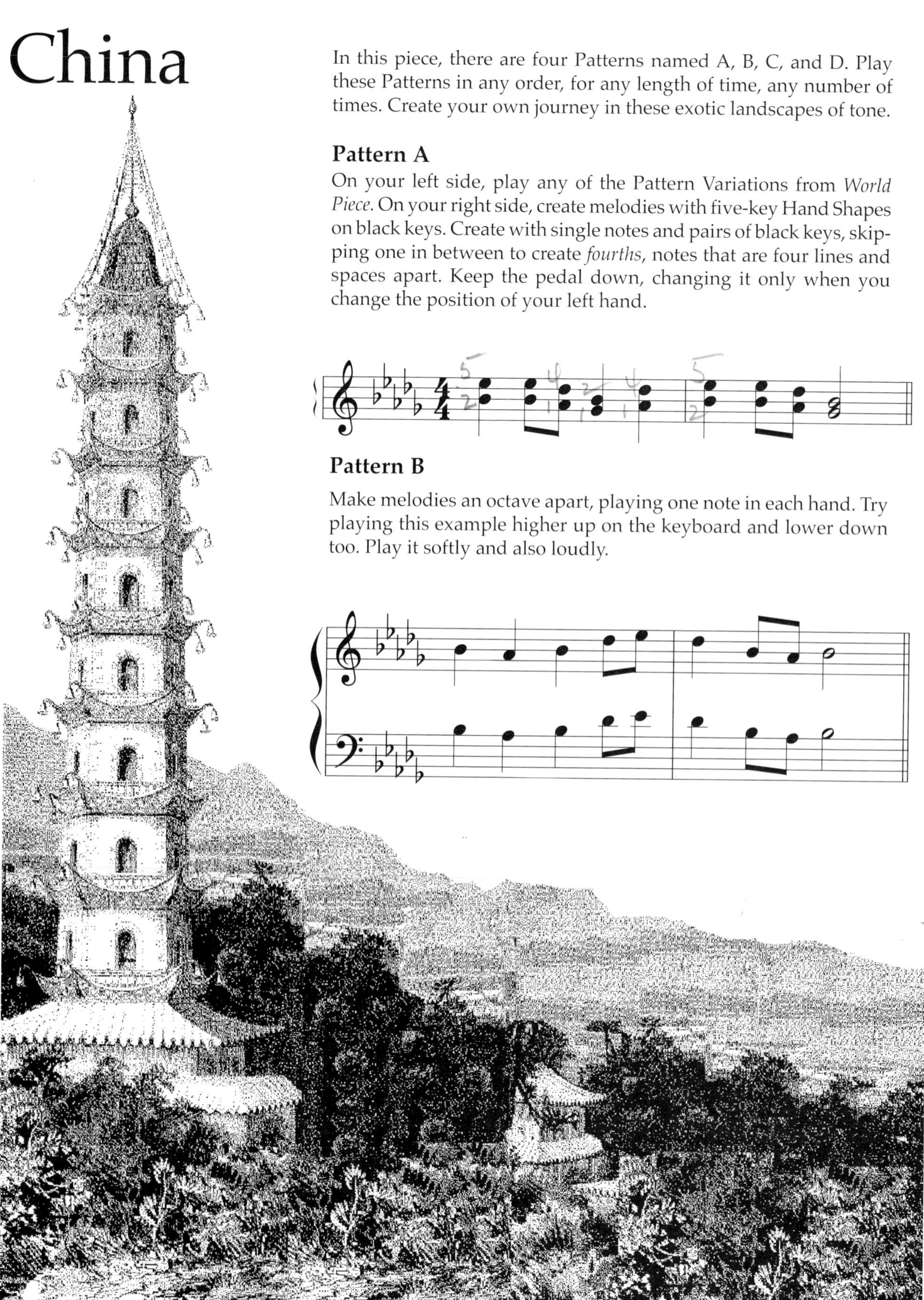

In this piece, there are four Patterns named A, B, C, and D. Play these Patterns in any order, for any length of time, any number of times. Create your own journey in these exotic landscapes of tone.

Pattern A

On your left side, play any of the Pattern Variations from *World Piece.* On your right side, create melodies with five-key Hand Shapes on black keys. Create with single notes and pairs of black keys, skipping one in between to create *fourths*, notes that are four lines and spaces apart. Keep the pedal down, changing it only when you change the position of your left hand.

Pattern B

Make melodies an octave apart, playing one note in each hand. Try playing this example higher up on the keyboard and lower down too. Play it softly and also loudly.

Pattern C

Play fifths or fourths with your right hand as an accompaniment while creating melodies with your left hand. Or, as in the second example below, make an accompaniment of flowing eighth notes. Below, I added *g flat* in the bass—play it whenever you want to add a rich dimension to the sound. For a change, play *e flat* in the bass rather than *g flat*. This changes the Key from Major Pentatonic to Minor. Keep the pedal down, changing it only when you change bass notes.

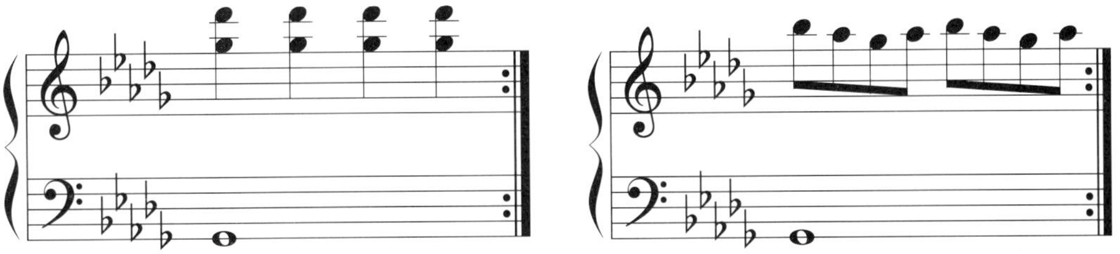

Pattern D

Here, an extra note has been added above some of the fifths to add color. Roll these notes from the bottom note to the top, or just play them normally as you create melodies above them. Try playing them softly and also forcefully. Note the different clefs.

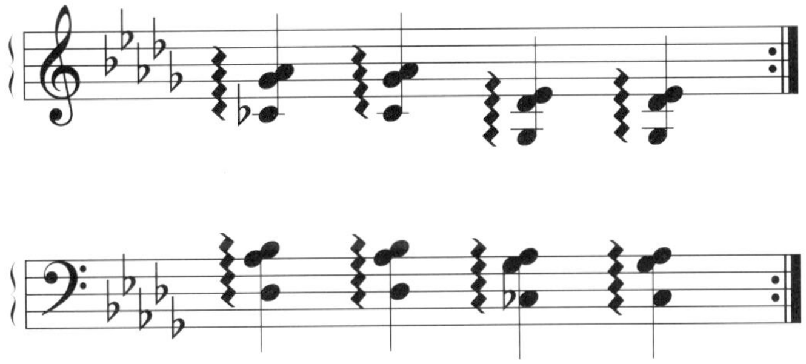

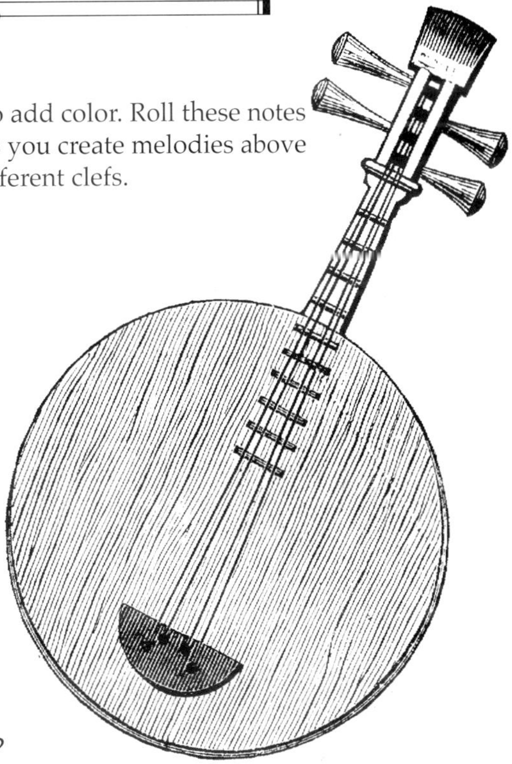

Why does this piece sound like music from parts of Asia?

The five black keys make a scale similar to the Pentatonic scales used in many Asian countries.

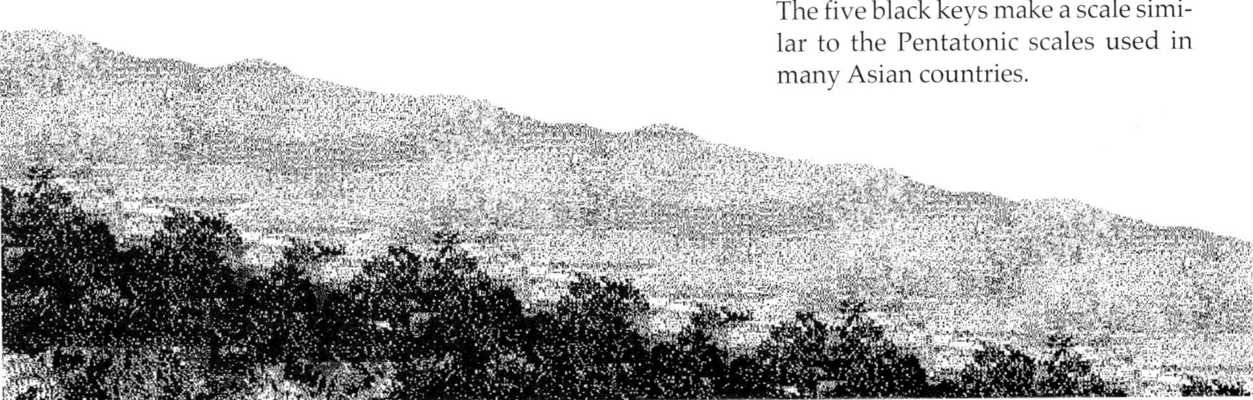

The Form of Your Musical Journey

Unless you are going to perform this piece in public and are nervous about it, I suggest you avoid planning out the form in advance. Let this piece unfold differently each time you play it. This is like traveling into a new country with an open schedule and an open mind. When you look back on your journey after it is over, then you can see the form it has taken. This way, your music will not be stitched together by your thoughts beforehand, but will grow naturally from itself and your feelings.

The architect Mies Van der Rohe wrote, "Form is not the aim of our work, only the result." The final form your piece takes ends up being the result of many decisions you made along the way. All travelers face four main decisions at each stage of a journey.

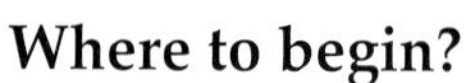

Where to begin?

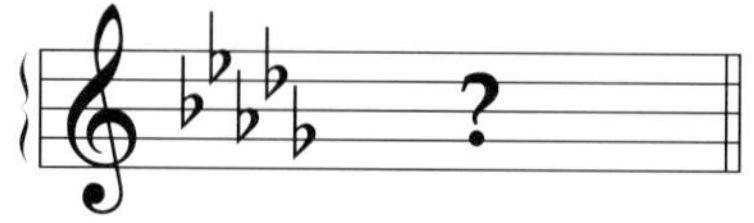

How about starting with a Variation of Pattern A, making simple melodies that have no beat? Then, how about moving into Pattern D very quietly? Or start with Pattern C, play a melody in the bass, and gradually move the melody up the piano until it turns into a melody played by both hands, as in Pattern B. Or start with a majestic theme using Pattern B. Of course, you could start with Pattern D.

Do I move on or stay?

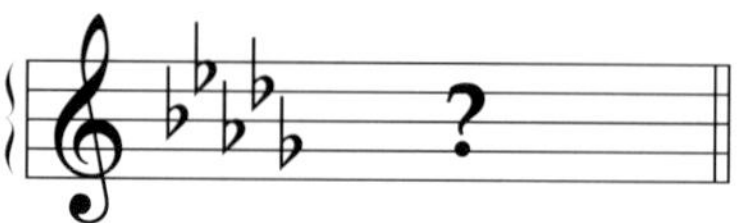

Do I stay in one place, exploring all the endless details of it, or do I move on to the next place? When I first discovered this piece, I stayed with Pattern D and explored it more than any of the other Patterns put together. But just today, I stayed with Pattern C and didn't want to budge for quite a while. Each day will bring different feelings, and with them, different decisions, journeys, and musical forms. Feel free to stay with one Pattern all day or just for an instant.

How do I get to the next place?

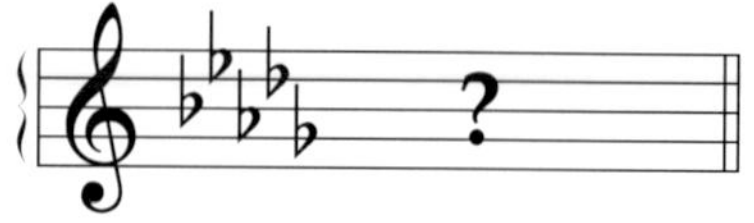

We can travel by foot, slowly moving from one place to another. Or we can get there by plane, and suddenly be in quite a different place. Both ways of travel have their pleasures. Try moving abruptly and dramatically between the different Patterns of this piece. Also try making the Patterns flow into one another, so that a listener would only realize afterward that you have come into a new place.

When does this journey end?

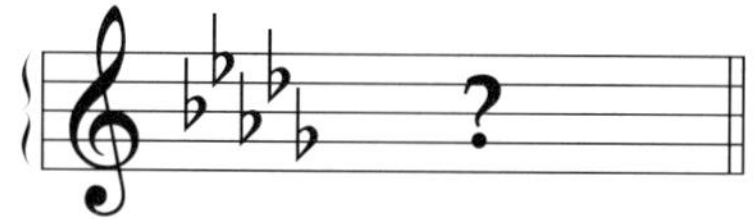

A journey ends when you have no desire to go on to another place. You might be tired, so your playing just fades gently away. Or it might be that you have found your favorite place, a place to call home, and you want to end the piece in this place with calmness or celebration. Where and how do we end a journey? Who can say in advance without ruining the adventure? If we knew how a journey would end before we began, wouldn't that spoil the fun of it?

What If I Can't Find Talent?

Think you may be short on talent? Don't worry. When it comes to creating, it's not important.

During the time I was writing this book, I took a vacation to the southern part of Oregon. I drove by this sign on the freeway. Now, I'm sure this town called Talent is a nice place with nice people. But the place called Talent along the *Creator's Road* is not the place it's cracked up to be. To be blunt, it's just a tourist trap. A lot of flashing lights and that's about it. Nothing much.

What is talent, anyway? Isn't it just the ability to perform certain recognized skills easier than most other people? But what has this to do with discovering the unique music that we alone are meant to discover? Not much at all. It doesn't matter whether some recognizable skill is easy for us, but whether we love what we are creating and whether we stick with it. If we have these two rare items (love and stick-to-itness), then we will certainly discover our own music in time.

Consider the painter Vincent Van Gogh. He did all his painting in the last decade of his life. If you look at his very first paintings, you might think, "There's not much talent there." And yet, he has become the most beloved painter of all time. Why is this? He had such a strong *desire* to paint, a *commitment* to paint, a *love* of painting, and the *patience* to stay with it. These qualities are far more important than mere talent.

Lack of talent probably *helped* Van Gogh learn the patience necessary to bring forth his unique vision. Same with Einstein. He once wrote, "I know quite certainly that I myself have no special talents. Curiosity, obsession, and dogged endurance, combined with self-criticism, have brought me to my ideas." Edison, Beethoven, Helen Keller, and many others overcame great personal disabilities to offer the world their great gifts. These creators became great because, in many cases, they didn't have a lot of the common talent, so they learned to persist and be patient. Over time, they went further down the road than anyone had gone before them. People call this "talent" but it is really love, commitment, and patience that do the work and create the magic.

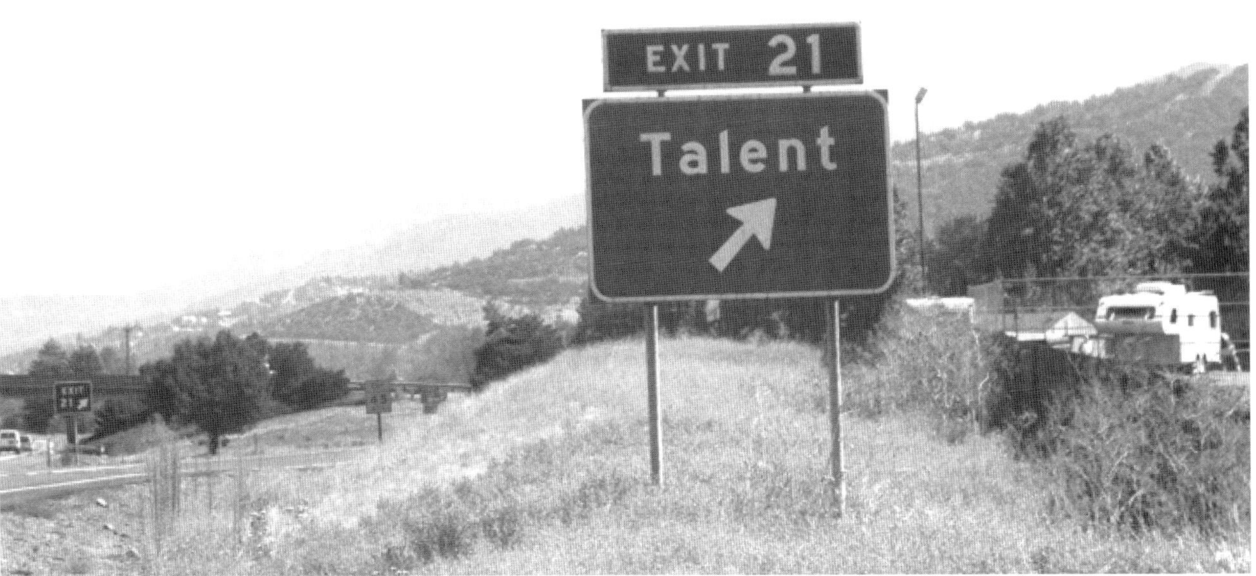

Japan

The two scales you've been creating with so far (Major and Minor Pentatonic Scales) are the most popular five-note scales, though not the only ones. Here you can create with a haunting five-note scale that comes from ancient Japan. This scale is called the *Kumoijoshi scale.* You can explore more ways to create with this exotic scale in Volume 3-A.

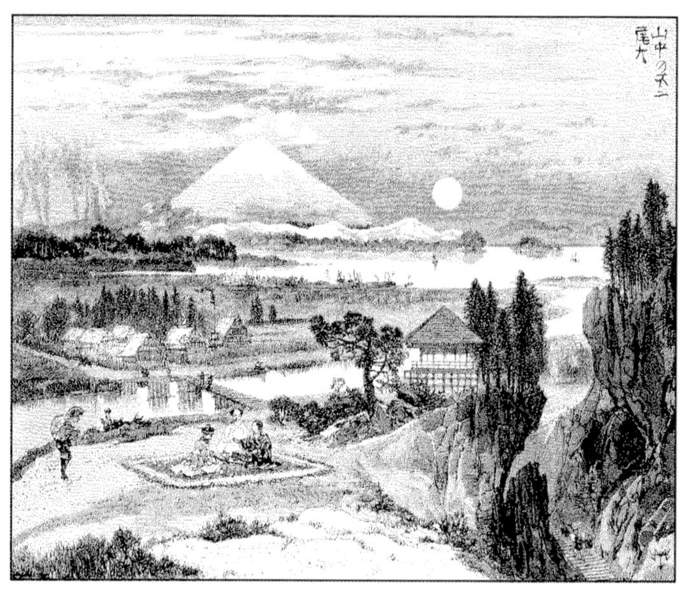

The smallest distance between pitches in Western (European) music is a *half step*, such as the distance between *e* and *f*. We cannot play half steps on black keys even if we want to! This is because the smallest distance between two black keys is a *whole step.* For scales that have half steps, we must use white keys.

Pattern (Right Side)

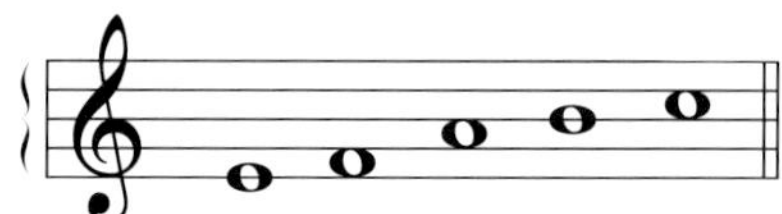

Place your fingers and thumb over these five notes. This is the five-key Hand Shape for this piece. You can play this same Hand Shape up an octave, or up two octaves, or up three octaves. Plus, you can play it down an octave. Make melodies and sounds with this Hand Shape using single tones and combinations of tones.

Pattern (Left Side)

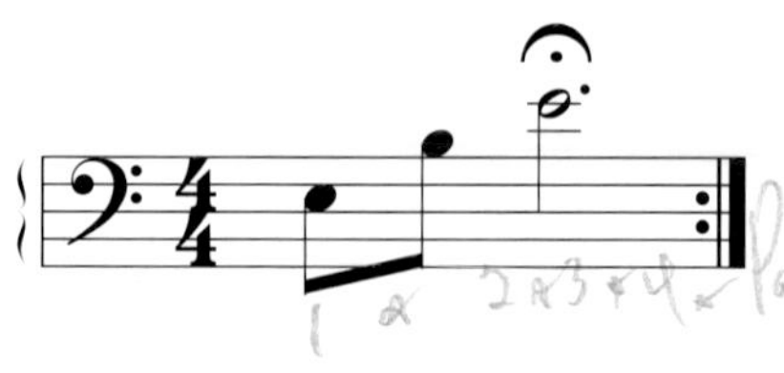

This accompaniment Pattern and both Vacations are simple drones, made by playing a fifth with an added octave. Play these softly, with the pedal. Your hands will sometimes have to share that *e* above *middle c*. To create a more resonant, full sound, add a low *e* in the bass occasionally and sustain it with the pedal.

Vacation One

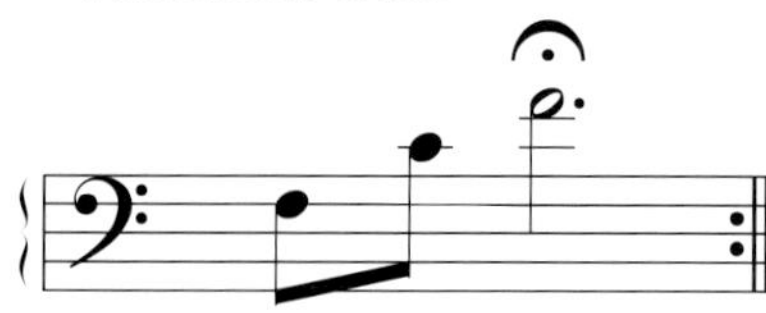

Experiment with other ways to play these three tones. Play these Vacations or the Pattern an octave lower when you want a thicker, deeper sound. Or try playing them up an octave for a sound as thin as rice paper.

Vacation Two

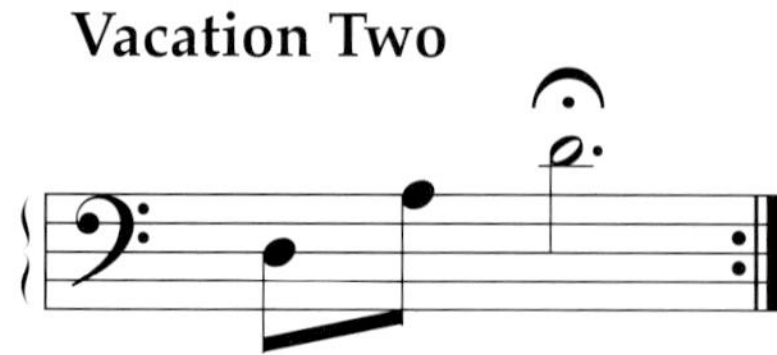

Because the *d*'s in Vacation Two are not in the traditional five-note scale, this Vacation freshens the sound of the scale. Feel free, as usual, to play this Vacation any other way you like—repeat tones, change the order (why not play the top note first?), play it faster and slower, louder and softer, and so on.

Musical Expressions

If music were a chocolate cake, then pitches and rhythms would be the flour and the sugar. These are essential ingredients, but what is a chocolate cake without milk, eggs, and the chocolate? Our way of writing music makes pitches and rhythms appear to be the most important ingredients, but music would be just tasteless dust without other ingredients. This page explores some of the flavors and fluids that make music so delicious. Some of these ingredients have standard names you may already know: dynamics, tempo, phrasing, and articulation. With music and language, it's not *what* is said (the pitches and rhythms) but *how* it is said (the expression) that carries the deeper meanings.

Dynamics

Play this melody loudly, and then play it softly. The personality of the melody is completely changed. Then *gradually* get louder and softer. Also try *accenting* certain notes in the melody, emphasizing them more than the others. This changes the meaning of the melody, just as the meaning of the following sentence is changed when you change the emphasis: I *like* him. I like *him*.

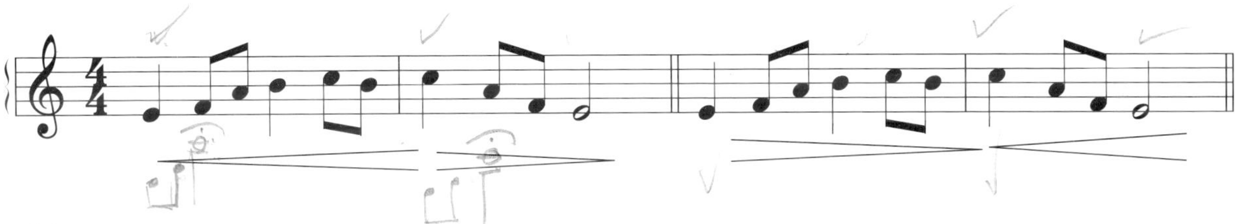

Tempo

The *tempo* of a piece has to do with its manner of moving. Try playing this melody quite slowly. Then play it much faster. Experiment with becoming slower (*ritardando*) and faster (*accelerando*).

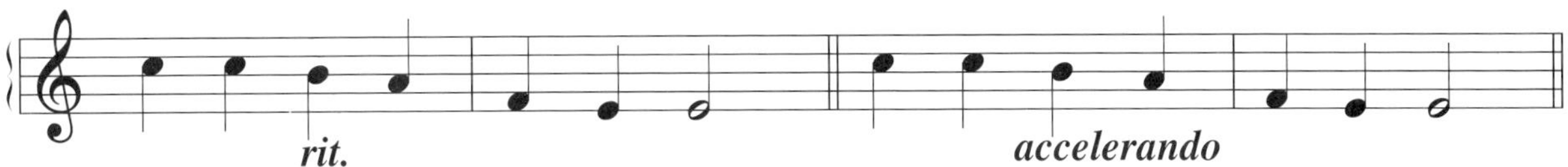

Phrasing

Consider this sentence: "I'll help you too." Now pause after "help" and emphasize "too." The sentence becomes: "I'll help. You too?" The meaning is changed. It's the same with melodies. The two melodies below are the same except for their phrasings. The slurs mark the beginning and ending of a "sentence." At the end of each slur, lift your hand early to create a moment of silence—a "breath"—without stopping the rhythm. By grouping tones differently, we create different musical "sentences."

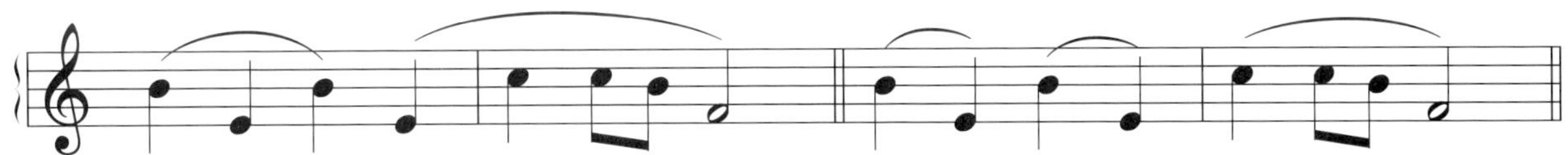

Articulation

Articulation has to do with the different ways of touching the keys. If you play a key as if you don't want to let it go, this gives the tone emphasis. This is indicated by a *tenuto* mark (-). There is also *staccato* (quick touch), *legato* (sustained), and *portato* (sustained yet detached). There are many other ways of touching a piano that don't have names or marks yet. Perhaps you will discover some.

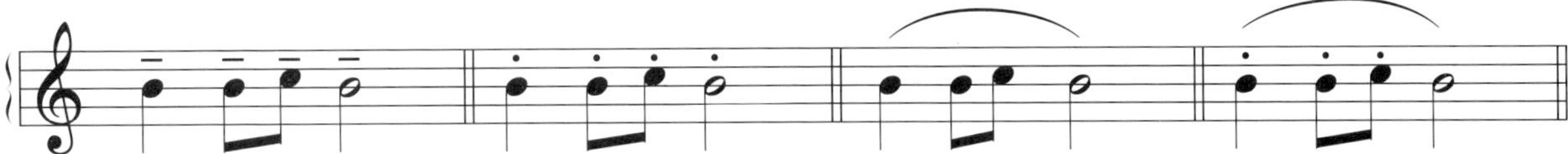

Patience Is Everything

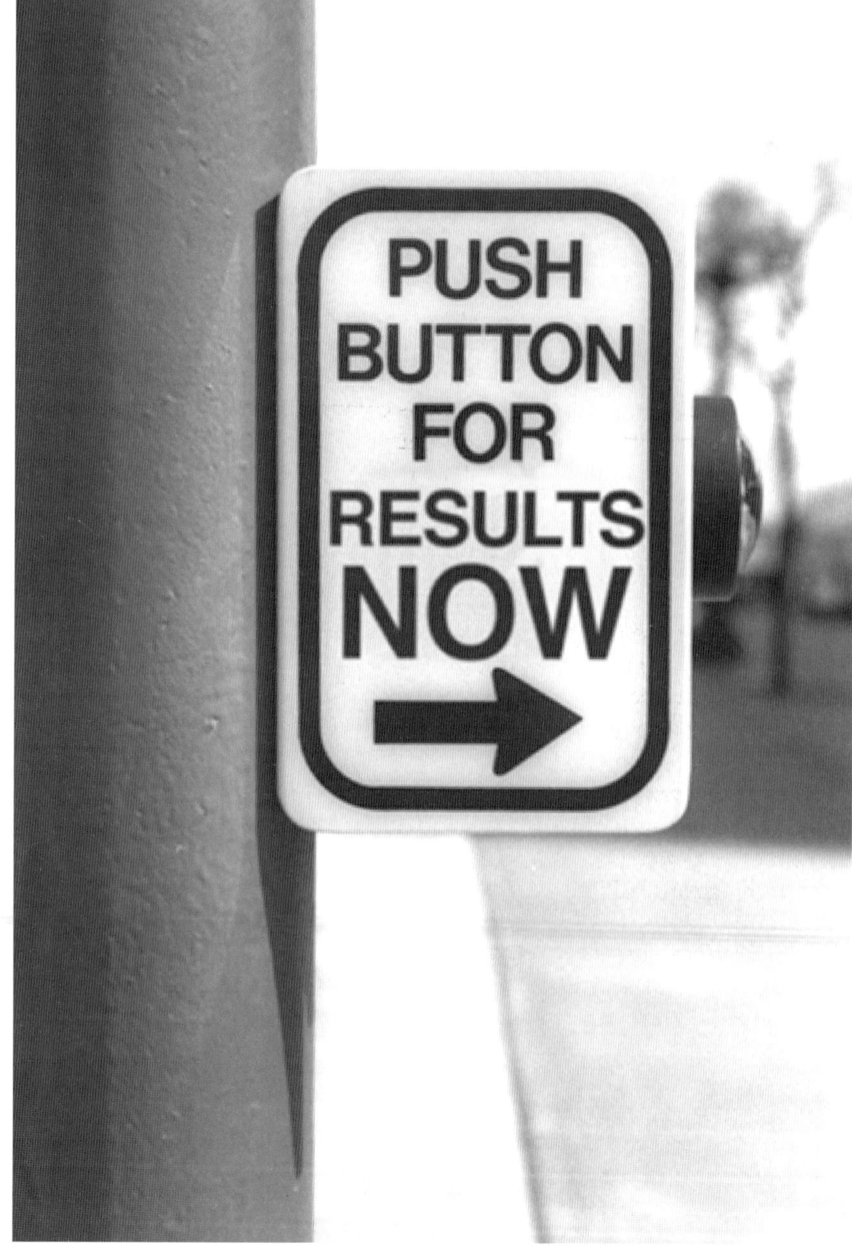

With the push of a button, we clean our clothes, cook our food, wash our dishes, and bring images from around the world into our homes. Our machines are designed to give us the quickest results with the least amount of effort.

As we get older, our abilities and skills become like these efficient machines. We can walk, talk, ride a bike, and do so many other things with hardly more effort than it takes to push a button. Since our skills feel so easy and natural now, we forget just how long it took to gain that competency. We expect that we will soon develop this same sort of competency with this new skill of creating music. But playing the piano is an unusually complex task. If we want to learn to create our own music, we will often have to feel like a beginner all over again.

Few activities in our lives prepare us for the complexities of piano playing. First of all, to play the piano requires that we tune into our feelings and inspirations, and then translate these into finger movements. This involves coordinating our body in new and difficult ways, using muscles large and small. Plus, piano playing also requires us to use our minds in new and complex ways. As if this weren't enough, piano playing requires that we do all this—feelings, mind, and muscles—*simultaneously.* Can you think of another activity that requires this many diverse abilities at once? It's no wonder that those who play the piano are admired by others. The piano will always have an enduring mystique about it.

Always a Challenge

Not only is piano playing a challenge now, but it will never cease to be a challenge, as long as we are playing creatively. The painter Degas said, "Painting is easy when you don't know how, but very difficult when you do." The same is true for the piano, or any art. We discover more and more possibilities as we go along, until we are embraced by infinity. The difficulty of turning the impossible into the possible keeps us inspired.

For our musical journey to be satisfying, it *must* be challenging. "A good writer always works at the impossible," wrote John Steinbeck. And yet, we hear recordings all the time where performers make it all sound so easy. We overlook the fact that these people have been practicing all their lives to sound this way! We hear the end results, but not all the challenges that they had to overcome along the way.

What Good is Frustration?

In all my years of teaching and helping people to create, I would say that the hardest thing for people has been to remain patient in the heat of all these challenges. "Why can't I do this? Why am I so hopeless? Where are the results? I seem to be getting nowhere." Most people get frustrated because they want to be competent right now, as competent as they are in the other activities they do each day. But what good is frustration? It only hurts us. We have to trust that, even though we can't see many results today, our skills and sensitivities are growing each time we play.

The Master Gardener

Patience is the most important quality to have in the practice of any art. The poet Rainer Maria Rilke said it this way: "Every day I learn with pains, for which I am grateful: Patience is everything!" Why have so many creators in so many different fields come to this same conclusion? It is because they feel that patience is a master gardener—it is the one quality that can grow any other.

Are you lacking talent? If you have patience, you can develop it. The great writer Flaubert said, "Talent is long patience." Are you not a genius? Michelangelo (speaking from experience) said, "Genius is eternal patience." Are you slow to learn? "Patience surpasses learning," says an old proverb. Want to create great art? "Good art is nothing more than infinite patience," wrote William Wallace Kimball.

Patience is far more important than creativity, musicality, talent, good looks, money in the bank, a nice car, or anything else. Ben Franklin, speaking for all creators, said, "He who has patience can have what he will."

The Years Teach

Our creative gifts and abilities have their own timetable. They take their own time. If we don't rush our musical gifts, they will emerge healthy and fully formed, and have a long and happy life.

Whenever I get frustrated, I try to remember this beautiful quote by Ralph Waldo Emerson: "The years teach what the days never know." What we desire will come in time. We look back and say, "I don't remember learning that, but I did." The years will teach us. In the meantime, we can enjoy the journey as it unfolds day by day.

Patience is bitter, but its fruit is sweet. —Rousseau

Old Scotland (Introducing Arranging)

This book is filled with Patterns that create environments in which your own melodies can come to life. However, often the Patterns musicians create with are not accompaniments but popular *melodies*. Pianists will often transform popular songs such as *Happy Birthday to You* or *Silent Night* into piano pieces. When music is changed from one medium to another, it's called *arranging*. Arranging is explored in detail in later volumes (especially Volume 2-A) because a knowledge of chords is necessary for this art. For now, I'd like to introduce some main ideas. This is the only piece in this book where the Pattern is a popular tune.

Auld Lang Syne ("Old, Long Time") is an ancient Scottish aire that traveled to America hundreds of years ago. It's a good tune to know because 1) It's a fine melody; 2) It is made out of a Major Pentatonic Scale and can be played on black keys alone; and 3) It's often played at special occasions, notably New Year's Eve and wedding anniversaries.

This tune was first composed and played on bagpipes. If you would rather play it on piano (a good idea, especially if you have grouchy neighbors), you will have to change the tune into a piano piece.

"What a lovely afternoon! Those poor pianists sitting inside on a such a fine day as this!"

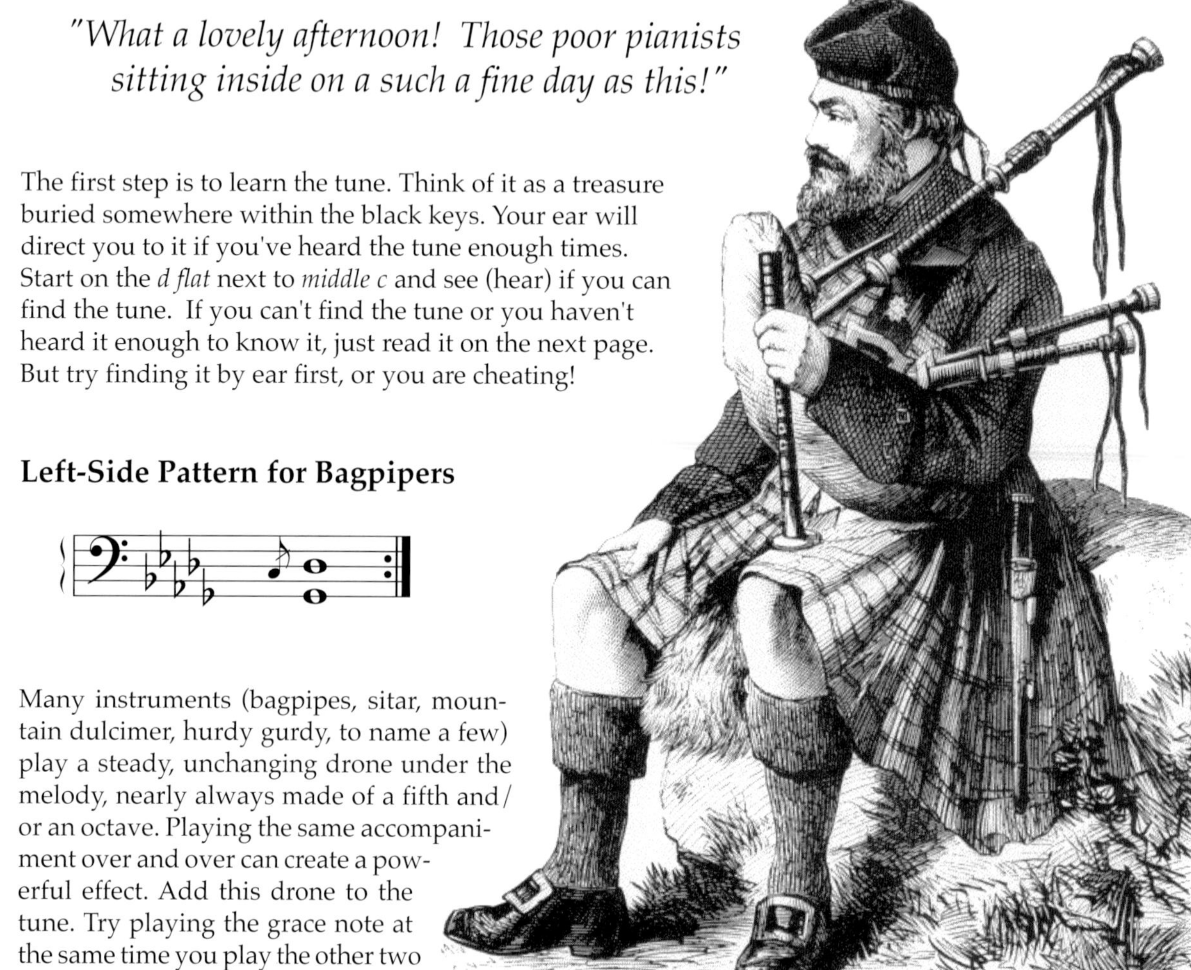

The first step is to learn the tune. Think of it as a treasure buried somewhere within the black keys. Your ear will direct you to it if you've heard the tune enough times. Start on the *d flat* next to *middle c* and see (hear) if you can find the tune. If you can't find the tune or you haven't heard it enough to know it, just read it on the next page. But try finding it by ear first, or you are cheating!

Left-Side Pattern for Bagpipers

Many instruments (bagpipes, sitar, mountain dulcimer, hurdy gurdy, to name a few) play a steady, unchanging drone under the melody, nearly always made of a fifth and/or an octave. Playing the same accompaniment over and over can create a powerful effect. Add this drone to the tune. Try playing the grace note at the same time you play the other two notes, and then release it quickly.

Pattern (The Tune of *Auld Lang Syne*)

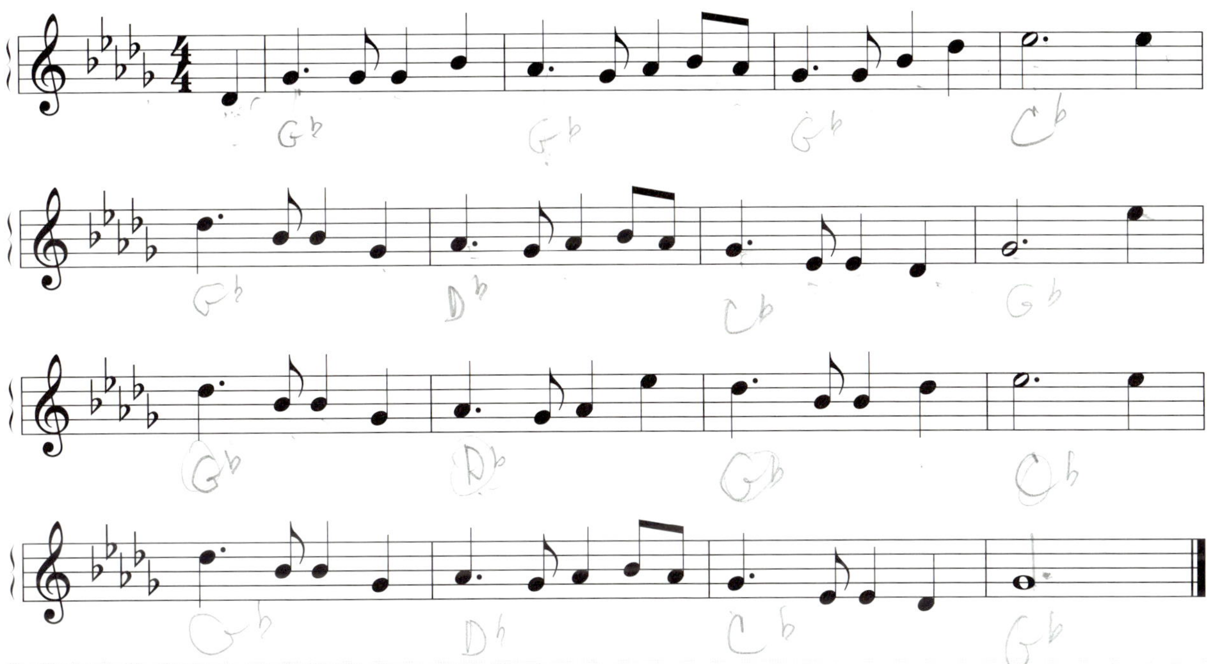

Changing the Scenery in the Left Side

Unlike bagpipers, we pianists are not able to stroll around lush Scottish hillsides while we play. To make up for this unfortunate situation, we can change the scenery in our left-side accompaniments more often. Use the three fifths below to create a fancier accompaniment to *Auld Lang Syne* than the bagpiper's drone. By doing so, turn this into a *piano* piece. Play the melody with your right hand and, any time you feel like it, play one of the three fifths shown below. Find the fifth that sounds best in each measure. How do you know when you are playing the "right" sound? When it sounds interesting to you, it's right.

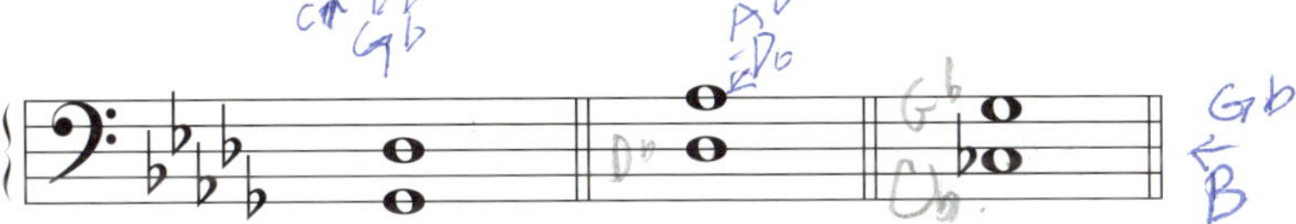

If you like, you can add a third between the fifths to make a chord. Once again, fit these chords with the melody in a way that sounds good to you. You can break up the notes of these chords to make a more active accompaniment, as shown in the examples at the bottom of the page.

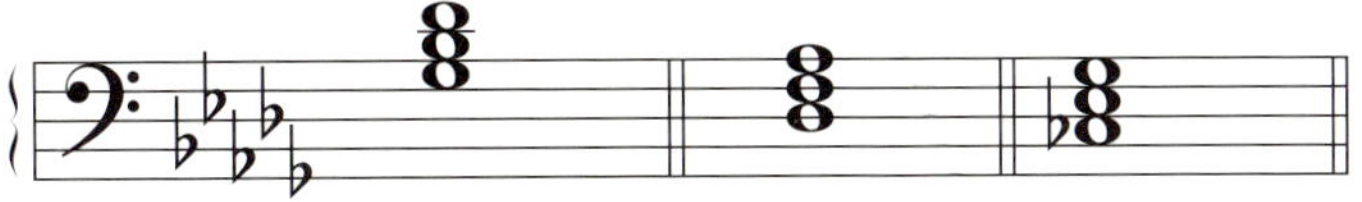

When making arrangements, we always have the freedom to change the left-side sound to make the melody sound fresh again. Just as we feel fresh and alive when we travel to a new environment, so a melody feels refreshed when it travels amidst new accompaniments. Here are some ways to play the accompaniments shown above. The second example adds an octave above the bass note.

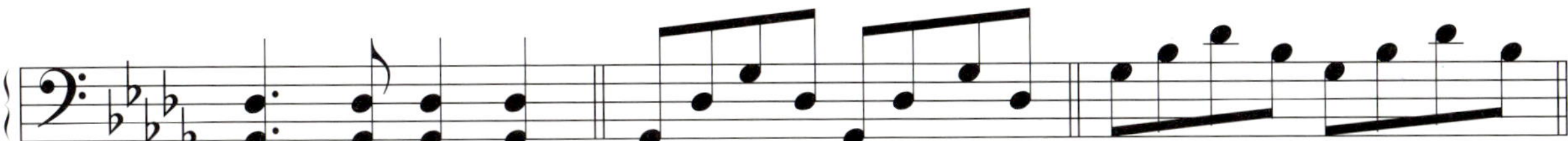

Another Way to Make an Old Tune New Again

To arrange a tune is to make it sound new again, even a song as old as *Auld Lang Syne.* Musicians use three main approaches to freshen up old tunes. The most common is to change the accompaniment Patterns, just as we did on the last page.

A second way to revive a tune is to think of the melody as being like a bare Christmas tree that can be decorated with various musical ornaments. The tune stays *basically* the same but sounds different because of all the new ornaments added to it. This is a very common musical practice throughout the world (Asian music, jazz, etc.), and was done in classical music until modern times. This page explores ways to ornament tunes. On the next page is a third way to make old tunes new again.

The most common way to ornament a tune is to add harmonizing tones below the melody to create a fuller sound. Think of the melody tones and the bass accompaniment as being like the outlines in a drawing, while the added tones "color in" this outline with harmony. How will you know what notes to add? Any black key will work and sometimes *f natural*. Your ear will tell you. Here's one way.

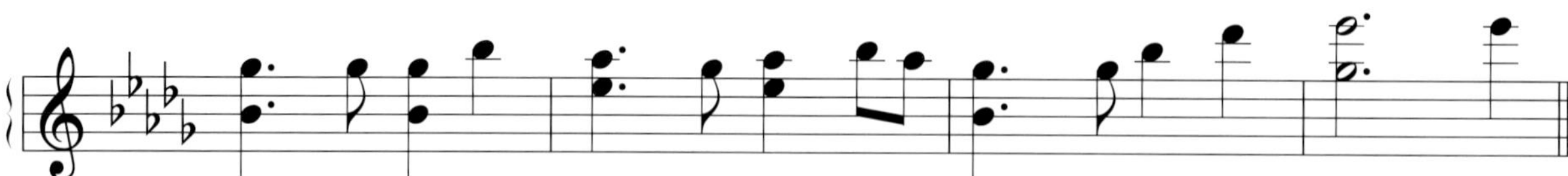

You can ornament the melody by adding notes *above* the melody note. Below, I added some *upper neighbors* to the melody and played them as grace notes. (Sounds bagpipey.) Your ear will tell you which neighbor tones sound good.

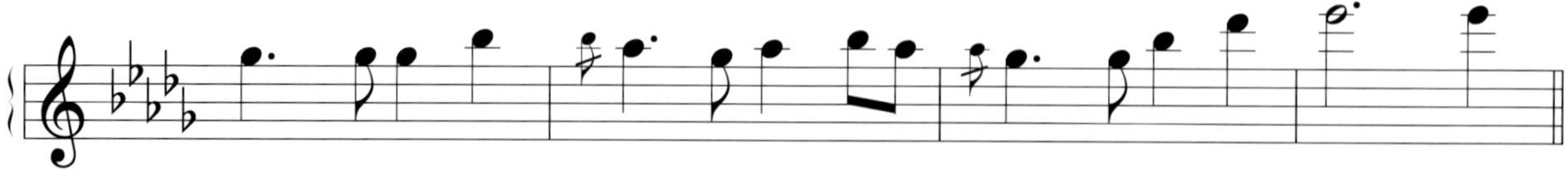

Here I added in some *lower neighbors* to the melody. Lower neighbors are the tones right below the melody tones. I ended up changing the rhythm of the melody to add them. Though I limited myself to black keys, you can also experiment with white-key lower neighbors.

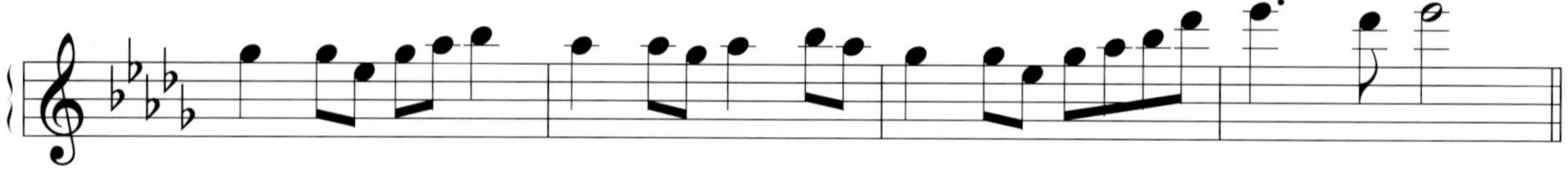

Here, I added both lower and upper neighbors. This was commonly done in Bach's time. Jazz players in the "bebop" style sometimes add so many lower and upper neighbors that they hardly have room in their melodies for the original melody notes at all! Notice how I used an *f natural*—though this note takes us out of the Pentatonic Scale, it sounds good.

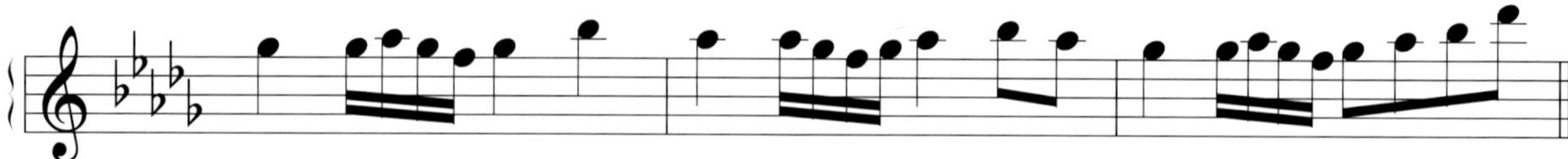

As you add tones to the melody, the rhythm of the melody may keep changing. One of my favorite ways of playing this tune is to add tones until I have a steady stream of eighth notes. This way, the melody is still there but it's woven into a steady stream of tones. Hearing the tune becomes a game of hide-and-seek for the ear. Below, I have marked the original melody tones with *tenuto* (-) marks.

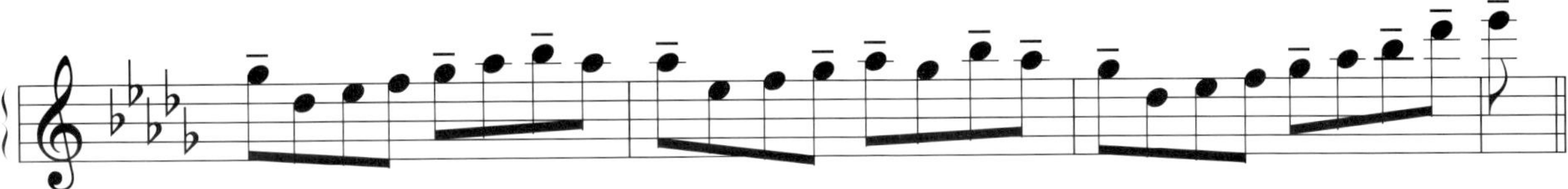

Often, singers will sing lyrics of songs on pitches other than those expected depending on how they feel at the moment. This is why there are often so many different versions of the same folk tune. There is no "final" version even after it has been written down. As your feeling for this tune grows, you will find that the melody wants to travel beyond its normal pathways. Below, the melody reaches out to other black keys, yet sticks to the most significant tones of the original melody.

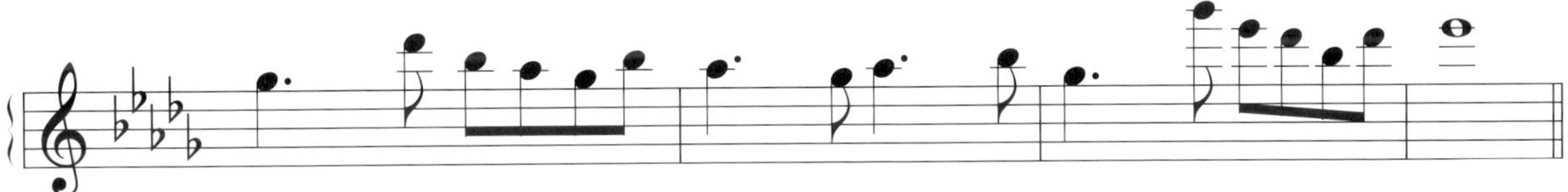

The Third Way to Freshen Up an Old Tune

First play the tune in the old, familiar way and then, keeping your same accompaniment pattern, let the tune grow into something completely new, something that doesn't resemble the original tune at all. This goes beyond arranging a tune. Now you are *improvising* new tunes as you have done in the other pieces in this book. On the previous pages, the tune was recognizable while the accompaniment changed character, but now the accompaniment is recognizable while the melody is not.

This is the basic approach of most jazz musicians. They first play a recognizable tune, then they improvise new melodies while playing the accompaniment patterns of the tune. Jazz artists call these repeating accompaniment patterns *changes* or *chord progressions*. To complete the piece, the jazz player usually finds a way back to the original tune, and brings the piece to an end. If you listen to much jazz, you will hear this approach over and over again.

So now, the recurring Pattern is not the *melody* of *Auld Lang Syne* but the left-side *accompaniment* of *Auld Lang Syne*. I wrote this below in the most basic form (just fifths lounging around on whole notes), but play these notes any way that sounds good to you.

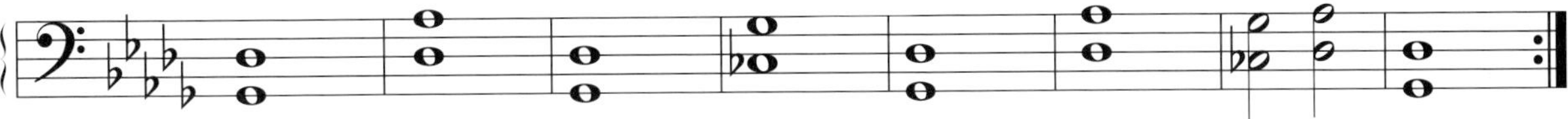

By now you can see why *improvising* and *arranging* are often confused. Jazz musicians move seamlessly from an arrangement of a tune into a free improvisation on the tune's accompaniment pattern. But these are really two quite different ways of making music—arranging is revisiting a melody that already exists, while improvising is discovering a melody that has never existed until now.

How Long 'til I'm There?

You may be asking, "How long 'til I'm good? How long until I get there?" The truth is, whenever we are on a creative journey, there is no *there* there! There is no place where we can say, "I have arrived. I'm done." For a creator, the only thing that matters is the journey of discovery right now. There is no *final place* called Piano Paradise. The sign below doesn't really exist. It's a fake. I made it on my computer by scrambling the letters on a picture of a nearby road sign.

On his deathbed, Beethoven said, "Strange, I feel as if up to now I had written no more than a few notes." After writing and performing hundreds of masterpieces, even Ludwig van Beethoven didn't feel he was *there* yet!

After creating for a while, we learn some tricks, we know more vocabulary, and we become better able to express some of what we feel. However, there will always be a gap between what we feel and what we are able to say. It is this gap between what is *possible* and what is *actual* that energizes and drives the creative spirit. The more we journey onward, the more we feel the infinite possibilities of creative expression, and the more we feel that we are moving far, far away from ever being able to express even a fraction of them.

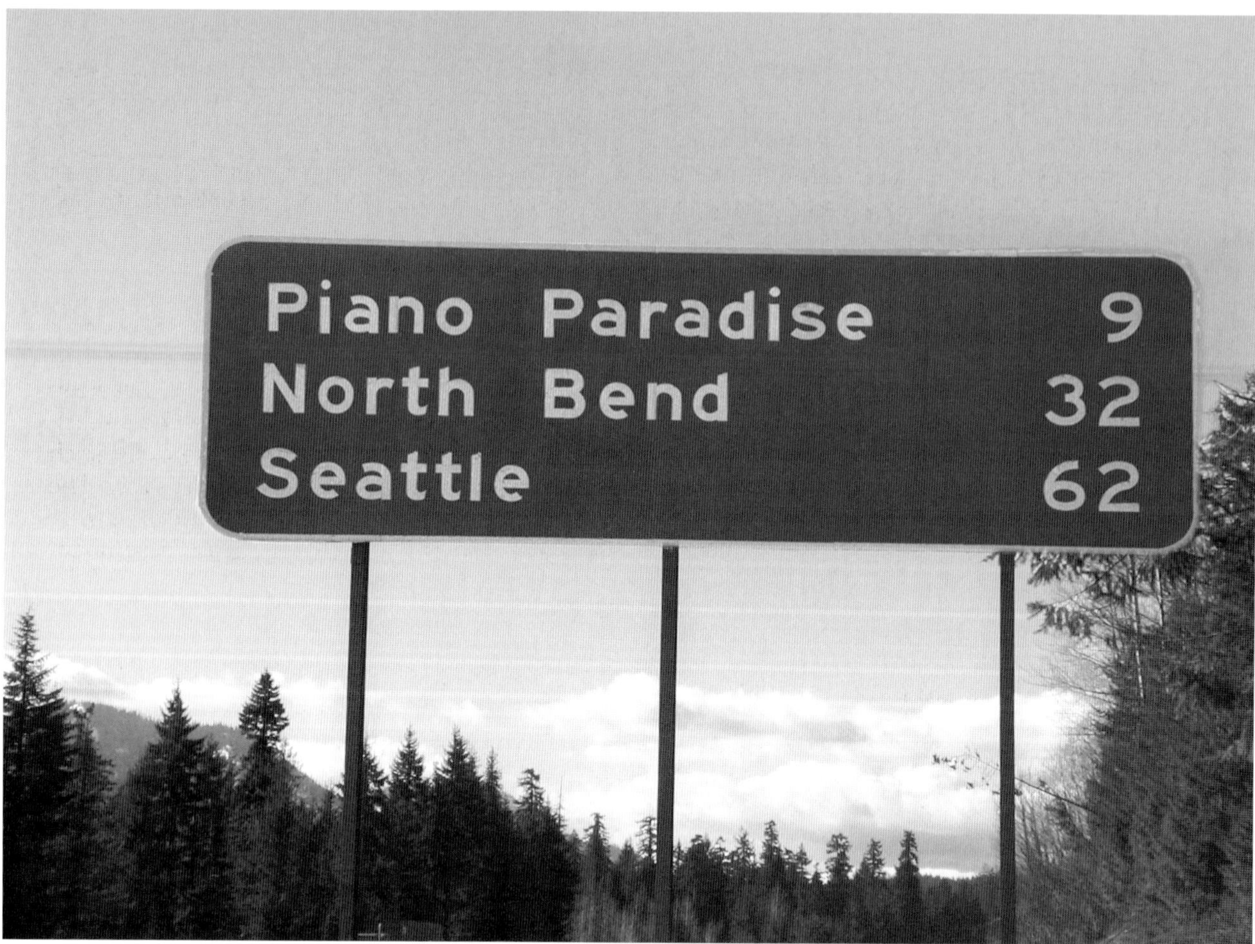

What is good, anyway?

After creating music for most of my life, I no longer believe that music is "good" just because the performer has attained a certain level of expertise. I don't even think it matters that much whether the music is complex, polished, or makes people scream and faint. To me, what matters is whether the music reveals and expresses something new and true. *Then* it's good, whether the performer is a beginner or a veteran with fifty years of experience. No matter how good we are, our expertise is made of old news. Creativity is all about discovering something new, something unheard of until this very moment.

Why rush?

When we are reading a great book, we don't want it to end. We savor each page. I think it is fantastic that it takes a whole life to discover our own music. This is an adventure that never ends! What a shame if we could do it all in a month or a year. What's the rush? The best part of creating is not in arriving, not in being "good," but in hearing things for the first time.

Always something more to learn!

One of the great composers of the 20th century, Igor Stravinsky, wrote, "I love whatever I am now doing, and with each new work I feel that I have at last found the way, have just begun to compose." Haydn, when he was in his early sixties, after fifty years of composing, fell dangerously ill. He prayed to God to spare him because, as he put it, "I finally just learned how to compose."

If we are creating truly, we are always learning new techniques, always revising what we did yesterday, and always exploring new ways to honestly express ourselves. Think of Beethoven, writing the simple *Ode to Joy* theme a hundred times to get it right, constantly striving to improve himself, even after attaining mastery in other's eyes. It was Beethoven who wrote, "Let every person do that which is right, strive with all his might towards the goal which can never be attained, develop to the last breath the gifts which a gracious Creator has endowed him, and never cease to learn."

The end keeps getting farther and farther away.

When we are enjoying our creative adventure, walking down what I call the *Creator's Road*, we keep discovering more and more pathways off to the side. Each one can be traveled without end, and each has more pathways off to the side! All these pathways could take many lifetimes to explore. On such a creative road, we find that our destination does not get closer with each step, but farther away. The end of the road disappears into the mist ahead. This is a good thing! This means we are on a truly creative path. We are fortunate that there remain all these possibilities to explore, all these unanswered questions, all these adventures.

Piano Paradise can exist.

I said there's no place called Piano Paradise where we can kick back on the sofa and say, "I'm done. I'm here." And yet, there is a state of mind called Piano Paradise that does exist. If we are deeply enjoying what we are doing right now, learning, discovering our own music, then we are there. Paradise is in discovering the true expression of this moment. We can be there, right now.

The Healing Harp

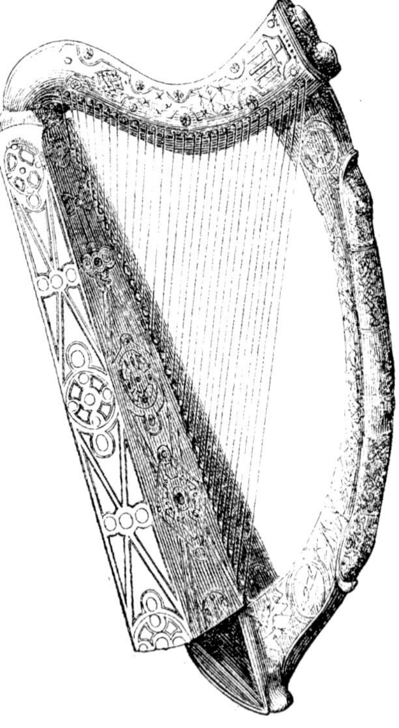

Harps are ancient instruments played in Sumeria at least five thousand years ago. They were played in temples to heal and comfort the sick. This piece evokes the ancient origins and purposes of harp music.

The piano can be thought of as a distant descendent of the harp. It is essentially a harp that has been placed in a large wooden case with a sound-board. Instead of our fingers striking the strings directly, they now push keys, which move hammers to strike the strings.

If you find this piece to be too difficult, try playing it slowly, focusing on making your movements as flowing as possible. Or just skip over it and come back to it later.

Pattern

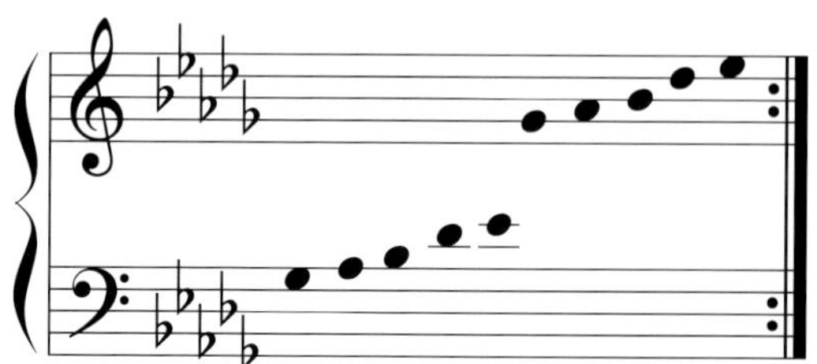

Play the five keys of the G-Flat Major Pentatonic Scale with both hands. Put the pedal down and roll the keys from the bottom key to the top, as if you were strumming a harp. Play these ten keys over and over, until you feel that the two sides of your body move in a single, flowing motion. You should feel like ocean waves, rolling up on a beach of black keys, falling back, rolling up the beach, falling back again.

Creating a Piece

Now that you feel this movement in your hands and arms, play other groups of five black keys (such as the ones below), moving between them to create pieces. Play in the upper reaches and lower ranges of the piano. You can leave the pedal down the whole time, or change it whenever you play a different tone in the bass. Hold down some keys longer than others to create new rhythms. Or omit some notes to create different Hand Shapes. Play the wave-like movement of the arms very slowly, and also very quickly. Drop your arm weight into the keys to make loud sounds, and also hold back your arm weight to make softer sounds. Explore the possibilities.

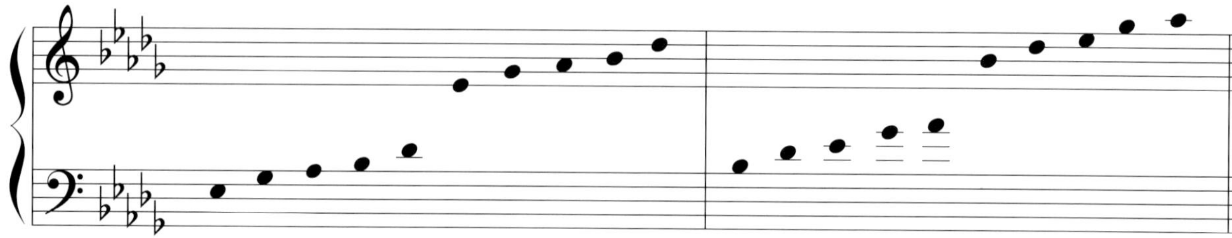

Other Movements

Roll the five keys in each Hand Shape in different ways. In the first example below, I rolled the left hand from bottom to top, and the right hand from top to bottom. In the second example, I rolled both hands from top to bottom, as though strumming a harp from the high strings downward.

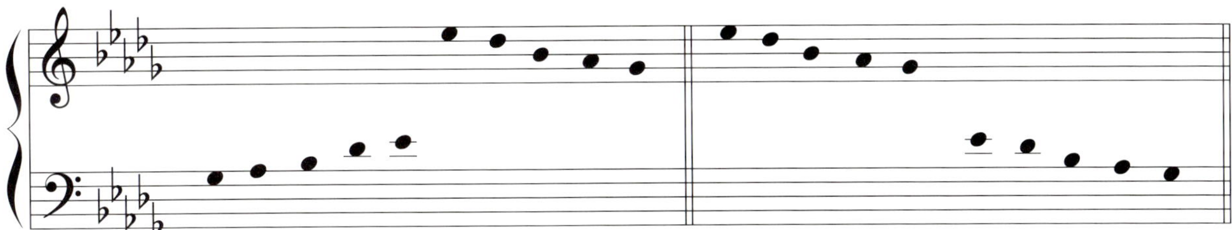

Longer Waves

Once you really feel the flowing motion in your arms, you are ready to make a longer wave. Play the keys the same way as in the original example, but then move both hands up an octave and play the keys again. Don't lift the pedal. Here's how that would look.

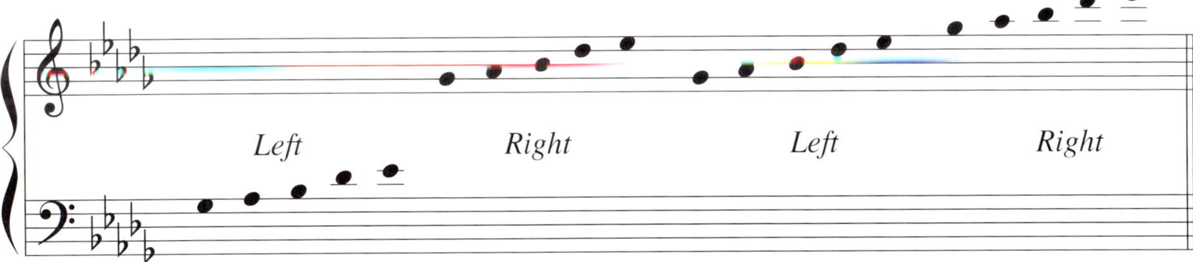

Melodies

Try adding a melody: Using the fifth finger of your right hand (your little finger), play a melody tone when you play the first tone with your left hand. Keep the pedal down, and it will sustain these melody tones for you. You could also invite a friend to create melodies with you, either on the piano or some other instrument. A flute fits this Pattern perfectly. Keep a gentle flow in your playing. Here's an example to try.

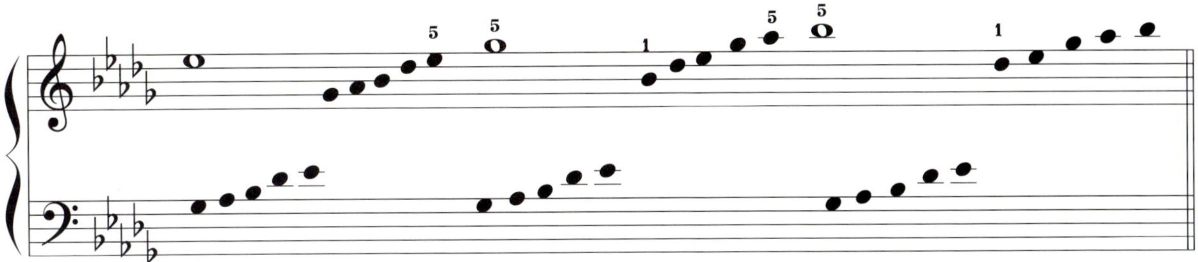

Music is the medicine of the mind. —John Logan

Simultaneous Playing

Rather than playing your hands one after the other, why not play them together? In the first example below, both hands play from the bottom note to the top. In the second example, the hands are both moving from the little fingers toward the thumb. As you move toward the thumbs, let your wrists move downward. This makes life more relaxing for your wrists.

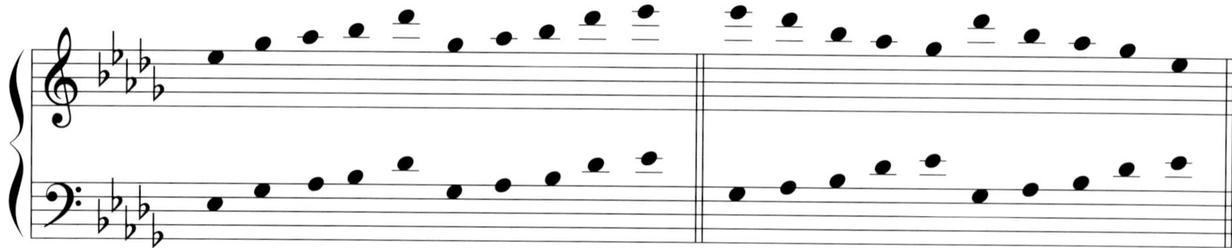

Melody and Accompaniment

For a different yet related sound, play pairs of keys on your right side instead of making the harp-like motions. Keep the harp-like movement on your left side to serve as an accompaniment.

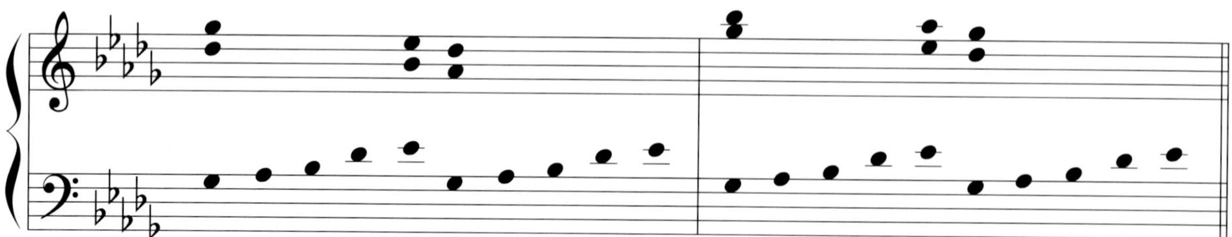

Adding Bass Tones

For a fuller sound, play a black key in the bass while you hold the pedal down. Or try playing a *b natural* or an *e natural* in the bass to create an intriguing sound. Notice how the bass tones sustain for a much longer time than the higher tones.

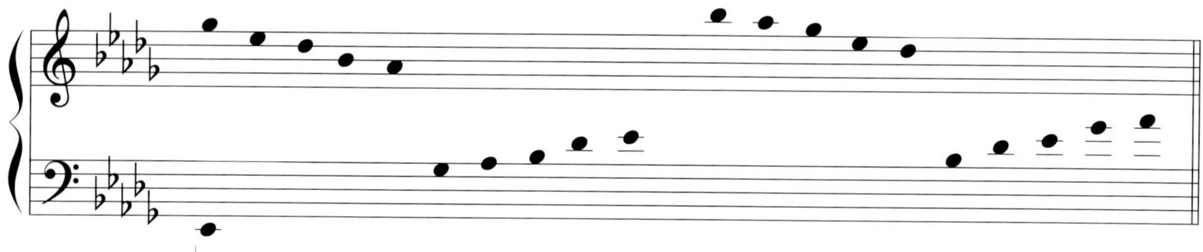

Other Sounds

For a Vacation from these harp-like Patterns, why not create melodies above some of your favorite accompaniment Patterns from *World Piece*? If you are playing this Pattern on a synthesizer, try the sound of a *koto* (a Japanese string instrument), classical guitar, or some other exotic string sound.

The Pedal: The Soul of the Piano

The pedal on the right is sometimes called the *damper pedal* or, just as often, the *sustain pedal*. Since it is the only pedal that is used regularly, it is most often simply called *the pedal*. Why is it called a "damper" pedal when it actually "sustains" the sound? The name doesn't seem to make sense. And why did Chopin and others call this pedal "the soul of the piano"?

If you have ever played a harp or a guitar, you know that the strings continue vibrating and making sounds after you strike them. You must press your hand against the strings to stop the vibrations. So why don't the strings of the piano keep vibrating after we play them?

Pressing up against each string is a piece of white felt that keeps the string from vibrating. This piece of felt lifts *off* the string each time we press down a key so the string is free to vibrate. When we release the key, the felt again presses against the string to *stop* the sound. These felts are called "dampers" because they dampen the sound. (I was just wondering if "damper" is related to the word "dampen" meaning "to make moist." My dictionary says they are. They both come from a word meaning "mist or fog." Damp, gray weather dampens our spirits.)

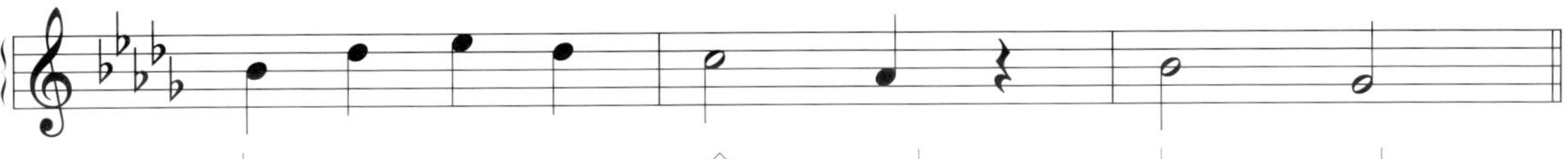

Modern pedal markings: The horizontal line means to keep the pedal down. The vertical line on the left means to press the pedal down, and the vertical line on the right means to release it. The triangular shape means to lift the pedal up and put it right back down again. This is called "clearing" the pedal.

Whenever we press down the damper pedal, this lifts *all* the dampers away from the strings. Over two hundred strings are now free to vibrate and make their own sounds, just like the strings of a harp. All strings in the piano vibrate slightly even when we play just one key.

It is this free vibration of the strings that gives the piano such a rich tone. All these subtle vibrations intermingle in the air, creating soft tapestries of sound. The more you listen to this soft play of vibrations, the more you will hear music in these endless shades of resonance. This explains why people who have played piano for years often find electric and synthesized sounds to be lacking, despite their incredible array of sounds. What is missing in electronically generated sounds is this rich play of intermingling tones in the air, the "soul" of the music, the soft dance of barely audible music.

As a pianist, you are right next to the strings when you play. This enables you to hear shimmers of tone that an audience member would never be able to hear. The sounds I am talking about are so soft that you almost need to put your ears next to the strings to hear them. As performers, we can play any Pattern in this book over and over, hearing new colors in the sound with each repetition, while someone standing across the room will hear just the same darn thing over and over! We are able to hear so much more music than a listener. So press down the damper pedal and play these Patterns, and enjoy the resonating rainbows of tones.

What are the other two pedals for, anyway? Since I'm out of room here, I'll explain their various functions on page 107.

Creating with Glissandos

Until now, we've been playing Patterns like the one below with two hands—the first five notes with the right hand and the second five notes with the left. However, any harpist will tell you that you can accomplish this by playing all the notes with one hand, making a sweeping gesture with your arm. Try playing the example below with just your right hand. Place the palm of your right hand on the black keys, fingers pointing up the keyboard, and then sweep down the keys while holding the pedal down. This is called playing a *glissando*.

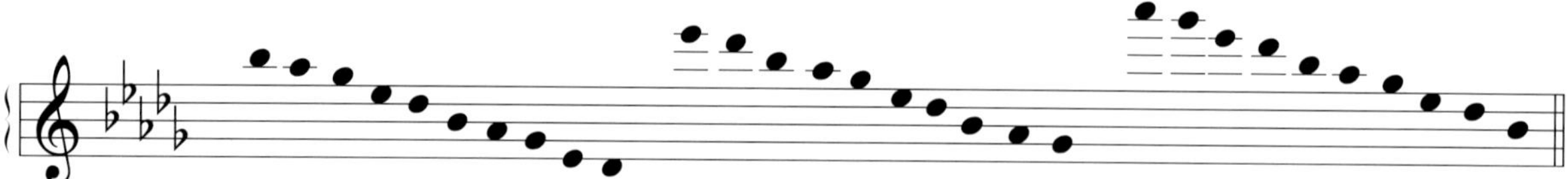

You can play one glissando with your right hand, the second with your left, and the third with your right. In the example below, RH means right hand and LH means left hand. This alternation allows us to play the glissandos quickly, creating a swirl of cascading tones. Try making falling cascades with both hands while creating melodies with octaves on your left side.

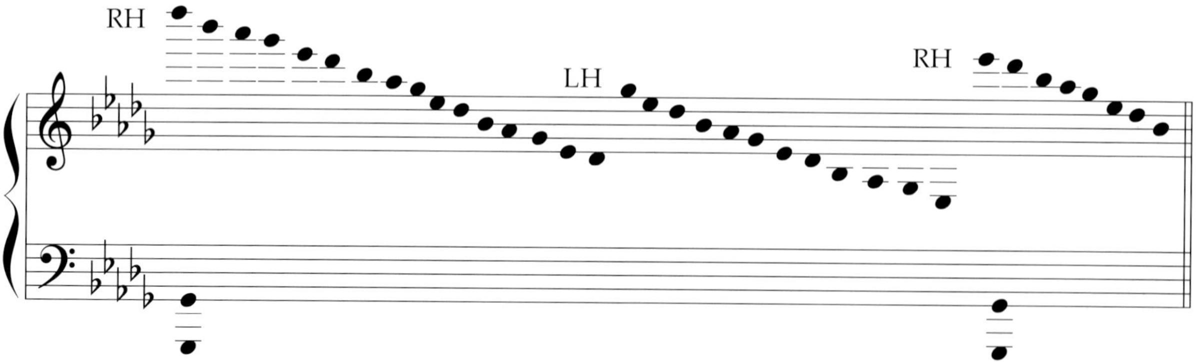

What goes down can also go up. To play the glissandos in this example, turn your right hand over so you can see your palm, and then make rapid movements up the keyboard with your fingernails making contact with the keys. Create bass lines and other sounds on your left side.

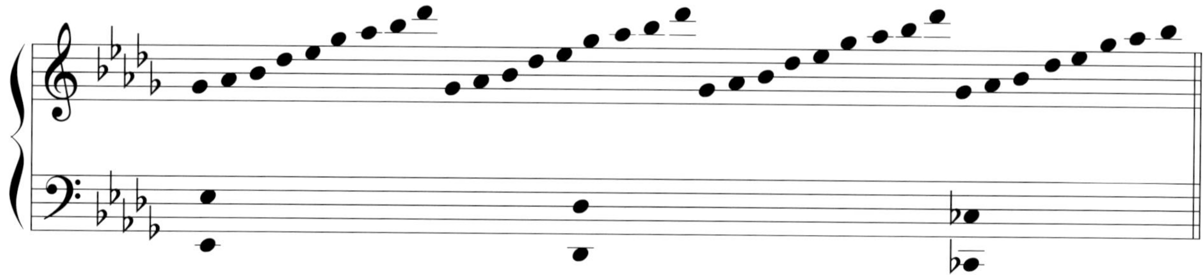

To make a duet, you could play swirling glissandos with both hands while your partner plays melodies below *middle c* with the right hand and bass tones with the left. Or you could play glissandos on your right side and bass tones on your left, while an instrumentalist plays melodies. Though your friends may at first complain about all the flats, they will be silenced by the rich sounds you make.

More Creating with Glissandos

Now try creating with glissandos that go both up and down, flipping your right hand over each time you change directions. Play octaves or single notes on your left side, using black keys or *c flat (b natural)* or even *e natural.* (In the next section on Major Scales, you will see why these particular white keys belong with the black keys.) Keeping the pedal down, make rainbows of colorful sounds by sweeping your right hand up and down over any black keys.

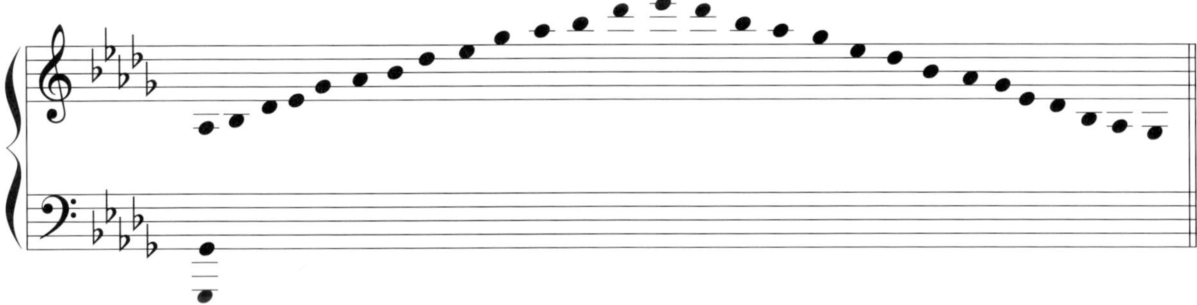

Try making quick bursts of cascading glissandos with your right side while playing octaves in the low bass. Then, holding down the pedal, create melodies in the mid-range of the piano.

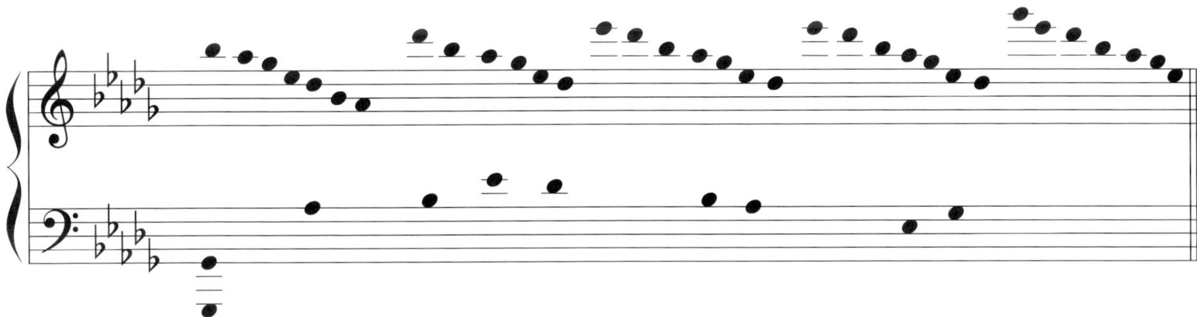

Press the pedal down and then make two rainbows of colorful sounds at once. In the example below, your arms will be moving in opposite directions, contrary to one another. Try moving them in the same direction too—both going up or both going down at the same time. Try playing these glissandos at different times rather than simultaneously.

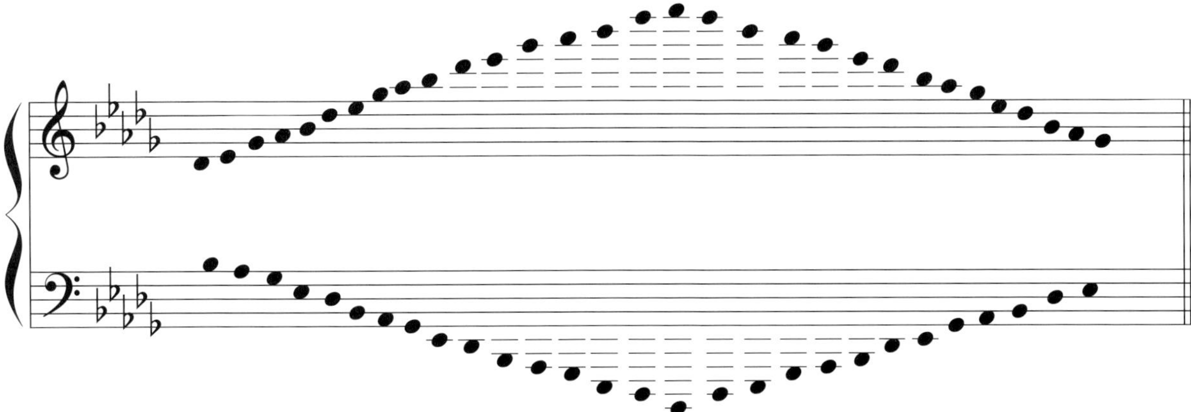

Africa

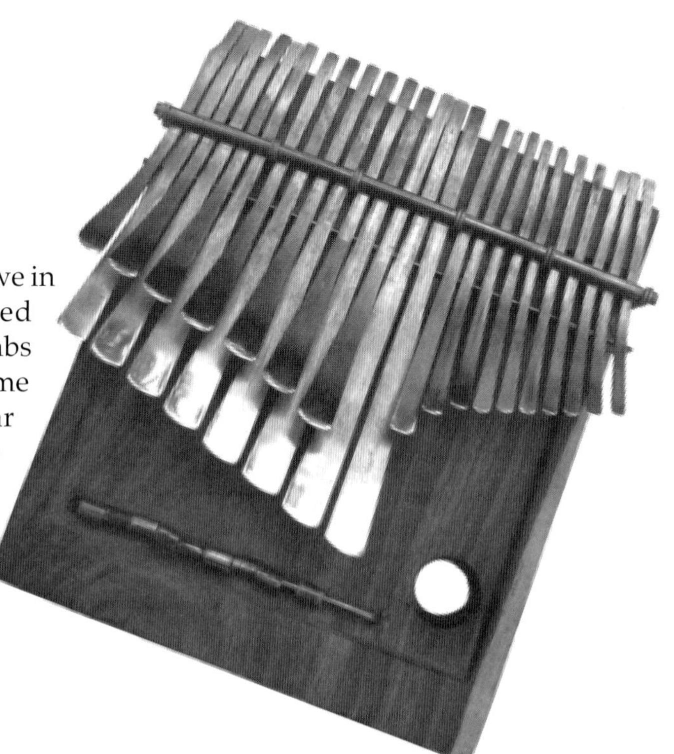

This is a musical instrument from Zimbabwe in Africa. It's called an *mbira,* pronounced *imbeera*. The keys are played with the thumbs and right index fingers. Big music can come from this small instrument! The irregular shape of the keys and their odd arrangement is a reminder that music doesn't have to be perfectly shaped. If it is true to our feelings, that is the important thing. What matters is whether the tones fit our spirit as we create them.

Pattern

This Pattern is meant for two people. One person (a piano teacher?) plays this Pattern while the other person makes rhythmic melodies on black keys. Introduce the bass line first, then bring in the right-side chords, and then bring in the melody. In case no one else is around, you can play this solo by playing just one of these lines with your left hand while you create melodies with your right.

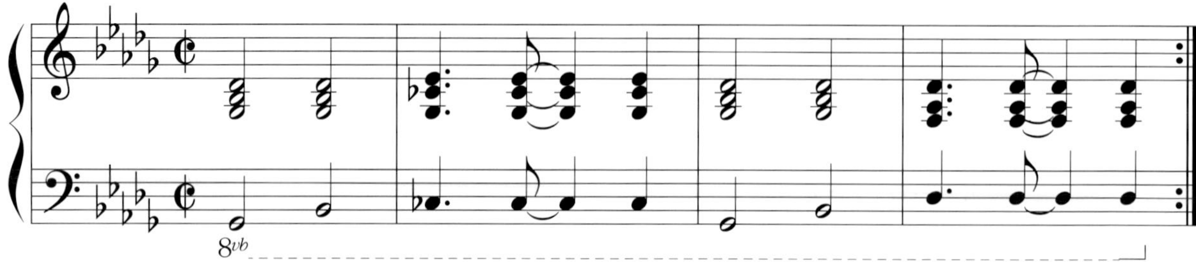

Pattern One Variation

Here the notes of the Pattern are broken up, creating a steady stream of eighth notes. However, the basic rhythm is the same, as indicated by the accents.

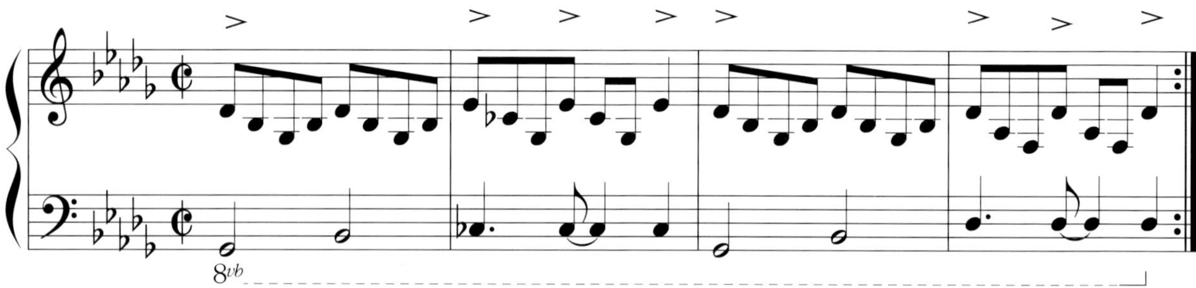

Pattern Variation Two

The same notes of the Pattern are played differently once again. Notice how, in this Pattern Variation, the first measure sets up a rhythmic feeling of "one two three" and the second measure plays against this with a "one two" feeling. This contrasts with the original Pattern where the first measure sets up a feeling of "one two," and the next measure plays against this with a feeling of "one two three." One of these two fundamental Rhythm Patterns is at the root of most of the music from Zimbabwe I have heard, always varied in astonishingly diverse ways.

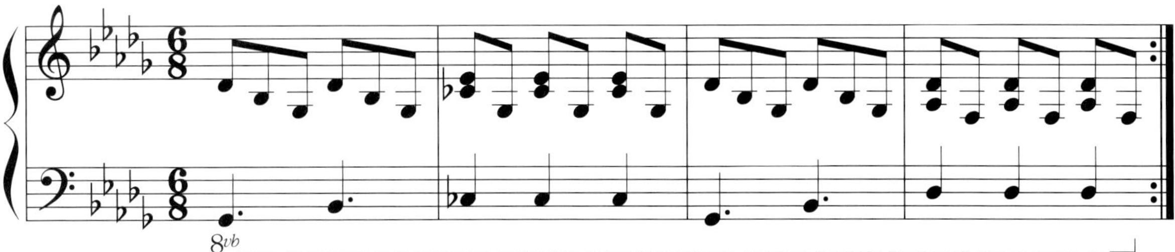

Vacations

For a simple Vacation, begin to play the Pattern more softly and slowly each time, until it nearly stops. Then, gradually get louder and faster again, or quite suddenly. I once heard a marimba band playing music from Zimbabwe, and they did this repeatedly—it created quite a wonderful effect when, after grinding to a stop, they suddenly resumed playing at the original volume and tempo.

rit. 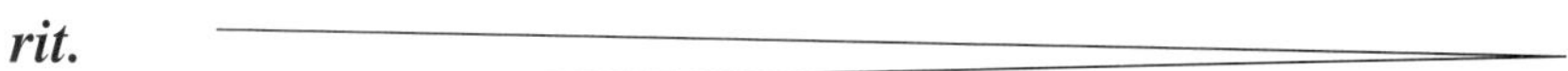

In African ensembles, different players drop out at different times, allowing others to be heard more clearly. For example, in that marimba ensemble I heard, the bass marimbas would often drop out, leaving the high-pitched marimbas all alone. When the bass marimbas came back in, it gave a tremendous boost to the music. So, as you play this with others, drop out the bass part for a few repeats, or the right-side chords, or even the melody, and then come back in again.

Creating Rhythm Patterns

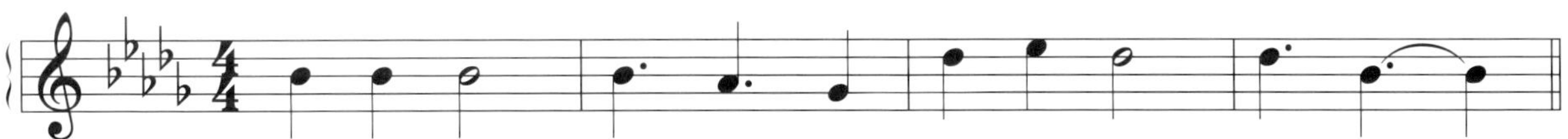

When we are making music, our melodies will sometimes move around freely, without a beat or a rhythmic wave to carry them along. More often, our melody tones are connected by a *Rhythm Pattern* played over and over, usually four or eight beats long. The melody above is made of an eight-beat (two measure) Rhythm Pattern repeated on different pitches with a slight change at the end.

To create your own interesting Rhythm Patterns: First create a simple melody that lasts for two measures, such as the one above. Play this melody over and over with the Pattern, until you feel its rhythm as a whole pattern. Then move to other pitches, creating other melodies while playing this same Rhythm Pattern. In other words, change the pitches while keeping the rhythm the same, as in the example above. Then create a new melody that has a different rhythm, play it until you feel the Rhythm Pattern, and then make a new melody with this same Pattern. And on it goes.

New Rhythms: The One Finger, One Key Approach

How do we come up with new rhythms? They grow naturally out of simple rhythms that are played over and over again, rhythms that we feel strongly. New rhythms emerge from rhythmic movements, not from thinking, so it is important that we move freely and rhythmically as we play.

Here's one of the best approaches I know for creating simple, strong rhythms that can grow into complex rhythms later. Play on just *one key* with *one finger* while you play the bass line of the Pattern, or while someone else plays the Pattern. If someone else is accompanying you, you may want to play with one finger in both hands. The point of limiting ourselves to one finger is to be able to focus on feeling the rhythmic movement in ours arms rather than being distracted by a lot of notes and fingers.

Since we can't create melodies using just one key, this challenges our imagination to create new Rhythm Patterns. Once you discover a new Rhythm Pattern you like (and you will, if you stick with this for a while), play it over and over. Then make melodies out of it. When you run out of inspiration, go back to playing just one key with one finger to invent another new Rhythm Pattern. As an example, here's a complex, eight-beat Rhythm Pattern on just one key.

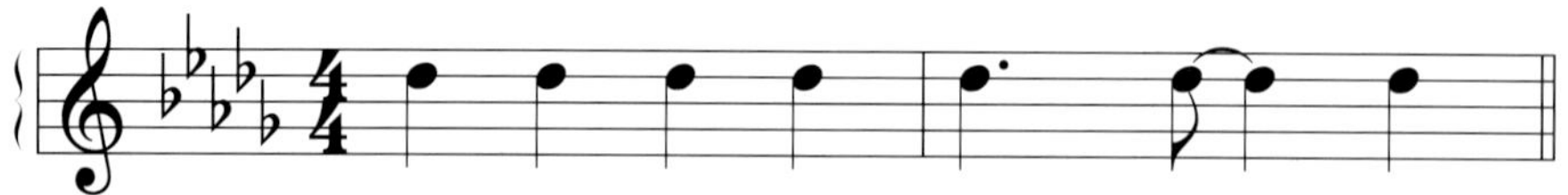

In the first example below, this Rhythm Pattern has officially become a melody. Hold on! It's already changed into another melody, as shown in the second line. Both melodies are created out of a five-key Hand Shape. You may find that your Rhythm Pattern changes slightly as you go along, as happened at the end of the second example. That's natural. In the third example below, the Rhythm Pattern altered itself a bit more. This is the way new rhythms often emerge—as slight variations on Rhythm Patterns that we already know.

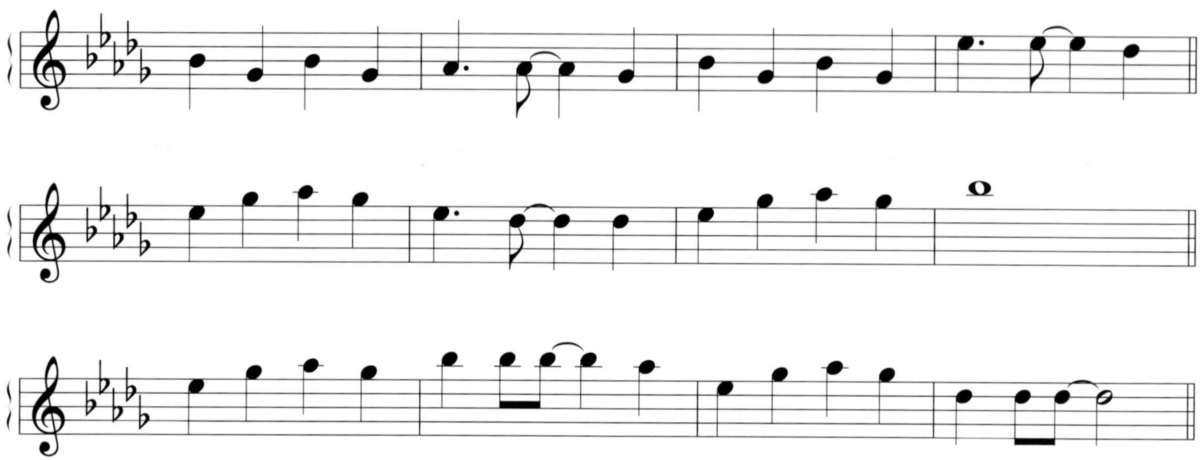

Repetition Brings Surprises

Some people object to playing the same Rhythm Pattern over and over. While it's true that repetition in music making and other areas of life can dull our minds, this is only when we repeat something *mechanically*. If we repeat a Pattern with an alert mind, then the repetition can focus our attention and relax our muscles, and this invites creative ideas to flow right into us. For this reason, music made of short, repeating Rhythm Patterns is extremely common throughout the world.

How Rhythms Grow: Variations Upon Variations

This page continues telling the life story of that Rhythm Pattern on the last page so you have a clear illustration of how simple Rhythm Patterns can grow and change. In the first example, notes have been added below the melody tones, creating harmony. Use any black keys to add harmony.

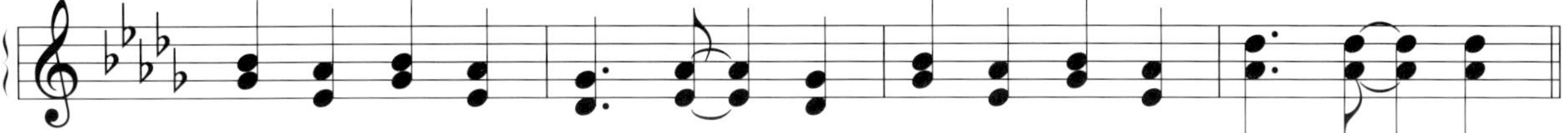

The two examples below are still the same basic Rhythm Pattern, even though they sound quite different. Rests have simply taken the place of some of the notes. This is one of the most effective ways to create new Rhythm Patterns instantly—substitute silence for sound.

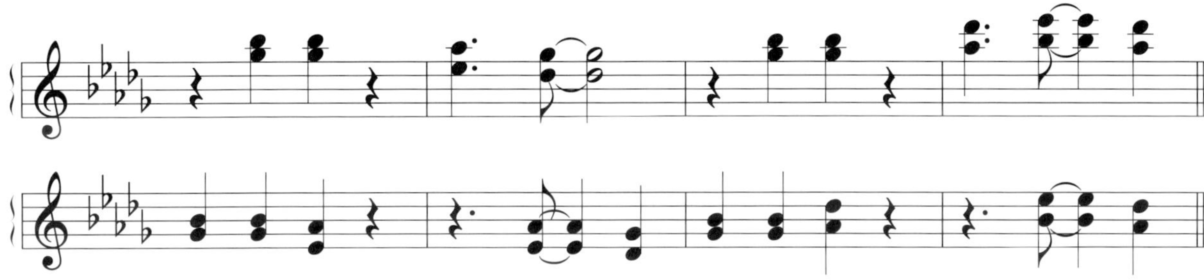

As I kept playing this Rhythm Pattern, tones suddenly appeared in between the usual notes of the Pattern. This is perhaps the most common way for Rhythm Patterns to grow. In both examples below, the quarter notes in the original Rhythm Pattern have been replaced by eighth notes.

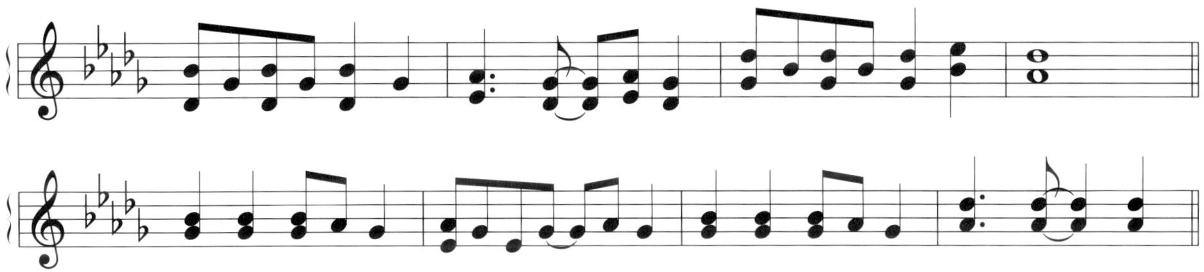

By the process of musical evolution, a Variation on the Rhythm Pattern becomes a Rhythm Pattern of its own. Then Variations on this new Pattern grow, and so it goes, forever. The first example below is a Variation on the previous example. The second example is a Variation on this Variation. Where will it grow next?

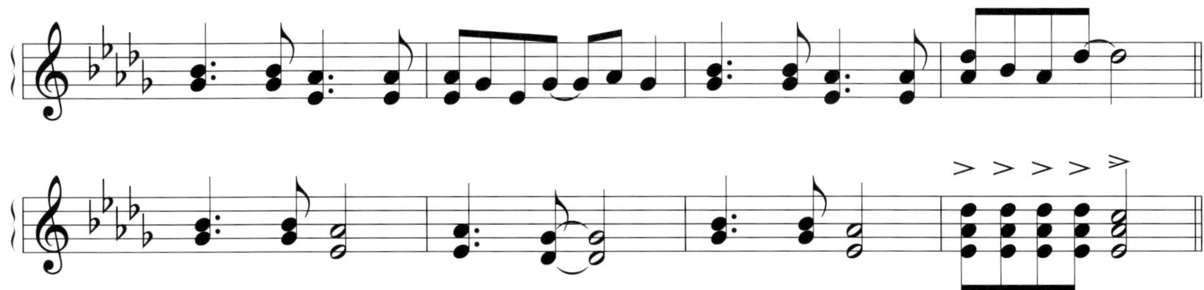

Free Play (on Black Keys)

Where did all the Patterns in this book come from? Where will your own new Patterns come from? New Patterns emerge from a state of play. When we are responding to the piano, listening and feeling at the same time, new ideas are invited, and they come.

For this piece, there is no Pattern but the Pattern that you discover as you freely play. So, for this piece, play the Pattern that is forever yet to be born. Place your hands on the black keys and your right foot on the damper pedal, close your eyes, open your ears, open your mind, and just play without concerns. Play is the source of creativity. Go with the direction of the music and your mood, and you may discover something surprising along the way. This is always where the real joy lies—in that moment of discovery.

Before you begin playing, forget what you created yesterday and the day before, even if it was special. This creates room for new Patterns.

Patternless Play

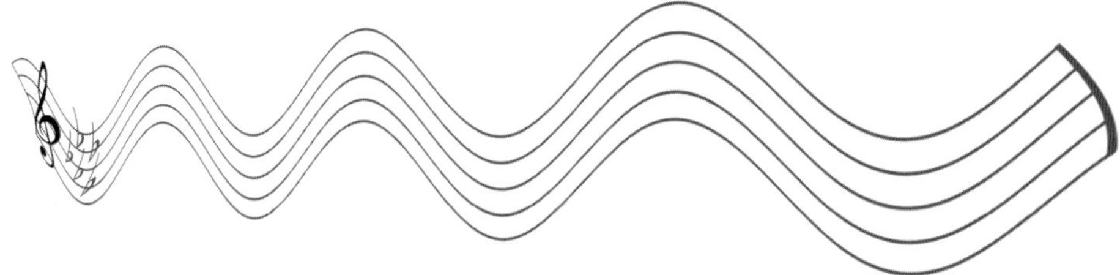

It doesn't matter whether the music sounds original or even good, at least not for now. Most often, Patterns that you already know will come to you (probably even Patterns from this section), sometimes in new combinations. Occasionally something completely new will visit you, too.

Will today's music be like falling leaves or volcanic fire? Will it flow like water or move like a dump truck? Will it travel to Japan or the moon? It's time to find out…

Creating with Major Scales

For over 300 years, the most popular scale in Europe and the Americas has been the Major Scale. In churches, dance halls, and living rooms, everyone from Bach to Duke Ellington to the neighborhood rock and roll band has been making most of their music from it. Since European-based music has spread around the world, the Major Scale is the most popular seven-tone scale in the world. As you will see (hear), this scale is closely related to the Major Pentatonic Scale.

There are twelve pieces in this section, all made out of Major Scales. Many of these pieces pay tribute to our musical ancestors, those pianists who played such a large role in shaping music as we know it: Beethoven, Mozart, Chopin and others. These composers wrote the vast majority of their masterworks using Major Scales. The last four pieces are more challenging to create with because of the complexity of their left-side accompaniments.

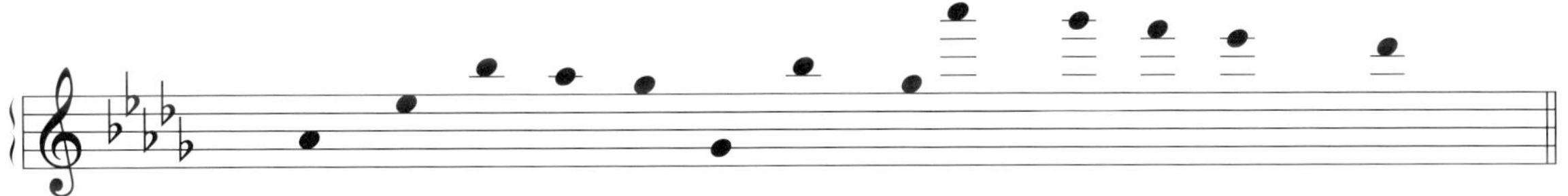

The word *scale* comes from a Latin word meaning "ladder." When people think of scales, they usually think of bored, weary piano students climbing up and down the keyboard, over and over. But as a creator of music, you will develop a very different notion.

A scale is the group of piano keys that you are creating with at any moment. Within this group, a million possible melodies are waiting to be born. The possibilities are endless! You don't have to trudge up and down the ladder of a scale, but you can leap, dart, and fly around between the different tones, as in the free-spirited melody written above. So, whenever you hear the world "scale,"remember that a scale is not a ladder to climb up and down, but a place where endless melodies can be born.

Major Steps

The Major Pentatonic Scale (shown below) was the first scale introduced in this book. The distance between most of the tones is a whole step (two half steps), although there are larger gaps between some of the tones, a distance of three half steps.

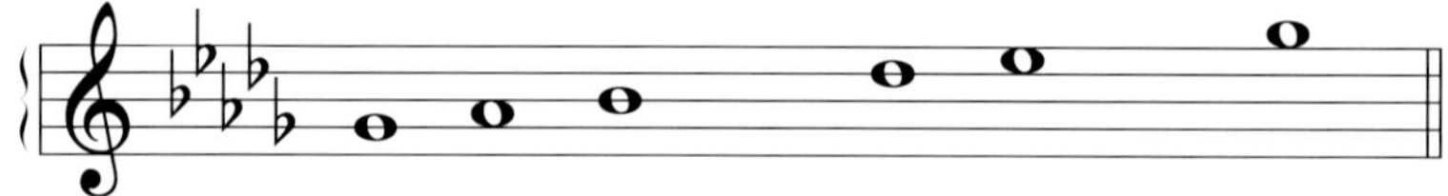

At some point, people began to fill in the large gaps with other tones, creating a seven-tone scale now called the Major Scale. This was truly a "major step" in the evolution of music. The wedges below mark where the tones have been added, creating half steps. So the Major Scale is made of whole steps (W) and half steps (H) in this order: WWHWWWH. Another way to say this is that it's mostly made of whole steps, with half steps between the 3rd and 4th notes, and the 7th and 8th notes.

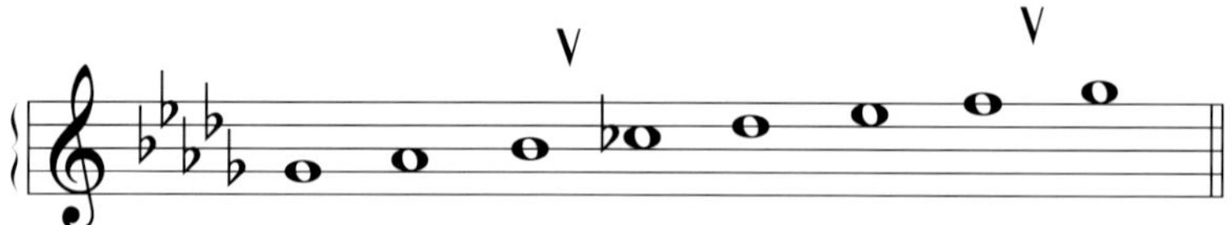

G-Flat Major Scale

The scale above is called a G-Flat Major Scale. Since it has a *c flat* in it, one flat is added to the key signature on the *c* line (see below). *C flat* is used rather than *b natural* so we don't have to repeatedly flat and unflat the *b*. Though harder to read than C Major, this is the best Major Scale for learning to create melodies. This is because half steps can be tricky to create with and, with this scale, the half steps are clearly marked by being made with the only white keys in the group.

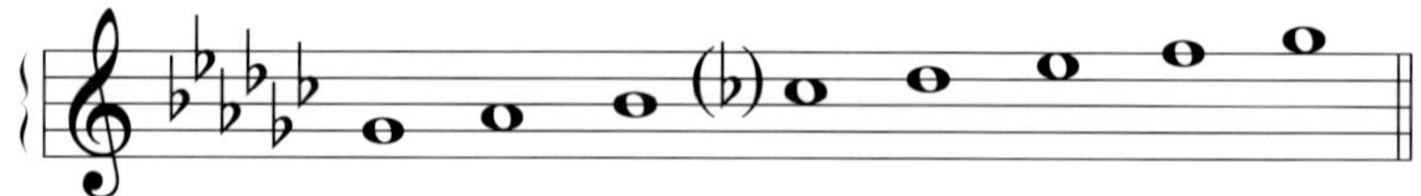

C Major Scale

As you probably know, you can make a Major Scale on just white keys by starting on C and moving up the keyboard. In doing this, you create the same pattern of WWHWWWH. As for creating melodies with this or any Major Scale, you are generally "safe" when creating melodies with the notes in the Major Pentatonic Scale (*c,d,e,g,* and *a* in C Major) while the two added tones (*f* and *b*) often require some special handling, especially the fourth note of the scale. This is because these added tones can create some surprisingly harsh and expressive sounds, as you will soon hear.

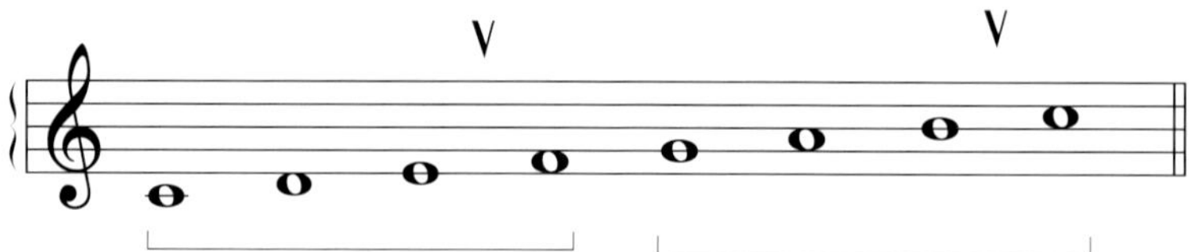

Twelve Major Scales

Since there are twelve pitches within each octave, we can make twelve different Major Scales. Each scale has its own particular character because it is pitched differently (higher or lower than the others) and also because it is made up of a different arrangement of black and white keys. I decided to limit this book to the Major Scales starting on G-Flat (for the reasons just given) and C, G, and F because these are easiest to read. Also, the white keys are larger than the black keys, and so the Keys of C, G, and F are easier to "get a feel for." For now, I think it's better to explore a few Keys in depth rather than all the Keys. That's what Volume 1-B is for. Here is a G Major Scale and an F Major Scale.

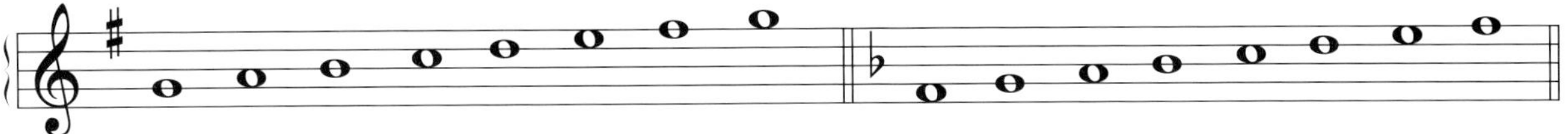

The usual way of organizing the twelve Major Scales is by the *Circle of Fifths*. This is shown below. This Circle shows the Key signatures for all the Major Keys. If you move clockwise around the circle, you will be moving down a fifth each time. And so it goes, until you come back to where you started. The Keys of G-Flat Major and F-Sharp Major are considered the same scale because the pitches are the same, though they are spelled differently—*g flat* is written as *f sharp*, and so on.

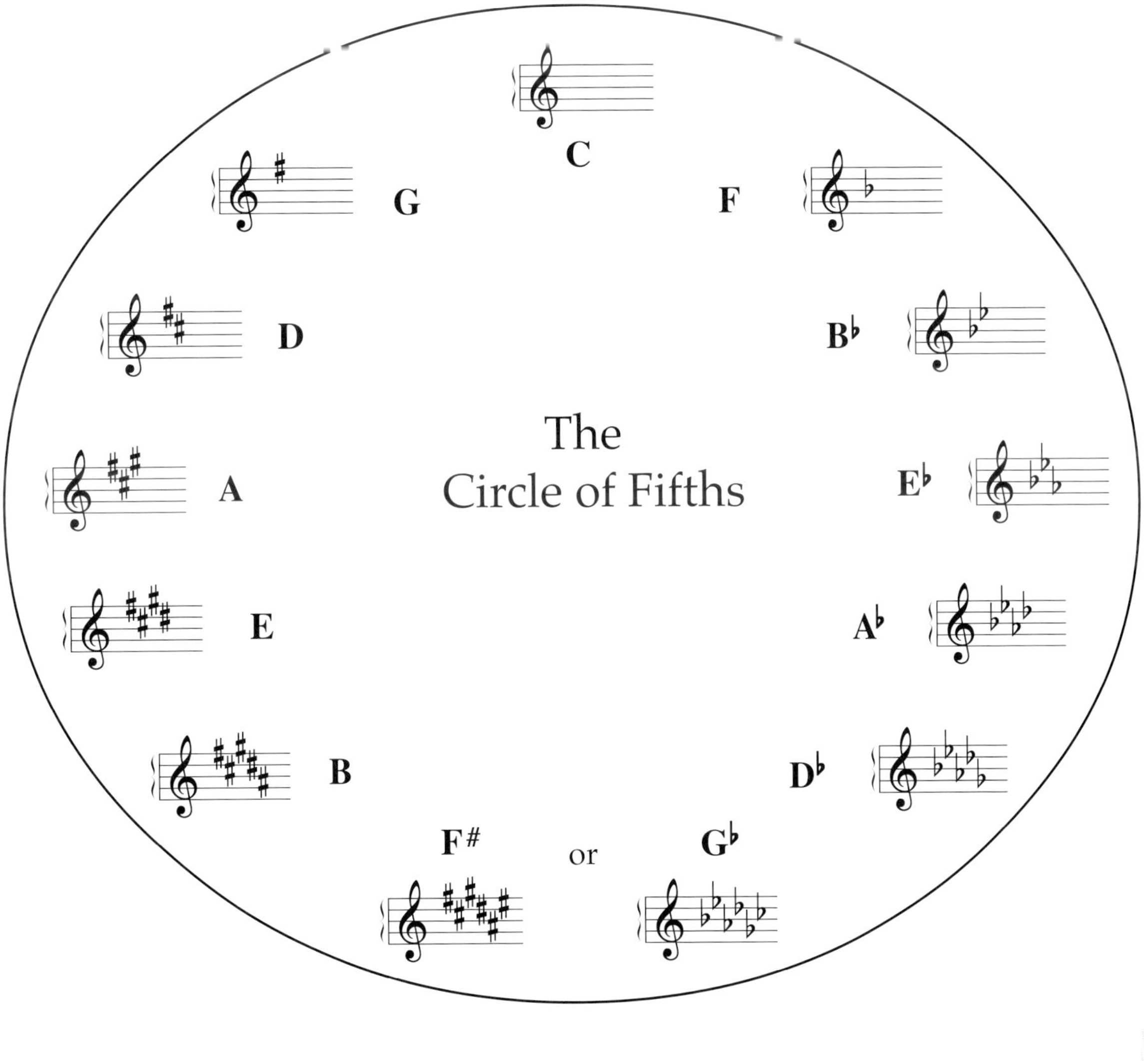

Spirals

When stuck in a rut, we are said to be moving in "vicious circles," round and round, always coming back to the same old place in the same old way. To learn is to move in spirals rather than circles. When we learn something new (say, a new scale), we reach beyond our familiar routines, create more creative options, and make our world a larger place.

Revisiting *World Piece* in G-Flat Major

The expressiveness of this melody is largely due to the notes marked with *. These notes are *c flat* and *f*, the two white keys in the Key of G-Flat Major. At the bottom of this page, these new tones are used to create harmonies below the melody tones, again revealing their expressive range.

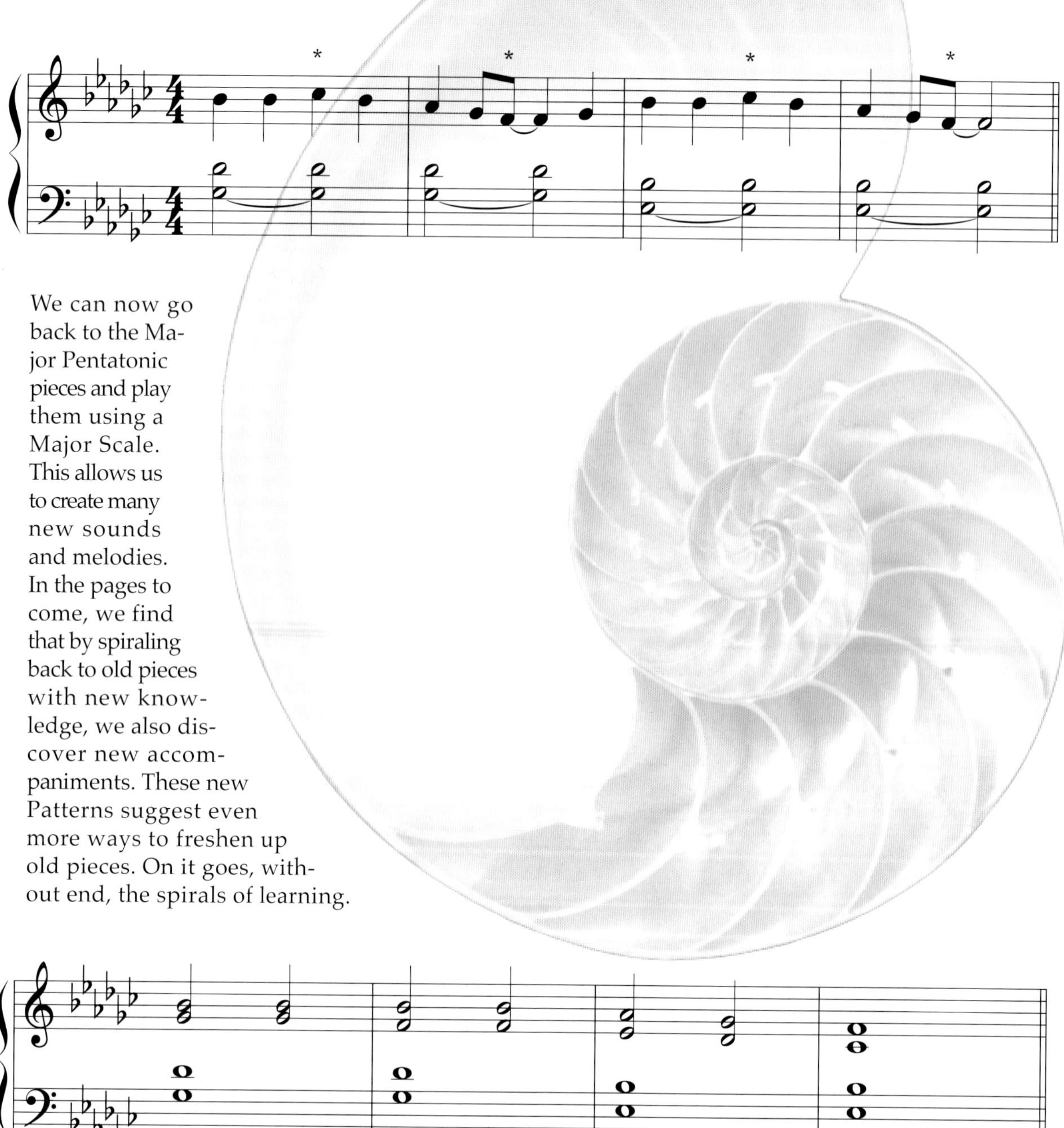

We can now go back to the Major Pentatonic pieces and play them using a Major Scale. This allows us to create many new sounds and melodies. In the pages to come, we find that by spiraling back to old pieces with new knowledge, we also discover new accompaniments. These new Patterns suggest even more ways to freshen up old pieces. On it goes, without end, the spirals of learning.

Old Pieces, New Possibilities

The accompaniment Patterns of *World Piece* are made of fifths played on black keys. Now that we have added the white keys of G-Flat Major to the mix, this means we have other fifths we can play as accompaniments, such as in the third measure below. There are seven fifths in any Major Key (one starting on each of the notes of the scale), which suggests that we can create new accompaniment Patterns with these fifths, an idea explored further on the next page.

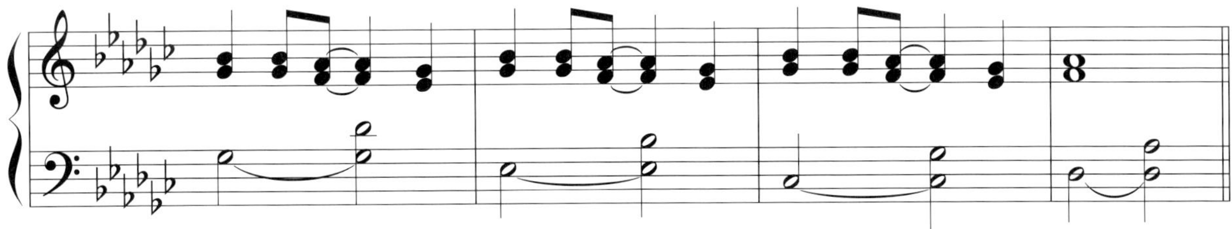

This version of *Healing Harp* includes the *c flat* and *f* of the G-Flat Major Scale. The rich sound created by the *f* in the melody and the *g flat* in the bass cannot be created on black keys alone. Neither can the movement of the bass tone, which moves down a half step in the third measure.

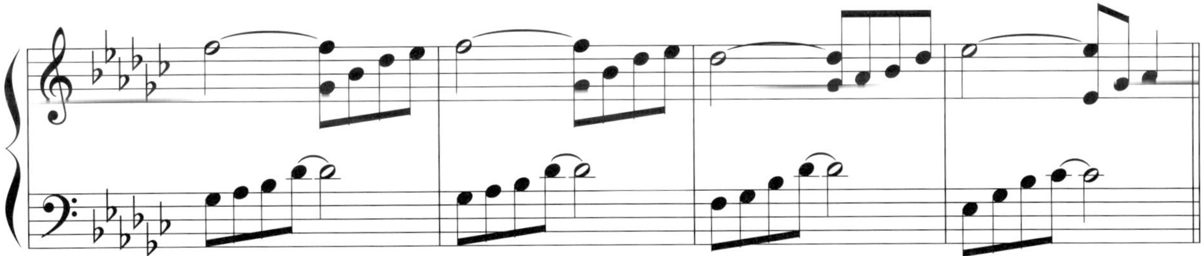

Here is *Africa* revisited in the Key of G-Flat Major. Below, I created melodies using neighboring tones in the scale. Once again, white keys are needed to make the sharp and spicy sound of the half step featured in all but the second measure.

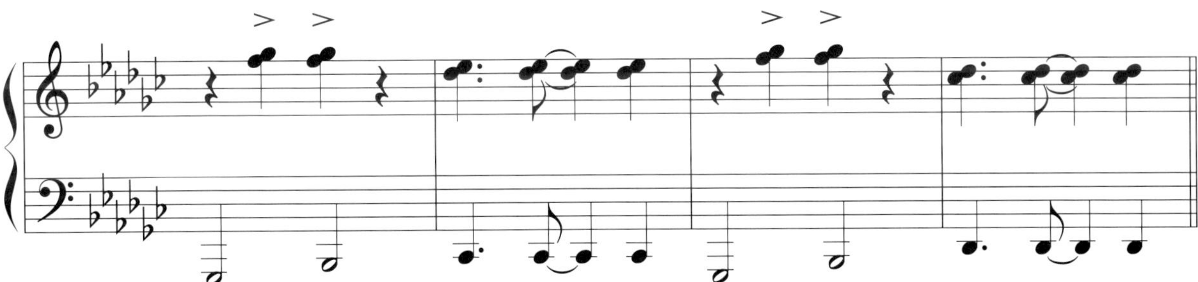

Revisiting *China, Japan,* and *Scotland*

Though the melody to *Auld Lang Syne* featured in the piece *Old Scotland* uses just a Major Pentatonic Scale, we already used the *c flat* of the Major Scale while playing fifths in the accompaniment, and when improvising new melodies. These added tones sound good. However, when we turn to *China* and *Japan* and add the extra tones of the Major Scale, this dilutes the character of these pieces, stealing their distinctive sound. So, "more" is not always better! Each scale has its particular range of expression, and sometimes it is better to play with just five tones, as is clear in the pieces *China* and *Japan*.

Creating with Fifths in C Major

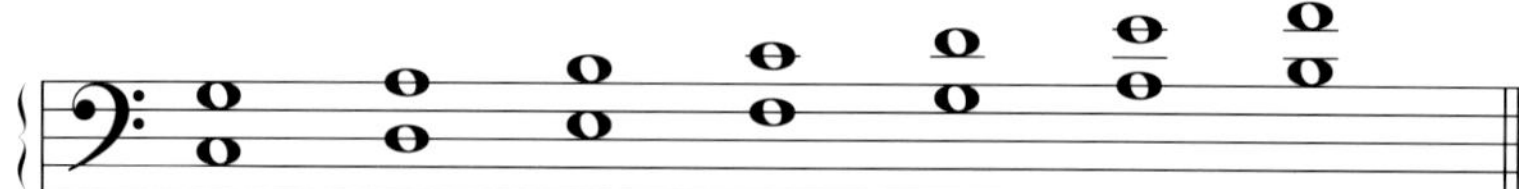

These seven fifths in the Key of C Major allow us to create endless accompaniment Patterns by simply playing them in different orders and different ways. One of these fifths is usually avoided—the one made of *b* and *f*. This is an interesting sound but not, by nature, a common accompaniment sound. Below, I've written some melodies accompanied by fifths in the Key of C. I particularly like the sound of sixths played with the right hand while fifths are played with the left. See the second example.

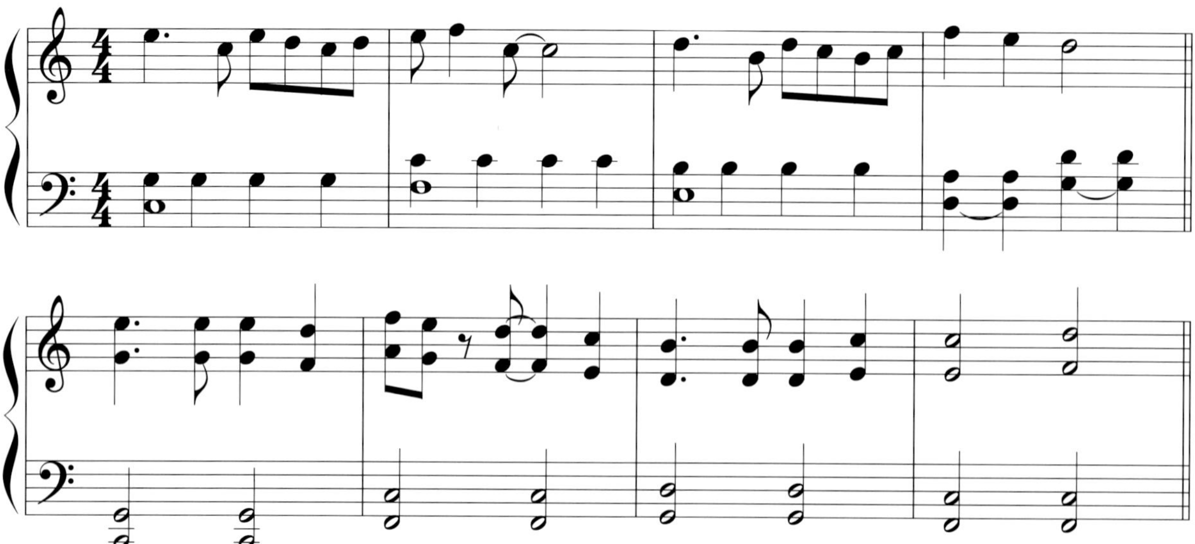

Creating in G Major and F Major

Now create in the Keys of G Major and F Major, even moving between these Keys in the same piece. Turn back to *World Piece* for more ways to vary how you play the left-side fifths.

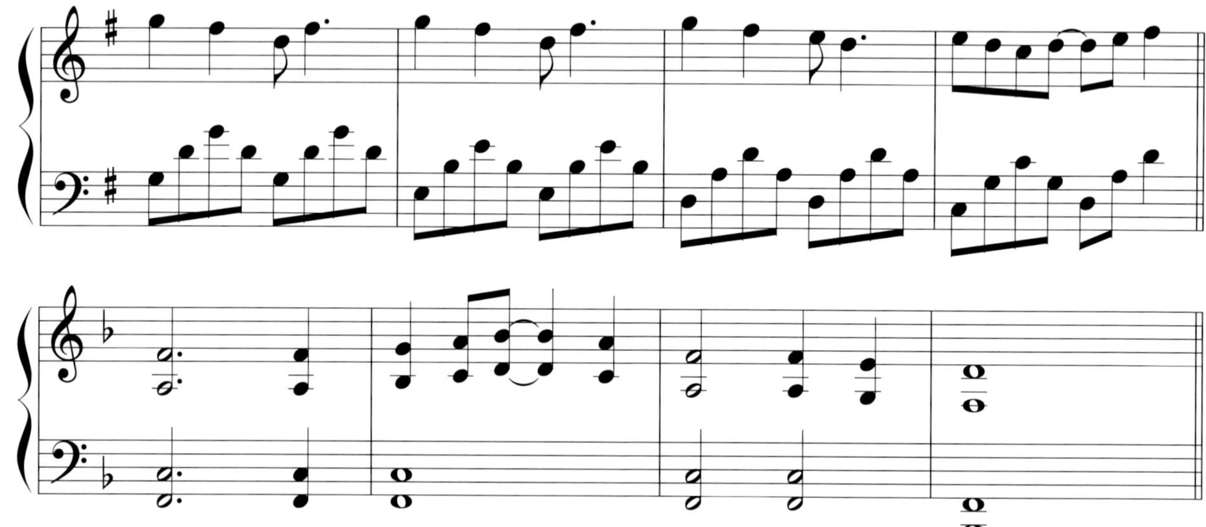

Old Pieces in New Keys

Now that you have a feel for creating in the Keys of C, F, and G Major, this new ability suggests a new way to freshen up old pieces. And so, we again spiral back to *Healing Harp*, but this time playing it in the Key of G Major. Try playing this piece in the original Key of G-Flat Major and then move up to G Major. In the second example below, I moved from G Major to F Major in the middle of a melody.

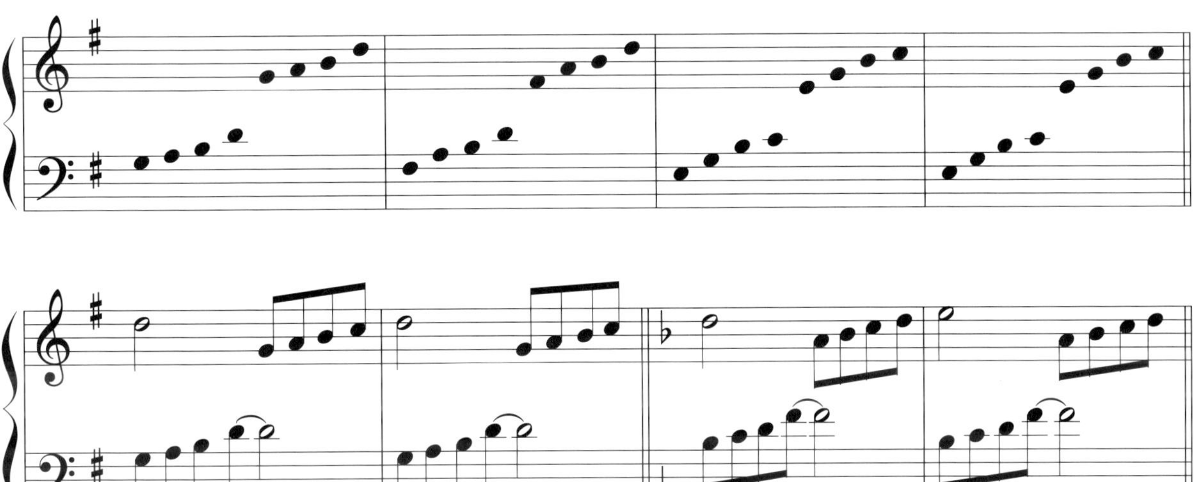

Revisiting *Africa*

Below, I have written the two main accompaniment Patterns from the piece *Africa*, one in G, and the other in F. Find a duet partner, or play just the bass line as an accompaniment, or perhaps just the chords. Create rhythmic melodies using all sorts of various Hand Shapes—sixths, thirds, and so on.

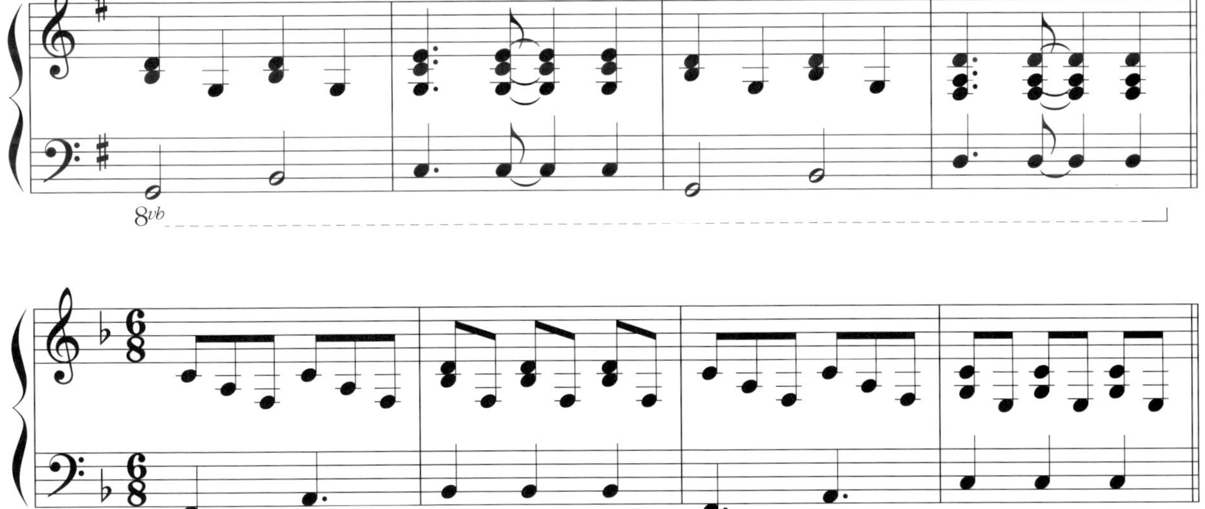

Each Major Scale has its own character, so when we play a piece in a new Key, it is infused with a unique flavor. In the companion volume to this book, *Volume 1-B,* you can explore the sounds and shapes of all the other Major and Minor Keys, and create your own music in their different worlds.

Electric Waters!

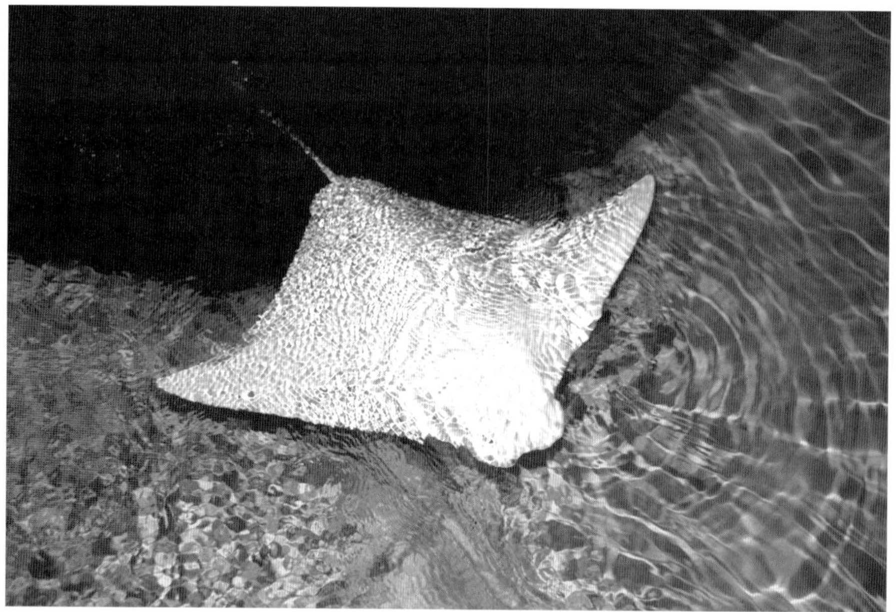

The black keys get along with one another. Try as you might, you can't make really harsh sounds while playing on black keys alone. This is why it's good to start creating melodies with them—we can freely experiment and explore, and yet we don't sound like we are completely tone deaf or clueless.

The water in this picture looks full of electric tensions. Some stingrays (not the one pictured here) can discharge an electric shock of over 220 volts to stun their enemies or their upcoming fish dinner. The Major Scales are like those charged waters. They have all sorts of electric tensions in them that the black-key Pentatonic Scales just don't have. They have sounds that can be shockingly harsh at times. The secret is to know how to put these harsh sounds to use, to be able to use them *expressively*.

In this piece, you first swim in the calm waters of a black-key Pentatonic Scale, and then you jump into the electric waters of the C Major Scale. You will experience the difference between creating with these two kinds of scales. It's as different as … well, black and white.

Part One: Swimming in Calm Waters (Black Keys)

With your left hand, make an accompaniment by softly and slowly playing *pairs* of black keys. Notice that, even when you play black keys right next to each other, the sound is not harsh. Calm waters.

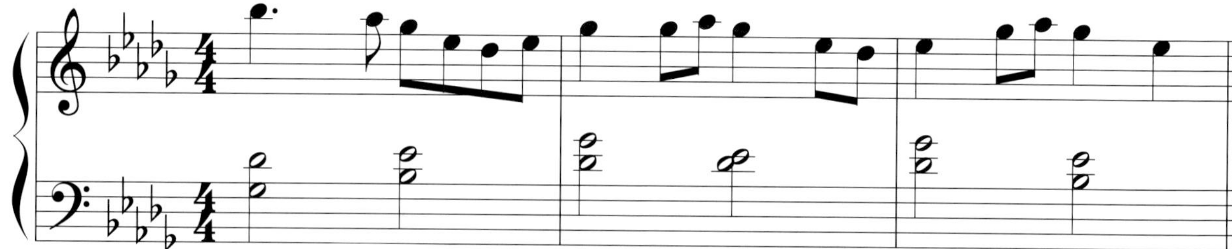

Part Two: Swimming into Electric Waters

Switch to white keys. Softly play fifths (such as the ones below) with your left hand. With your right hand, create soft, ominous, weird sounds with the pairs of keys shown below. These pairs of keys create strange, harsh sounds that you will *never* be able to create on black keys alone unless your piano is very, very sick. Yet, these discordant sounds are common in all the Major Scales! Using them expressively is the key. In this case, the soft, strange sounds express an ominous feeling.

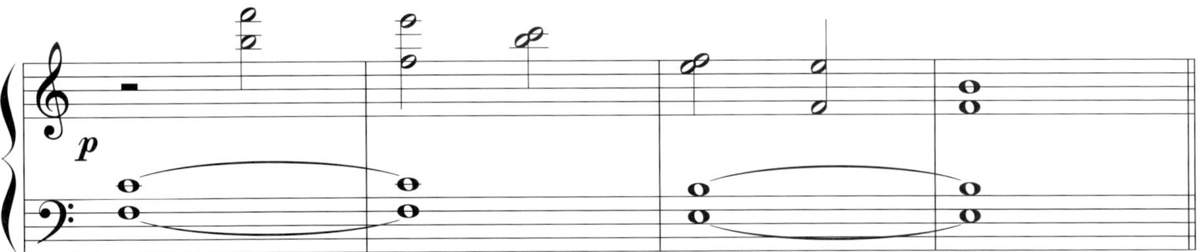

Part Three: It's Shocking

The quickest way to overcome the fear of making "mistakes" with the discordant sounds in Major Scales is to use them creatively. That is, use them to express something energetic and edgy. So now, for a third section of this piece, create something that uses these sounds, such as the music below. Or create a simple left-side accompaniment out of some of the pairs of keys played by the right hand above, and then add melodies above your accompaniment using tones in C Major, G-Flat Major, or both. Now and then, hit five keys at once. *Clusters* have the highest voltage of any sounds.

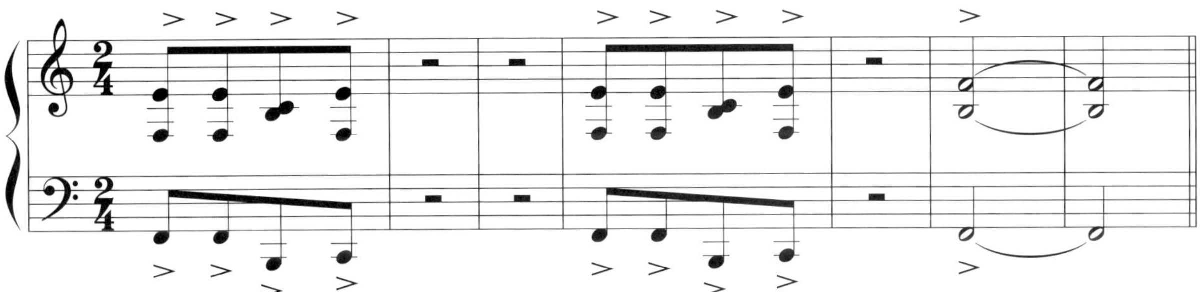

Now, to complete the piece, return to Part Two to suggest a release from the shocking experience, and then to Part One and the calm of the black-key Pentatonic Scales. To make a longer piece, you could move between the calm Pentatonic Scales and the shocking Major Scales a few times.

Creating with Dissonance

The harsh sounds in this piece are called *dissonant* sounds, or dissonant intervals. In Latin, *dis* means "asunder" or "apart" and *sono* means "to sound." Dissonant tones "sound asunder." Yet they are a vital part of music. They are intense and expressive. They provide the tension in music, while the release is called *consonance*. (This means "to sound together.")

Most people have difficulty at first when creating with dissonance because it often sounds "bad" or like mistakes. So it's usually best to work with it in small doses for a while. In this piece, you played one dissonant sound after another, using them to express something ominous and then something edgy. In the next piece, you can explore a much more common way of dealing with dissonance—moving dissonant melodic tones toward consonant ones, creating waves of tension and release.

Strange Attractions

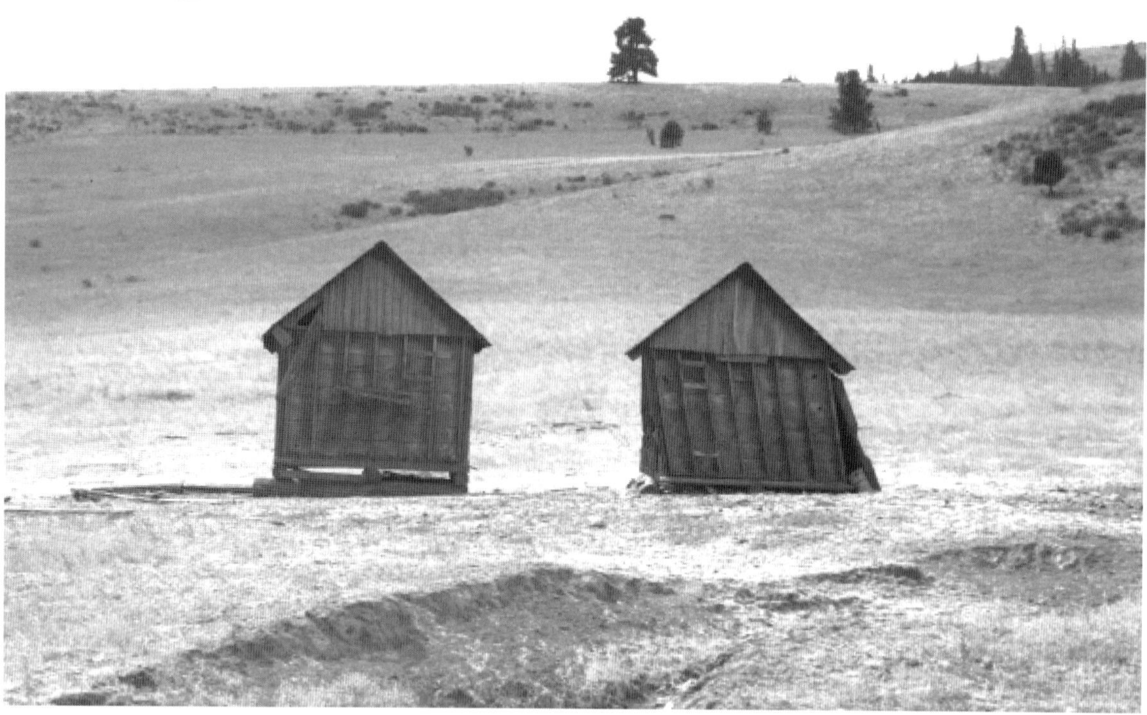

Why are you attracted to one person while another might fall for someone completely different? Why is one person drawn toward art while another toward engineering? The mystery of attraction is another way of saying "the mystery of life." Music has the power to express our inner lives because it is made of such strange attractions. Music is made of the love and hate between tones, the various ways they are drawn toward each other and pushed away.

Pattern and Variations

Create in the Key of C Major above this Pattern. On the second line below, I wrote three Variations on the first measure of the Pattern. Just play the other measures of the Pattern in the same way.

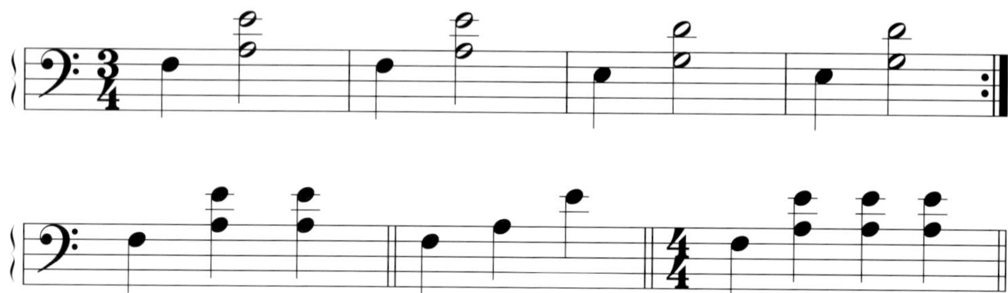

Vacation

After repeating the first part of this Vacation as many times as you like, either go straight back to the Pattern or play the second part first. When playing the second part, create in the Key of F Major.

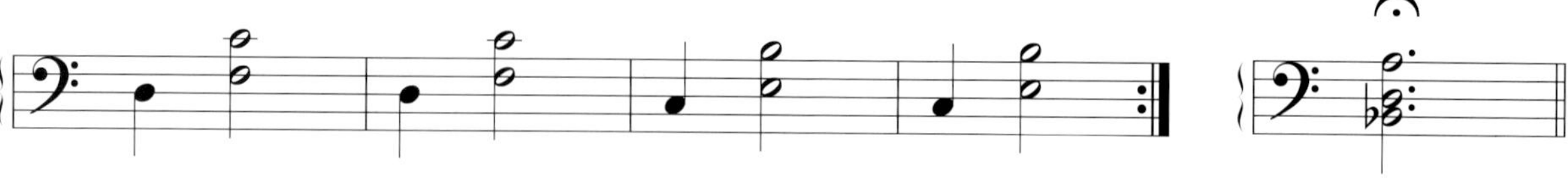

Moving Towards Consonance

To prepare yourself for creating melodies, slowly play each note of the C Major Scale with the notes of the Pattern. (See below.) Listen to whether each melody tone sounds dissonant or consonant. For example, notice how *c* sounds consonant when *f, a,* and *c* are played on the left side, but dissonant when *e, g,* and *b* are played. Likewise, *b* is "attracted" to *e, g,* and *b* but "repelled" by *f, a,* and *c*.

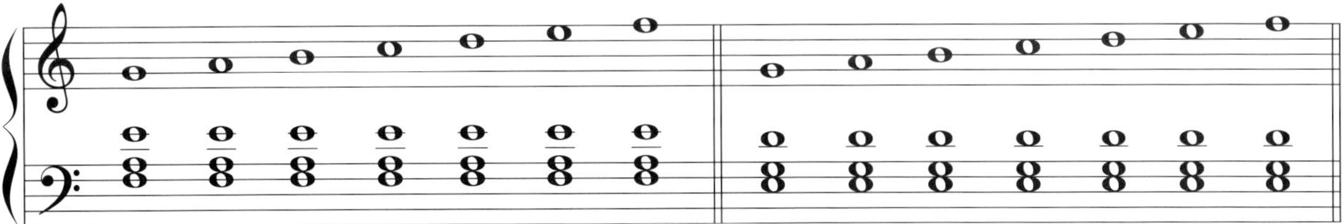

In *Electric Waters*, you dealt with dissonant sounds by using them expressively, by celebrating—even flaunting—their brashness. Another way to deal with harsh sounds is to follow them with calmer sounds. Resolve dissonance into consonance. Play as if the harsh sounds are *attracted* to relaxed sounds. After all, when we are tense or upset, aren't we attracted to people and places that are calm?

In the melody below, play the dissonant notes a little louder and then "back off" as you release into the consonant notes. This play of dissonance and consonance is what makes melodies so expressive.

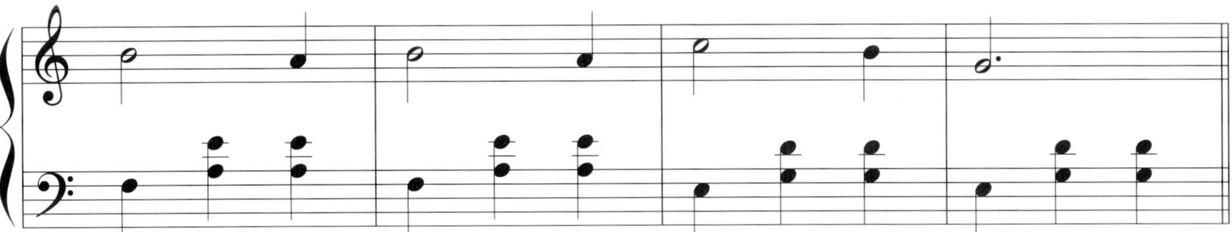

Now play this same melody with the Vacation rather than the Pattern. The melody sounds so different! This is because notes that were formerly consonant may now be dissonant and vice versa. Each accompaniment provides a new environment for a melody, and this changes the attractions that the melody tones have to the accompaniment and to one another. The personality of the melody changes because the attractions all change under the spell of a different accompaniment. In cold weather, we are attracted to a thick coat that would repel us on a steamy, summer day. It's the same with music. Change the environment and you change the pattern of attractions.

What feeling—what personality—does your melody have today? Somber or upbeat? Rude or shy? Is it made of fire or ice? The most important musical question of all: what is the melody that fits best in your hands in this unique moment?

Key of F Major

The Pattern and Vacation played in F Major sound much lighter, full of air. The dissonance isn't as strong at this higher elevation. Try making a longer piece by starting in C, then moving to this Key.

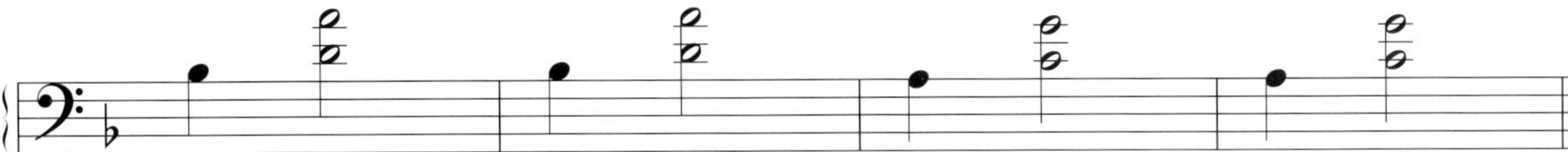

You're a Winner!

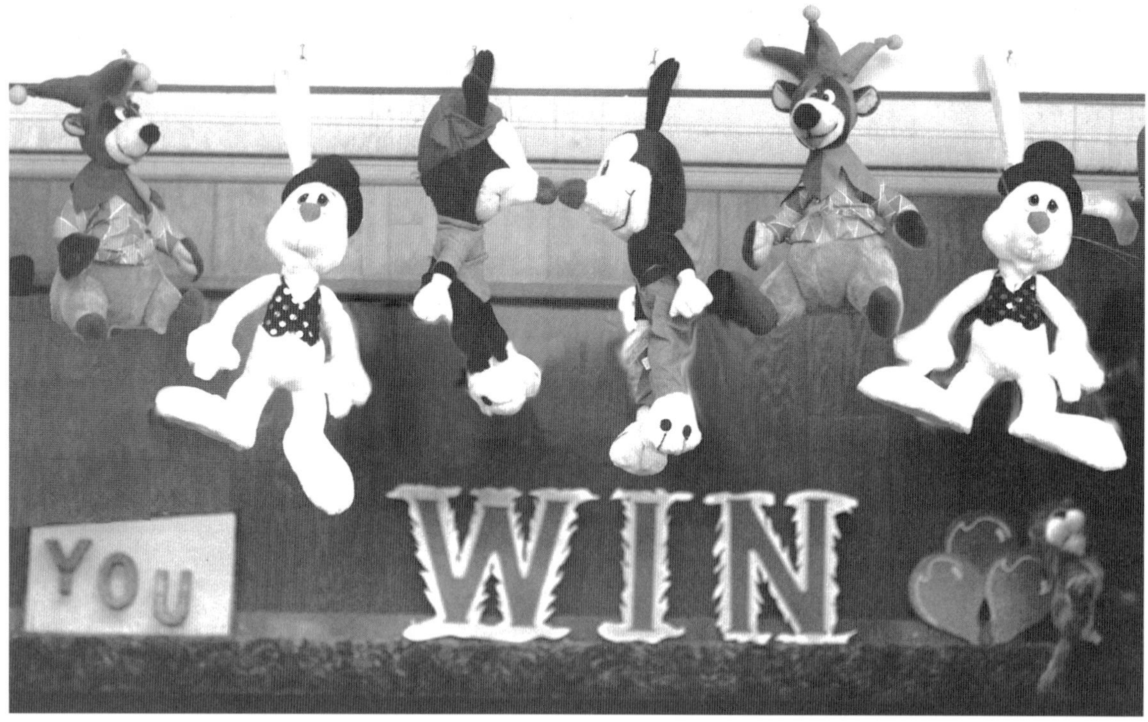

I took this picture at a local carnival because I was struck by the syncopated (off-beat) rhythms suggested by the three pairs of stuffed animals. I also liked the Eskimo kiss of the two in the center. The Patterns of this upbeat piece have a sound that captures the spirit of fun at such a place.

Pattern

Create melodies above this Pattern while keeping your right hand in the shape of a *sixth.* A sixth is created whenever you play notes that are six lines and spaces apart. For example, *e* and *c* make a sixth. There are two kinds of sixths: *major sixths* have nine half steps between the notes, while *minor sixths* have eight. These sixths look and feel the same but sound different. Also create with *thirds,* which are sixths turned upside down. That is, *e* and *c* make a sixth, while *c* and *e* make a third.

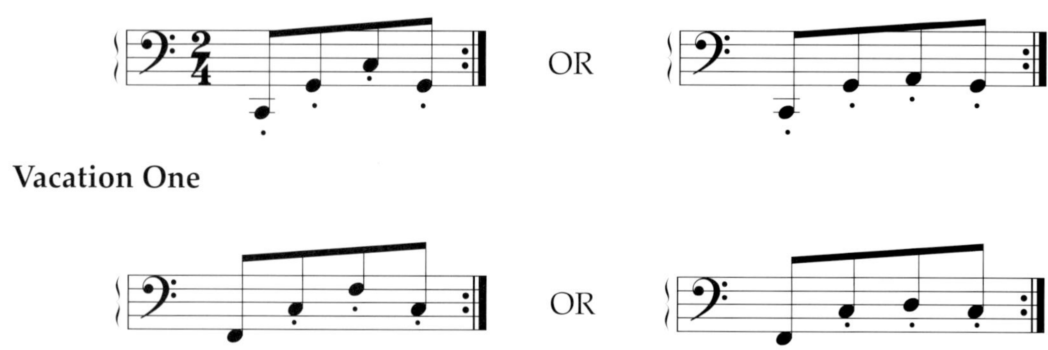

Vacation One

The sound here is lively and crispy. Never tired. Jumpy, not lumpy. Keep your foot off the pedal. If it sounds good on your piano, play the Pattern and Vacation One down an octave.

Vacation Two

During all those beats of rest, your right side takes a solo. Keep the beat during these rests. In this style of music, it is advisable to tap your left foot. Better yet, tap your left *heel* to really feel the beat. You can shorten these rests if you like. Turn the page for some ideas on what to do during this long Vacation.

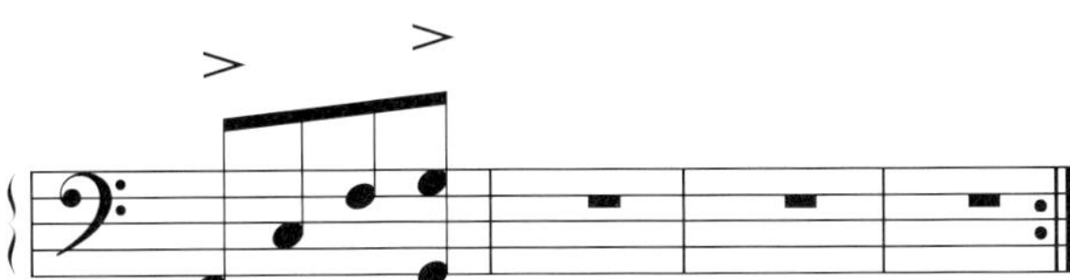

Vacation Two Variation

A good way to begin creating with these two Vacations: Instead of playing notes during the rests, play a "drum solo" using the piano case for a drum, or your legs, or the bench. The idea is to feel the beat strongly and not lose it by worrying about a lot of notes. Then, when you feel a strong beat, go back to being a pianist.

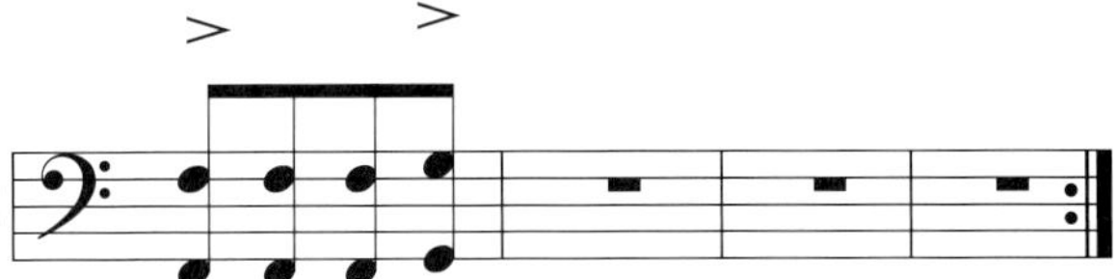

Ways to Play

Move back and forth between the Pattern and the Vacation until you need a longer Vacation. Then move to Vacation Two or Vacation Two Variation. Move between these three sections as many times as you like. I usually end by playing Vacation Two, and then playing a low *c* in the bass.

Keep both your wrists loose so your hands can bounce around freely. Think of the keyboard as a kind of trampoline. Shake any stiffness and tightness right out of your hands.

Pattern Variations

An interesting and popular Variation is to alternate between adding a *c* above the fifth, and then an *a*. In the second line, I played the same notes in a different rhythm, making it sound more like the popular piano piece *Linus and Lucy*.

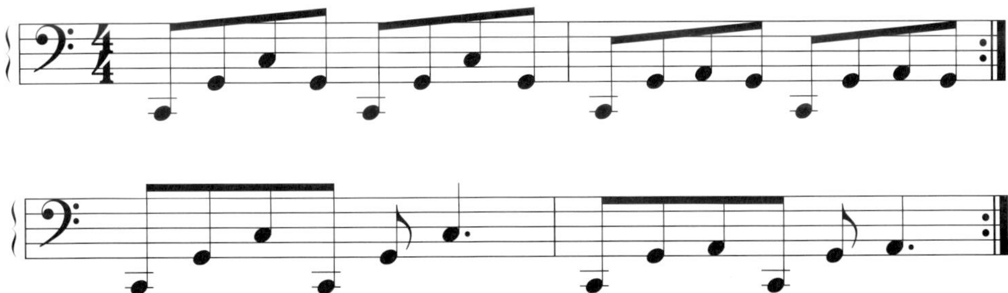

Feel free to change the rhythm of the notes in the Pattern in whatever way you like, as long as the beat is strong and steady. Here are three more Variations.

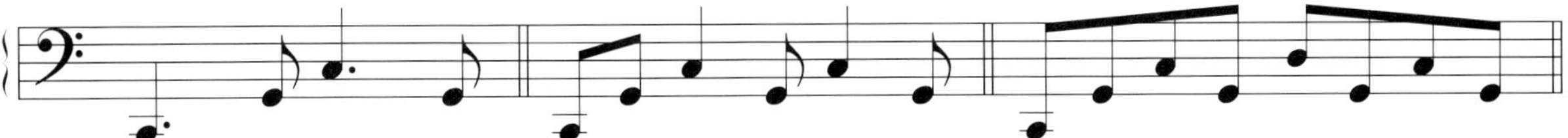

Another way to vary this Pattern is to change Keys. If you know how, move these Variations into the Key of G Major or the Key of F Major, or any other Key you know.

Fancy Rhythms

When creating with this Pattern, the whole secret is to strongly feel the beat. Start creating with rhythms that land right *on* the beat. This means playing quarter notes on your right side, as in the first example below. Get the feeling of the beat in your bones. Then, without making any extra effort, more complex rhythms will start to come your way.

In complex rhythms, tones will land *between* the beats as in the second example, *before* the beats as in the third example, or *after* the beats as in the fourth example. The more you play simple rhythms to *feel* where the beat *is*, the more you will be able to *play* where the beat *isn't*.

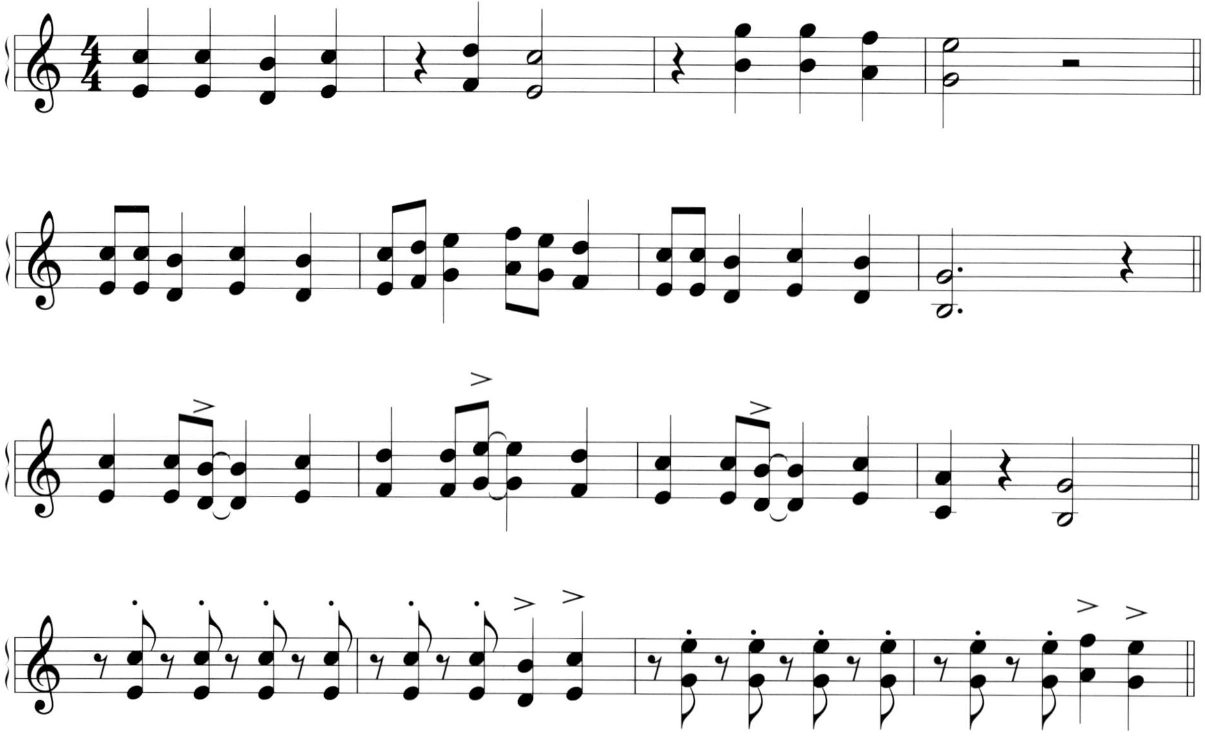

Creating with Rhythm Patterns

The first melody below is made of the same one-measure Rhythm Pattern played three times in a row on different pitches. Try creating other melodies out of this Rhythm Pattern or with a Rhythm Pattern of your own. Though most melodies are made of repeated Rhythm Patterns, some melodies consist of one different rhythm after another. The second melody below is of this kind. Play it with the Pattern. Then make up some melodies that have patternless rhythms.

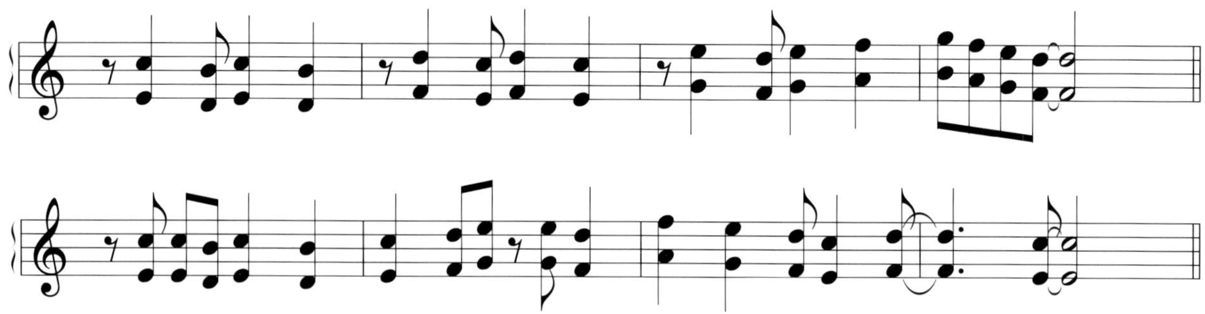

Ideas for Vacation Two

Here, the sixths on your right side "lock in" with the left-side notes to make a chord. (More about creating with chords in Volumes 2-A and 2-B.) Then, the right side takes a solo using thirds.

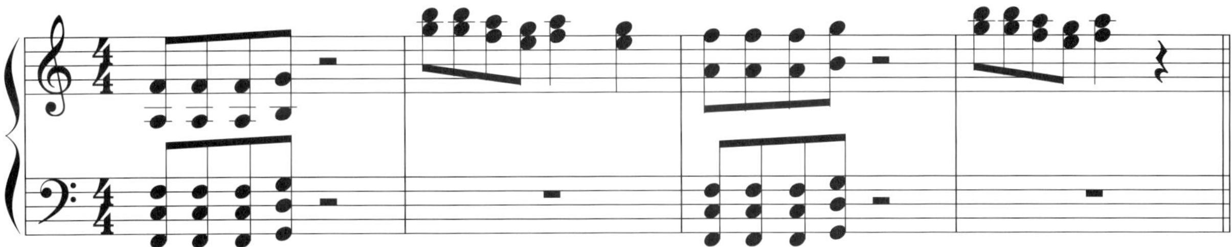

Play the examples below with the same left-hand Pattern as above. In the first and second examples, I added a lower neighbor below an *a* and *e* before I played them. In jazz styles, lower neighbors are usually played a half step below the note. Create with lower neighbors below other white keys, too. They add spice. In the third example, I played lower neighbors as grace notes.

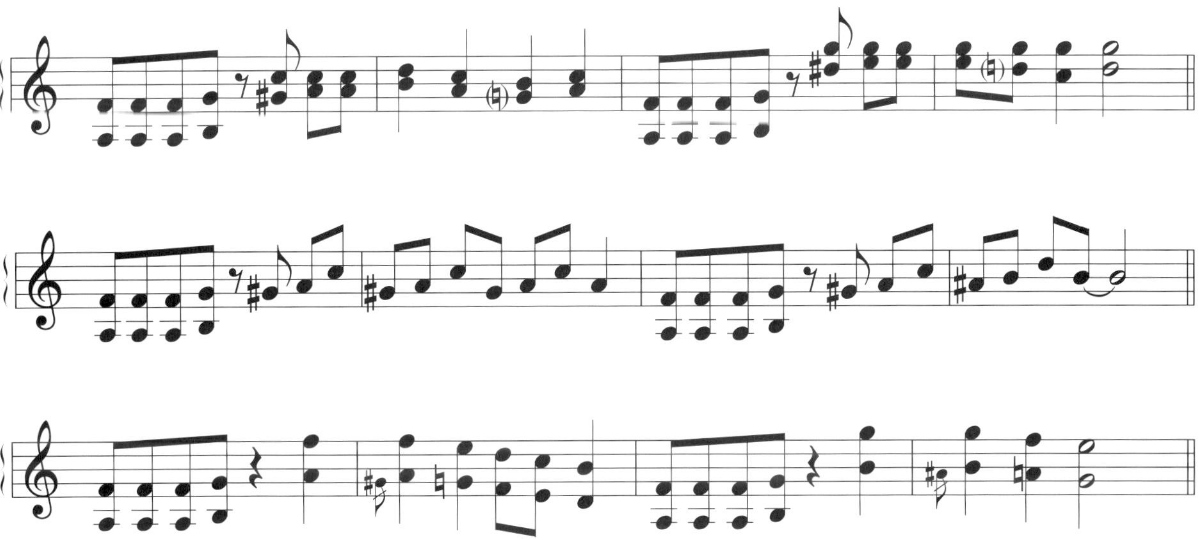

Ideas for Another Vacation

Need another Vacation? What about moving the Pattern rapidly into and out of other Keys? In the example below, I moved the Pattern to the Key of G, then I went back to the original Vacation in the Key of C, and then to the Key of F (playing *b flat* in the bass). At this point, it sounds good to move back to the Pattern in the Key of C. The Key of E-Flat also makes a good Vacation, if you know it.

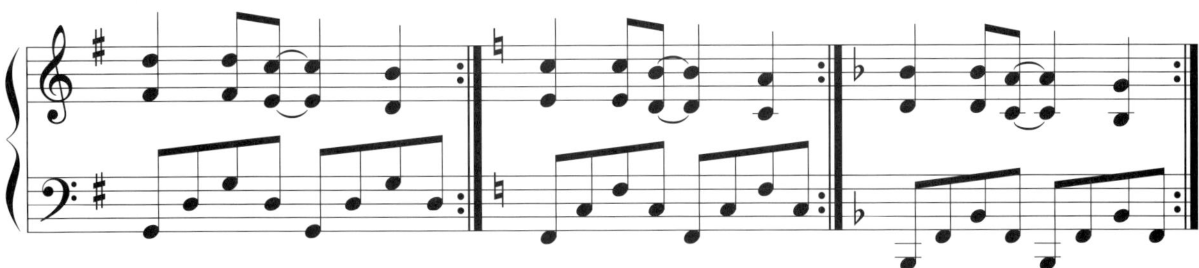

Color Waves

Perhaps you have heard Bach's famous *Prelude in C.* It has no real melody, and it uses the same Rhythm Pattern in all but the last of its thirty-six measures. Yet it is a beautiful piece with its waves of moving harmonies. In this piece, you create a similar kind of music, creating waves of audible colors.

Pattern

In this piece, you are creating your own Patterns from scratch. To begin, play the example below—each hand is held in the shape of a fifth, and these two fifths are played right next to each other. Now, keeping both hands in this same Hand Shape, move all over the piano, listening to the different sounds this same Hand Shape makes on different keys. Once you feel comfortable in the Key of C, do the same thing in F Major and G Major, molding your hands to the fifths in these Keys.

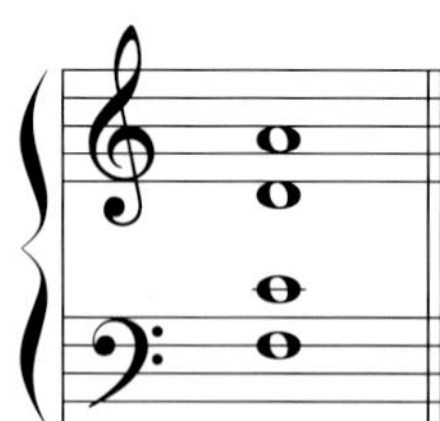

Now that your hands have gotten "in shape," you are ready to begin creating color waves. Play the four notes in the Hand Shape broken up, one after another, at different speeds, with different touches and dynamics. See below for ideas.

As you create sounds, move freely between the keys of C Major, F Major, and G Major. If you know other Keys, go to them too. Keep the fifths in each hand.

Each of the following seven examples is a different way you can break up this two-handed Hand Shape. There are endless ways of making this Pattern into moving waves. Try creating a piece with one Variation, and then another piece with another. Try alternating between them in the same piece. Make a Vacation by playing the notes blocked and perhaps in a different Key.

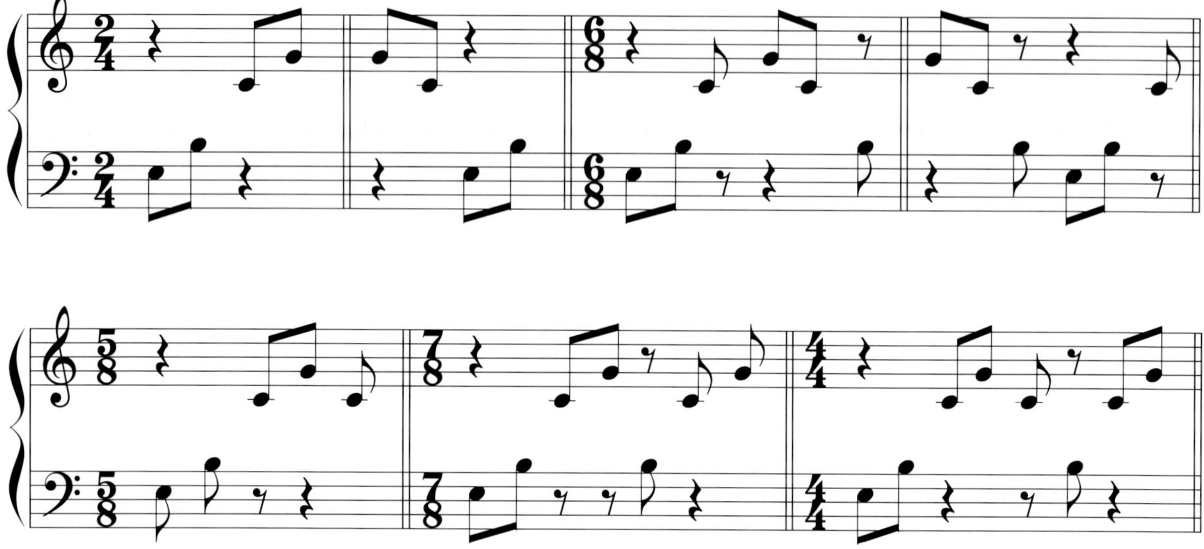

A little music theory: Each Key has seven fifths, six of which are consonant and called *perfect fifths*, and one which is dissonant and called a *diminished fifth*. In C, the diminished fifth is between *b* and *f*. In every Key, the diminished fifth is created by playing the seventh and fourth notes of the scale.

Two-Octave Waves

Press the pedal down and play the notes of the Pattern, and then play them again, up an octave. This creates a harp-like sound. Here are three possible ways to do this.

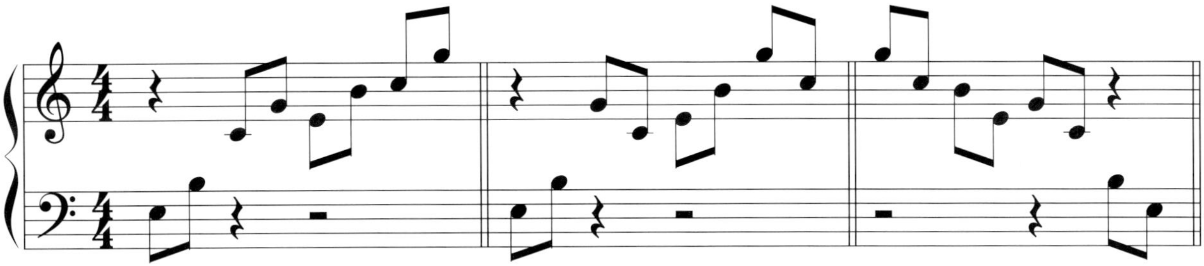

Melodies Riding the Waves

Once you have created waves of moving harmonies, you could create melodies that surf along the tops of these waves. In the music below, I created a melody by emphasizing the first note of each measure and by changing it to other pitches. All the other notes stayed within the old Hand Shape.

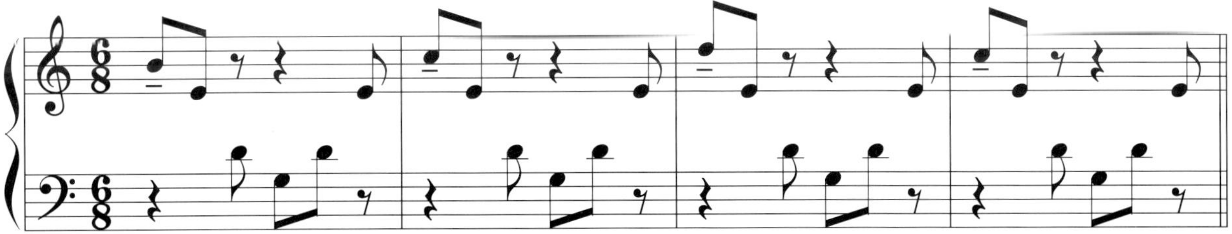

Triads

Add more color to your sound by adding a note between the fifths. Here I added a third. The resulting shape and sound is called a *triad*, the most common chord in European-based music. Triads and their endless potentials are explored in Volumes 2-A and 2-B of *Pattern Play*. Also try adding seconds between the fifths (making *c, d,* and *g*, for example) or fourths (making *c, f,* and *g*).

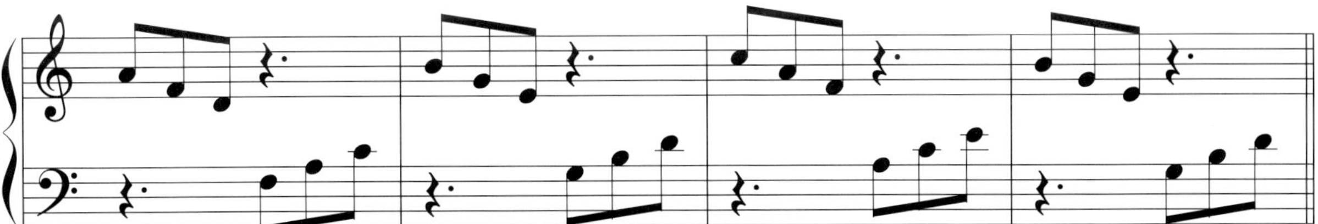

Other Waves

All this music was created by just playing neighboring fifths! You could create waves of different colors by playing the fifths a third apart or a fourth. You could also play sixths right next to each other, or different distances apart. Try creating with fourths, thirds, seconds, and sevenths. Play one shape with one hand and another shape with another—a third with your left and a fifth with your right sounds good. Add tones in the bass now and then. The possibilities are limitless. As usual.

Beethoven

Ludwig van Beethoven (1770-1827) was one of the greatest creators the world has ever heard. He was great because he dared to be himself. This suggests that we find our greatness when we have the courage to be who we are. Beethoven first made his fame in Vienna performing at the parties of the rich and the royal. He would spontaneously create long pieces based on themes given him by audience members. Later in life, his fame rested on his ability to compose and publish his profound musical thoughts. He once wrote:

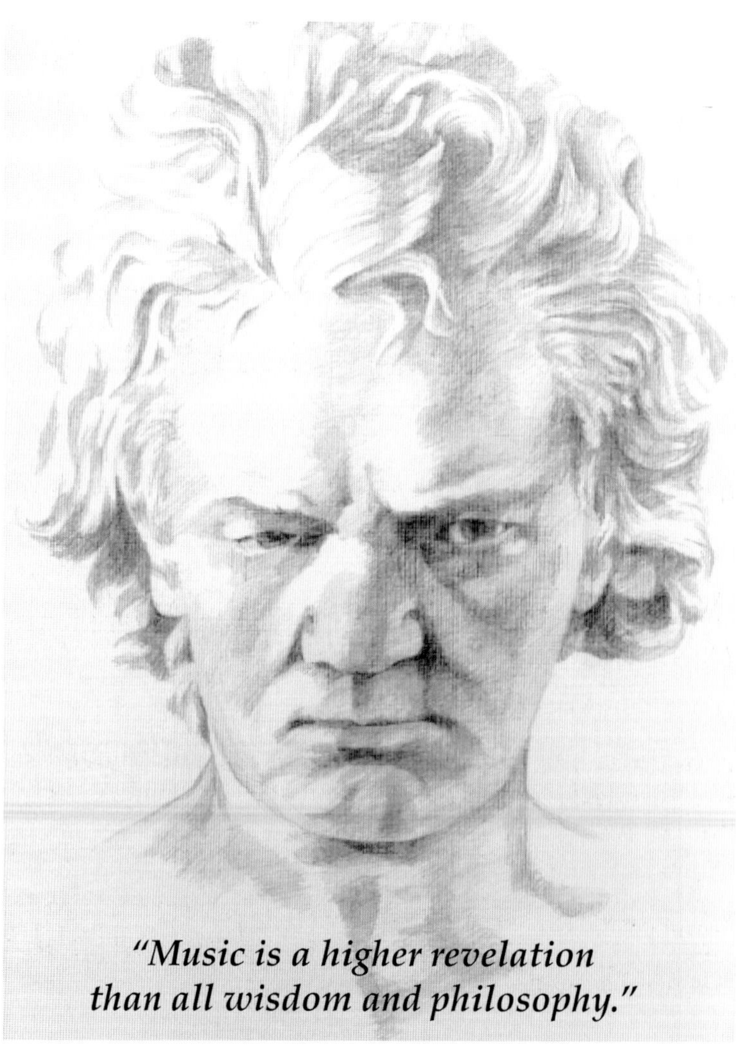

Pattern

Play this Pattern slowly and loudly. Fill the room and the world with deep, confident sounds. Or repeat each measure, playing the Pattern quickly, impetuously.

Vacation One

As a Variation, play these chords as two half notes rather than four quarters.

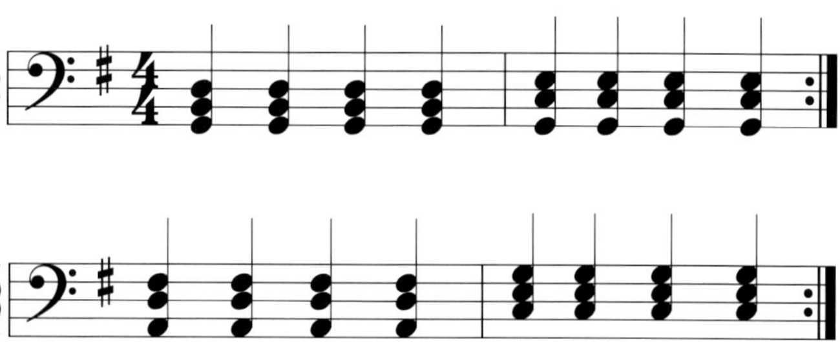

Vacation Two

Choose the Vacation you like, and play it softly. During this quiet time, gather energy for further outbursts of Ludwigian creation. You could move every note down a half step and play this in G-Flat.

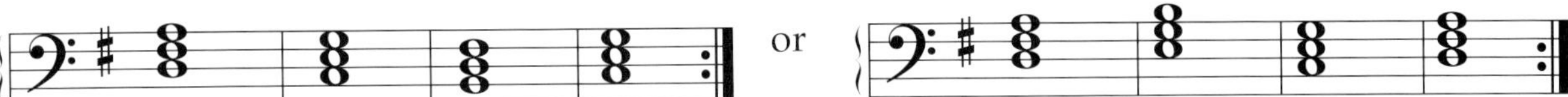

Making Variations

Variations occur naturally as we repeat a Pattern over time. This is a sure sign that our music is alive and growing. Beethoven particularly enjoyed spinning out variations on a theme, as evidenced by his *32 Variations on a Theme in C Minor* and other sets of variations.

Here are some ways you might vary this accompaniment Pattern. First, a more energetic variation than the original.

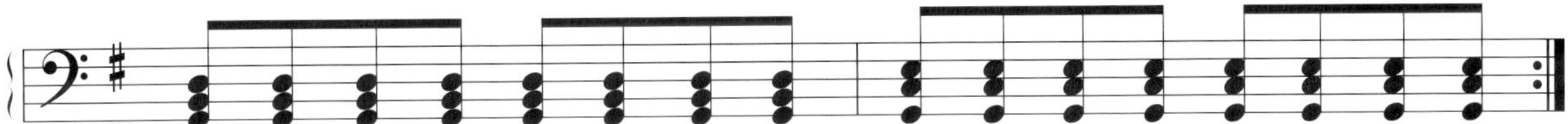

You could play the notes of the Pattern in various Rhythm Patterns rather than the steady plodding of quarter notes. Here is a favorite Rhythm Pattern of mine.

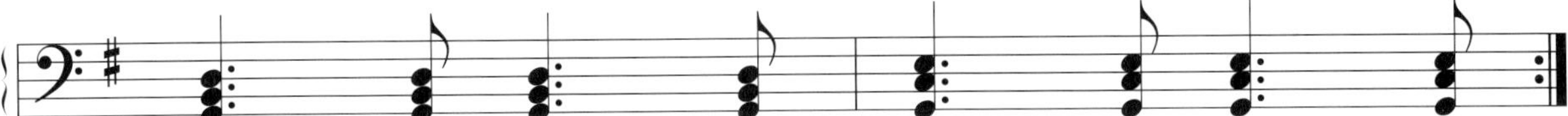

You could also break up the notes of the Pattern in various ways to create more active and melodic accompaniment Patterns. In the second example below, I broke up the notes of the first two measures of the first Vacation at the top of this page.

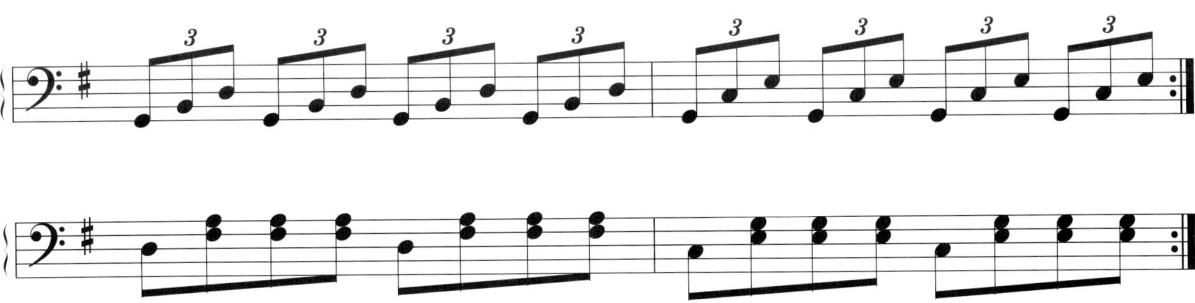

How To End?

You could play the Pattern softly, die away, and end by sustaining the first chord of the Pattern. Or you could play the first Vacation at the top of the page, and then end with the first chord of the Pattern. You could play Vacation One loudly and more forcefully, ending with the first chord of the Pattern. Or?

Ideas for the Right Side

Create melodies in the Key of G Major. With a strong Pattern such as this one, what is needed is a melody that can hold its own. You could play melodies in a deeper range of the piano than usual.

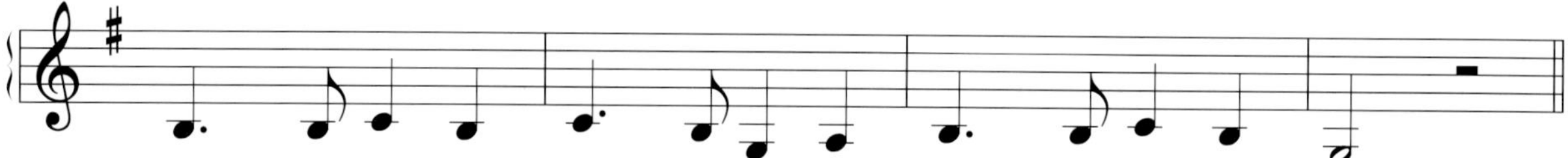

You could also create melodies that move quickly and demand attention. As in the second example, you can put to use any scale practice you may have done by flying around a G Major scale.

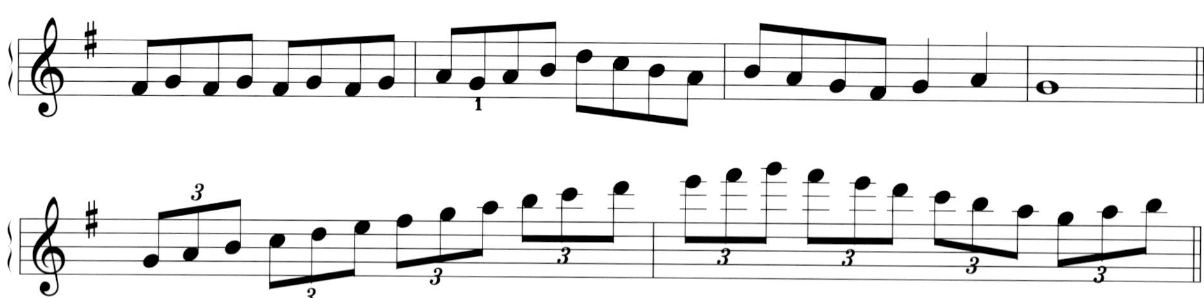

If your hands are big enough, create with octaves. Octaves can cut through the thick din of the bass like a knife. Beethoven used octaves a great deal in his piano music, often *broken octaves* as in the second example below. Broken octaves have not only the power of octaves, but also the quickness and rhythmic vitality of eighth notes. Plus, they are playable by smaller hands. However, they are difficult to play, requiring experience, coordination, and patience.

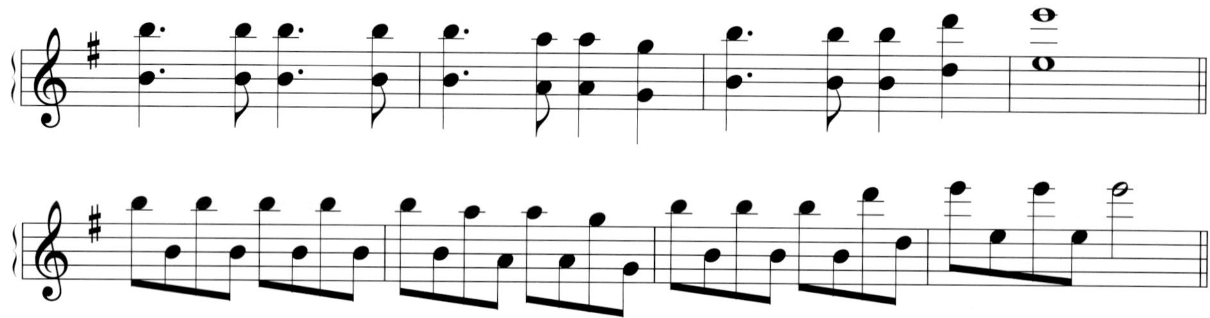

Also create with broken sixths—easier on the hands and sweeter sounding. For greater rhythmic vitality and complexity, play them in triplet rhtyhms, as in the second example below.

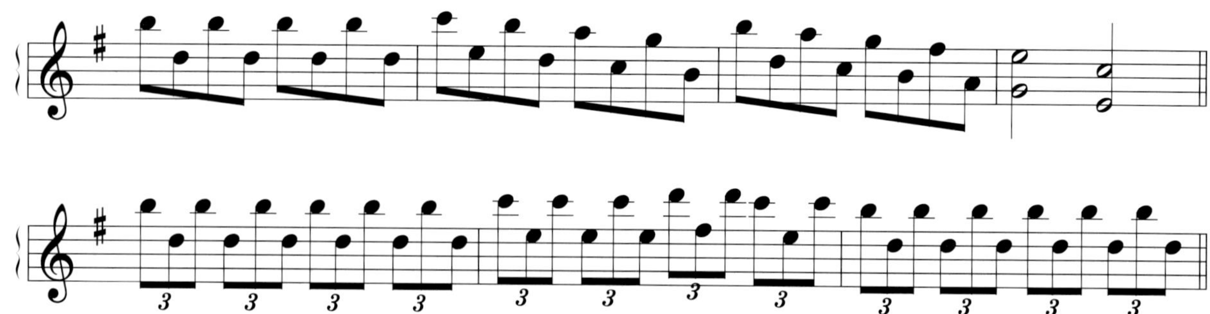

New Beginnings

When asked to play, Beethoven would usually play music he created fresh rather than music he had already composed. He preferred to discover the music of the moment, the music that was always beginning, the "higher revelation." This page explores ways to create new beginnings.

Habits can be healthy or unhealthy, and ruts are habits of the unhealthy variety. A creator is always trying to root out ruts, always seeking new beginnings, new ways of being alive.

New Fingers

Do you begin your melodies with your thumb most of the time? With your hand in any five-finger Hand Shape, start a melody with your thumb and see (hear) where it goes. Then start a melody with your second finger, then your third finger, and so on. Try the examples below with the Pattern. I didn't write rhythms so you could make your own.

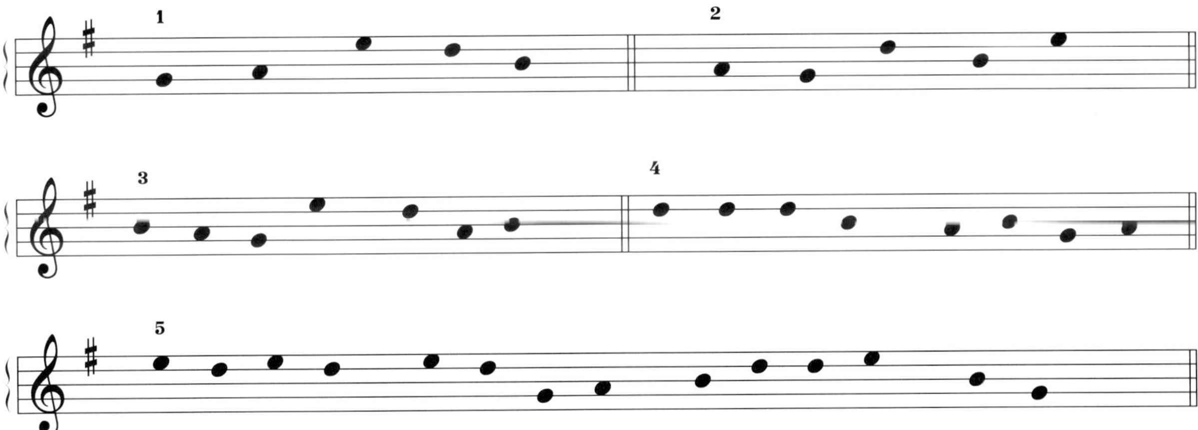

Try playing one of these measures right after another to make a longer melody. Or repeat any note a number of times before you go on to the next note. Also, create with a five-finger Hand Shape different than the one above.

New Entrances

Most melodies begin on the first beat of the measure. Why? What about the other beats? Below are four melodies, with each melody starting on a different beat of the measure. Play these examples with the Pattern, and then make your own melodies that start on these different beats.

It feels good to break out of ruts. It feels like opening the curtains in the morning and letting the light of the world illuminate the room.

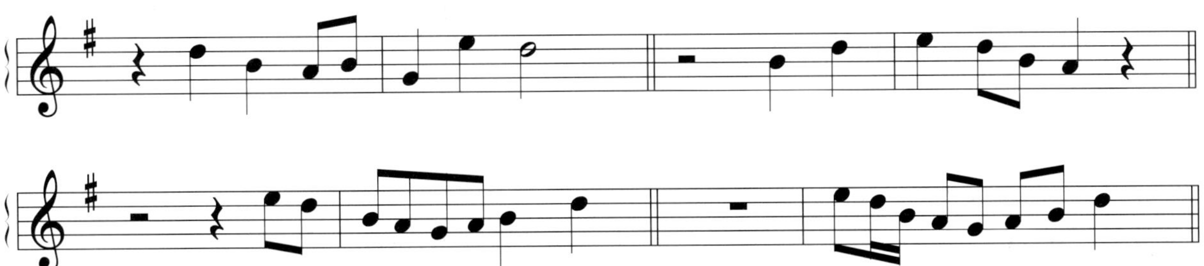

Gentle Rain

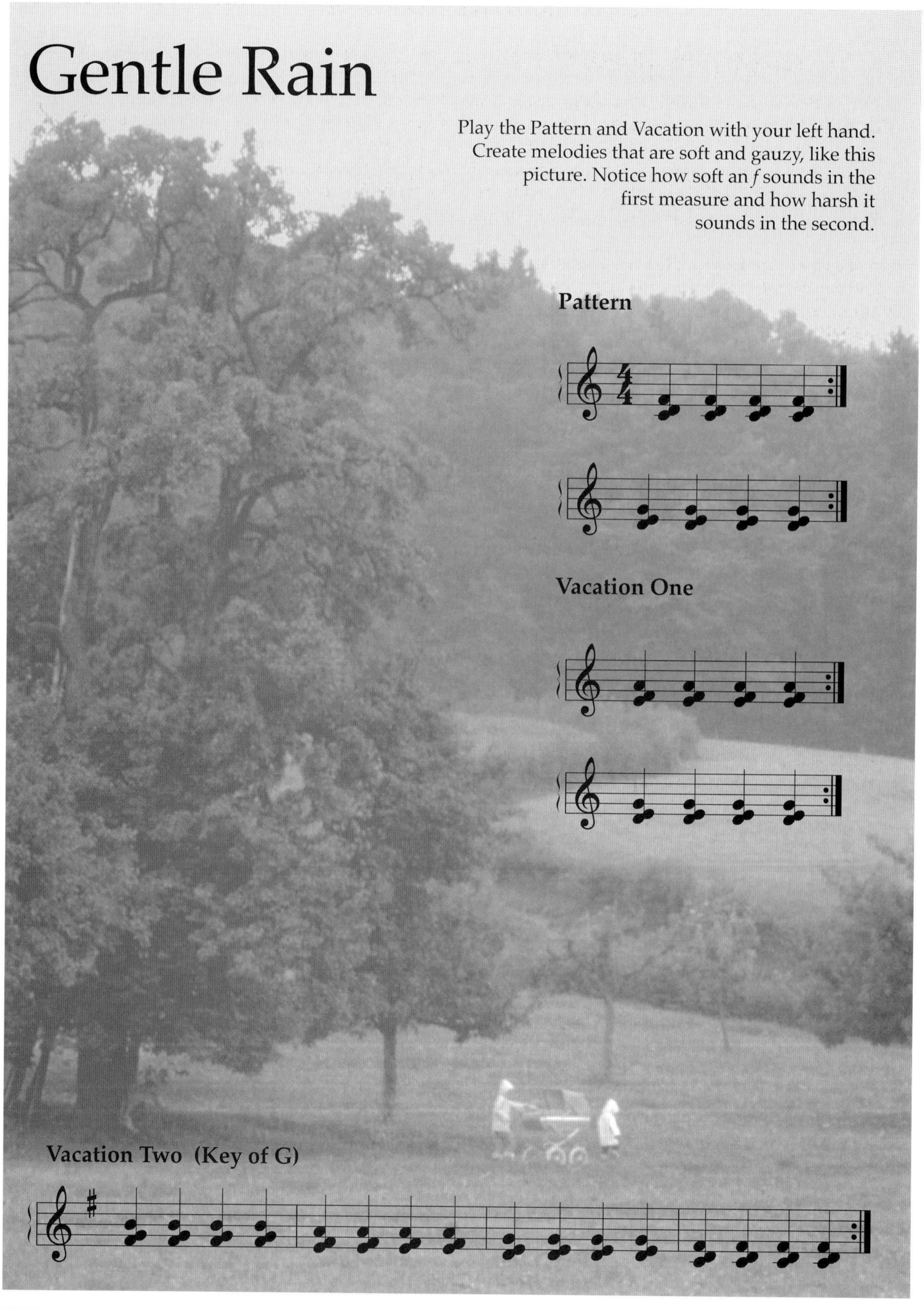

Play the Pattern and Vacation with your left hand. Create melodies that are soft and gauzy, like this picture. Notice how soft an *f* sounds in the first measure and how harsh it sounds in the second.

Pattern

Vacation One

Vacation Two (Key of G)

Same Shape, Different Sounds

The Pattern and the Vacations of this piece are all made of the same shape—a fourth with an added second. While playing this piece, your left hand is like a cookie cutter pressing into a mass of white-key dough. Now that you have this shape in your hand, try making up some Patterns of your own with it. Also, try changing Keys in the middle of your piece, playing this same Hand Shape in the Keys of F Major or G-Flat Major, and creating melodies in those Keys. If you are familiar with other Keys, consider those, too. This piece sounds especially nice in Keys with lots of black keys.

Just as there are two kinds of fifths, there are two kinds of fourths: *perfect fourths* (five half steps apart) and *augmented fourths* (six half steps, same as diminished fifths). Perfect fourths sound consonant while augmented fourths sound dissonant, like a car horn. The only augmented fourth found on white keys is made by *f* and *b*. There are also two flavors of seconds: *major seconds* (a whole step apart) and *minor seconds* (a half step). These sound quite different, though they look similar on the page. The added second in the first measure of each Vacation is a minor second. In the Pattern, it's a major second.That's why the Vacations of this piece sound so different from the Pattern, despite being the same shape.

Same Shape, Different Ways To Play

Once we pianists have a shape in our hand, we have something to create with. Here are six different ways to play the Hand Shape used in this piece. Create your own Variations.

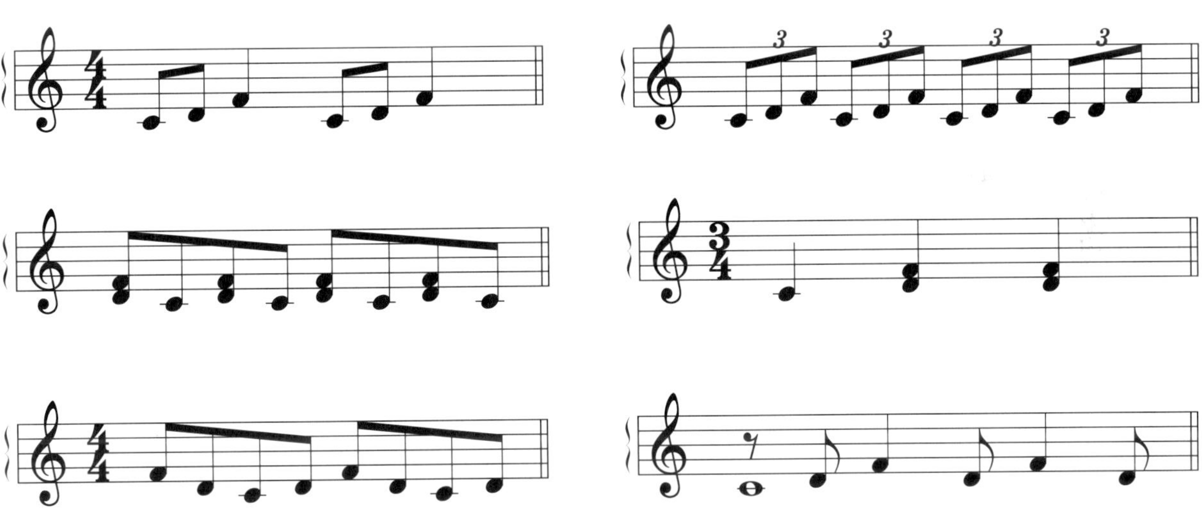

Different Shapes and Sounds

I took the top notes in the Pattern and Vacation One and moved them down an octave. This changed the Hand Shape. It's somewhat the same sound, but the shape is a sixth with an added second.

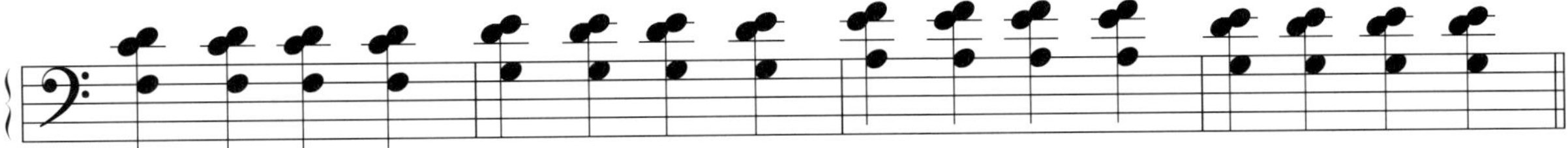

Though single notes sound just fine for melodies, you could also create with pairs of keys. Try shapes such as seconds and thirds. Why not try playing the Patterns with your right side while creating melodies and sounds with your left side? This would make a nice Vacation in a longer piece.

Patterns of Patterns

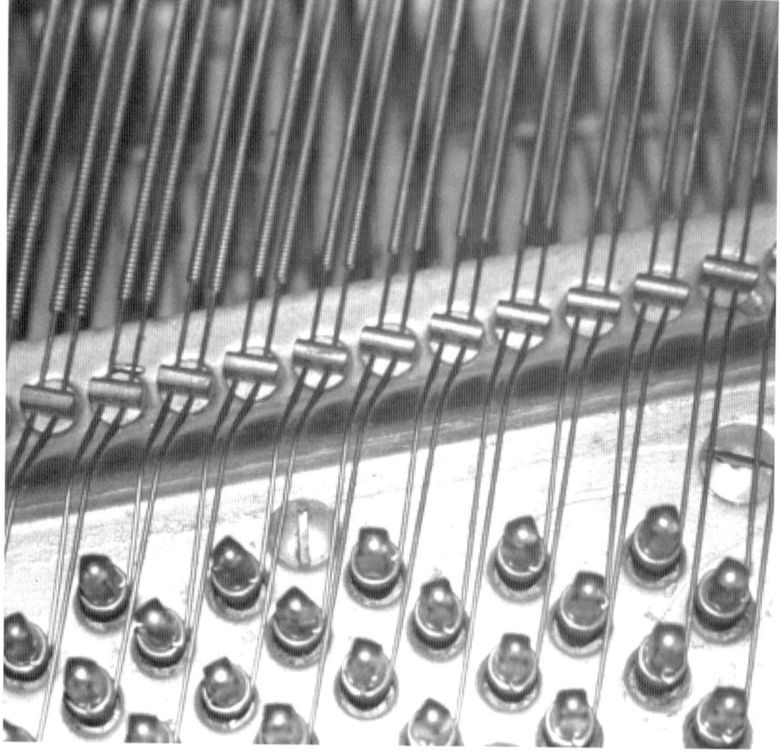

When I look at this picture of the inside of my piano, I see many individual shapes as part of three groups of shapes. In other words, smaller patterns group themselves into three larger patterns. In this piece, you will be exploring the same idea. Composers develop the ability to think in terms of *groups* of notes rather than just one note at a time. They begin to hear the simple patterns underlying hundreds of different tones.

Pattern

This style of accompanying is called an *Alberti bass*. It's named after Domenico (you guessed it) Alberti. He lived in the first half of the eighteenth century. Mozart's pieces often feature this sound in the accompaniment. I call this a "Mozart left hand" for that reason. This piece recognizes Wolfgang Mozart, one of the greatest composers and improvisers of piano music. Create melodies above this in F Major.

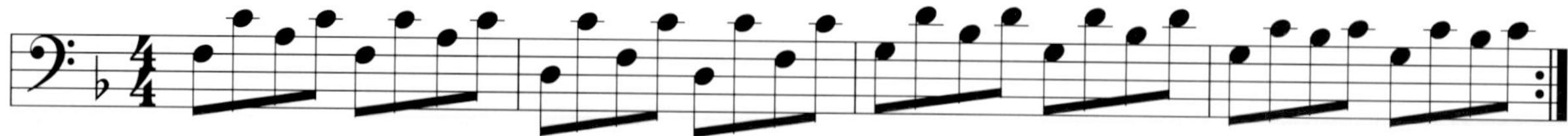

Instead of thinking of this Pattern as thirty-two unrelated notes, think of it as four families of eight notes each, with each family having just three different notes. If you think about the Pattern this way, it will be much easier for you to discover different ways of playing it. Once you get the feel of these four Hand Shapes in your left hand, create other ways of playing the individual notes.

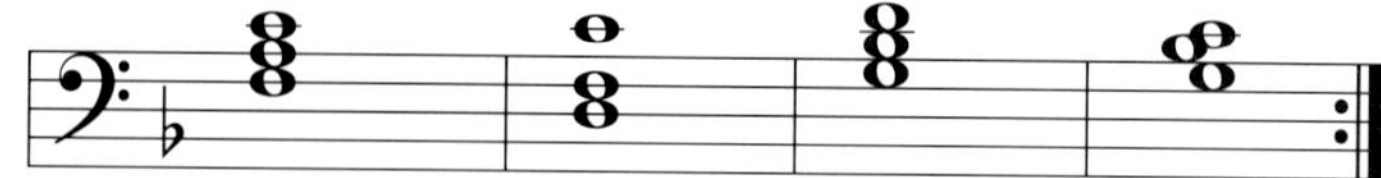

The secret to playing the Alberti bass easily is to play these four Hand Shapes blocked (as written just above) until your hand can move between them quickly, without your fingers having to reach for individual keys. Then all you have to do is smoothly roll (rotate) your forearm, and the Pattern almost plays itself. Otherwise, you end up reaching for each key with separate finger motions, and there is no feeling of flow. A flowing motion brings all the notes together to form musical patterns of Patterns.

Pattern Variations

Here are nine different ways to play the notes of the Pattern. Though there are four measures in the Pattern, I only wrote the first measure in each Variation to save space. Just change the remaining three measures in the same way.

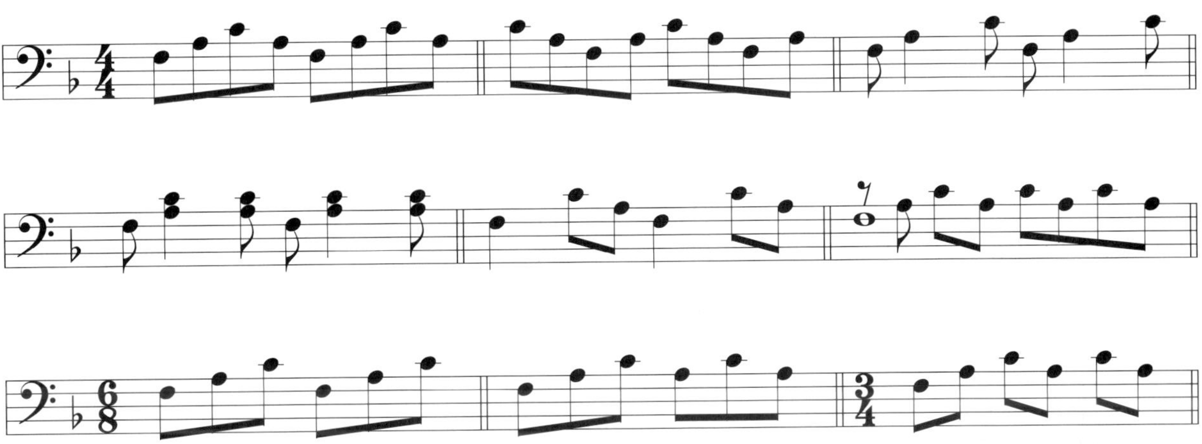

Alternate Pattern

Here's a Pattern that has four notes in each measure rather than three. The harmonies are more contemporary, and it's a bit harder to play. As before, create your own ways of breaking up these groups of notes. Try time signatures of 6/8 and 3/4, too. I often start this piece by playing the Pattern and the Vacations for a while, and then I'll move to this Alternative Pattern as a new section of the piece.

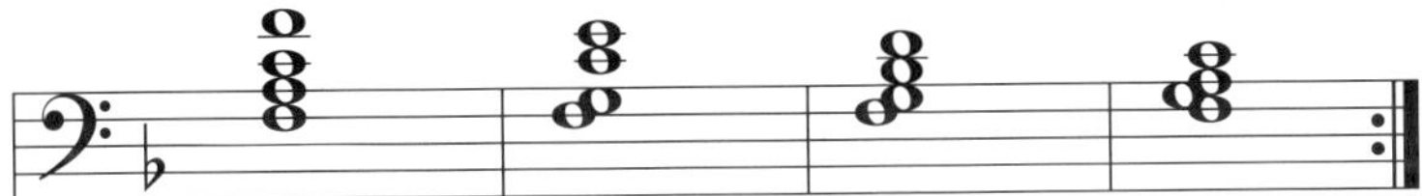

Four Vacations

After learning these Vacations as written below (blocked), vary the ways you play these groups of tones as you did with the Pattern. Two of these Vacations begin in the same place, while two end in the same place. Two are short, two are long. Which sounds best today?

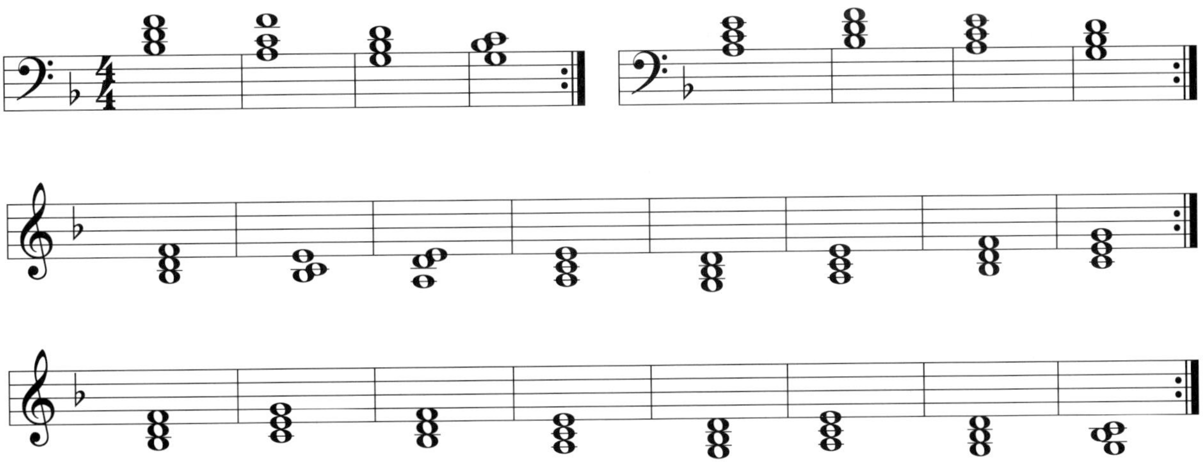

Painting the Dance

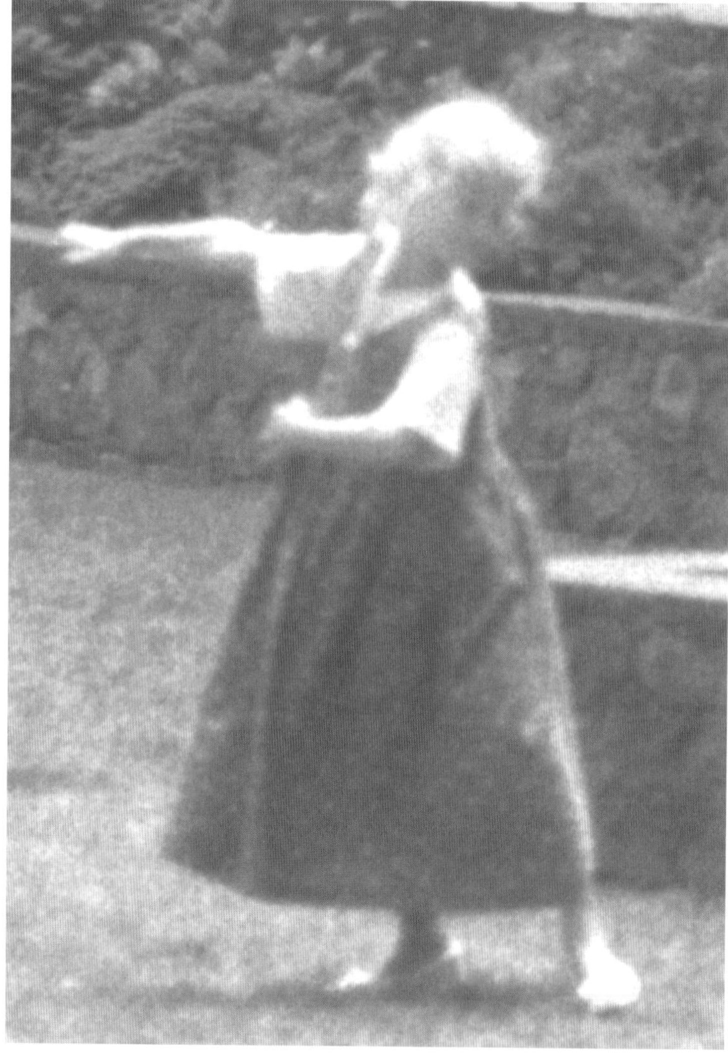

This soft-focus photograph reminds me of the paintings of the French Impressionists. These painters created a new kind of art by, first of all, stepping out of their studios into daylight. They saw color as light's passing moods, and they wanted to capture these moods with oil paints. They wanted to paint the play of light *in the moment* rather than make a realistic representation of a scene. A painting might take only a few hours to make. Of course, this approach offended the realistic painters who painted indoors and often worked on a single painting for weeks. The realistic painters had different understandings and, as a result, different techniques.

By making music in the *Pattern Play* way, by improvising, we are creating with an understanding like that which guided the French Impressionists. We are exploring and expressing the fleeting essence of each moment. As those painters celebrated the colors that sparkled in the various dances of light, so we are making the melodies that live only in this moment. We are making music that moves with the dance of life.

Pattern

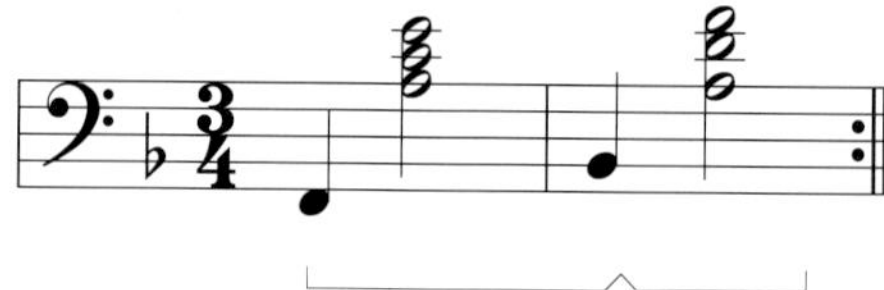

This Pattern sounds as if it were composed by Eric Satie, a French composer who wrote music that was often simple and appealing. He lived at the same time as the French Impressionist painters. Create melodies with this Pattern using tones in the Key of F Major. The Pattern Variation has some extra color tones added and a lower bass tone.

Pattern Variation

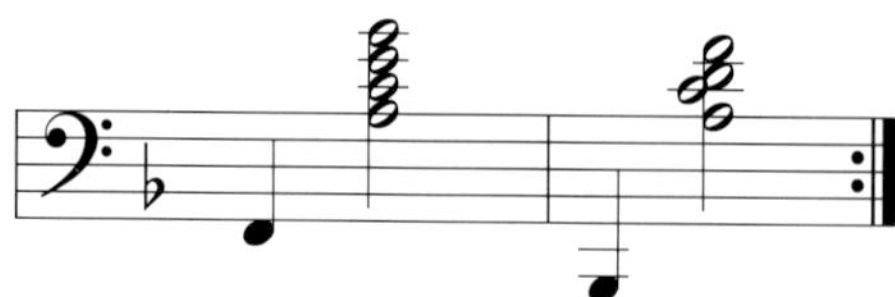

Vacation If you like, repeat each measure.

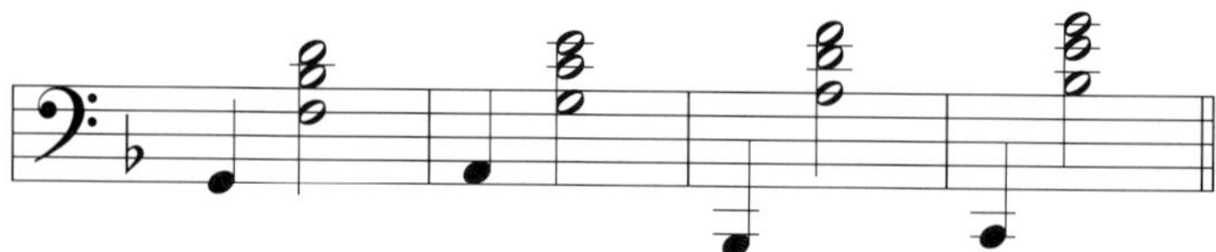

Voicing

Play the melody louder than your left-side accompaniment. This is called *voicing the melody*. If you can, voice the top key when you play pairs of keys with your right hand. Here's a fine technique that will make this possible: Play the top note of any pair loudly, and then the bottom note softly. Keep doing this, playing them a little closer together each time, until you are playing them simultaneously but at different volumes. This is the most effective technique I know for learning voicing.

Different Rhythmic Feelings

When starting to create melodies with this Pattern, keep them simple. Simple melodies with long-held notes work nicely because the sound of the left side is so full. I suggest creating simple melodies made of dotted half notes at first. Then a quarter-note feeling. Quicken your step with eighth notes. Then take a trip with triplets.

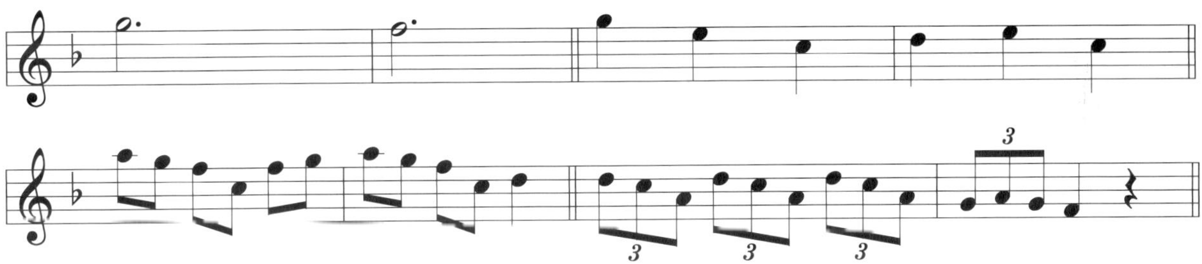

Different Colors

A painter has many different colors to play with, while a pianist has many different Keys to play in. You can move any Pattern to any Key and create a fresh effect. Try creating with this Pattern and Vacation in the Major Keys you know. Below, I've written them in G Major, G-Flat Major, and C Major.

Notice that I changed the Pattern slightly in order to keep it from becoming too low or too high. These Patterns are made from *seventh chords*. You can learn how to create your own Patterns with seventh chords in Volume 2-A and especially in Volume Four of *Pattern Play*.

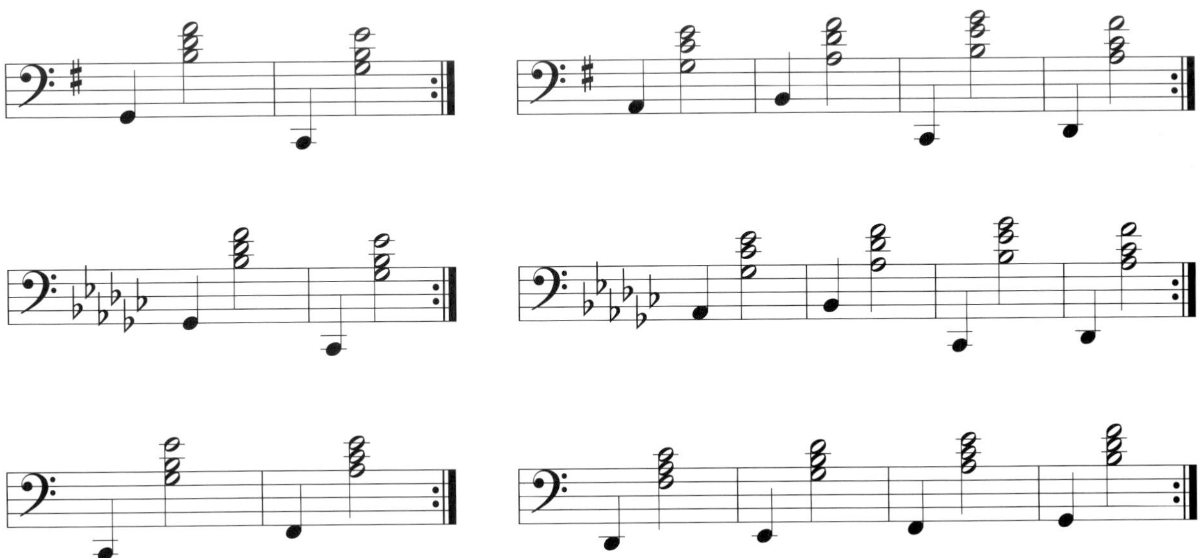

Season of Play

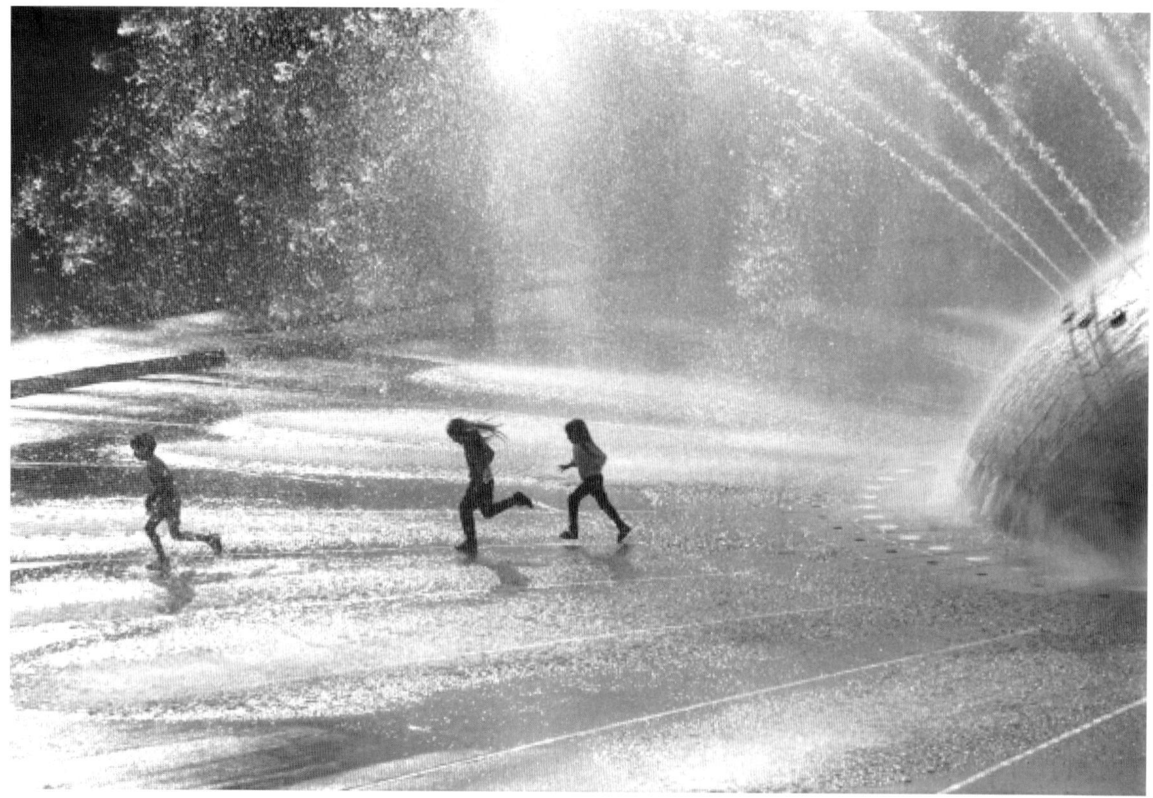

Last August, while the afternoon sunlight streamed into my room, this Pattern beamed right into my hands. When I play it, I feel the bright, childlike happiness I feel when I am creating something new. To be a creator is to be able to make your own seasons. This piece is summer, the season of play.

Pattern

Play this Pattern with a strong, fast beat. A good way to start creating is to keep your right hand in the Hand Shape of a G Major Pentatonic Scale (*g, a, b, d,* and *e*) and to stay with one Rhythm Pattern for quite a while. Try creating melodies with pairs of keys, and even more at one time.

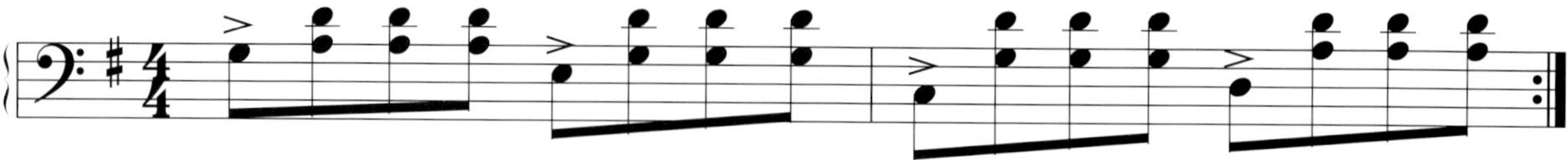

Pattern in the Key of G-Flat Major

This piece was born in G-Flat Major, and only later moved to G Major. I can't decide which Key I prefer. Usually, I'll play it in G-Flat for a while and then move it up to G Major. If you like the Key of G-Flat, simply play all the Vacations on the next page down a half step.

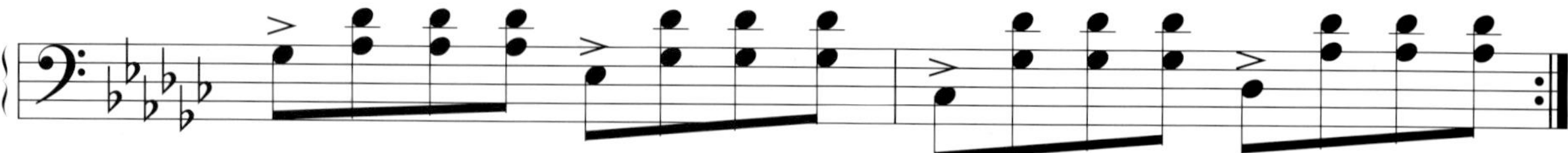

Vacation One

Each time you play these octaves, you may want to play them in a different rhythm. As long as the underlying beat is strong and steady, anything goes. See the next page for ideas. If your hand is not big enough to reach an octave, play just the bottom note, using your middle finger for extra power.

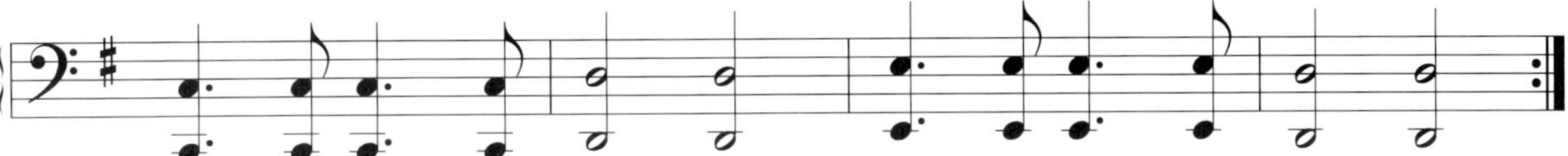

Pattern Variation

Same notes, new rhythm. Make up your own rhythms using the same notes, or keep the same rhythm and play some new notes. Oh, go ahead—play some new notes and new rhythms at the same time!

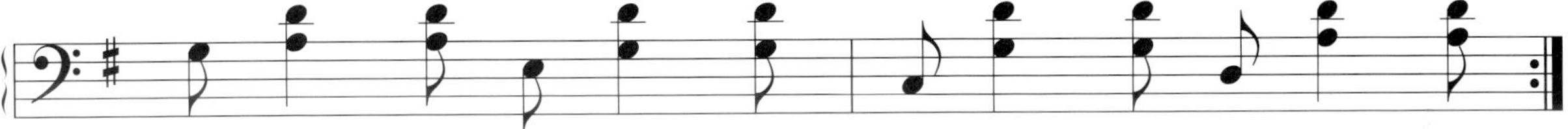

Vacation One Variation

Here's an eight-bar Vacation that begins and ends with the same sounds as Vacation One, but takes you to other places in between. Again, play these octaves in any rhythms you like.

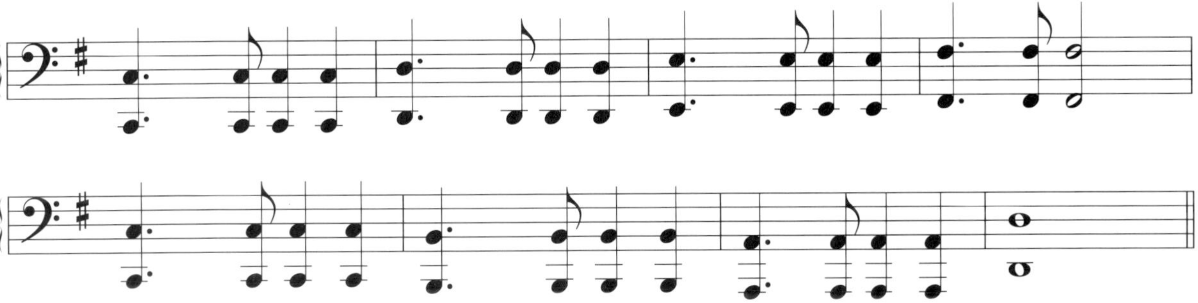

Vacation Two and Variations

I usually play this Vacation four times, getting more active each time. Try adding a low *d* in the bass now and then to create a fuller sound. Change the rhythm of these two chords in any way you like.

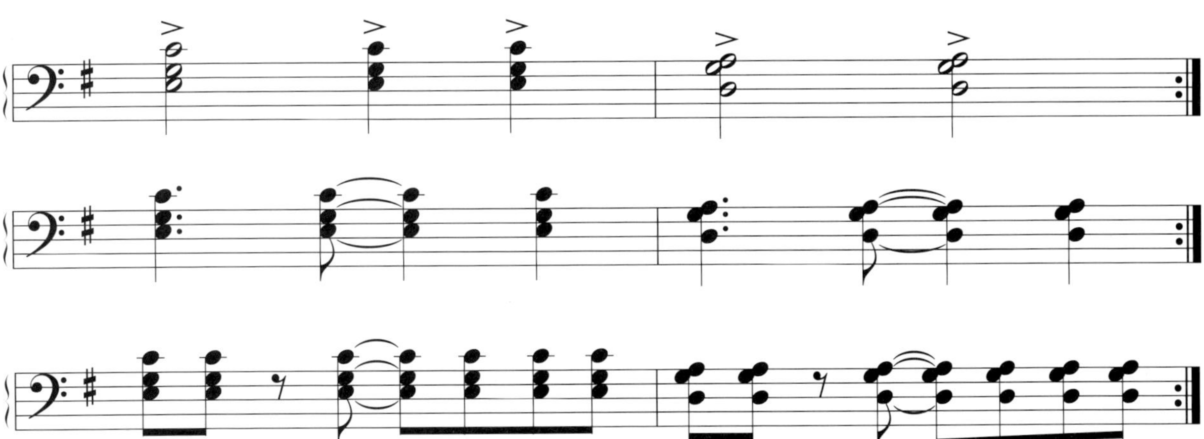

Rhythm Patterns

This is a very rhythmic piece, so it sounds especially good to play melodies with short Rhythm Patterns, over and over. Here's a new approach to try: Play the same four-beat (one-measure) Rhythm Pattern three times, and then do something completely different for a measure. Anything different. The resulting four-measure Pattern is strangely satisfying. This approach works especially well with the Pattern of this piece.

Below are five of my favorite ideas that follow this design. They are all made out of the same five-finger Hand Shape. You could play these same Rhythm Patterns using different Hand Shapes.

I wrote all the rhythms on this page in cut time to make them easier to read. That means that you play them twice as fast as they are written. Each of these four-measure examples should last as long as the two-measure Pattern of this piece.

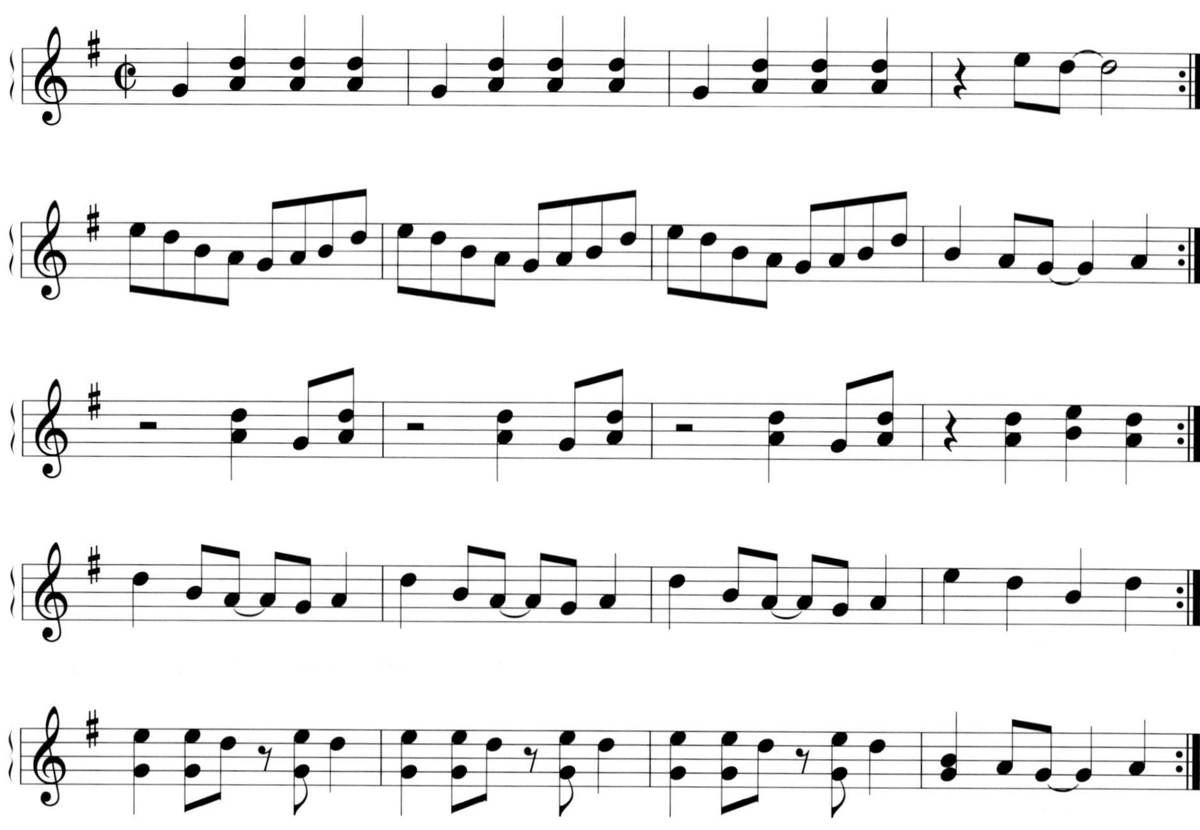

Here are eight more Rhythm Patterns that sound good with this Pattern. As you just did, play these ideas three times, and then do something different (strange, surprising, silly) in the fourth measure.

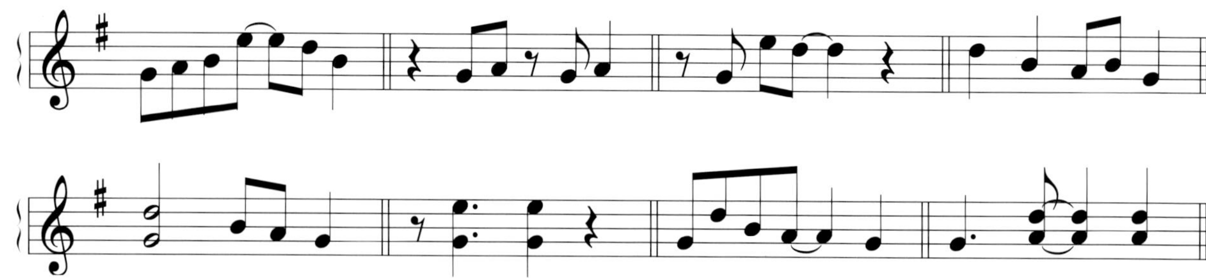

Longer Rhythm Patterns

Why not create longer Rhythm Patterns? Each of these five melodies features an eight-beat (two-measure) Rhythm Pattern that is then repeated with some sort of variation. Play these with the Pattern, and then make up your own eight-beat Rhythm Patterns that vary when they repeat.

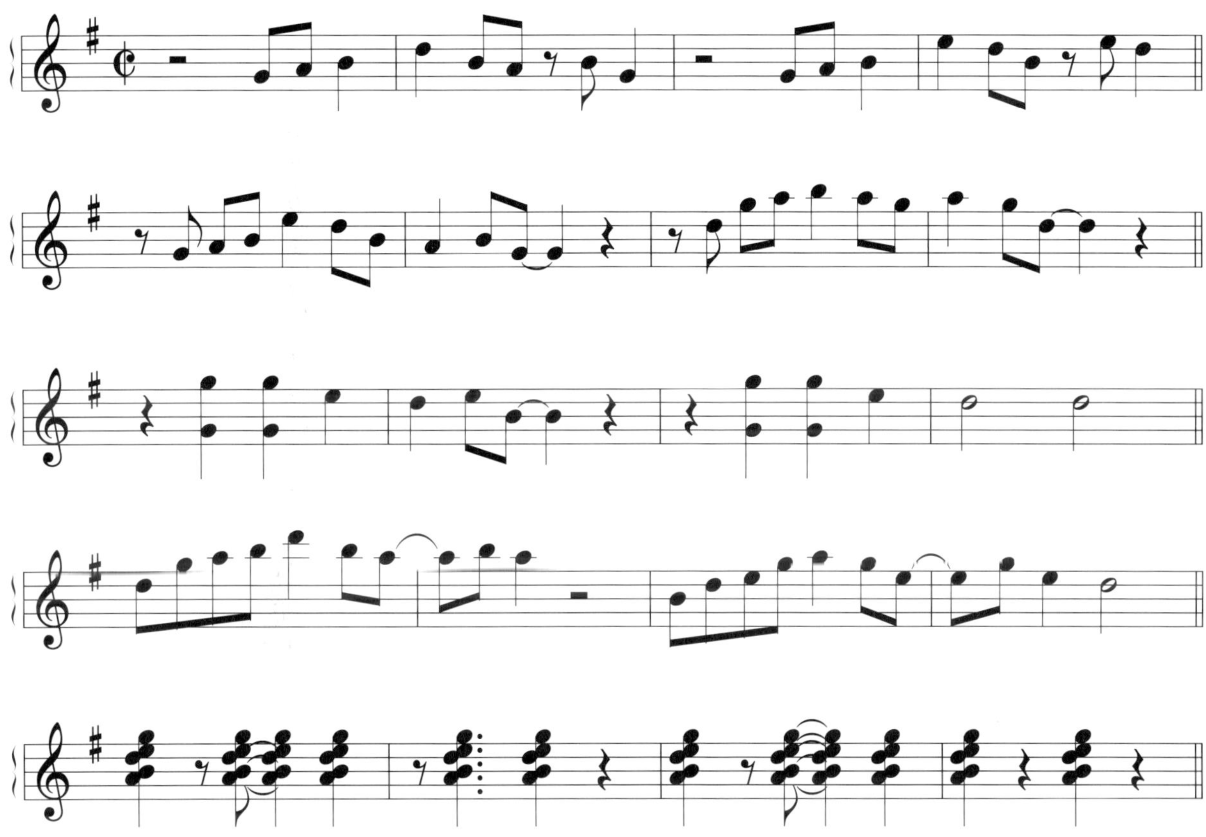

Of course, not all melodies want to fit neatly into four-beat or eight-beat Rhythm Patterns. Here are three such melodies. If you like, you can think of them as being sixteen-beat (four-bar) Rhythm Patterns, and then recycle the rhythm to make new melodies.

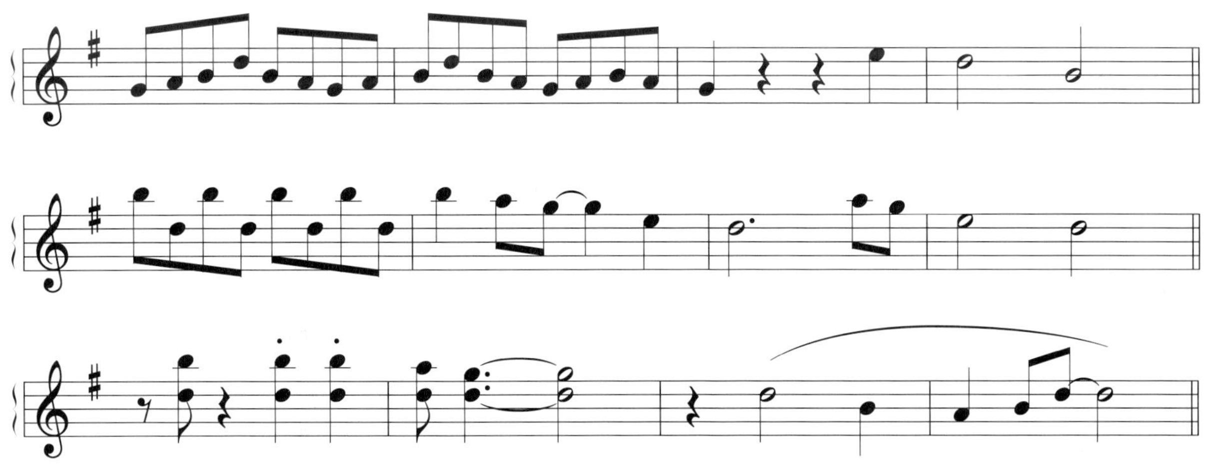

The creative mind plays with the objects it loves. —Carl Jung

Medieval Fantasy

Pattern A *The Journey*
The sun rises, touching the fields of wheat with vibrant, golden light. A long shadow stretches behind the castle as an entourage sets out on a long journey.

Repeat this Pattern many times. Use pedal. Create melodies in the Key of G-Flat Major.

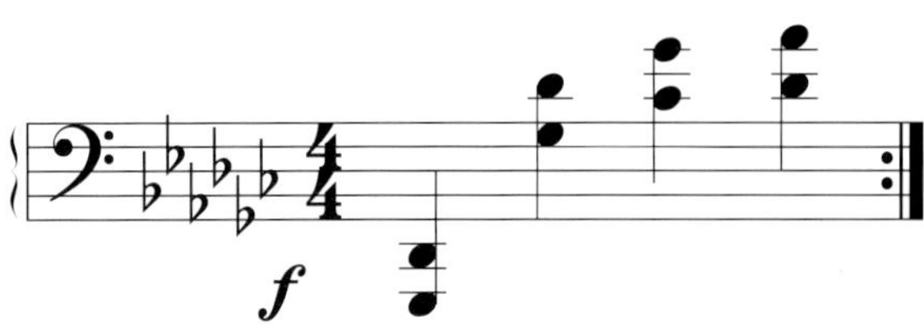

Pattern B *The Return*
After many days of travel, the distant kingdom has been reached. After many festivities, everyone turns toward home.

Each time you repeat the first measure of this Pattern, play it more softly. For different ways to play this Pattern, see the next page.

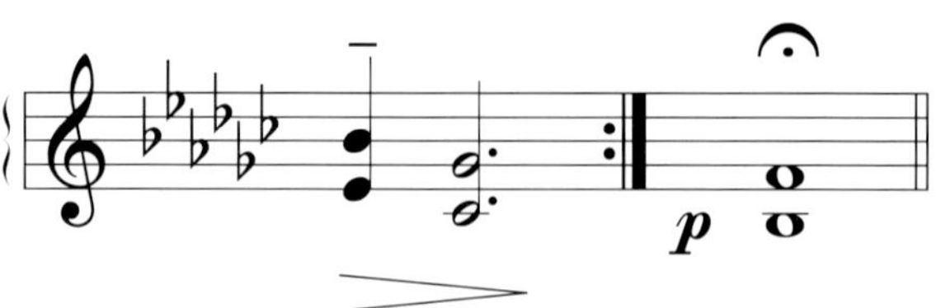

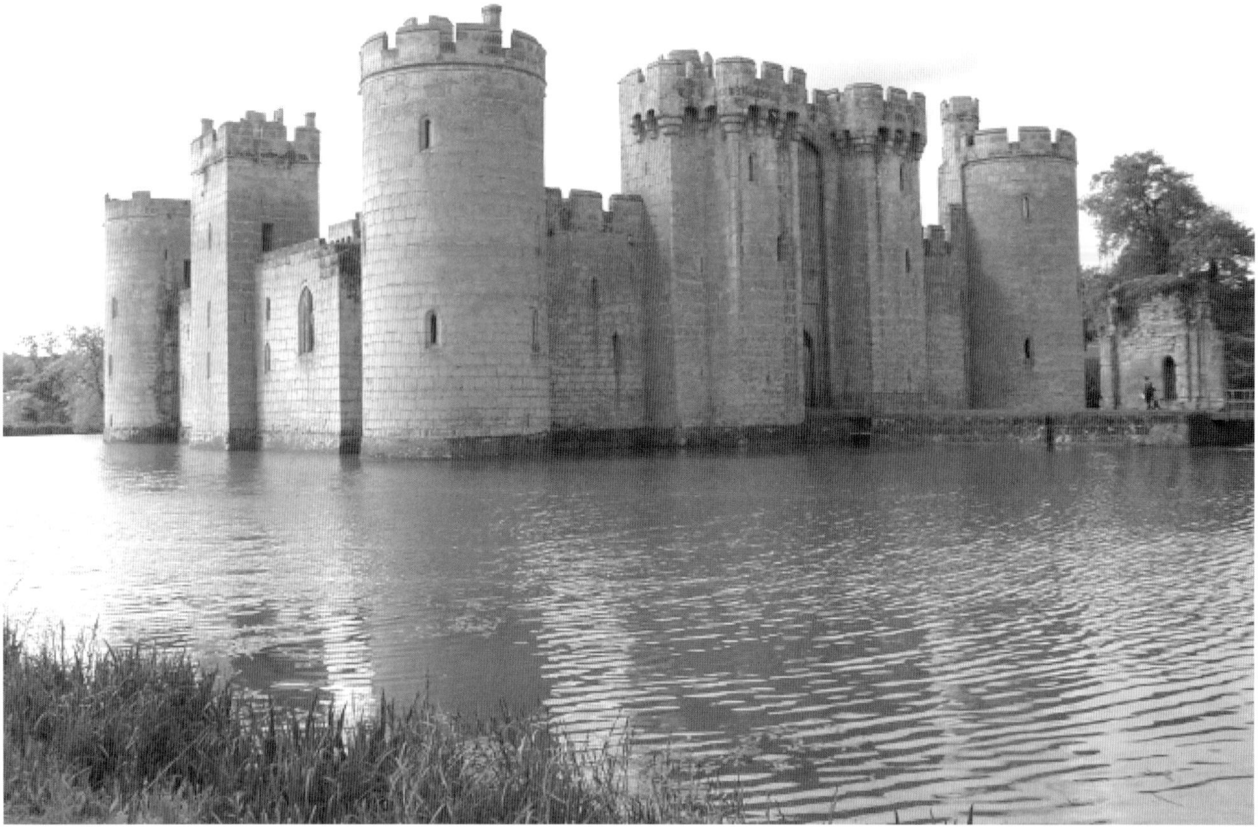

Pattern C *The Dance*

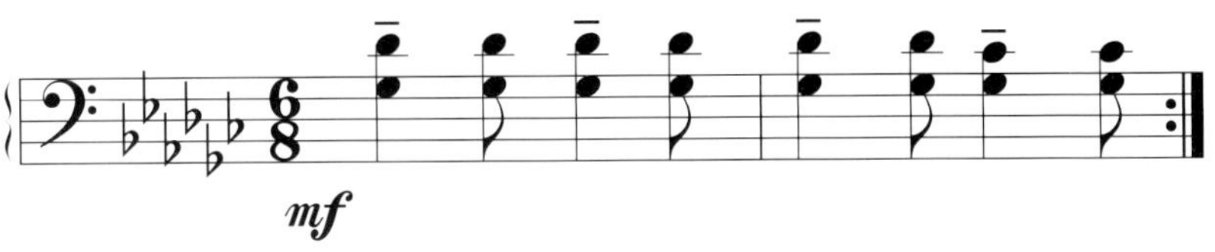

The long journey is over. Everyone has returned with gifts. Let the celebration begin!

Here, create in the Key of B Major. This Key also uses all five black keys, though the white keys are now *e natural* and *b natural*. To end this piece, slowly come to a stop. Or return to Pattern A and begin another journey.

Vacation for Pattern C

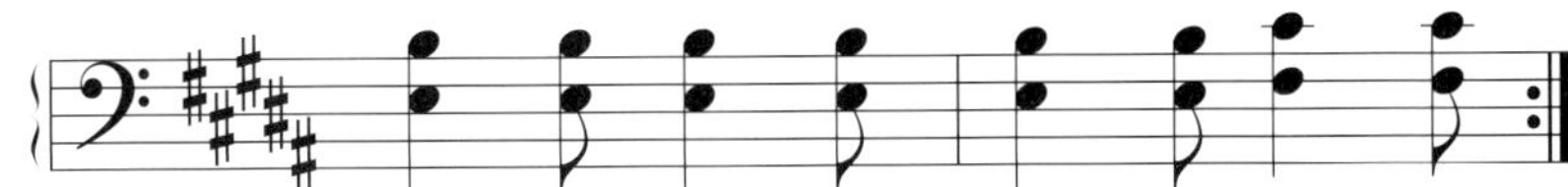

Pattern A Variations

Any of the fifths below can be substituted for the fifth (*g flat* and *d flat*) on the first beat of Pattern A. Play the rest of Pattern A as written. These variations sound especially good when returning to Pattern A after playing Pattern C. The new bass tones initiate a new musical journey. When you play *e natural* and *b natural* in the bass as in the first measure below, create in the Key of B Major, as you did in the Vacation for Pattern C. Some of these bass tones may sound "muddy" on your piano and you may want to avoid them for this reason. On the other hand, it can be fun to play in mud for a while.

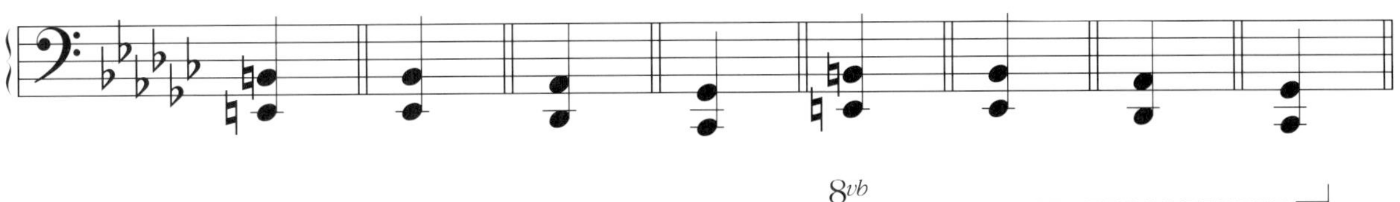

Pattern B Variations

Play the Pattern up an octave or down an octave. Play it in both hands at once. Create melodies in either side. This example shows the left hand moving freely between octaves.

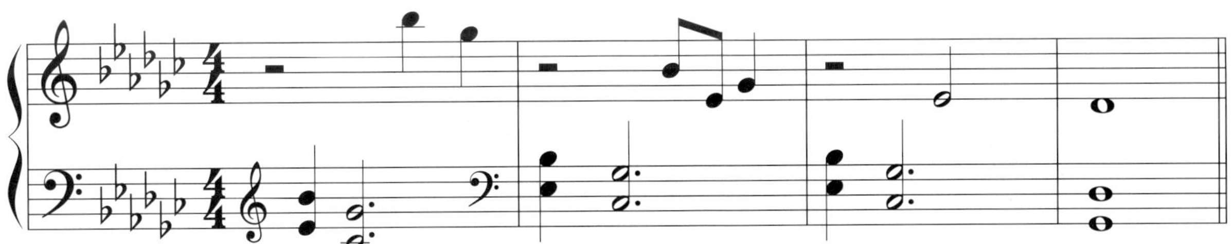

Pattern C Variations

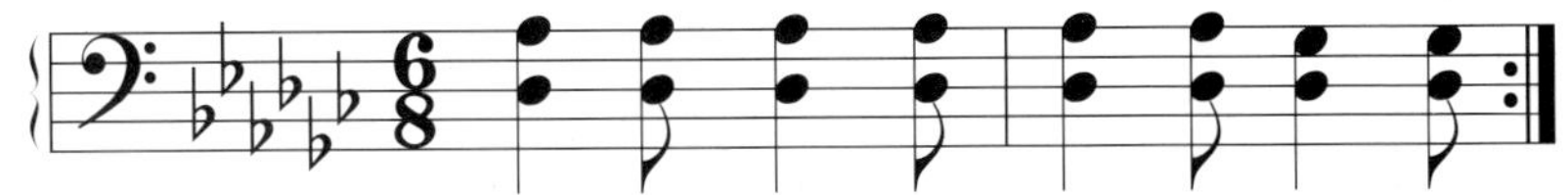

Substitute this for Pattern C or use it as a Vacation for it.

Different Rhythms Have Different Characters

Every Rhythm Pattern has its own distinct personality. The more we play music, the more we sense the unique character of every rhythm we meet.

The repeated rhythm of an eighth note followed by two sixteenths is my favorite Rhythm Pattern to play with Pattern A. To me, it has majesty, strength, and hopefulness. Here is a melody made mostly of this Rhythm Pattern.

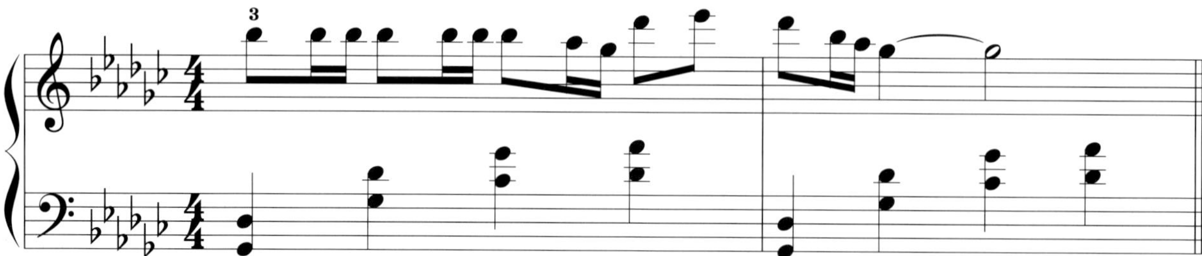

If you play that same Rhythm Pattern using the shape of a fifth, it sounds like a fanfare played on a couple of medieval trumpets. This rhythm then becomes the announcement of a long journey about to begin.

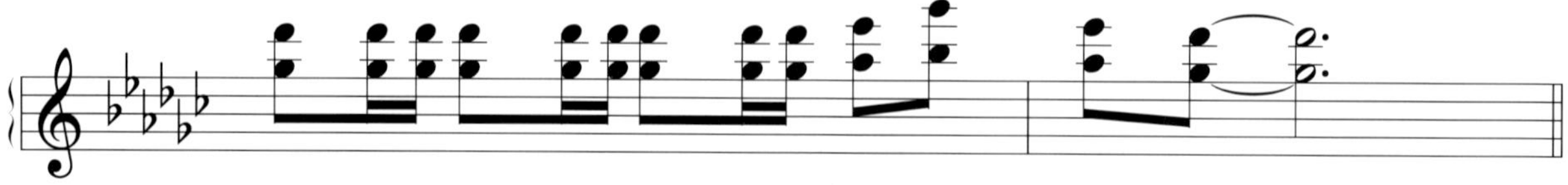

Below, the Rhythm Pattern breaks into a sixteenth-note gallop. The character of this Rhythm Pattern (an eighth followed by two sixteenths) is now changed by the rhythmic company it keeps. This melody occurs within a single five-finger Hand Shape.

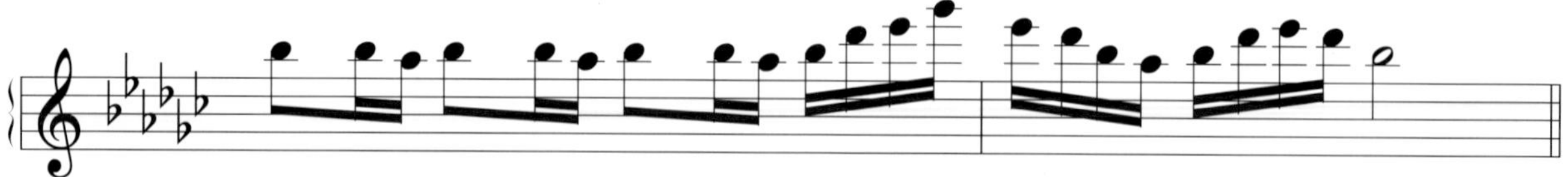

Pattern B on the last page has the feeling of something coming to a close, a journey ending. In this example, the same Rhythm Pattern is now played at half speed, and becomes a quarter note followed by two eighths. Then it is slowed down again, becoming two quarter notes and a half note. Playing the left side down an octave in the last measure also creates a "coming to rest" sound.

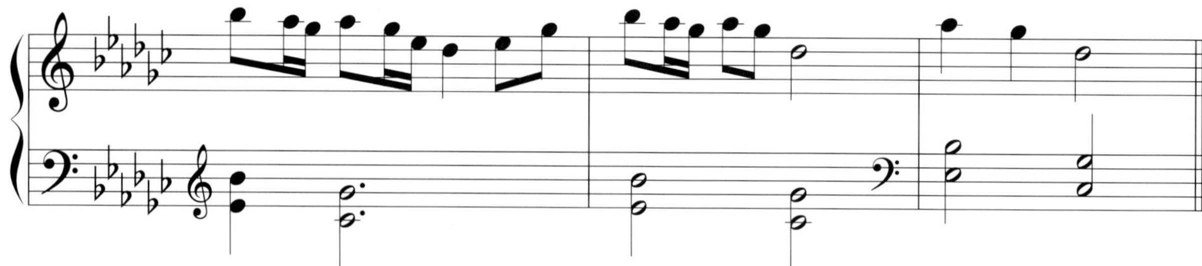

Ideas for Pattern C

Pattern C has the feeling of an evening dance following the end of a journey. Dances in medieval and renaissance times were usually in a triple meter such as this. Historians have discovered over 200 different court dances from the 15th century. Where did they all go?

The most natural way to start creating with this dance-like Pattern is to play the same rhythm in both hands for a while so you feel the rhythm in your whole body. Something such as this.

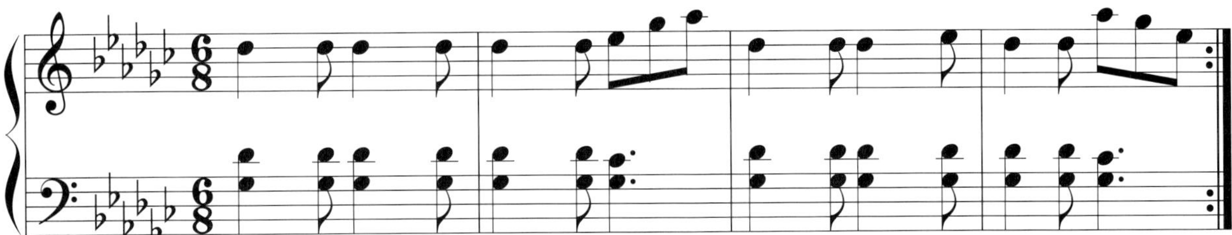

Then play melodies using different Rhythm Patterns. A good way to start creating your own Rhythm Patterns is to play a five-finger Hand Shape in a flowing eighth-note rhythm over and over with the Pattern, as in the first example below. Once you can play this effortlessly, you will find that different melodies naturally start growing out of it. The second example illustrates what might grow—in this case, a Rhythm Pattern made of eighth and sixteenth notes.

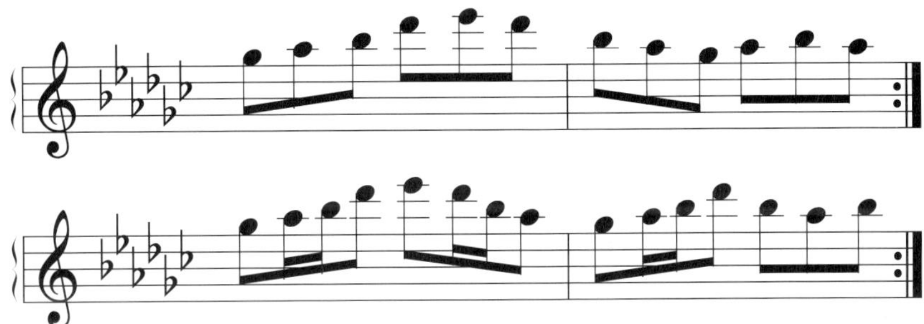

Day and Night, Duple and Triple

Just as there is light and dark, up and down, left and right, so in rhythm there's *duple* and *triple*. Duple rhythms have a feeling of two: ONE, two, THREE, four. This is the rhythm of marches and most classical and popular music. A triple rhythm has a feeling of three: ONE, two, three. This is the rhythm of waltzes and most dances in olden times.

All rhythms can be thought of as either duple rhythms, triple rhythms, or some combination of them. For example, 5/4 is a mixture of duple and triple. In some Eastern European countries, people dance in 7/8 and 11/8 time!

How Will This End?

You could end by slowing down Pattern C until you come to a stop. Or by playing the first notes of Pattern A, suggesting the beginning of yet another journey. Or by fading Pattern B toward silence, ending on the first notes of Pattern A, played very softly or unexpectedly loud. Or you could sustain the ending notes of Pattern B, and let them hang in the air like a question. Or?

Chopin

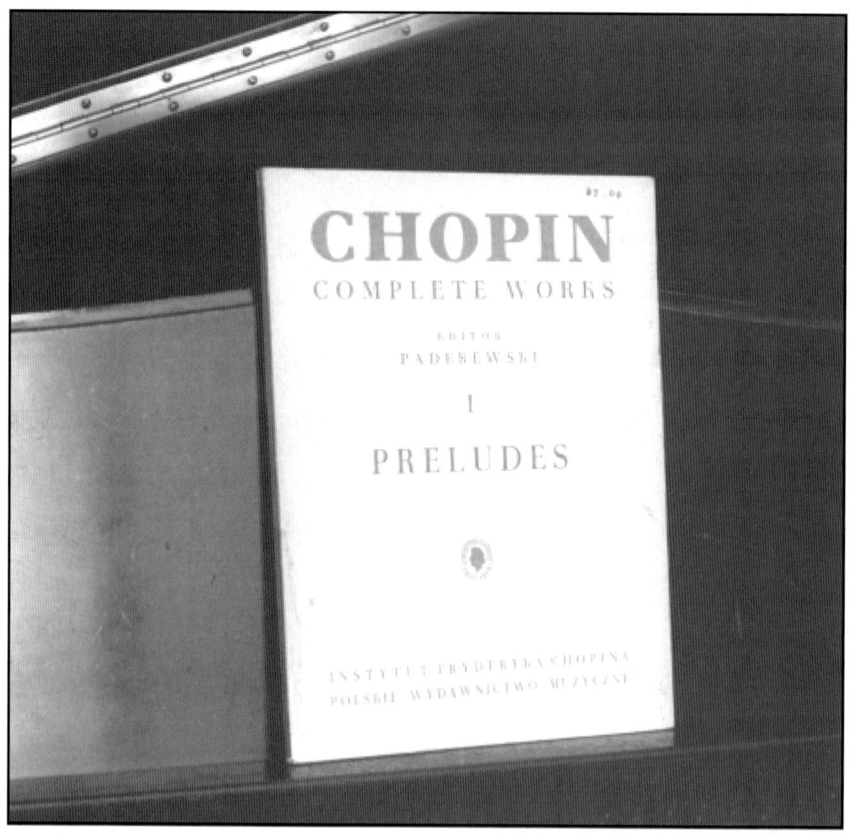

Frederic Chopin (1810-1849) was an astonishing pianist and creator of piano music. If I could own only one music book, Chopin's book of *Preludes* would be it. Each of the twenty-four short pieces in this book (in each of the major and minor Keys) is amazing for both its expressive depth and startling originality. The pieces are completely different from each other and unlike anything created before them.

During Chopin's time, the piano changed dramatically, nearly becoming the modern piano. It acquired an iron frame, more strings and keys, a larger size, and a weightier action. Patterns such as this one became possible.

Pattern

Think your hand is too small to play this? See the next page for some advice.

Chopin was one of the first to play this sort of accompaniment in which the hand spans a *tenth* (a total of ten lines and spaces) and then an *eleventh*. It's a very rich sound—the piano at its best. Pedal each measure. Create melodies above this in the Key of G Major.

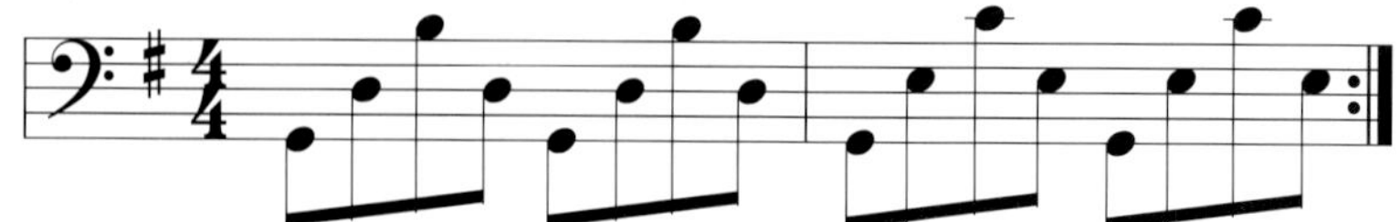

Vacation

Continue to create melodies in the Key of G Major. Repeat this Vacation if you like. All the sounds in this piece are made of triads (three-note chords) spread out to create a richer and fuller sound. I explain how you can create your own Patterns in this versatile style in Volume 2A of *Pattern Play*.

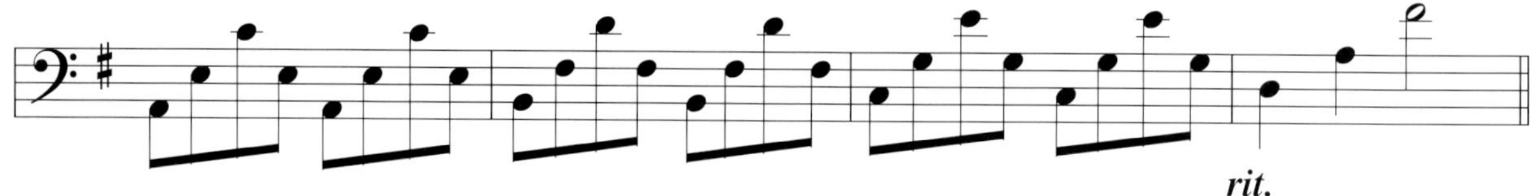

Pattern Variations

As always, there are endless ways to play the notes of this Pattern. Below, I've written six Variations on the first measure. Play the other measures of this Pattern the same way.

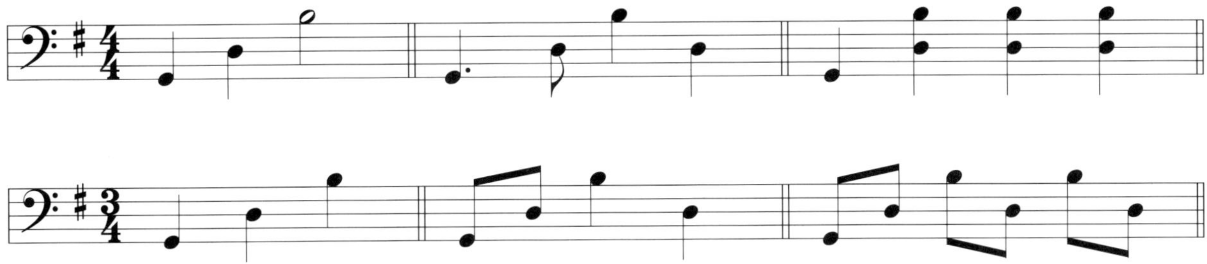

Alternate Pattern and Vacation

Here is an alternate Pattern and Vacation for this piece. It sounds less like Chopin and more like the accompaniment to a popular song. When you come to the Vacation in the second line, create in the Key of F Major during the first measure, and then return to G Major.

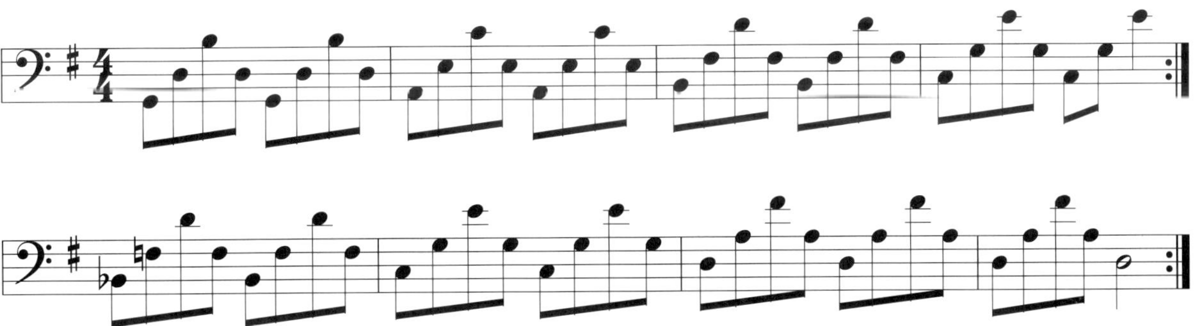

Give Yourself a Big Hand

You don't have a big hand to play this with? It doesn't matter, because you shouldn't try to play such Patterns with your *hand* anyway! Patterns such as this are to be played with your *arm.* If you play this Pattern while making a swinging, smooth motion of your arm, you'll be able to play it with comfort and ease. Try this approach: First play just the bottom and top note in each measure and feel your arm swinging left to right. Then add the note in the middle *without losing* that nice, easy swinging motion of your arm.

A piano teacher named Abby Whiteside wrote a valuable book called *Mastering the Chopin Etudes.* In this book, she argues that technical difficulties occur because we use small muscles (fingers) when we should be using larger muscles (arms). So play these Patterns with your arms and let your fingers spread out just enough to convey the weight of your arms into the keys. Piano playing should never be painful. It should feel as natural as walking and as easy as dancing.

Advice from Chopin

Chopin would tell his students that the left-side accompaniment is like a tree trunk, rooted in the earth, while the right-side melody is like the branches and leaves, moving freely in the wind. Let your right side move freely while your left side stays rooted in the ground.

Exploring Melodies

Chopin loved creating soaring melodies, so this page is about creating melodies that can fly. Since the Pattern is challenging to play, a good way to start creating with it is to stay in a five-key Hand Shape and a simple Rhythm Pattern. Complexity grows naturally out of simplicity if it isn't forced to grow.

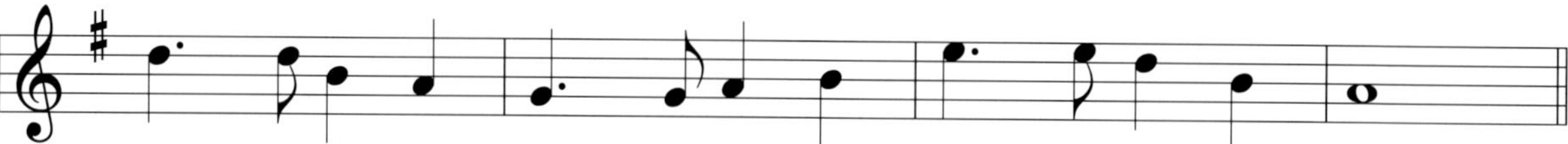

Chopin's melodies were at home on the full range of the keyboard. An easy way to get comfortable moving around the keyboard is to keep your hand in the same five-key Hand Shape as you move it between octaves.

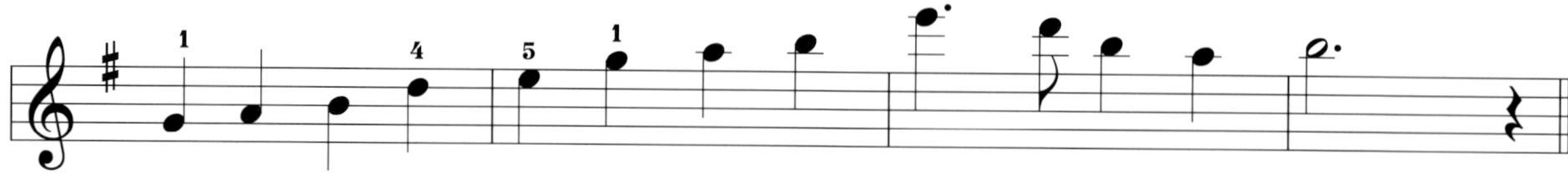

In this example, the same Hand Shape is moved between three octaves to create an *arpeggio*. This is a sound Chopin enjoyed and played a lot. If you have a swinging arm motion, this is not as hard to play as it looks or sounds.

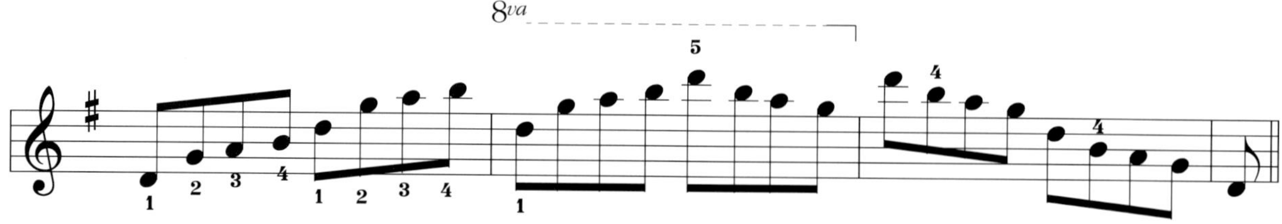

Octaves and "octave sandwiches" (my term for octaves with notes added between them) sound especially good with this Pattern. In the third and fourth measures, I broke up the octave sandwiches.

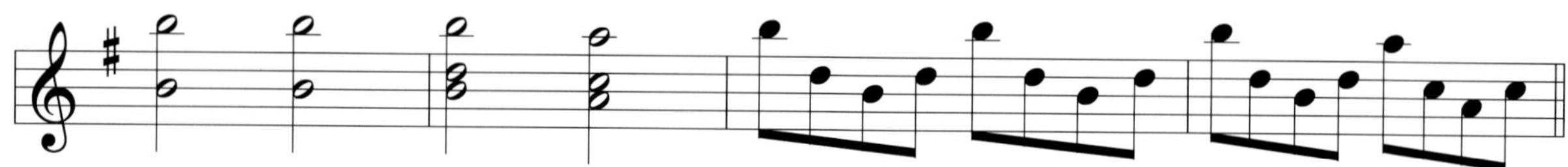

What If Chopin Had Owned a Tape Recorder?

Once Chopin played one of his *Nocturnes* for a group of people. Everyone wanted to hear it again, and Chopin said that he would oblige them. He then played the same piece so differently that most of the listeners didn't even recognize it! I don't think that Chopin *tried* to make it different. It was just that he was such a master speaker of the piano's language and so sensitive to the mood of each unique moment that he *naturally* created new music each time he touched the piano. It's no wonder writing down music *once and for all* was so difficult for him! His friend George Sand once wrote about him:

"His creation was spontaneous, miraculous ... but then began the most nerve-wracking labor that I have ever witnessed ... He shut himself in his room for entire days, weeping, walking, breaking his pens ... He might spend six weeks on a page... "

Phrases

Just as people fit themselves into groups and communities, and just as words fit themselves into sentences, so melody tones fit themselves into phrases. Like a spoken sentence, the end of a phrase tends to be played softer, and there is usually a brief silence before the next phrase begins. The beginning of a slur marks the beginning of a phrase, and the end of a slur marks the end of a phrase.

Also like sentences, phrases come in many different shapes and sizes. The most common phrase length is four measures. Play this four-measure melody with the Pattern of this piece. Phrases are also commonly two measures long, especially when the accompaniment Pattern is of the same length.

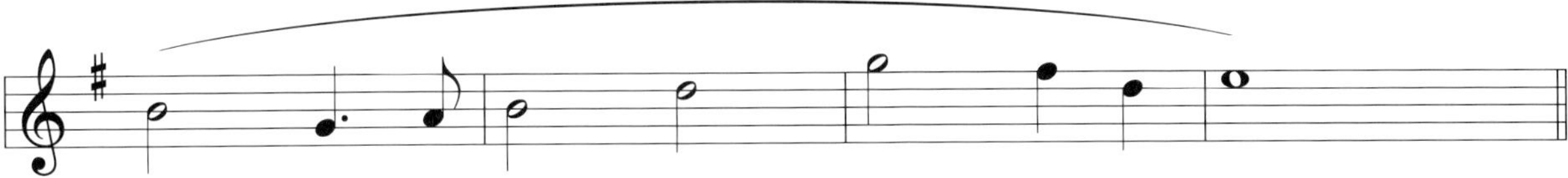

Melodies are as restless and curious as the people who play them. It doesn't take them long to feel that two measures is a cage, and even four bars is just a cage with more room. If you are listening to your melodies, sooner or later they will ask, "Why do I always have to end at the end of four bars like all the other melodies? Why can't I reach beyond that?" It's a good question. Melodies that soar beyond the normal phrase lengths are expressive and free. So let your melodies grow beyond the fence that sits at the end of the fourth bar. Push them into the fifth and sixth bars. Here's a melody to play with the Pattern or Alternate Pattern that pushes beyond that usual four-bar limit.

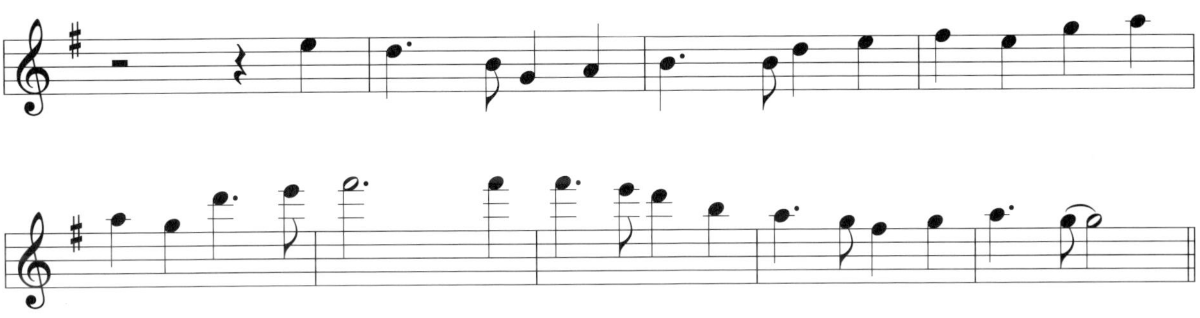

The same group of notes can have different meanings depending on the way we phrase them. Play this melody with the three different phrasings suggested below, and even make up more of your own. This will attune you to the various possible "meanings" that any group of tones can have, depending on how you phrase them.

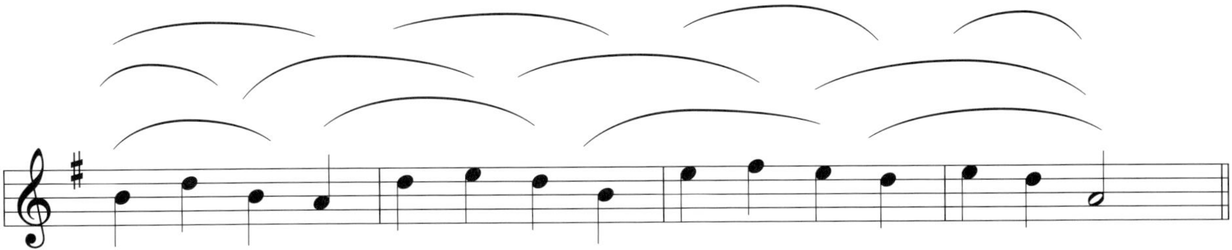

The best way I know to break out of phrasing ruts (which are, along with rhythmic ruts, the most common) is to begin playing melodies on different beats, the approach I discussed on page 72.

Free Play (on White Keys)

Now is the time to invite new Patterns into your hands. Press down the pedal and place your hands over the white keys. Close your eyes and open your mind. Allow yourself to hear sounds you've never heard before.

Don't worry about sounding bad or making mistakes—these don't exist in a state of free play. There is only exploring, experimenting, and discovering the sounds the piano is making today. Just keep going and flowing, trusting that such play is the doorway into your personal creative world.

Patternless Play

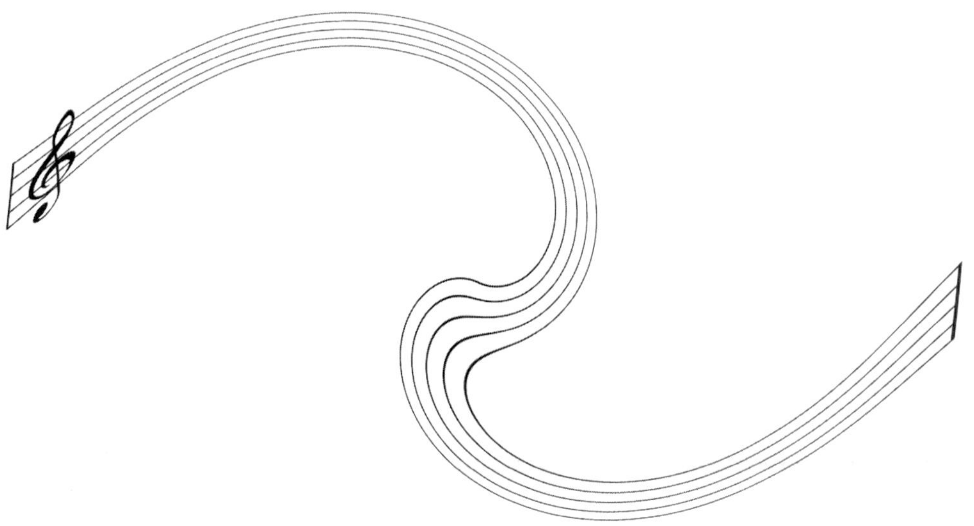

When we truly play, we are responding to *what is* rather than struggling to produce *what should be.* In such a state of mind, we are open to the possibilities of creation, and we can just explore them without fear. This is when new and original ideas come out from their hiding places and startle people.

Albert Einstein used to spend hours with his violin, improvising new music, just fooling around. Insights about physics would often ride in on his melodies. He would reward a good scientific theory by calling it "musical." A Portuguese proverb says an idea that Mr. Relativity himself could easily have formulated: "An hour of play discovers more than a year of conversation."

Creating with Minor Scales

Though the Major Scale has clearly been the most popular scale during the last three hundred years, the Minor Scale's contributions have not been minor. You've probably heard the two most popular piano pieces by Ludwig van Beethoven: The *Moonlight Sonata* and *Für Elise* (which some scholars believe was not actually composed by Beethoven). The *Moonlight Sonata* is in the Key of C-Sharp Minor, while *Für Elise* is in A Minor.

Speaking of Beethoven, perhaps the most famous symphony in history is his Fifth Symphony and this is in the Key of C Minor. His Ninth, his final symphony, is in D Minor. Mozart's most-played symphony, his fortieth, is in the Key of G Minor. One of Bach's most famous pieces, the *Toccata and Fugue in D Minor* is in the Key of … oh, you know! So, though the Minor Scale has been used far less than the Major Scale during the last three centuries, it has made a powerful contribution, and has been the second most popular scale overall.

In this section of the book, you'll be creating with the Minor Scale in a few different Keys. As you will hear, the Minor Scale is not merely the somber scale it is usually thought to be. It is capable of expressing a surprisingly wide range of feelings, moods, and emotions. Enjoy!

Minor Changes

You may recall from the first section of this book that the E-Flat Minor Pentatonic Scale has the same notes as the G-Flat Major Pentatonic, except that *e flat* is featured in the bass rather than *g flat*. This creates a different center of gravity—a different note that feels like "home"—and changes the flavor of the sound. This scale is the E-Flat Minor Pentatonic.

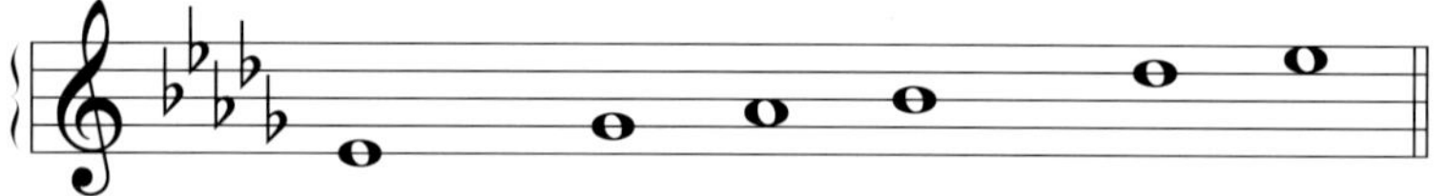

E-Flat Minor Scale

To make a Minor Scale, we fill in the gaps with two tones, just as we did with the Major Scale. In fact, we add the same two pitches we used in G-Flat Major—*f* and *c flat*. So, G-Flat Major and E-Flat Minor are made of the same notes, but each has a different bass note as the tonal center. Changing the bass note is a "minor change" which ends up making a major difference in the sound of the music.

Since these two scales have the same notes, they share the same Key signature of six flats. This raises a question: how do we know which Key we are in if the Key signatures are identical? We can tell by the bass note. If *e flat* is featured more often in the bass, the Key is E-Flat Minor.

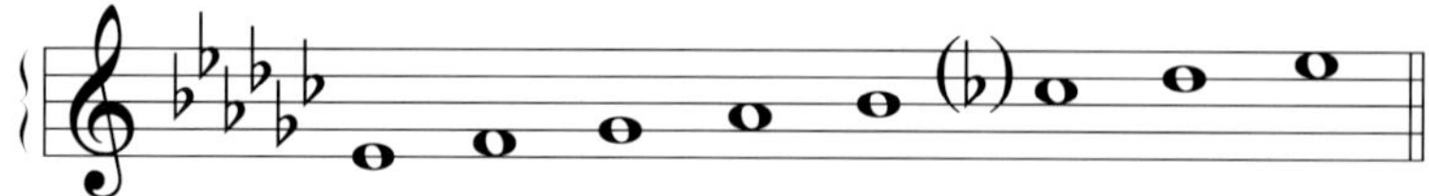

A Minor

Just as E-Flat Minor and G-Flat Major are relatives having the same notes and sharing the same Key signature, so are A Minor and C major. Each Minor Scale shares a Key signature with a Major Scale. The Minor Scale is always three half-steps below the Major. Here's A Minor Scale.

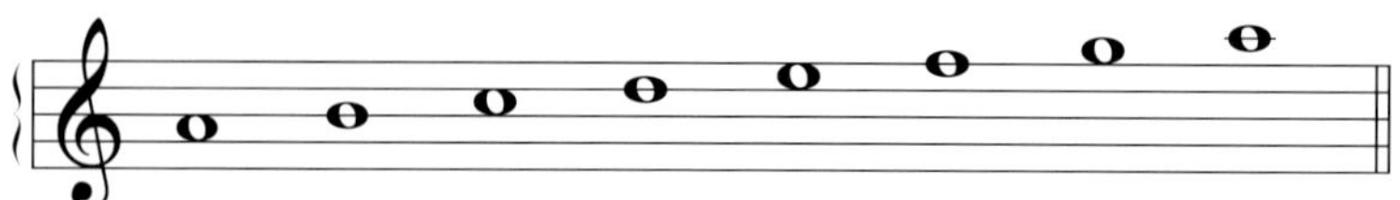

A Harmonic Minor

Composers often raise the seventh note of a Minor Scale to create what is called a *Harmonic Minor Scale*. In this scale, there is a half step between the last two notes, just as there is in the Major Scale. This alteration creates a gap between the sixth and seventh notes, creating an Arabic sound. In fact, there is an Arabic scale nearly identical to this scale. The normal Minor Scale shown above is often referred to as the Natural Minor Scale to distinguish it from the Harmonic Minor. Here is the A Harmonic Minor Scale. Note that the Key signature is the same as A Natural Minor.

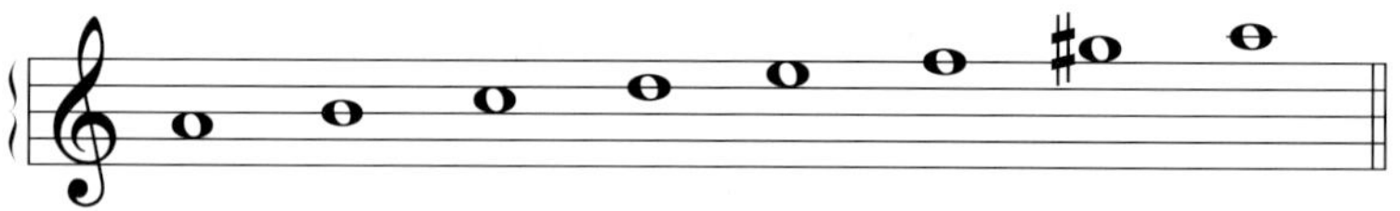

Melodic Minor

There is one other kind of Minor Scale, called a *Melodic Minor Scale.* This scale begins with a Harmonic Minor Scale (raised seventh note), and then also raises the sixth note to smooth out that large gap. This makes the scale more melodic and easier to sing. This Scale does not make an appearance in this book, but you can explore it in the companion to this book, Volume 1-B, *Melodies in All Keys.*

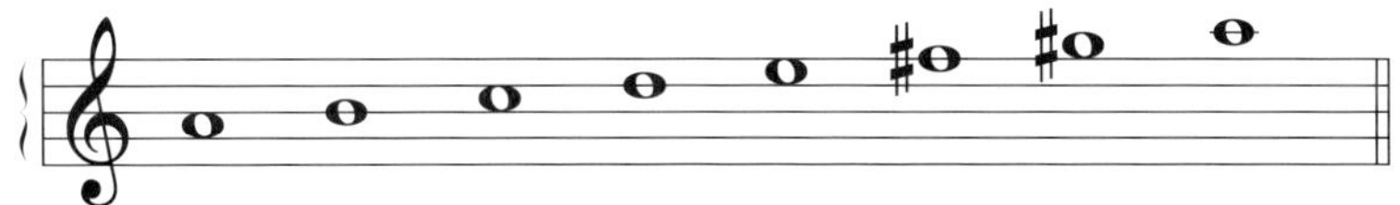

The Circle of Fifths

Like the Major Scales, the Minor Scales are usually organized on the Circle of Fifths. (I also call it a "Key Wheel.") Notice that you would say a piece is in G-Sharp Minor rather than A-Flat Minor and B-Flat Minor rather than A-Sharp Minor.

This section has pieces in the Keys of E-Flat Minor, A Minor, D Minor, and E Minor. That's enough for now. You can explore the sounds and moods of the other Minor Keys in *Melodies in All Keys.*

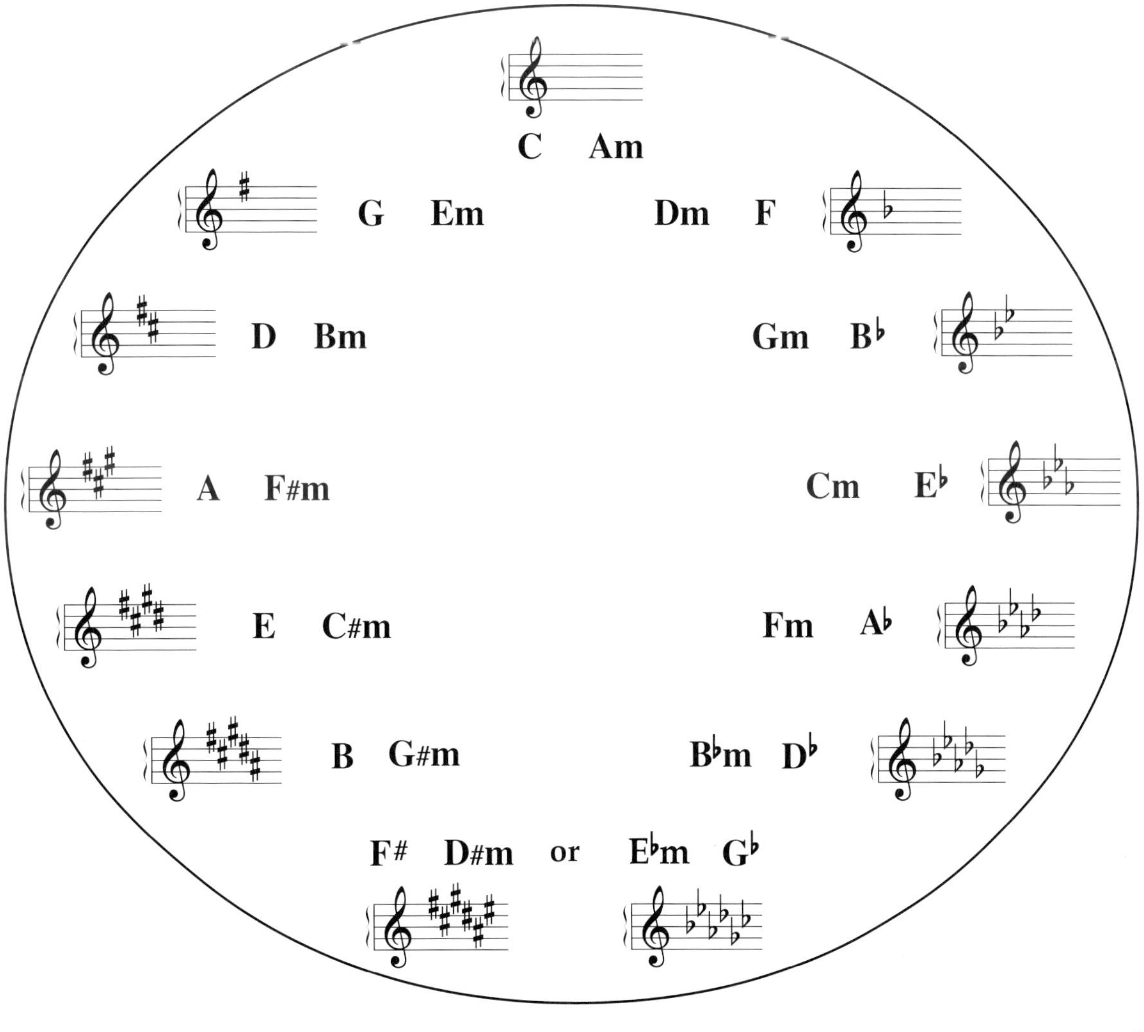

C Am

G Em

Dm F

D Bm

Gm B♭

A F#m

Cm E♭

E C#m

Fm A♭

B G#m

B♭m D♭

F# D#m or E♭m G♭

Simplicity

It is hard to simply be ourselves. The pressure is on to be complex, dazzling, and much, much better than we are. There are so many comparisons and expectations to live up to! But can we simply be who we are? Can we gradually unfold our own gifts, and not force ourselves to be something we are not? Perhaps this is one of the greatest challenges before us: to simply and honestly be ourselves.

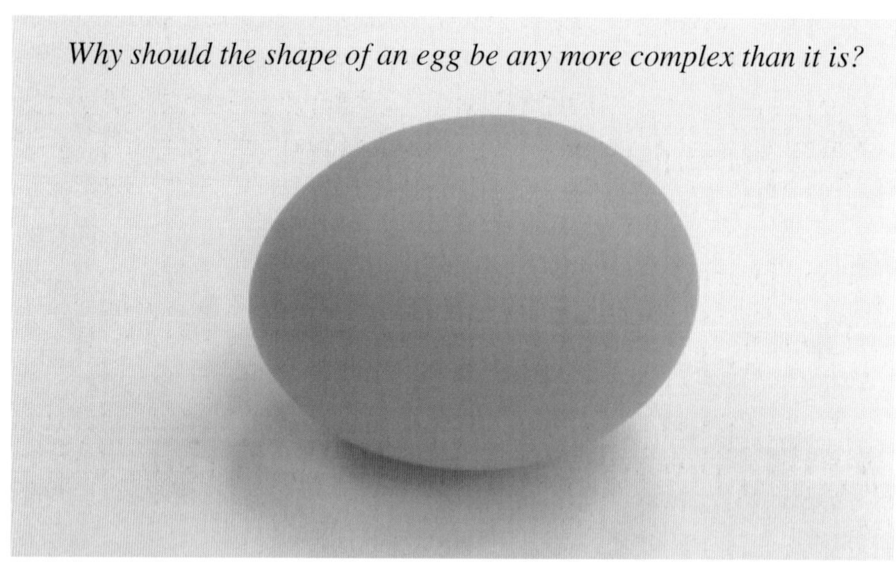

This piece has a simple Pattern made of fifths in the Key of A Minor. Simple Patterns give complex feelings more time and space in which to grow. Because they are easier to play, they allow us to focus on these feelings. Create your own Patterns using fifths in A Minor, E Minor, or D Minor.

Pattern

Vary this Pattern any way you like (see the next page for ideas), as long as you don't disrupt its flow when you add melodies. If you have to stop or slow down to add melodies, it is probably because you are trying to do more than you actually can at that moment. In the Variation below, I added a note above the fifth, the note an octave above the bass note.

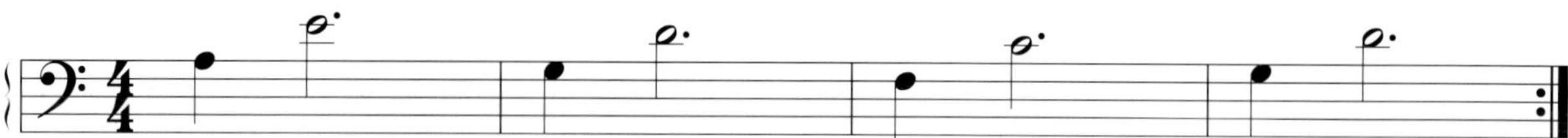

Pattern Variation

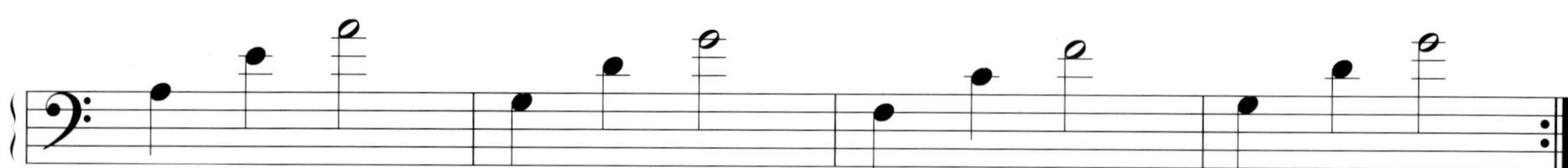

Vacation

Create your own Vacations using fifths, or just use this Vacation. In this Key, the diminished fifth (the harsh one) is created by playing *b* and *f*. It is the only fifth I haven't used on this page.

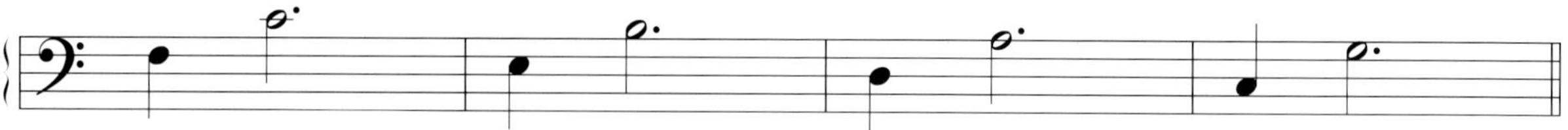

Pattern Variations

After playing the Pattern in simple ways for a while, you will find that more complex variations will naturally find their way into your hand. Here are some Variations to try. I wrote them in treble clef to minimize the number of ledger lines, making them easier to read. I wrote just the first measure of each Pattern to save space. Change the other three measures in the same way.

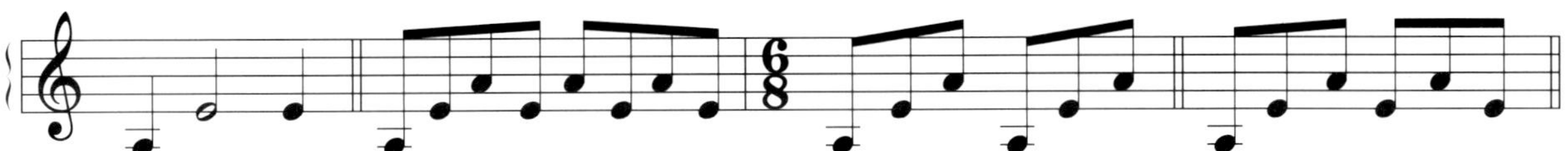

By playing with just two or three different notes, we can focus more on making the rhythms interesting. This way, simplicity allows complexity. Below, I have written some rhythms that you may find quite challenging even though there are just a few different notes to play.

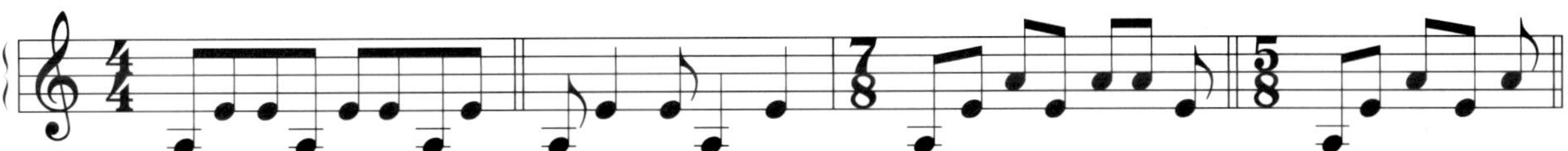

Ideas for the Right Side

If you want to create a different mood, use the notes of an A Harmonic Minor Scale in the first measure and even the third measure. (During the second and fourth measures, the *g sharp* in the scale would clash with the *g* in the accompaniment.) This new scale makes this piece sound like music from a distant land. This is especially true if you use the Pattern Variation in 7/8 time shown above.

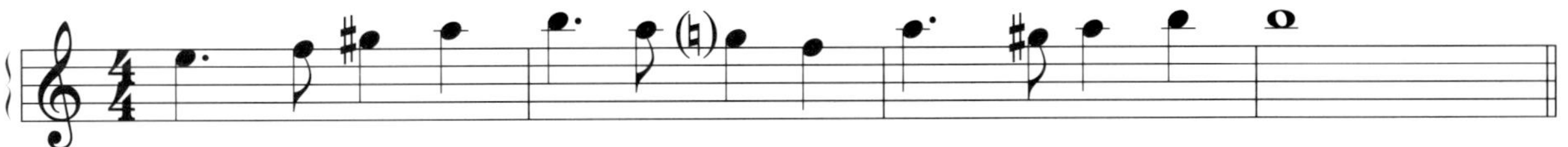

One of the nicest things about creating in A Natural Minor or C Major is that creating with Hand Shapes is so much easier than in other Keys. Adding a sixth below the melody note is simply a matter of keeping your hand in the shape of a sixth and moving it around. Here's a melody in sixths to play with the Pattern. Also try creating with the sounds of thirds and fourths.

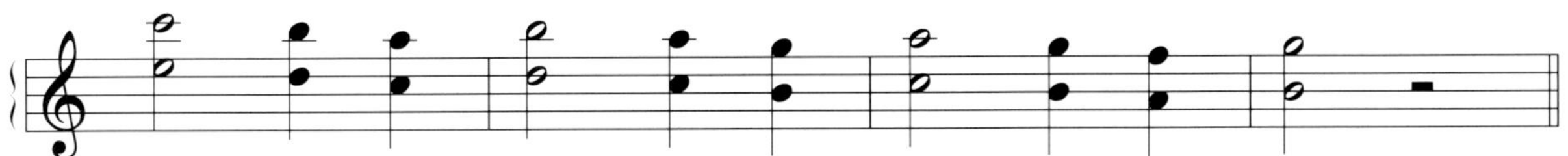

The two melodies above were made by repeating a one-measure Rhythm Pattern on different pitches. Notice how this gives coherence to the music, a sense of pattern and design.

A lot of music throughout the world grows from a single Rhythm Pattern repeated many times. For example, Chopin's *Prelude in A* and his *Prelude in C Minor* both grew out of a single four-beat Rhythm Pattern played throughout the piece. Make up your own four-beat Rhythm Patterns and create melodies with them.

Flow

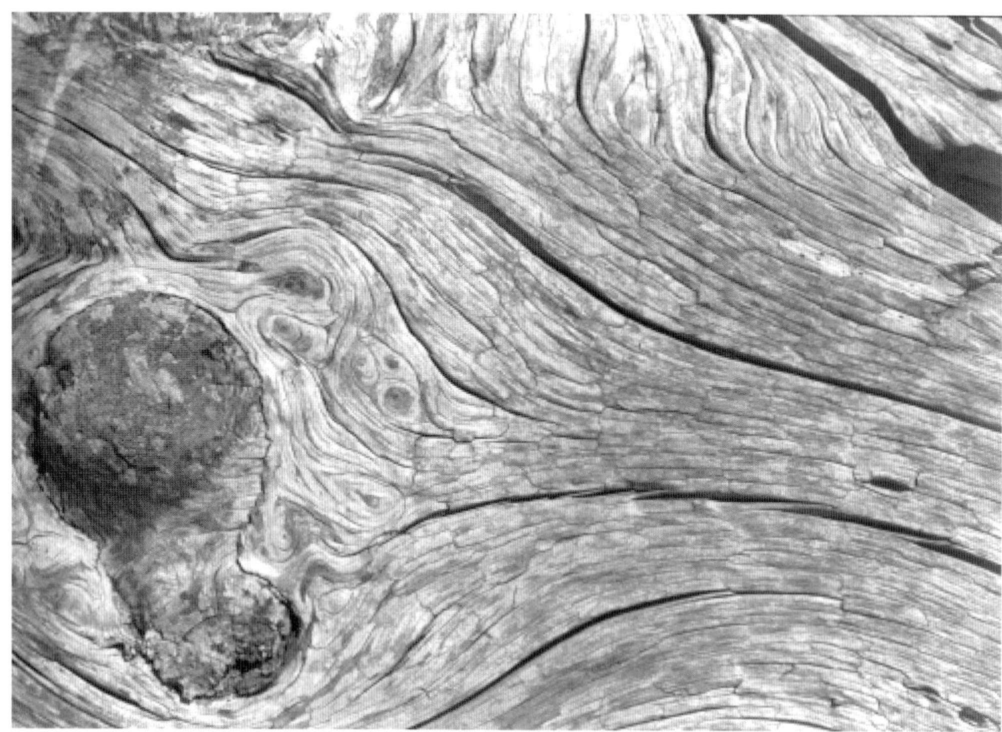

a tree is a slow river

Where do musical ideas come from?
How can I encourage musical ideas to come to me?

For musicians, these are the *big* questions. My answers are not scientifically proven, but they are encouraging. Musical ideas seem anxious to make a home in our hands and minds. They want to be heard. They are bored with being a good idea with nowhere to go and no one to know them. Musical ideas want to come to us and will gladly do so, but *they must be invited first*. That's the catch.

So how do we invite musical ideas to come to us? By offering them a home. The place they like best is a river of flowing movements. When we play with flowing circular motions, completely immersing ourselves in what we are doing, listening deeply to each sound, letting go of our anxieties and limitations, letting our arms flow over the keys and into the keys, then we become a river of music. Musical ideas are curious, colorful fishes and when we provide them with a new river to explore, they will come and keep coming.

This is why so many great creators have talked about flow. Mozart used to say that music should flow like oil. Chopin and Beethoven made similar comments. Provide musical ideas with a river made of flowing movements and you will never tire of all the wonderful ideas that will swim your way.

Pattern

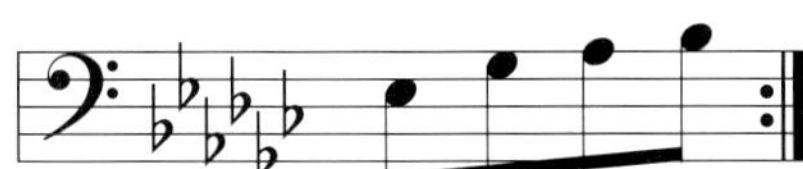

Play these four notes with a circular, flowing motion of your arm rather than with four individual finger motions. Your wrists should drop a little as you move toward your thumb and rise as you move toward your little finger. Keep the pedal down.

Vacation One

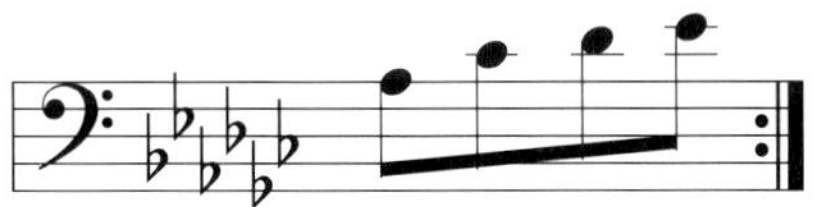

Move to this Vacation without breaking the feeling of flow in your arms. If you hit a wrong key, just keep going. Don't interrupt the flow for anything as trivial as that!

Vacation Two

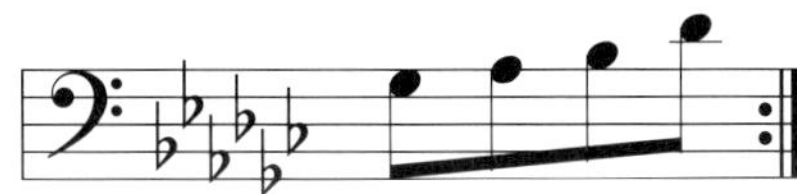

I hear Vacation Two as brighter and sunnier than the Pattern, while Vacation One is darker and "moonier." Explore the sounds of other four-note Hand Shapes in E-Flat Minor and in the other Minor Scales, and make up other Vacations.

Above and Below

After you have created melodies with various five-key Hand Shapes for a while, move around the whole upper half of the piano, freely exploring the sounds of all the tones in E-Flat Minor that lie above the left-side Pattern.

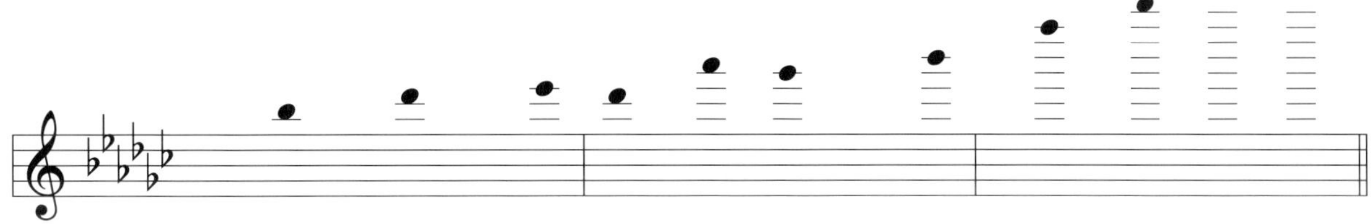

Here, your right hand (RH) flies over the top of your left to play a bass line. Explore the sounds of other bass tones in the key of E-Flat Minor. Also, try adding *e natural* in the bass with Vacation One for a rich and different sound. When you do that, create in the Key of B Major, which has an *e natural* in it.

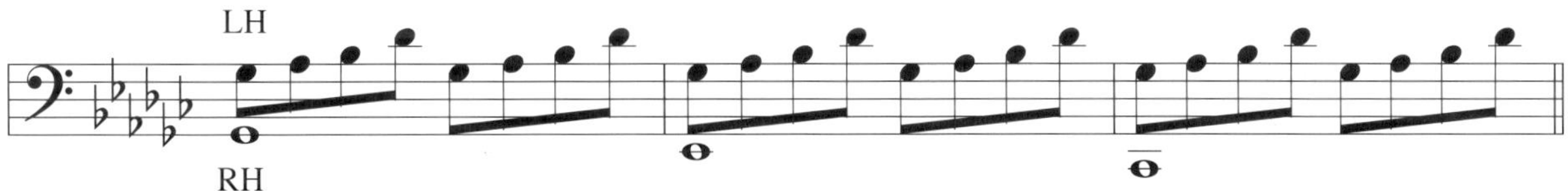

Here, your right hand is doing double duty, playing melodies above the left-side Pattern as well as bass tones below. Keep the pedal down. In this stream of sound, everything flows together.

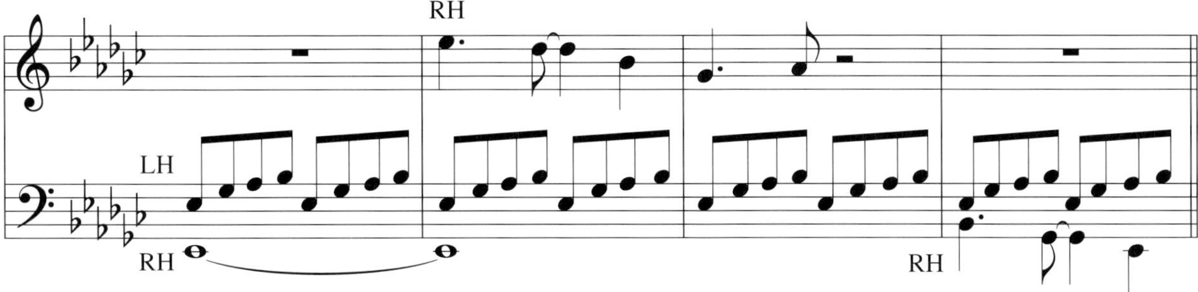

Loss

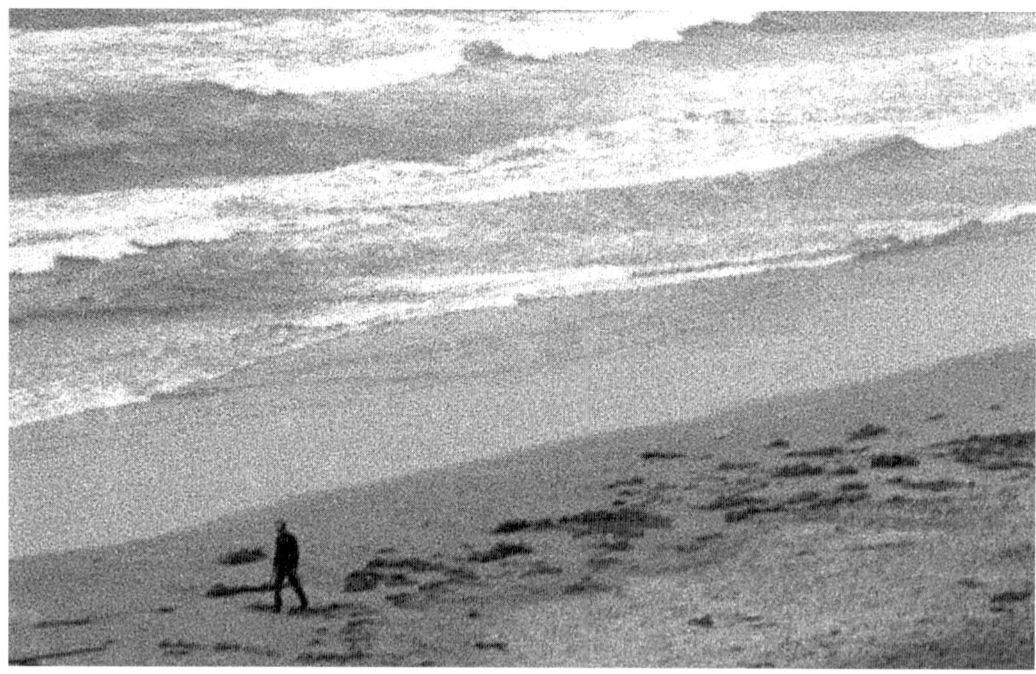

A loss creates a tide of emotion, bringing grief in waves. When we suffer a loss, do we choose cheerful music to lift us up or music that fits our torn feelings? Music can heal either way.

I usually make sounds that go *with* the direction of my feelings rather than against them. If I play music that fits my harsh feelings, if I don't try to hide my pain under something bouncy and cheerful, then my somber feelings eventually change into feelings with wider and brighter skies. This way, the piano has helped me through some hard times.

Pattern

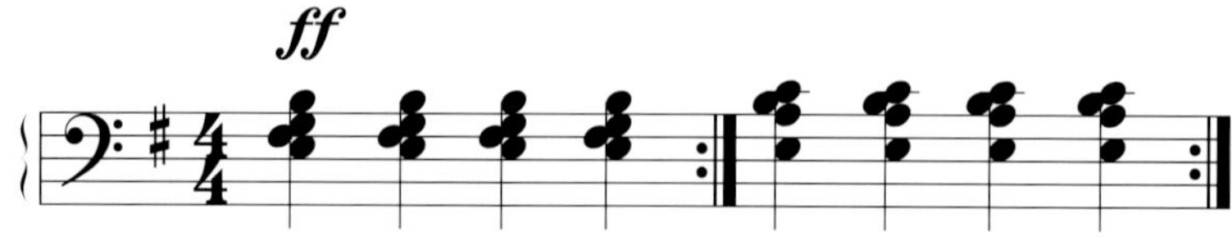

This left-side Pattern makes harsh sounds to fit harsh feelings. The clusters (closely spaced notes played at the same time) sound dense and confused. Create melodies and sounds on your right side in the Key of E Minor, using single notes, pairs of notes, and even five-note clusters.

Pattern Variation One

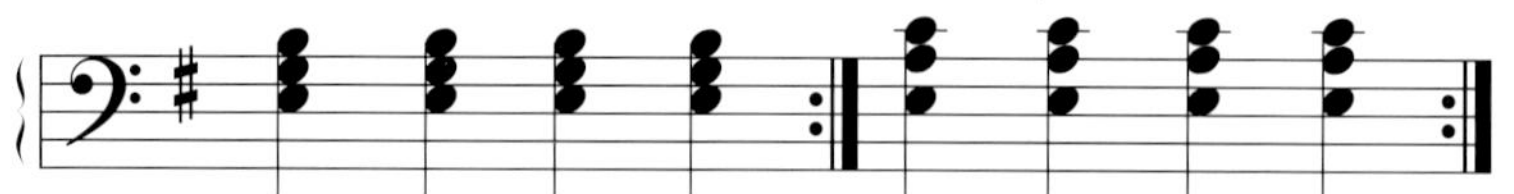

Here, I omitted one note from each cluster, making a much less dense and dissonant sound.

Pattern Variation Two

Just as in the last Variation, this Variation uses three out of the four original notes in each measure. This time, a different tone is omitted from the cluster to create quite a different effect.

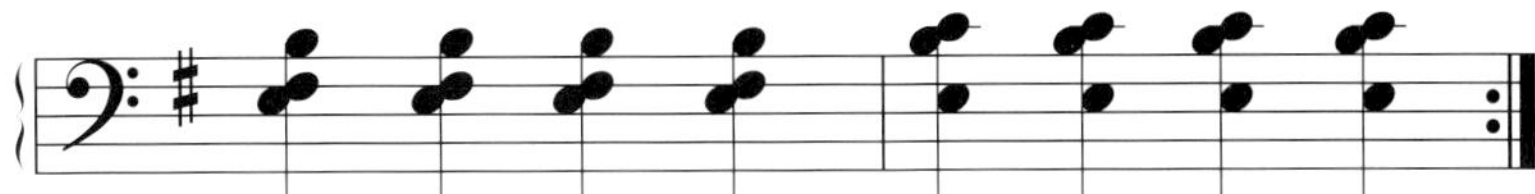

Vacation

With this Vacation, the tension of the Pattern is eased. Then, returning to the Pattern, you are back with the harsher feelings. Move between the Pattern and the Vacation many times.

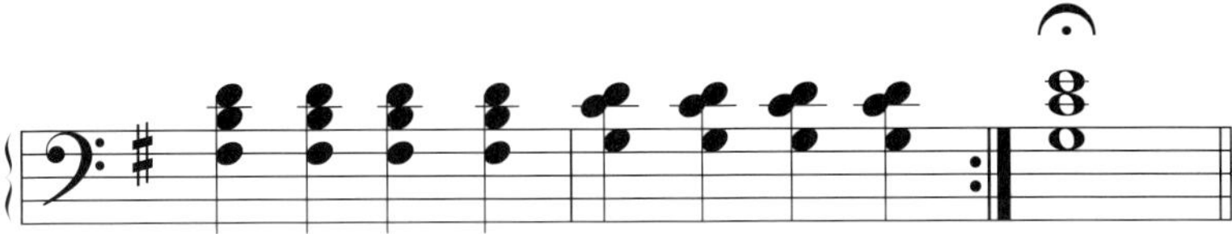

It's Not the Notes

When we are saying something heartfelt to a friend, the actual words we speak are rarely as important as our feelings and our sincerity. We can always express our feelings using different words, and this shows that the feelings are what is important. It's the same with music. The notes are not what is most important—it's the feeling, the sincerity, the mood behind the notes. This is why we can't let our concern with notes break the flow or taint the feeling.

Intensity

There is an intense sound I call "stuck notes." As you play pairs of keys, keep the top key the same as you change the bottom one. See the first two measures below. You could also make the bottom note the stuck one. I've already mentioned clusters, shown in the third measure below. Sometimes, nothing is as expressive as a whole fistful of keys.

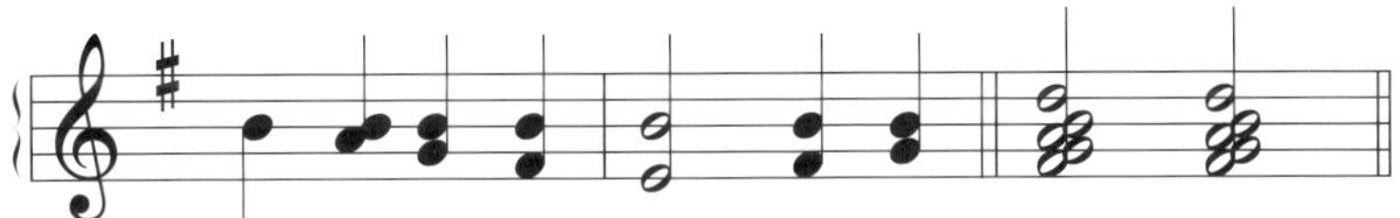

So Much More Meaning

Most people seem to think of music as being for entertainment. But this is a narrow view, like thinking of a forest as being just for timber. Music making can have *so much more* meaning. It can be a way of discovering who we are, and of growing into the confident and creative person we are able to be. The act of making music can be very empowering and healing.

We can't worry about whether our music sounds boring to others, at least at this point. Play what you feel, however long you feel it. Stay true to that. This way, you will develop the strongest connection between the feelings of your music and the music of your feelings. When that happens, music begins to have its real power.

We are healed from suffering only by experiencing it to the full. —Proust

No Limits

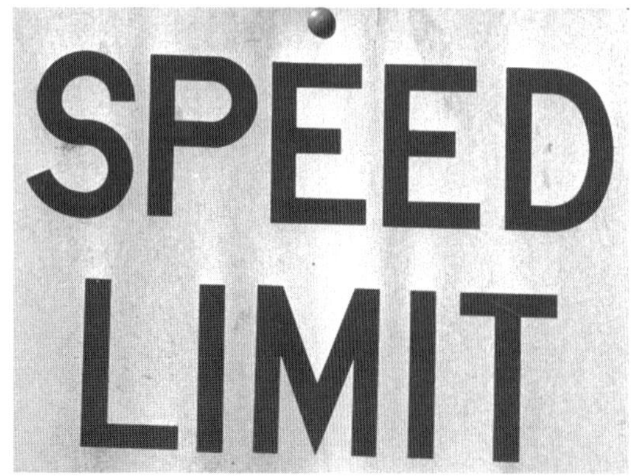

Do you feel limited at the piano? Are you unable to quickly find the sounds that express how you feel? How does a person attain a state of creative expression in which everything flows and there are "no limits"?

The answer is an odd one. We have to create within limits in order to become limitless. As the great composer Igor Stravinsky once wrote, "The more I limit myself, the more free I am." This piece explores this strange, liberating idea.

Pattern

The right side below is made of just one Hand Shape—a sixth with a third inside. Create with just this one Hand Shape for a while, and see how many new Rhythm Patterns you can discover with it. When you get bored with the same sound, keep playing it, and your imagination will generate more rhythmic ideas. Limit yourself to become unlimited.

Create in A Natural Minor (all white keys) but change to A Harmonic Minor in the last measure. Or play *g natural* rather than *g sharp* in the last measure to stay in the Key of A Natural Minor. Repeat each measure if you like.

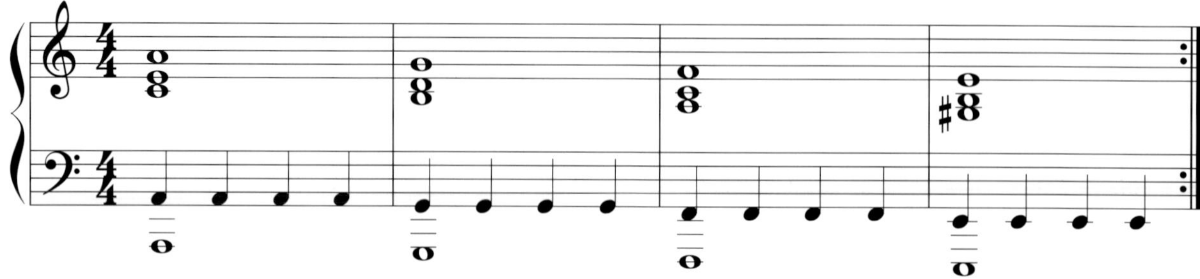

Vacation

This uses the same Hand Shapes as before but goes off in a new direction. Again, create Rhythm Patterns and melodies with the right-side notes, and vary the left-side octaves any way you like. Repeat each measure, and repeat the Vacation as a whole as many times as you like. Before returning to the Pattern, I usually play *e*'s in the bass rather than the *g*'s in the last measure.

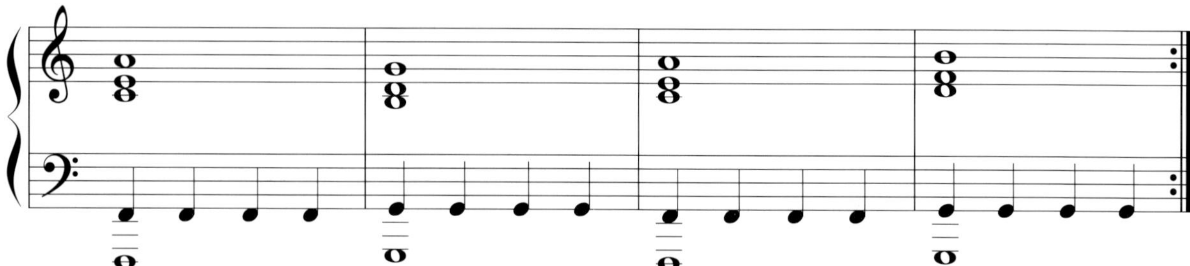

Rhythm Patterns

To get started, create with four-beat Rhythm Patterns played over and over. Below are two examples to try. The first one has accents, and the second features the same Hand Shape broken up.

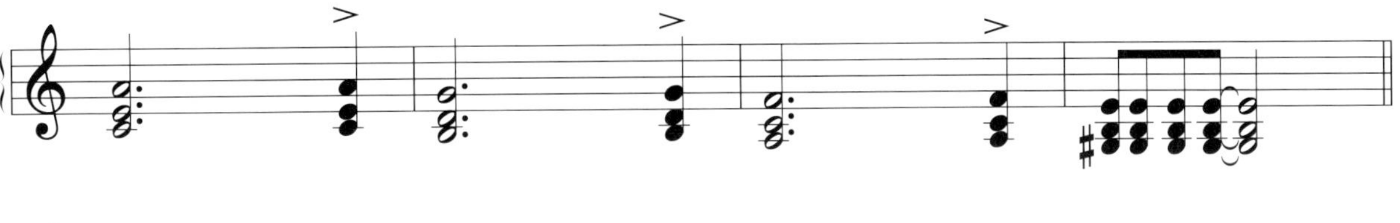

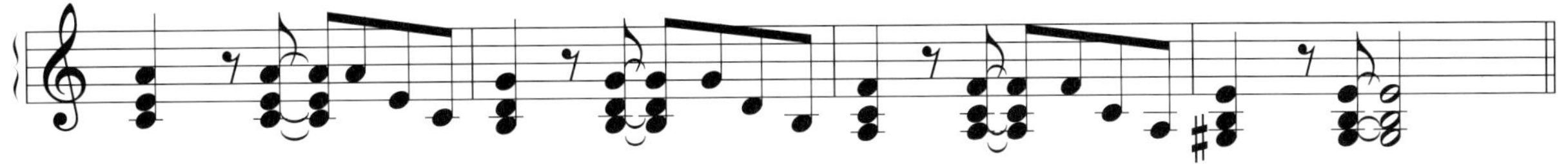

Making Melodies

After creating Rhythm Patterns for a while, change the top note of the Hand Shape to create melodies. Here's an example to play with the Pattern.

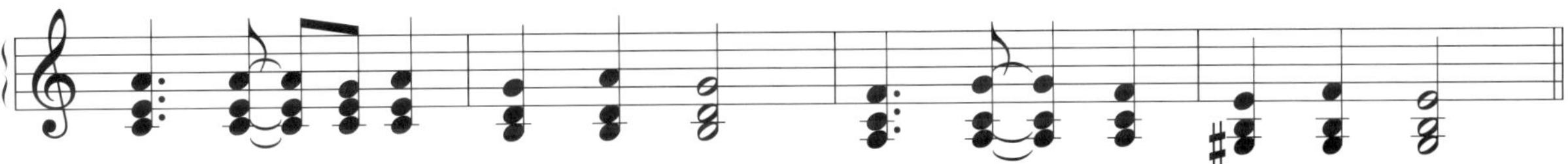

Making Pattern Variations

You may want to change the way you play the left-side notes of this Pattern. Here are three Variations to try. The last one features a very popular Rhythm Pattern used in rock music.

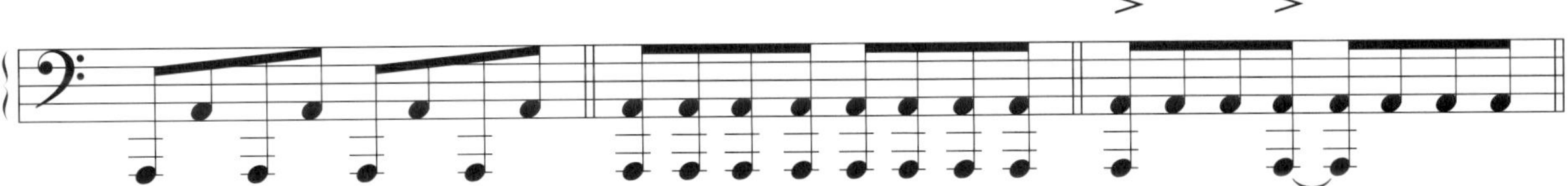

Now change your Hand Shape to create new sounds. Try fourths and thirds. If you know the A Minor Blues Scale (explored in the next section), you can create melodies with that, too. (I use it a lot on the CD.) Also, if you know about triads and inversions (explored in Volume 2-B), you can invert the Hand Shapes to create new sounds.

You can explore any Pattern for as long as you like, and you will always find new ideas as long as you stay with it. We live in an infinite universe. When it comes to exploring and learning, *there is no limit!*

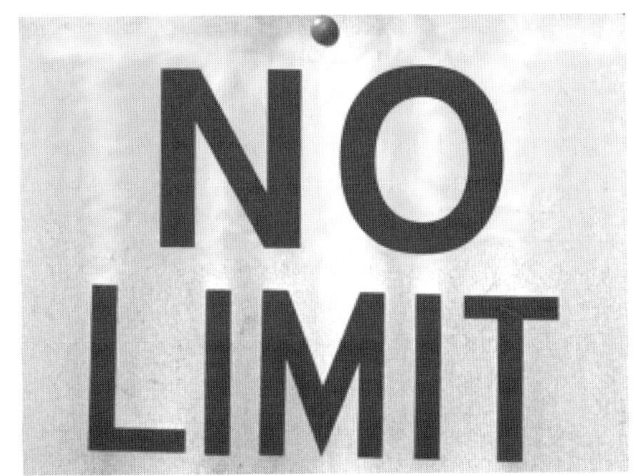

Reflecting

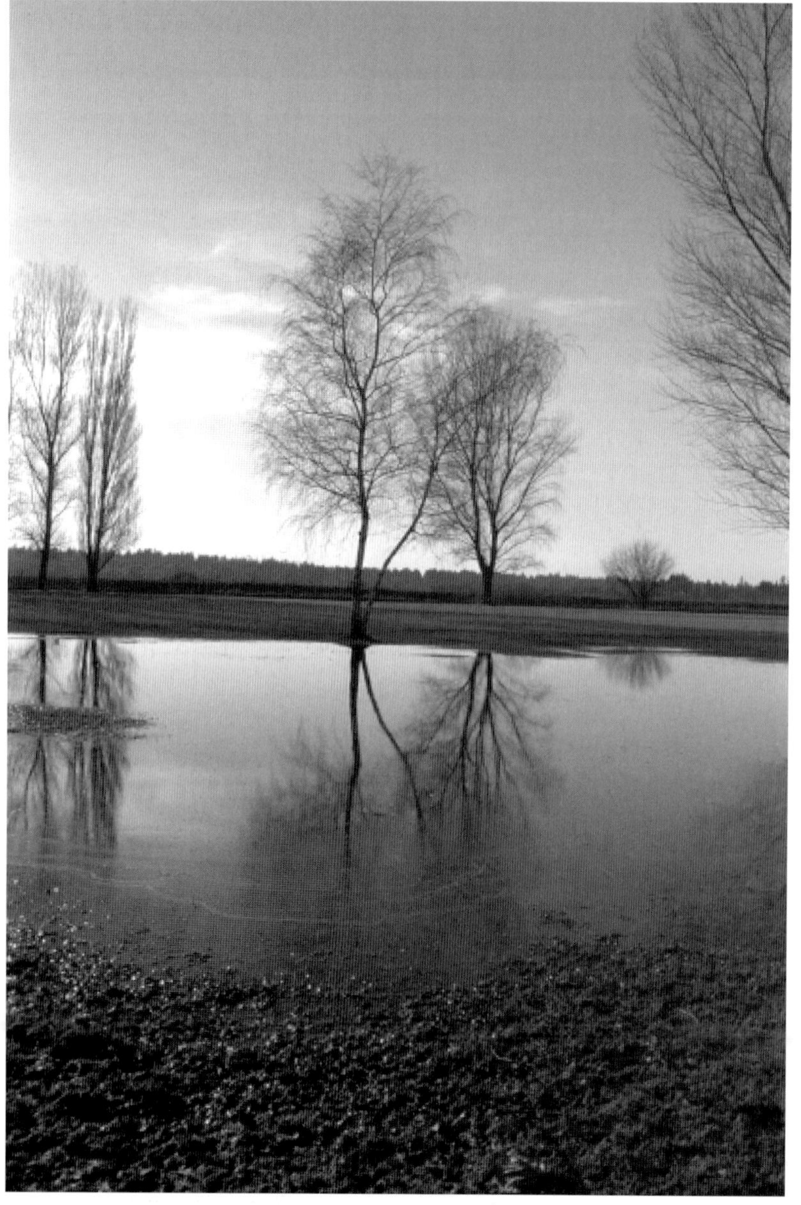

Only calm waters give true reflections.

When you look
into a mirror,
you do not see
your reflection—
your reflection
sees you.

– anonymous Japanese poet

The piano is a special kind of mirror. It gives reflections we can *hear* and *feel* rather than see. The piano sounds out the music and ideas hidden within us. After years of playing, we may appear to develop a deep friendship with our piano, yet our instrument remains only a shiny crate filled with wires, hammers, and keys. Our friendship is with the invisible self the piano reflects and reveals. I sometimes wonder how I ever would have discovered who I am without the piano's kind and deep reflection.

Pattern One

This is the most popular Pattern I teach. Create melodies in A Minor, using single notes, thirds, and sixths.

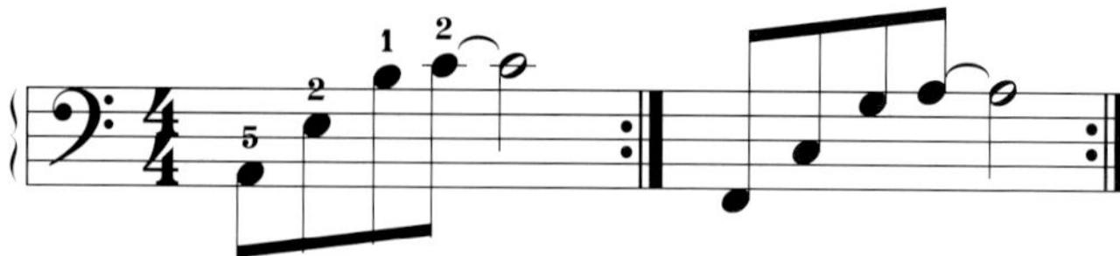

Vacation One

Sometimes I like to hold the *b* for an extra couple of beats.

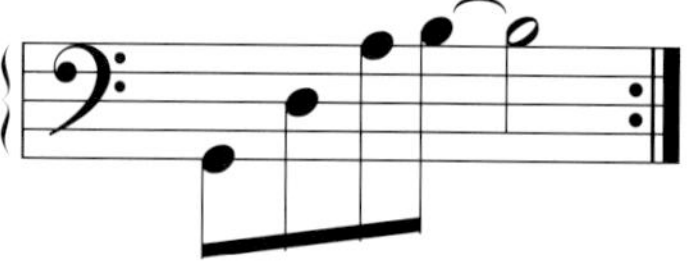

Vacation Two

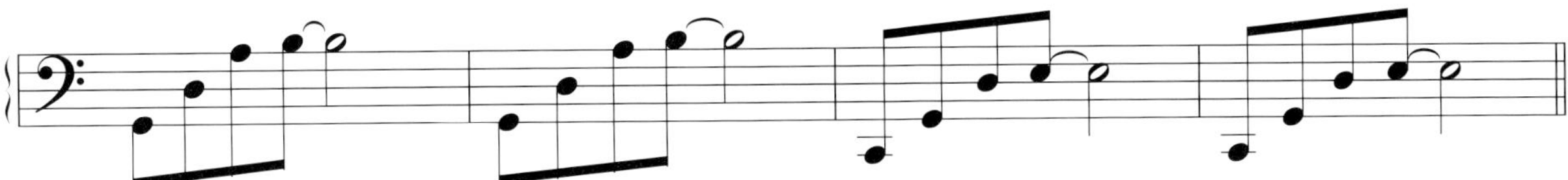

Vacation Three

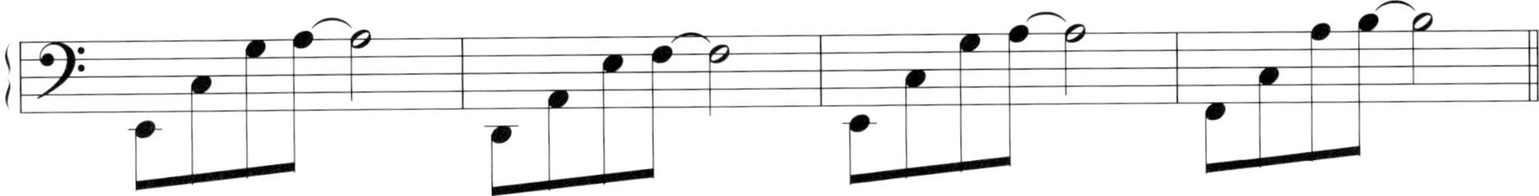

The Shape of A Minor

The best thing about playing in C Major and A Minor is that creating with Hand Shapes is easier in these Keys than in other Keys. There are no black keys to worry about, just the uninterrupted smile of fifty-two white keys.

Sixths fit with this Pattern perfectly. They have a ringing, sweet sound. If you can, play the top key of each sixth slightly louder than the bottom key. Voicing a tone this way makes the melody tone ring out.

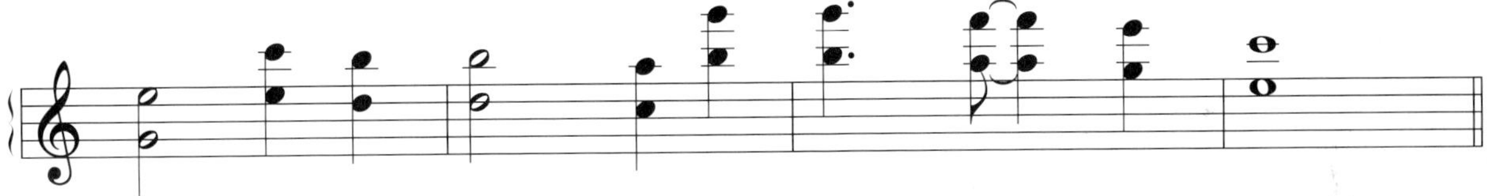

Notice how this melody leaps around. Composer Charles Ives once wrote, "If a song happens to feel like flying where humans cannot fly, to scale mountains that are not there, who shall stop it?" If your melodies feel like flying, don't let your concerns over a few missed keys keep these melodies from taking to the skies.

Try breaking up the sixth shapes. Fortunately, *playing* sixth shapes is easier than *saying* it. (It's a tongue twister.) Here, play the top key louder than the bottom key (the thumb key).

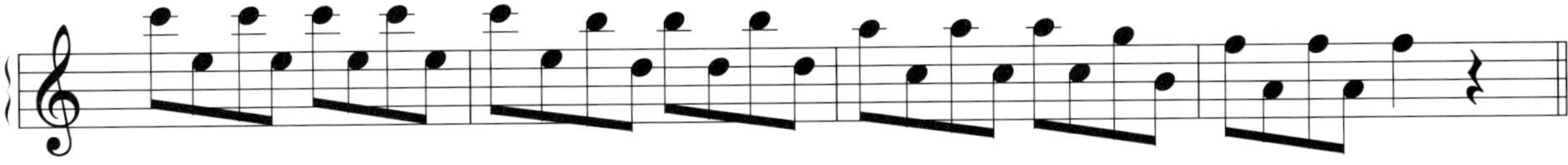

Other Shapes

Of course, there are other shapes besides sixths—thirds, fourths, and fifths. Also, you can sandwich notes inside these shapes to create three-note Hand Shapes. For example, you could play a sixth (such as *c* and *a*), and then play a third above the thumb (in this case, an *e*) to create a Hand Shape that you could then move all over the piano. Try playing a third inside a seventh, a fourth within an octave, a second within a fourth, and so on. Break up these Hand Shapes in various ways, and move the same Hand Shape freely between different octaves to create runs and expansive melodies.

Pattern Variations

As you know, any group of notes can be played differently at different times. Here are fourteen other ways you could play the four notes in the first measure of the Pattern. Play the second measure of the Pattern in the same way. Then again, if you play the first measure one way and the second measure another way, this gives you a hundred and ninety-six new ways of playing the Pattern on just this page. Which ways do you like best right now?

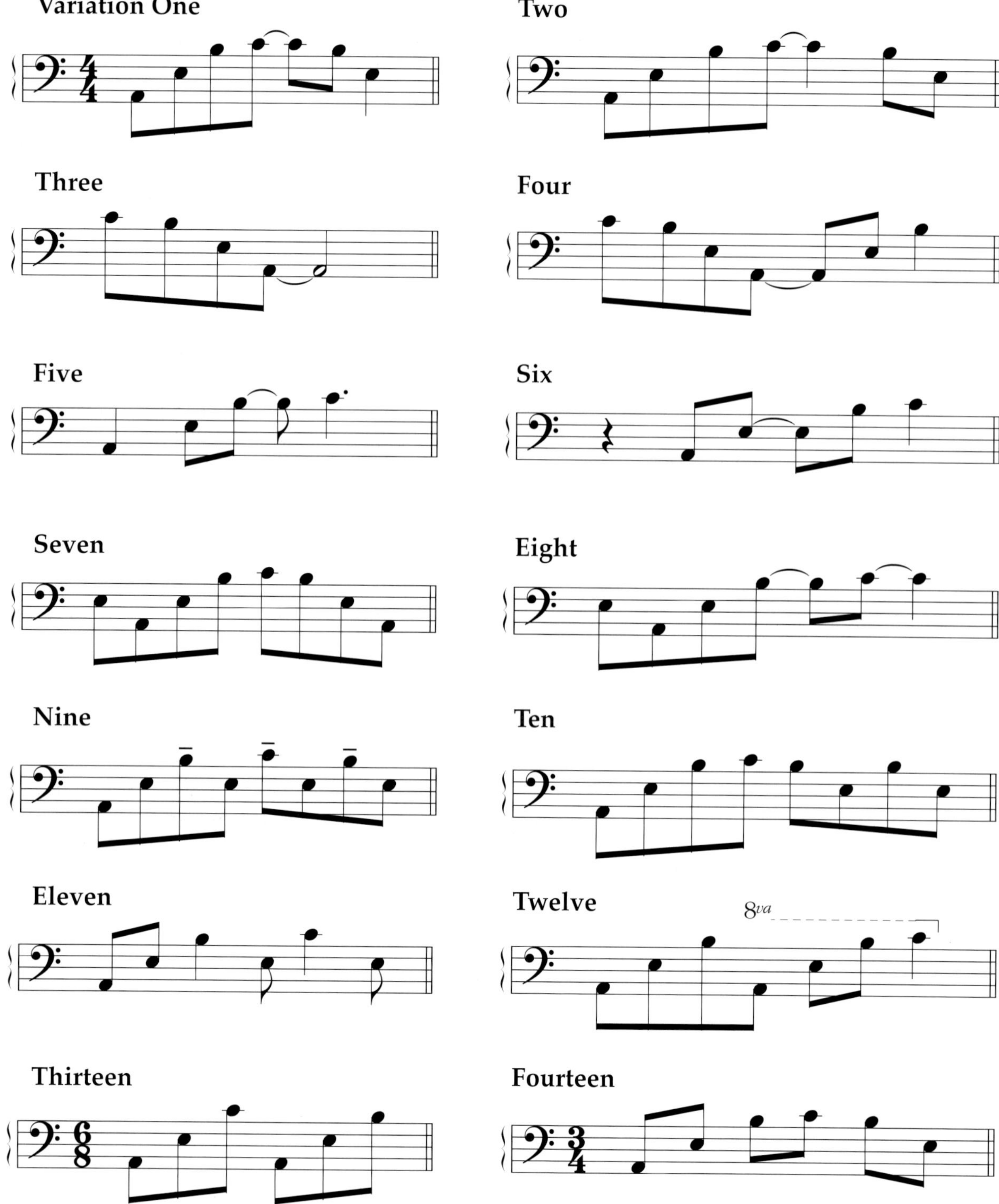

Reflecting on Black Keys

I often introduce this Pattern to people in the Key of E-Flat Minor and tell them, "Just create melodies with black keys while I play the Pattern." Later I tell them about the two white keys in the Key of E-Flat Minor, the *f natural* and the *c flat*, and I encourage them to create with those, too. Finally, I teach them how to play the Pattern and the Vacation, and encourage them to put it all together.

This is an especially good approach if you want to play this piece as a duet with a friend who doesn't have much (or any) experience at a piano. As long as you play the Pattern with a steady beat, your friend will sound good playing with just black keys. It's so much fun to create with people who have never made music before. They are often so excited and grateful.

Pattern One

I usually play each measure twice, sometimes four times. You can finger the second measure the same as the first, or use your thumb on both the *d flat* and *e flat*.

Vacation One

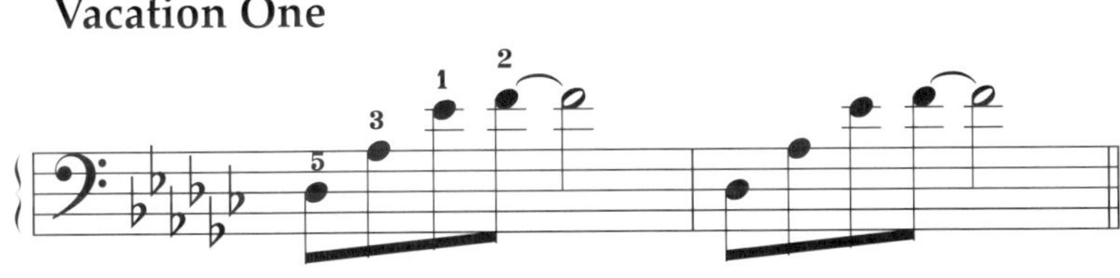

As you add melodies using tones in the Key of E-Flat Minor, begin by adding melodies during the long-held notes. This is an easy way to start putting the hands together *and* it sounds good.

Vacation Two

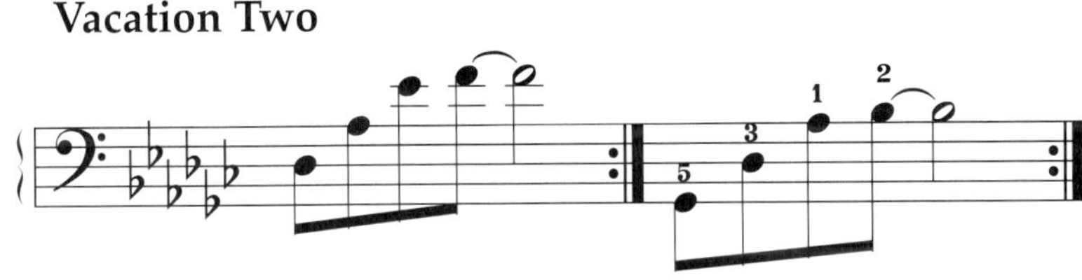

This Vacation begins in the same way as the one above, but it then travels to another location.

Vacation Three

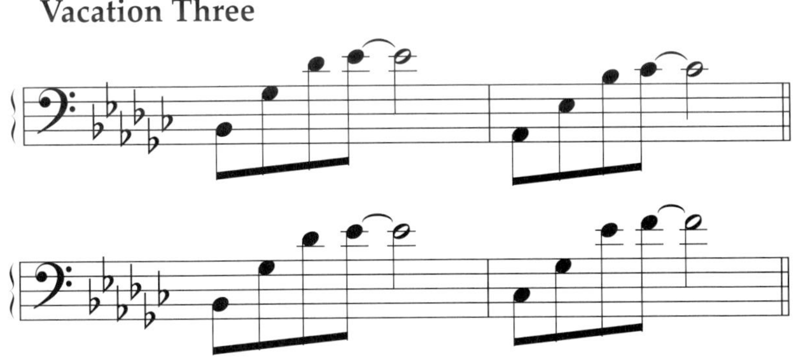

The last two notes in each measure make a counter-melody that leads your ear back to the Pattern. I often repeat the last measure (don't forget the *c flat*) a number of times before returning to the Pattern. The harmony of those notes seems to be asking a question, inviting further reflections.

Create your own Vacations in E-Flat Minor or in another Key such as D Minor. Also, try moving this Pattern to other Keys, even in the same piece. For example, move up a half step to the Key of E Minor.

Art is not the reflection of reality. It is the reality of that reflection. —Jean-Luc Goddard

Touch of Moonlight

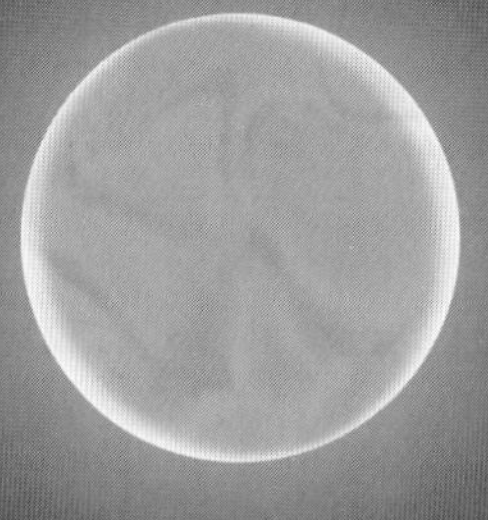

Pattern

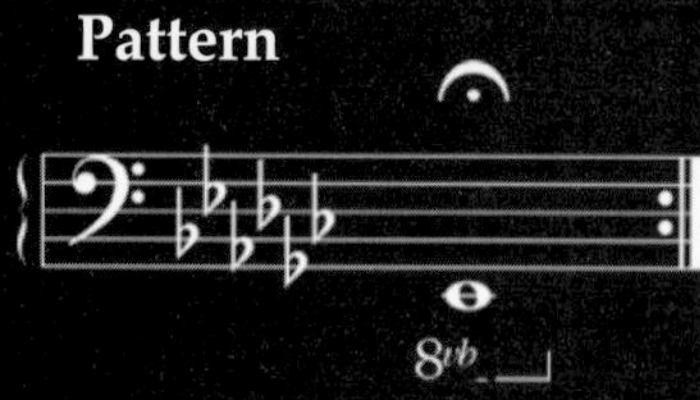

Begin by pressing down the pedal and softly playing *e flat* in the bass. Keeping the pedal down, play any keys in E-Flat Minor, alternating quickly between your right and left hands. Play in the upper reaches of the piano. As your fingers touch the keys, let them be soft moonbeams touching a lake.

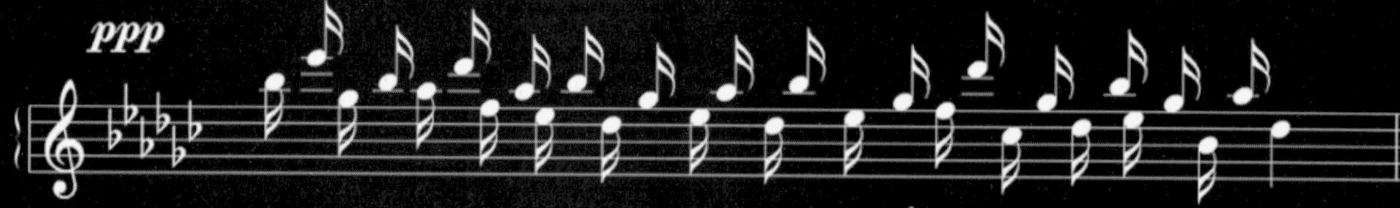

Try alternating at different speeds to create different effects. You could alternate unevenly between the hands to create rhythmic effects, or play many keys in each hand instead of just one. Become softer and louder. Consider all the gentle shadings of moonlight, the shadows, the way the same soft light gives everything a different glow.

Vacation

While in the Key of E-Flat Minor, play two keys with each hand in the higher range of the piano and let them ring in the air. (The higher the pitch, the faster the tone dissolves.) Roll the keys if you like. Add a bass tone, as you did with the Pattern. Try playing the hands closer together and farther apart. Note that both hands are written in the treble clef.

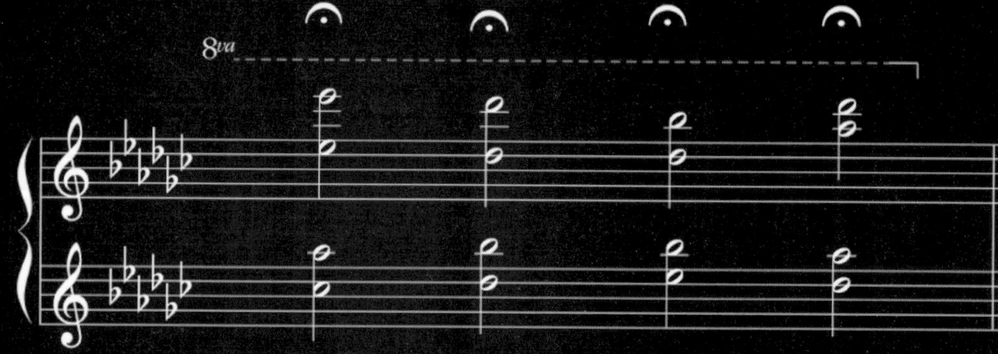

Three Pedals?

On most pianos, there are three pedals. What are they all for? If you have never used all three pedals in the same piece, there is no better time than right now.

As I explained in *The Healing Harp*, depressing the pedal on the far right (the damper pedal) lifts all the dampers away from the strings, allowing the strings to vibrate freely like those of a harp. If you are playing a grand piano, reach inside and gently strum the strings while pressing down the damper pedal. It sounds like a harp. Now that's a soft touch!

Try playing this piece with the damper pedal only halfway down or only a third of the way down. On some pianos, this creates distinctly different effects.

The Sostenuto Pedal

If your piano has three pedals, consider the pedal in the middle. What does this neglected pedal do? On many modern uprights, this is a "practice pedal" that drops a thick piece of felt between the hammers and the strings, muting the sound when we don't want our playing to disturb others.

More often, the middle pedal is the *sostenuto pedal.* It works like the damper pedal, but it only works on those keys we held down *before* we depressed this pedal. In the example below, you would first play just the low *e flat* in the bass and, while still holding down this key, press down the sostenuto pedal. Then lift your hand off of the *e flat* and it will still be sustained, *but no other key on the piano will!* You can now play staccato notes while still sustaining the *e flat* in the bass. Think of the sostenuto pedal as providing a third hand that holds down bass tones.

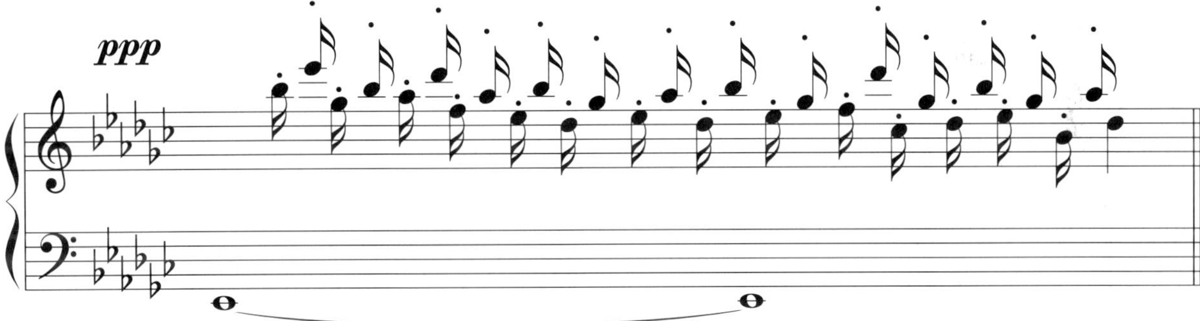

The Soft Pedal

The pedal on the left is called the *soft pedal*. On most upright pianos, pressing this pedal drops a piece of felt against the strings to mute the sound. If you are playing a grand piano, you will notice that the keys move slightly to the right when you depress this pedal. Why? Most hammers in a piano strike two or three strings at once, each tuned to the same pitch. When the pedal is depressed, the hammers move to the right and strike two strings instead of the usual three, or one string instead of the normal two. Back when pianos had only two strings per hammer, the soft pedal was called the *una corda* ("one string") pedal because when it was pressed down, only one string was struck.

Pressing down the soft pedal not only softens the sound but changes its personality because fewer strings are struck. Think of this pedal as a way of "coloring" the tones rather than merely softening them. Some pianists will even play *forte* while pressing the soft pedal just to get a loud but somewhat muted tone. This is a perfect piece for the soft pedal.

Endless Road

This is the last piece in this section. Why is such an easy-looking piece here rather than at the beginning? It's because this Pattern is played on your right side while you create melodies on your left. This can be quite a challenge! If you like, play the Pattern on your left side first, creating melodies on your right, and then switch.

When we are on a creative adventure, just when we think we have arrived somewhere, we see that the horizon is still ahead, always out of reach, suggesting an infinite number of places yet to go. The road ahead is endless. But why feel weary when we realize this? How wonderful that we can travel without end!

Pattern (Right Side)

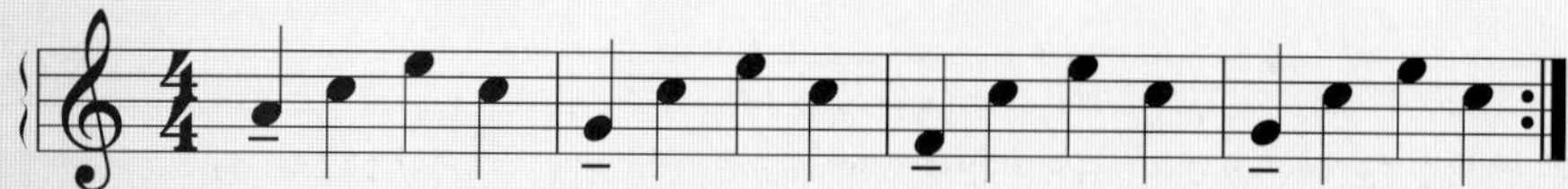

Create melodies in A Minor with your left hand playing both below and above the Pattern. See the next page for ideas.

Vacation (Right Side)

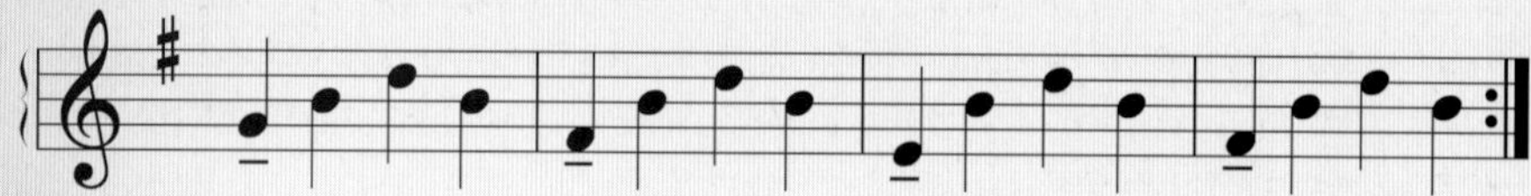

Create in the same way as the Pattern, but this time create with tones in the Key of E Minor.

When you're on a journey and the end keeps getting further and further away, then you realize that the real end is the journey.

— Karlfied Graf Durckheim

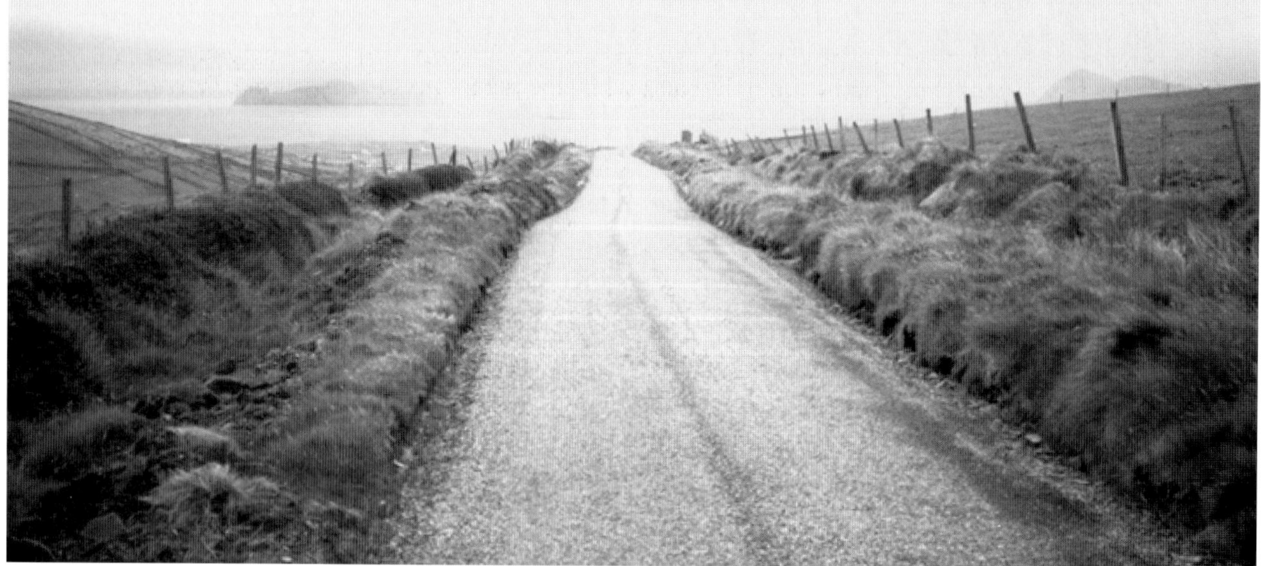

Other Vacations

With this Vacation, create melodies and bass lines in the Key of D Minor. You could also transpose this to the Key of E-Flat Minor pretty easily by simply playing every note up a half step.

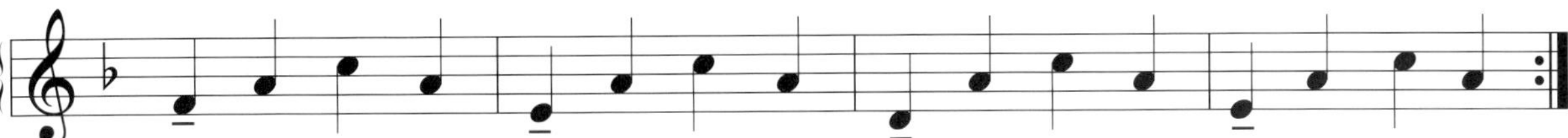

To create other Vacations, play a Pattern that starts on different pitches within the Key you are in. Here, create in A Minor. Try changing the first note of each measure to make other Vacations.

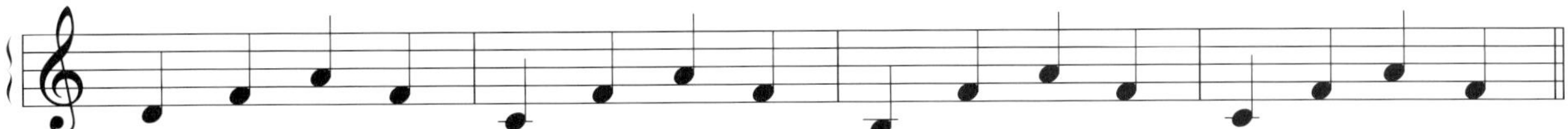

Ideas for Creating

Begin by playing melodies below the Pattern in simple rhythms—whole notes and half notes. Creating melodies with the left hand can be difficult, so simplicity is the "key," not A Minor or E Minor. In the example below, I first created a bass line and then added a melody below the notes of the Vacation.

This piece makes a very nice duet. You can play something similar to the example below while your partner creates melodies above it. In other words, you can play the Vacation with your right hand and add bass notes and melodies with your left hand. Meanwhile, your partner adds melodies above you using one or both hands. The following two pages are all about duet playing.

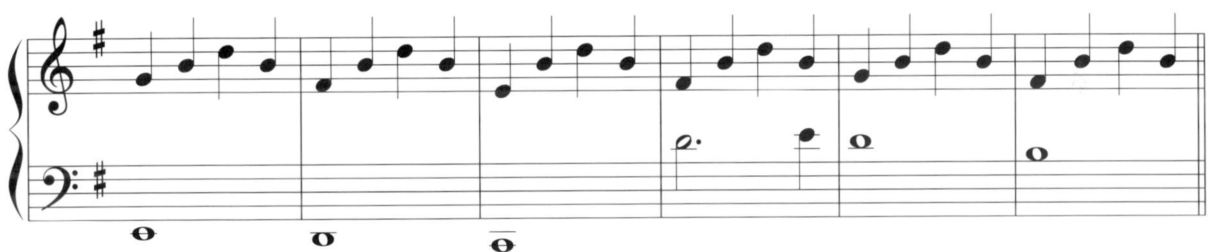

Eventually, you will develop the ability to play as many as four different parts by yourself. In this example, the Pattern is played by the right hand while the left first plays a bass tone, then a melody above the Pattern, and then a melody below.

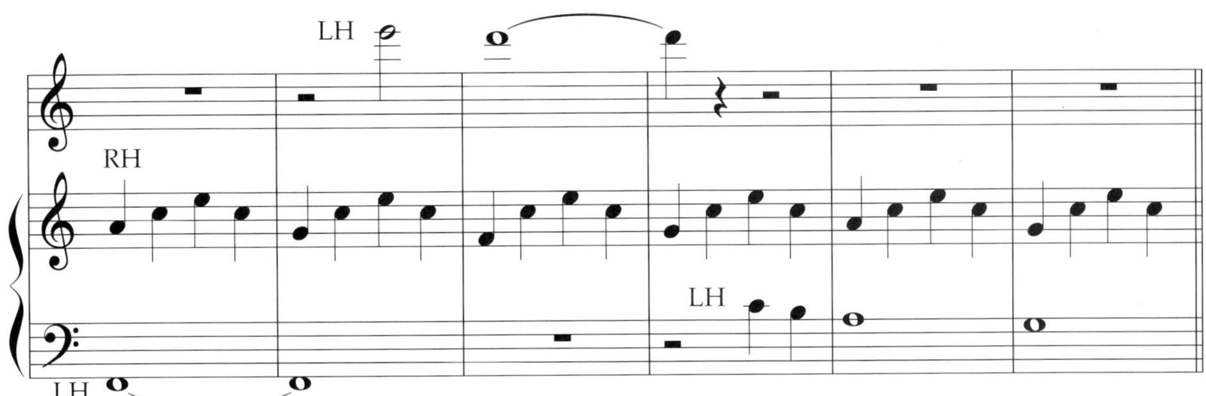

Endless Road as Duet

On the last page, I explained a way you could make this piece into a duet. Here's another: The player on top (playing the so-called *primo* part) plays the Pattern on the left side while creating melodies on the right. The player on the bottom (playing the *secondo* part) sustains a bass tone while playing a simple counter-melody such as the one below. This secondo part could be played by some beginners.

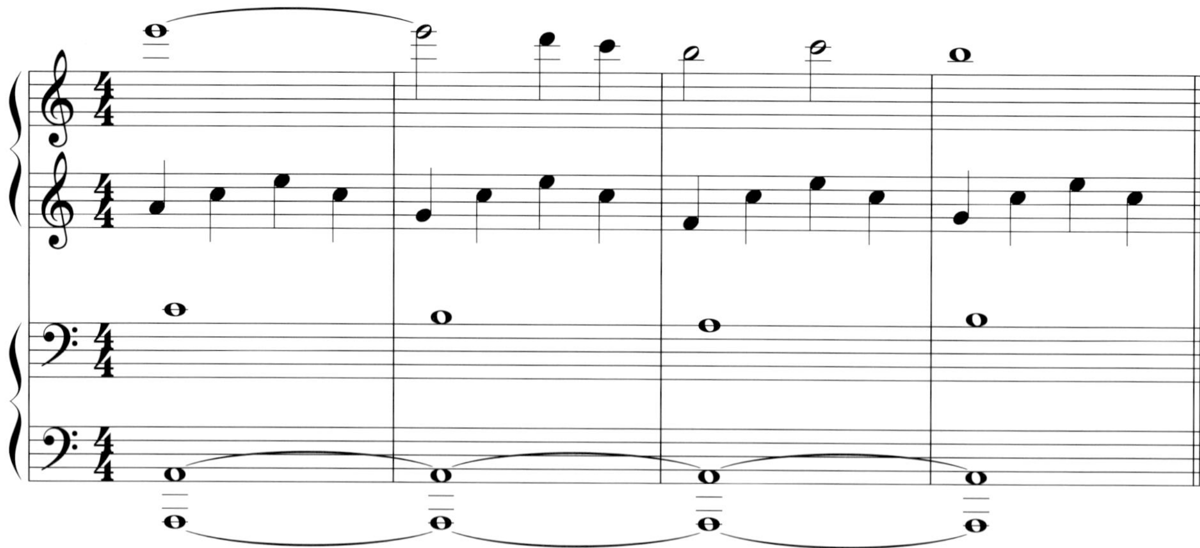

Here's another way *Endless Road* could be made into a duet. The player on top plays melodies and counter melodies while the player on the bottom plays the Pattern and adds bass tones.

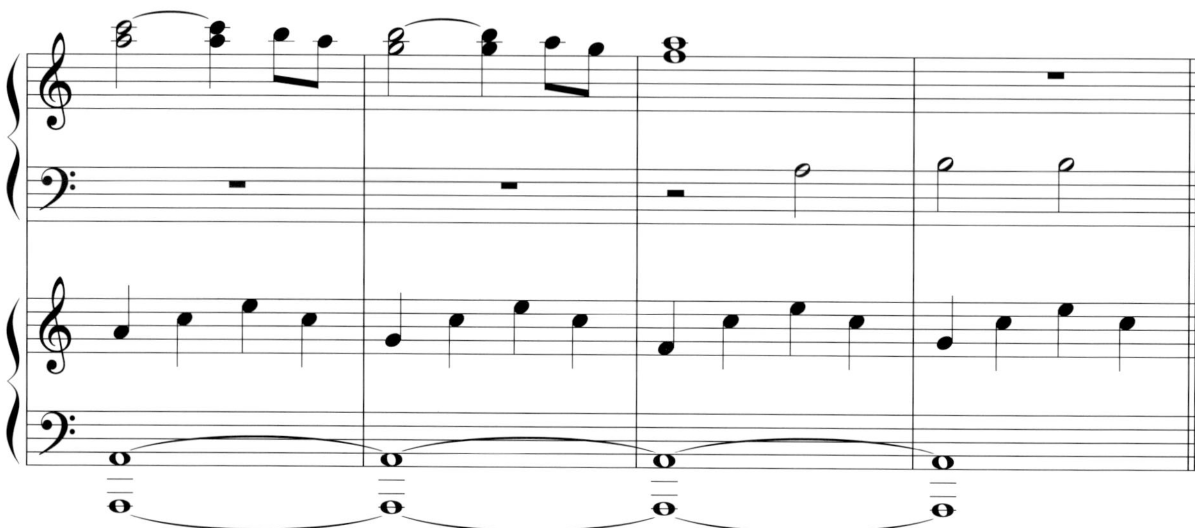

For a Vacation, your partner could play the Pattern while you create melodies below it. This piece sounds quite nice when played with other instruments—flute, clarinet, violin, cello, etc. When playing with these instruments, play an accompaniment like the secondo part in the example above.

The road is better than the inn. —Cervantes

As Long As You Have a Duet Partner Handy

As long as you have a duet partner on hand, why not play other pieces in this book with them? Below, I turned the Pattern from *Chopin* into a relatively easy secondo part. While the player on the bottom plays the two lower clefs, the player on top creates melodies such as the one below. This could also be played by three players, one on each part, all parts playable by beginners or near beginners.

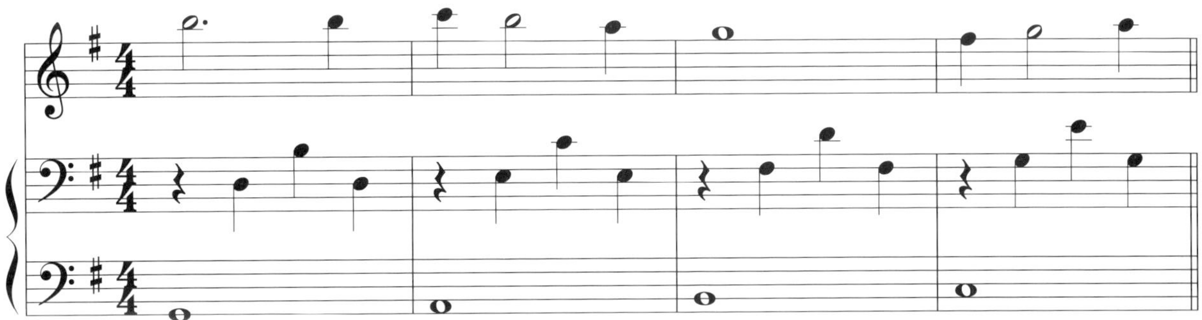

Here is a duet version of the piece *No Limits*. Once again, the bottom two staves could be the secondo part, or you could have three people playing these three parts. Trios are a lot of fun.

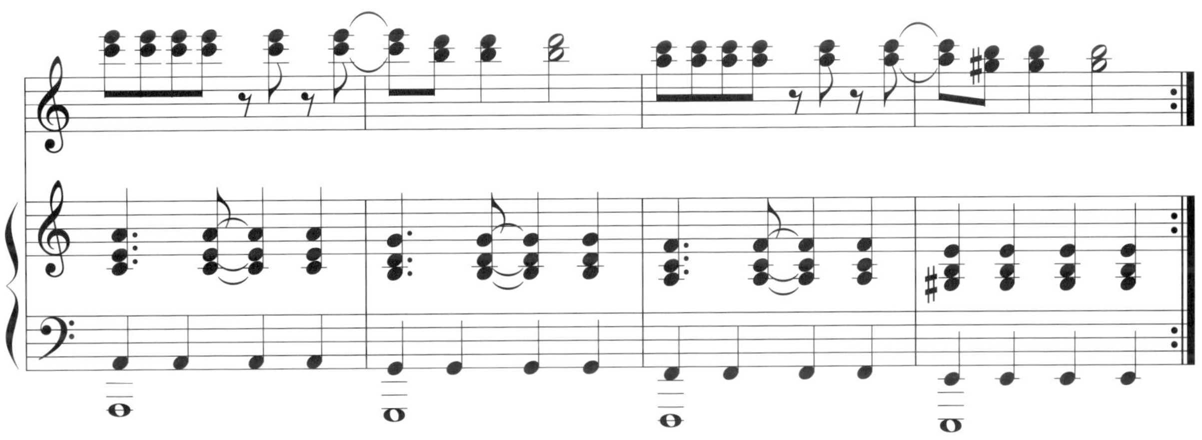

Here's a variation for when you want to play with a beginner. Have your partner play the bass line with one finger while you play the chords and the melody. There is always a way to include everyone.

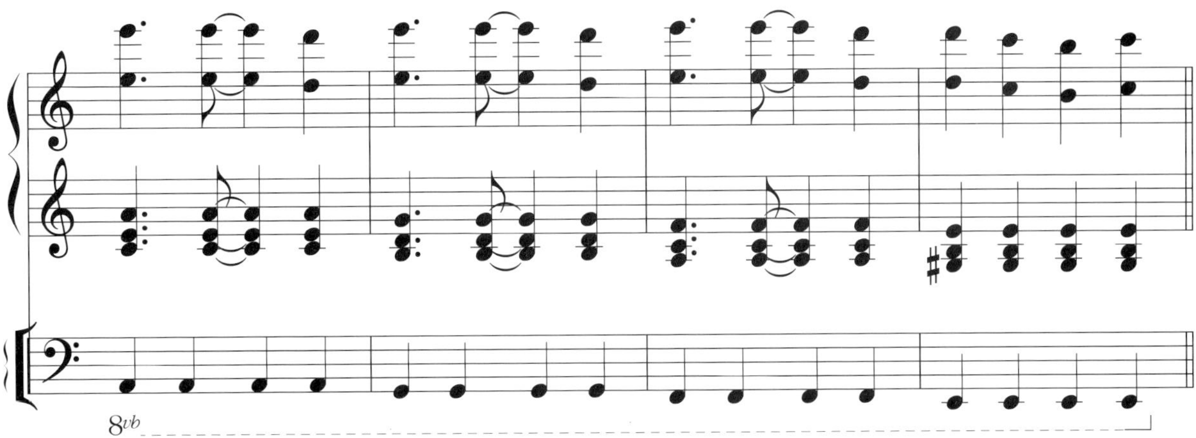

Free Play (on All Keys)

It's time once again to invite new Patterns into your hands. Close your eyes, open your ears, and forget all the music you've ever made. As you freely play, let your fingers roam over *all* the keys on the piano—black, white, or any color you might find. Eavesdrop on the arguments and conversations between tones. Just make sounds—weird sounds, ugly sounds, strong sounds. Make them wild, mild, bold, cold, spicy, mean, fat, and lean. Let "unheard of" sounds be heard at last.

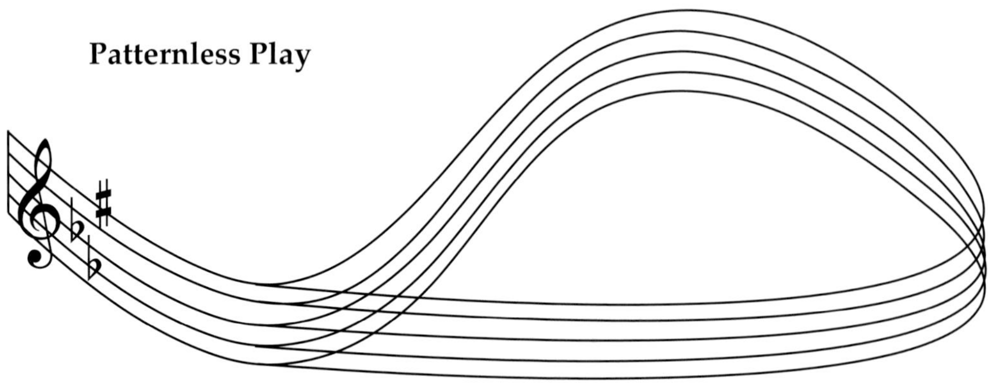

Children learn their abilities, their roles, and their ways of being through play. They imitate, model, and create all sorts of imaginary houses, offices, parties, and such. They learn by playing. If we adults are slower learners, it is because we have forgotten how to play.

Wild animals don't "learn to play"—they play to learn. Likewise, children in Africa or in Bali don't "learn to play" a musical instrument—they play to learn. They simply play along with their elders, learning as they go, gradually gaining skill. They do not feel they have to "learn to play" before they can play. This is how we can discover our own way of making music, by returning to a state of play, and enjoying all our work there.

Creating with Blues Scales

Though the Major and Minor Scales (as we know them) have been around for over three hundred years, the Blues Scale came to life in the 20th Century. Born in the souls and songs of African-Americans, it has become a popular scale, spreading from blues to jazz to rock and beyond. It is an extremely expressive scale, with a strange arrangement of tones, and a love affair with moody dissonance. It expresses what other scales cannot. To understand how to make a Minor Blues Scale, begin with a scale you already know, the E-Flat Minor Pentatonic.

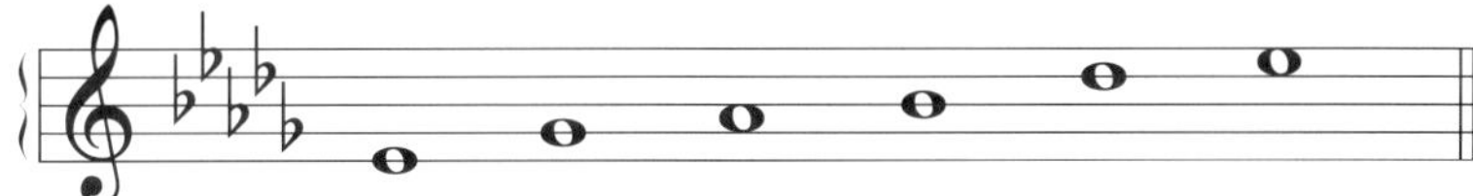

The *E-Flat Blues Scale* (also called the *E-Flat Minor Blues Scale*) uses these same tones but adds one more—an *a natural.* This one note changes everything! Sometimes players will also add an *f* to make the fingering easier. Two pieces in this section use this scale, the E-Flat Minor Blues Scale.

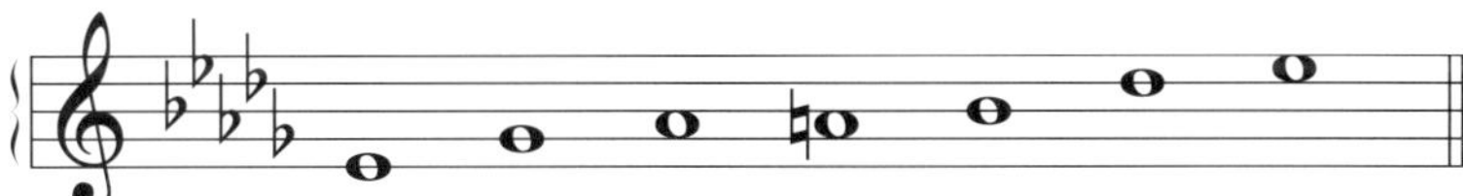

Another piece in this section uses an *E Minor Blues Scale*. While E-Flat Blues is made of black keys with one white, E Blues is made of white keys with one black.The *A Minor Blues Scale*, also used in this section, is another scale made of all white keys and just one black. Here's the E Minor Blues Scale. When you want to run up this scale quickly, finger it so that your thumb lands on *e* and *b*.

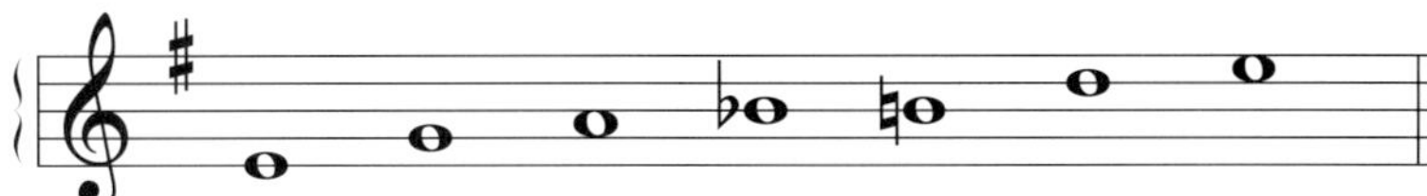

Just as there is a G Major Scale that has the same notes as the E Minor Scale, so there is a *G Major Blues Scale* that has the same notes as an E Minor Blues Scale. This section has one piece, *Lazy Days*, that uses this lesser-known, good-natured scale.

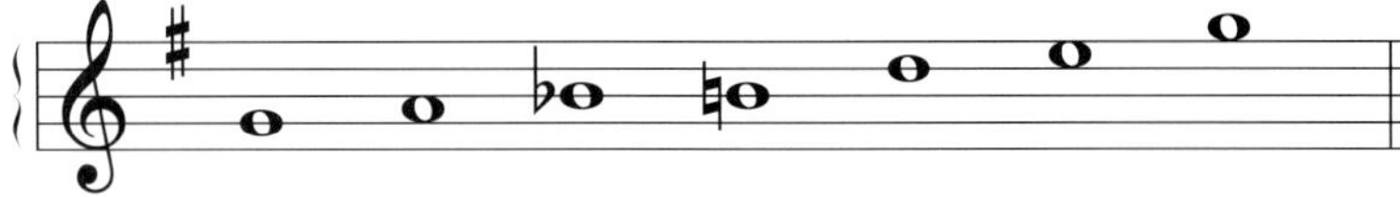

Too Late Blues

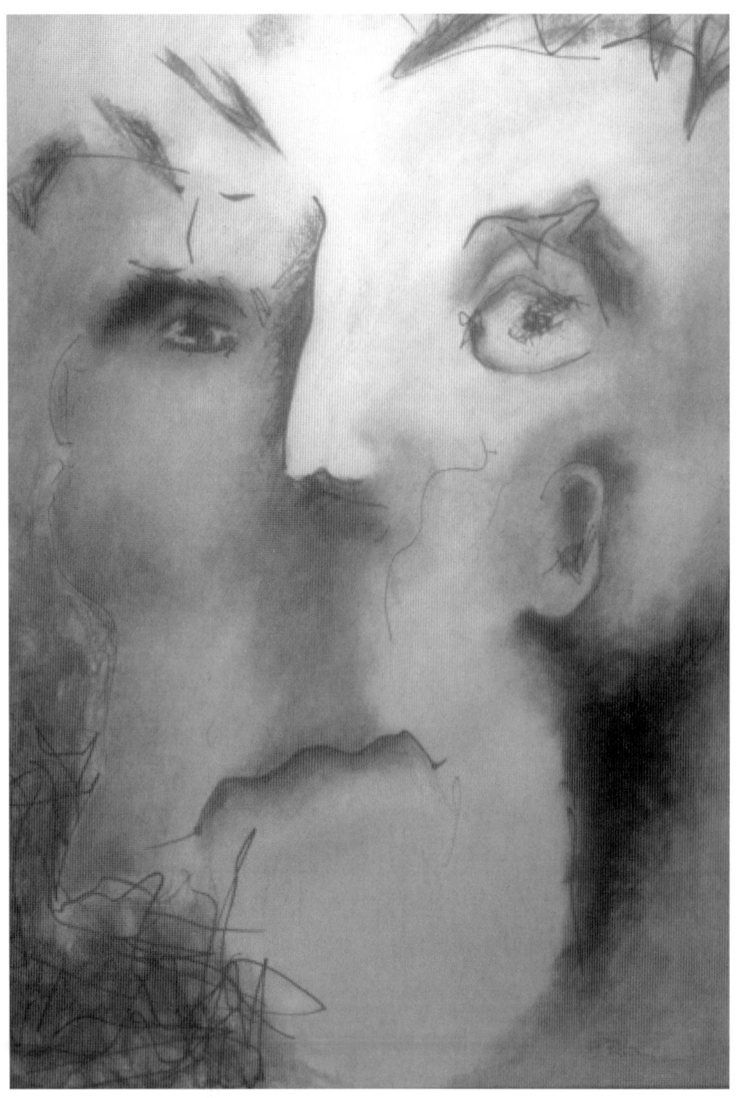

Pattern (Left Side)

Slow and steady. It's been a *very* long day. Settle into this left-side Pattern and soon your right hand will be saying, "Sometimes there is just no scale in the world like an A Minor Blues Scale." What in the world does it mean by this? See below.

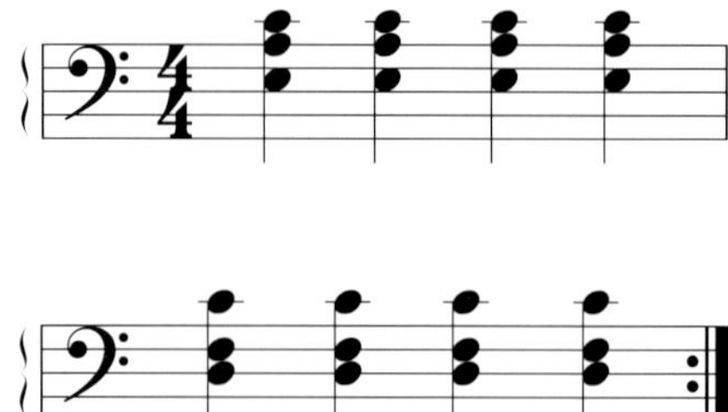

Vacation

When you add melodies to this Vacation, there will be some harsh sounds coming out of that first measure. That's the blues.

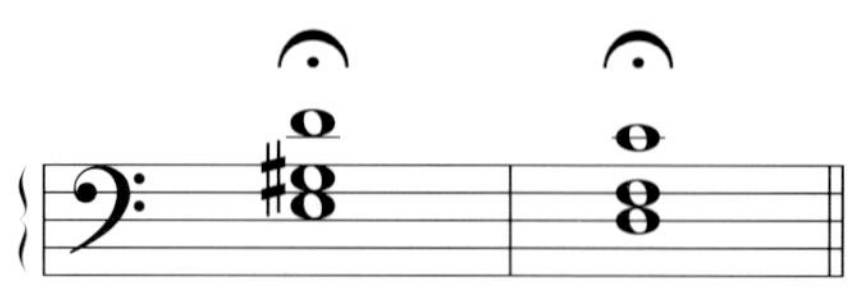

Create melodies above the Pattern and Vacation using the notes of an A (Minor) Blues Scale—the five white keys of the A Minor Pentatonic Scale plus the secret ingredient, an *e flat*. The clash created by the *e flat* and the accompaniment is a big part of the blues sound. You can use *b* and *f* too, but they are not part of the traditional blues. During the Vacation, you can also create with the E Blues Scale. (See the previous page.)

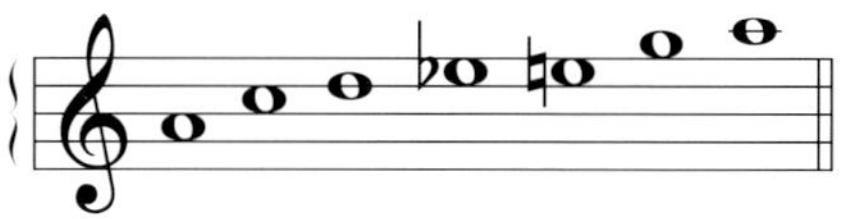

The blues have a triplet feel. To get this rhythmic feeling, play this melody over and over with the Pattern. Then make your own melodies. Though your melodies will be made of many other rhythms, keep the *feeling* of triplets.

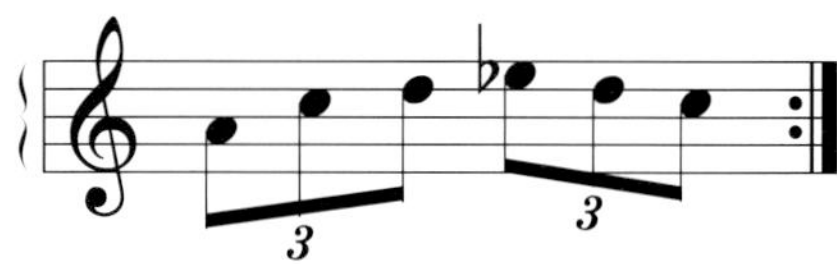

The traditional blues are played in a twelve-measure Pattern, which I will explain in the next three pieces. For now, just enjoy creating with this basic Pattern. Nothing fancy here—just true feelings.

Ideas for the Right Side

Sometimes the melody wants to move around in a hurry. A good way to become mobile with the A Blues Scale is to play it as written here, accompanied by the Pattern. Play the scale up two octaves and then back down again, in triplets. Finger this by keeping your thumbs on every *a* and *e*.

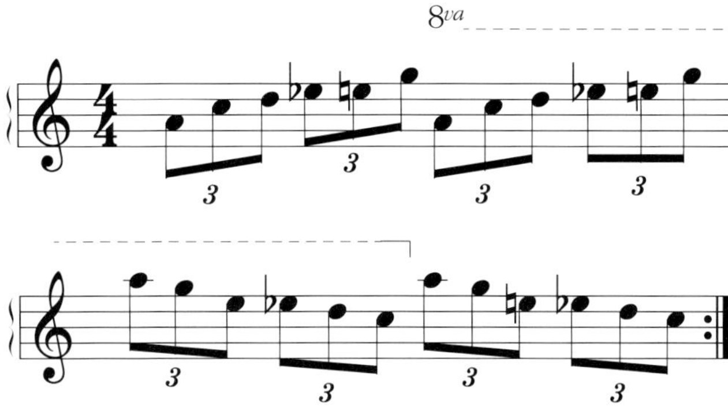

In the blues style, eighth notes (like those in the first measure) are played in swing rhythm, like the notes in the second measure. The first note of each pair is played about twice as long as the second. See page 126 for more explanation, and listen to the CD to *hear* this sound.

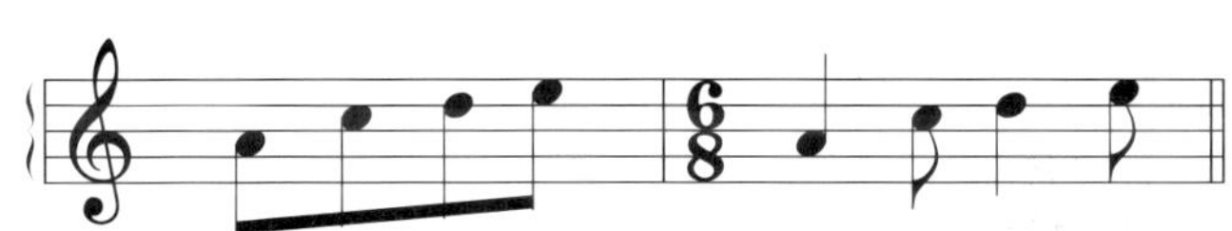

Try playing two notes at a time. Sometimes it is satisfying to get stuck on one note as I did on the *a* here.

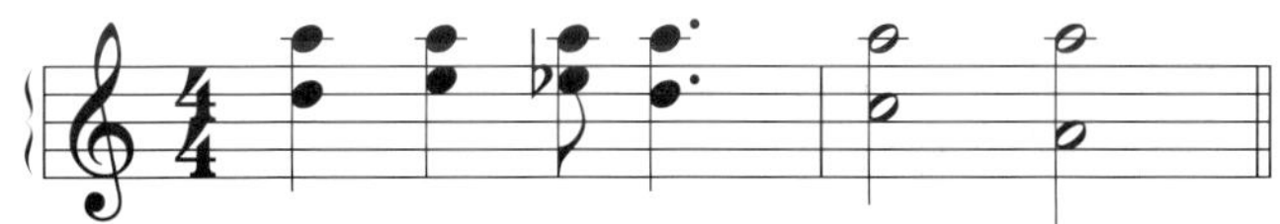

Play one or two keys quickly before you play a sustained note. This creates a common blues sound. These quick notes are called *crushed notes*. Classical musicians call them *grace notes*, though they don't often sound all that graceful when played in the blues.

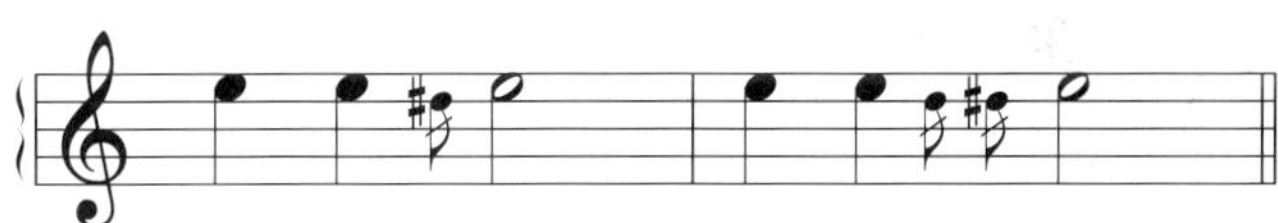

Playing melodies in octaves creates a penetrating sound that is quite fitting now and then.

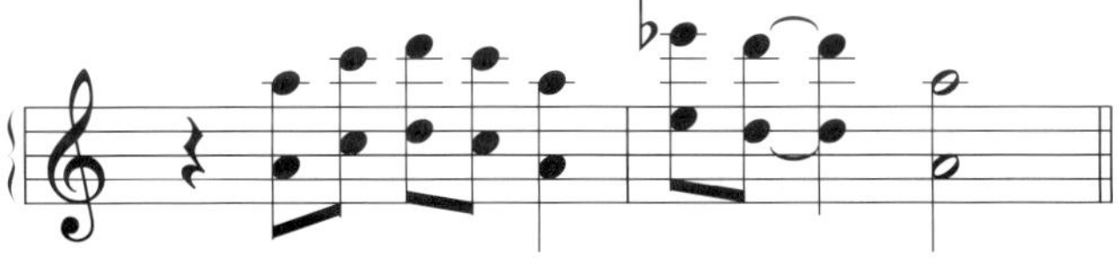

Rapidly rotate your forearm back and forth as you play two keys to make a *shake* or a *tremolo* (the common, classical name).

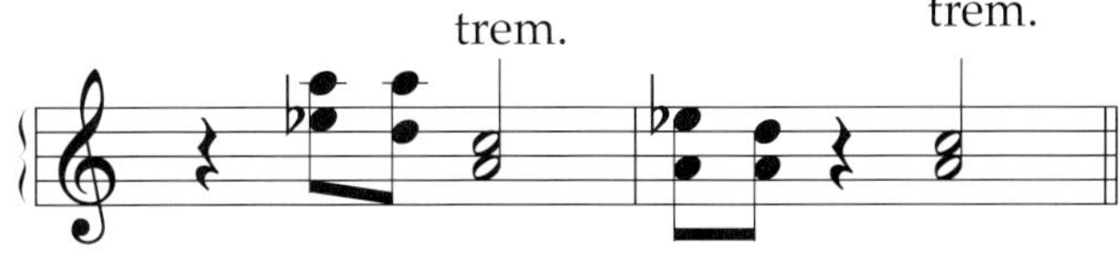

If you want to play the left-side accompaniment with a stronger triplet feeling, you can play the Pattern in this Variation.

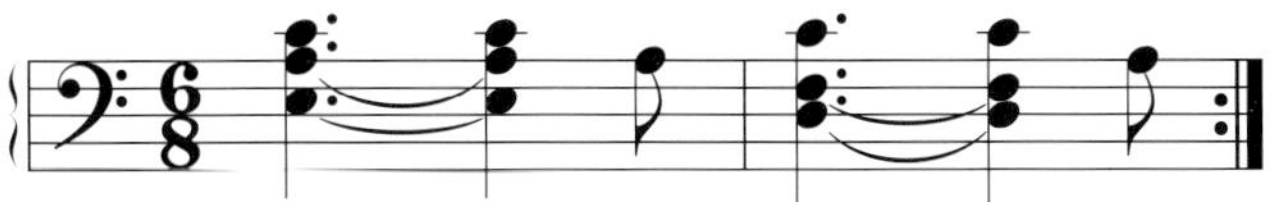

The *I'm Confused* Blues

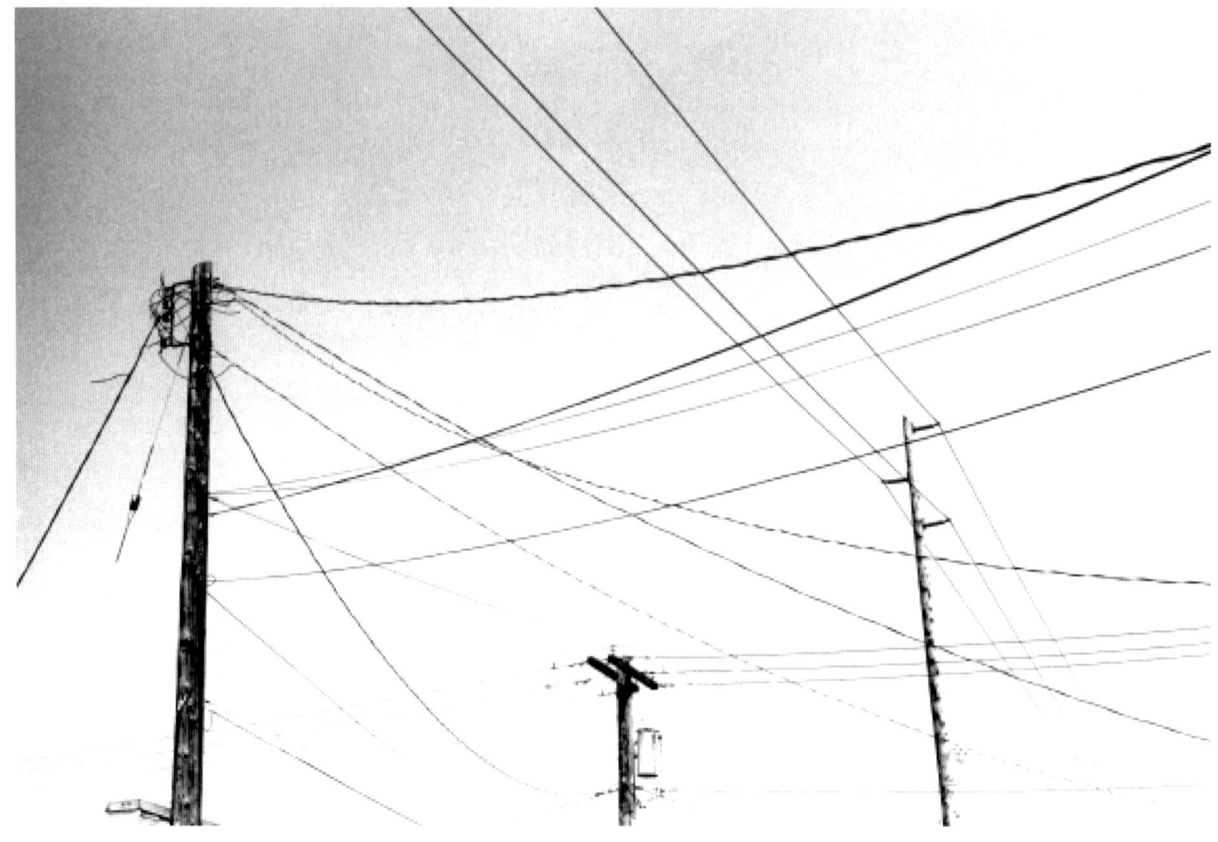

The blues are a feeling, a longing for some other state of mind. They are also a musical language for communicating these feelings and changing them. Feeling confused? Welcome to the blues.

The Pattern and both Vacations are made of the same Hand Shape (white key, black key, white key) played in three different places. Repeat each one as many times as you like before going on. Feel free to play these chords in any rhythm you like, as long as you keep a strong feeling of four beats per measure. Turn the page to see these chords arranged in the traditional 12-bar accompaniment.

Pattern

Vacation One

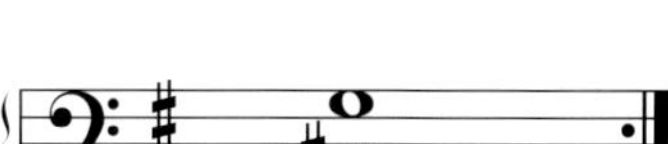

Vacation Two

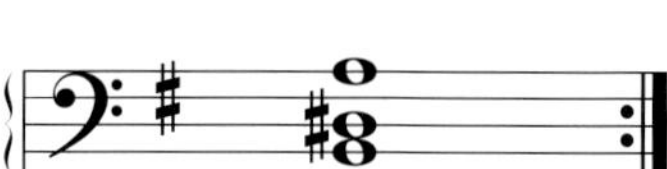

The Right Side (E Minor Blues Scale)

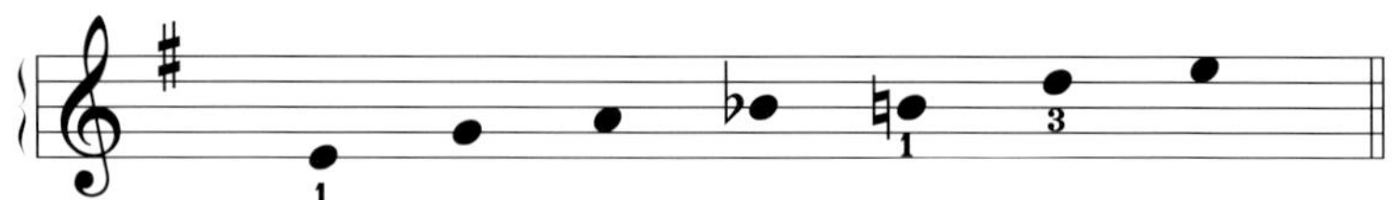

Create melodies above the Pattern and Vacations using tones of the E Minor Blues Scale. Remember to *swing* the eighth notes to get the traditional blues feel and sound.

Consonant or Dissonant?

Before creating, play each tone of the E Minor Blues Scale with the Pattern and the Vacations. (Below, I included an *f sharp* in the scale since that is sometimes added.) Listen to how many of them make dissonant sounds. Some are in agreement with the chords. This wide range of consonance and dissonance is what makes the Blues Scales so expressive.

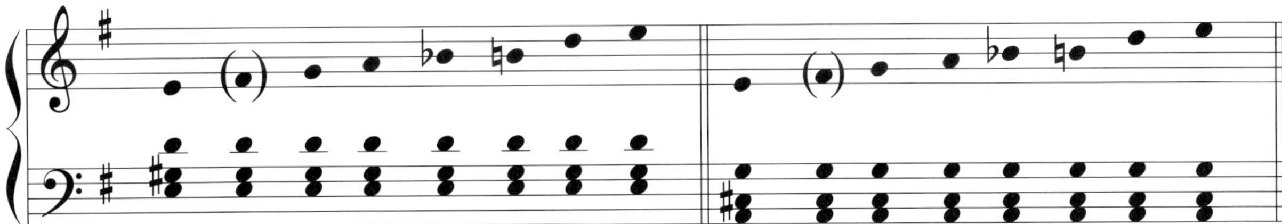

Variations

You may prefer to play the Pattern and Vacations in a more rhythmic way. Here are three different Variations to try. Make your own. As long as there are four beats to a measure and you feel the beat strongly, anything goes.

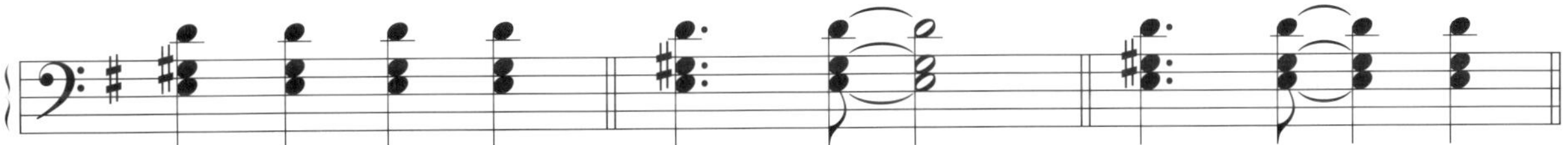

If you want to play the swing rhythm on your left side, try this Variation. This may not be easy to play at first, but if you feel *g sharp* and *d* landing on each beat, and the *e* coming *before* every beat, it's not too bad after all. Swing the eighth notes, as explained before.

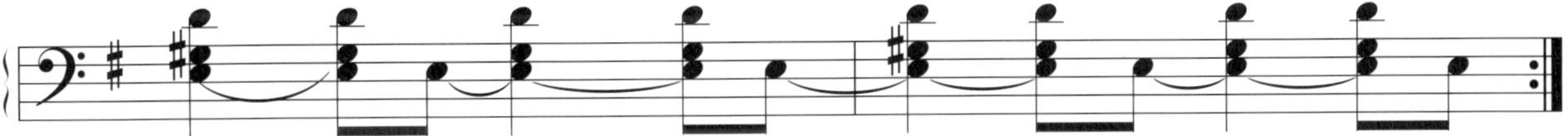

White Or Black?

Perhaps you would like to play this in the Key of E-Flat Minor Blues—all black keys with one white—and then move up to E Minor Blues. Here are the Pattern, Vacations, and Scale in E-Flat Blues. I added an *f* to the scale (commonly done) to make the fingering easier.

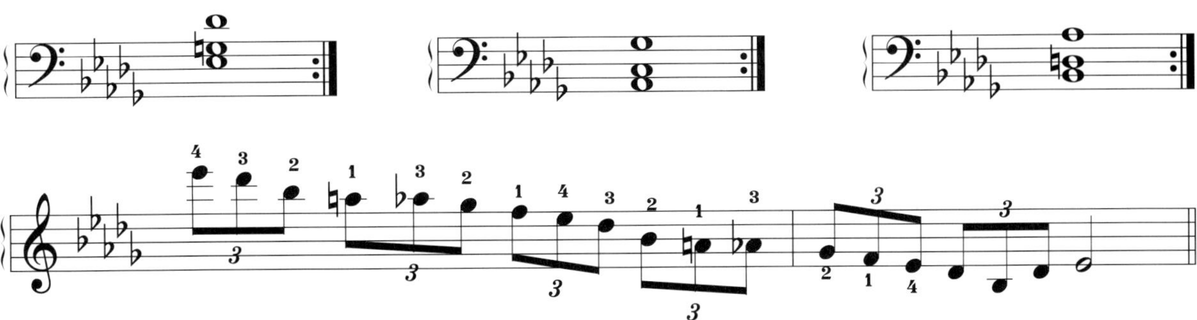

These days, if you're not confused, you're just not thinking straight. —Anon.

The Twelve-Bar Blues Pattern

Most blues players create melodies while playing a twelve-bar accompaniment Pattern over and over. You will probably recognize it when you hear it. Here's how to make the twelve-bar Pattern using the Pattern and Vacations of this piece. Though I played Vacation Two in the twelfth bar, some people play the Pattern there, and some people play only silence. The twelfth bar is a free-for-all sort of measure—do whatever you want.

Pattern four times.

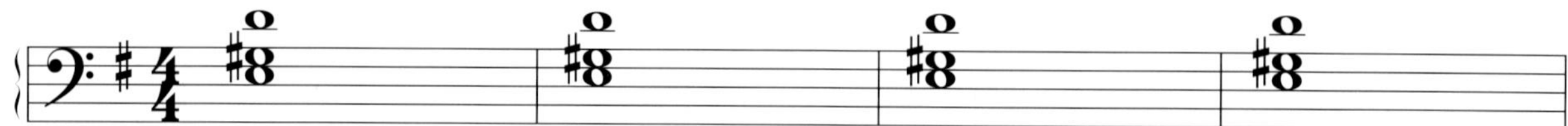

Vacation One twice. **Pattern** two times.

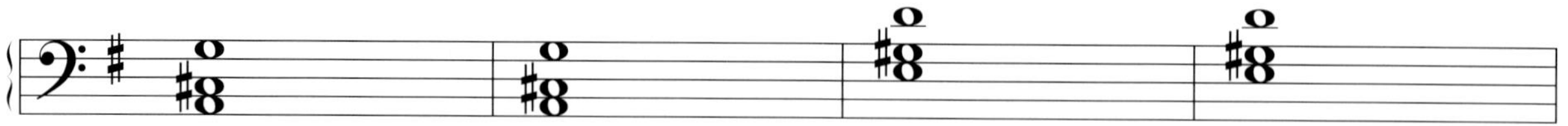

Vacation Two **Vacation One** **Pattern** **Vacation Two**

Why Twelve Bars?

To get a feeling for this longer Pattern (so your playing is guided by a *feeling* rather than a lot of thoughts), it helps to know about the original feelings from which this longer Pattern grew.

Say that you have a strong feeling, and so you say or sing, "I'm so confused, I don't know which way to go." When you hear yourself say this, you feel inside, "Yes, that's how it is!" and this makes you say it again with more feeling. "Well, I'm *so* confused, I don't know which way to go!" And then this leads you to a new feeling and understanding, and so you might then say, "An answer will come, and I'm waiting for the news."

The blues form is—in essence—a feeling, the feeling repeated with emphasis, and then a new feeling that grows out of this. Each feeling lasts for four bars. The first feeling is expressed with four bars of the Pattern. The repeated feeling is expressed with Vacation One. The new feeling that comes is expressed with a new sound, Vacation Two, and then goes back to the Pattern by way of Vacation One.

Though this particular musical form was originated by African-Americans, I think it is meaningful to all of us because of this universal pattern of feeling that is so perfectly expressed. How often do we feel something, feel it again even stronger, and then have a new feeling that comes out of this? This is something we all know.

To play the blues is to tell the truth about strong feelings and allow them to change into new understandings and make us feel better. This is what the blues are really all about.

An Example to Play

Though it began as a way of singing, the blues have also become a way of playing the piano. If you want your playing to have a more traditional blues sound, fit your melodies into the four-bar phrases I told you about on the previous page. These traditional melodies tend to be simple and short. Or you can just play whatever you feel using the Blues Scale on your right side, and it will still be the blues. Here's one of my creations for you to play. Remember to swing those eighth notes as I do on the CD.

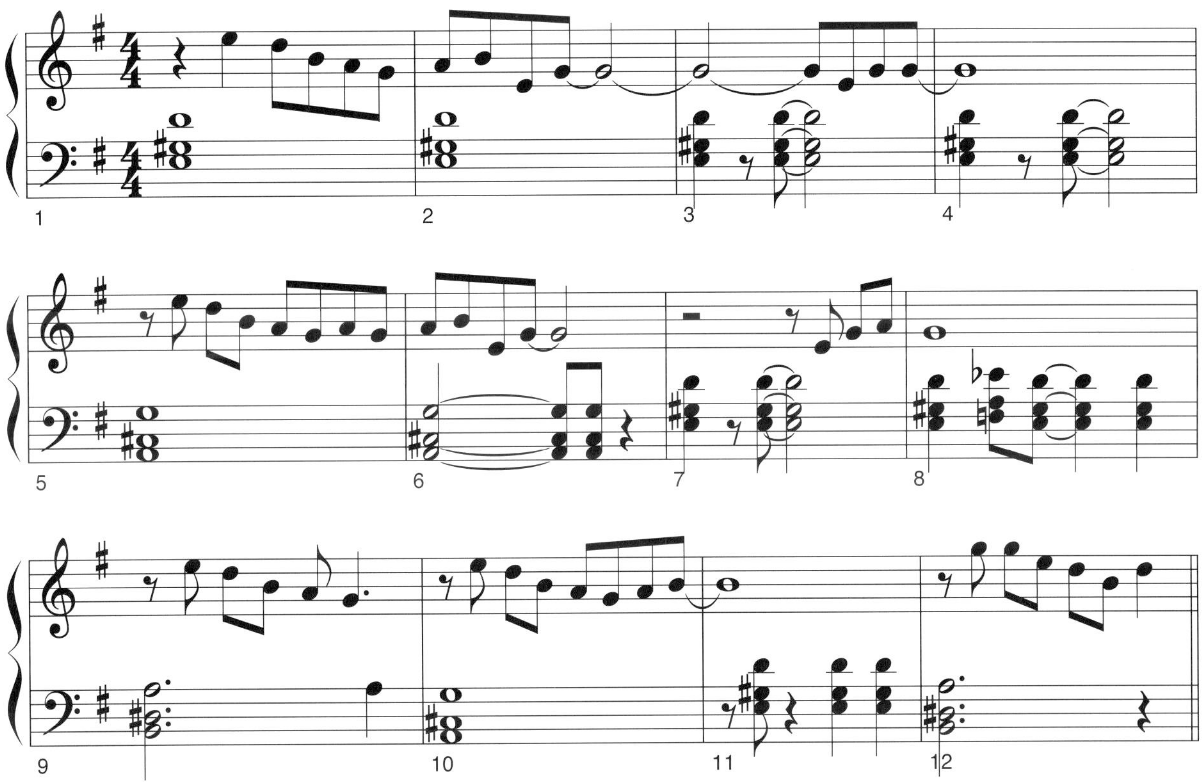

Comments

Left side: Notice how the Patterns and Vacations are played in simple ways whenever the melody is active. Then, when the melody comes to a rest, the chords become active to keep the music from losing its energy. In bar 8, I slid the chord up a half step and back down again for extra tension.

Right side: Notice how the melody in the second line (measures 5 - 8) is quite similar to the melody in the first line (measures 1 - 4) and how the third line is different from the first two lines. This is a traditional blues melody, the kind I talked about on the previous page. Again, you don't have to follow this design, but it is good to know about, especially if you are adding lyrics.

Clash of left and right sides: That *g natural* in the right side clashes with the *g sharp* in the left. This is not to be avoided. This is how it's supposed to be.

This is just one time through the twelve-bar Pattern. Play through this form as many times as you need in order to change dark blues into lighter shades of feeling. Usually, I'll play it 10 to 20 times.

Often, I will add a bass part. Consult *Blues on Black* for ideas. You can use that same bass line here, but you will need to play the tones a half step higher, moving them from E-Flat Blues to E Blues.

Lazy Days

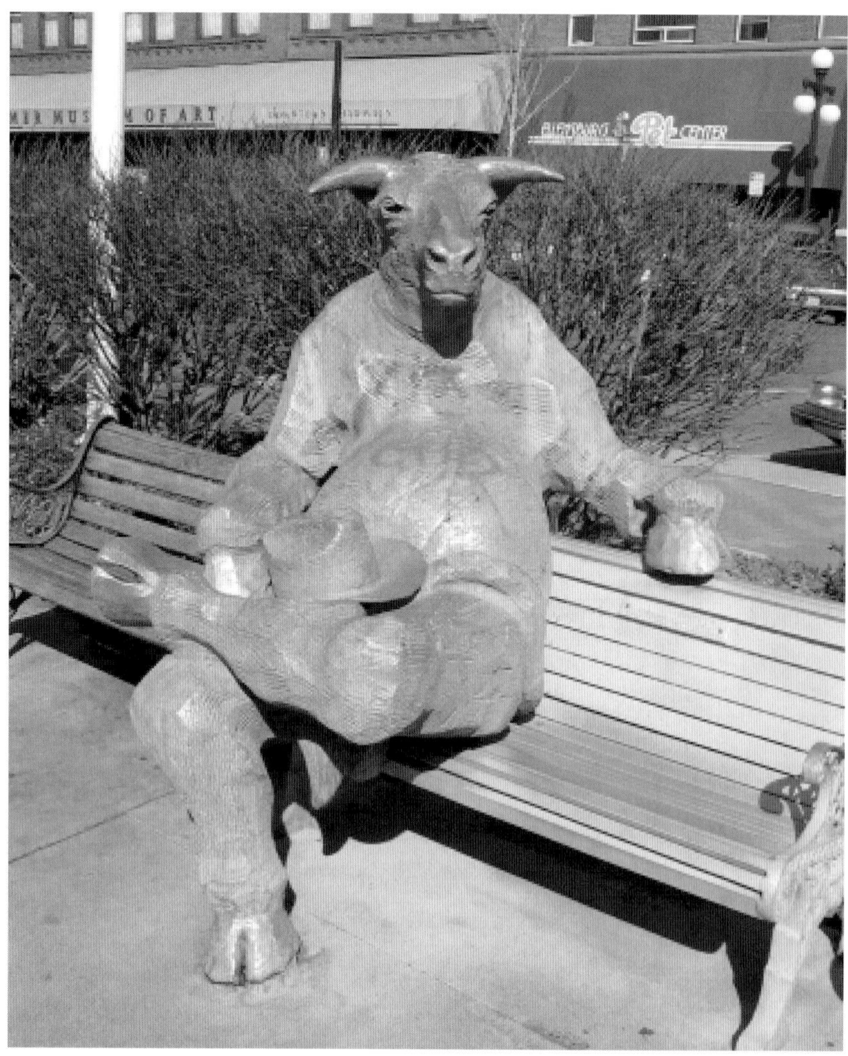

I have a friend who likes to say, "When you don't have time to relax, it's time to relax!" In this modern world, everyone is so busy. Where is the room for those creative insights that only visit us in free moments?

Ben Jonson wrote, "Ease and relaxation are profitable to all studies. The mind is like a bow, the stronger for being unbent." So, perhaps it's a day to unbend ourselves. Here's a soundtrack for such a lazy day. Take it nice and easy.

Pattern

This is the twelve-bar blues Pattern in another Key. As this Pattern pokes along, create lazy melodies in the uncommon Key of G Major Blues, made of the same notes as E Minor Blues. I usually repeat each measure—I'm in no hurry. Play all the measures that start on *g* down an octave if it sounds good on your piano. Play *d* in the bass in the twelfth measure if you like, in any rhythm.

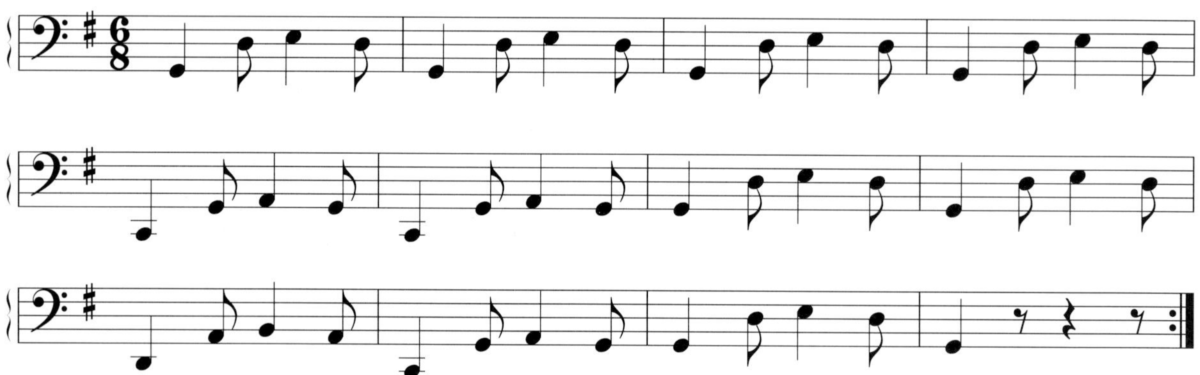

Ideas for Melodies

Though twelve-bar Patterns look long, they are usually made of just a single one-measure Pattern played in three predictable locations. In the case of this piece, the same one-measure Pattern starts on *g*, later moves to *c*, and then later, *d*. When you are playing the Pattern on *g*, the G Major Blues Scale is unbeatable for creating upbeat, blues-flavored melodies, but when C comes along, you may want to create with the C Major Blues Scale. It's not necessary to change, but it sounds good. This scale feels the same under the hand as the G Major Blues scale because it is made of all white keys except the third note. Though the C Minor Blues Scale is extremely popular, few people know about the cheerful C Major Blues Scale. Here's what it looks like.

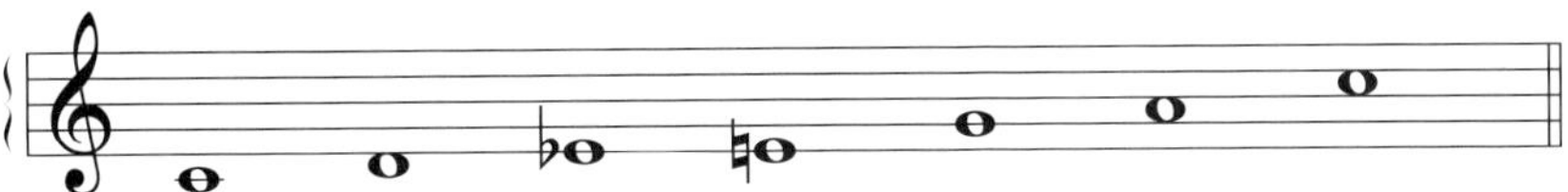

When I come to the one measure with *d* in the bass, I like the sound of the G Major Scale and G Major Blues Scale combined. Another way to say this is that I like playing the G Major Scale with a *b flat* added to create that blues sound. The combined scale would look like this.

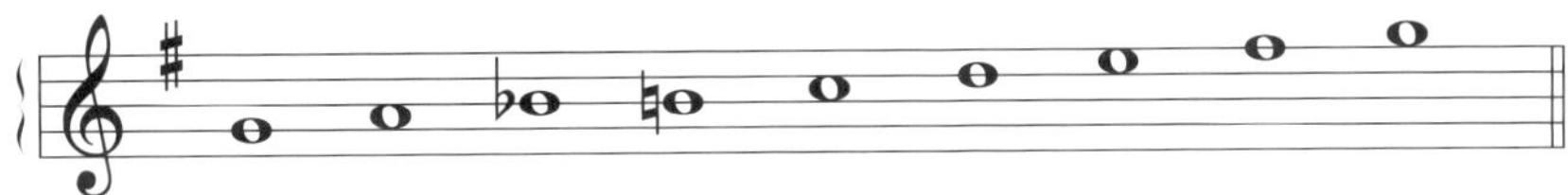

Pattern Variations

Here's another way to play the notes of the Pattern in its three locations. This is a *boogie woogie* Pattern that has more energy, but if you play it lazily, it fits the mood nicely. How slow can you go?

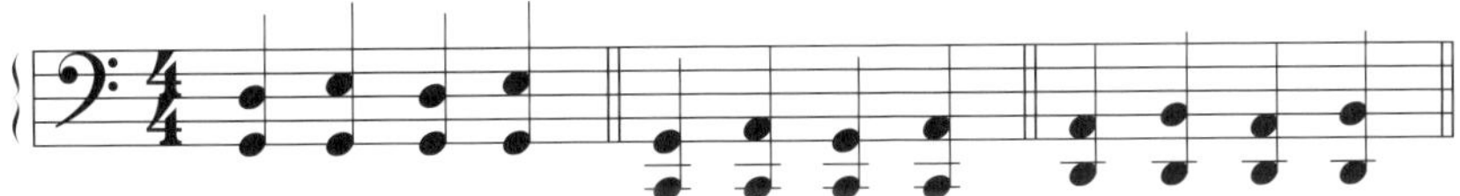

Backbeats

Most of the time, the first beat of a measure is given more emphasis than the others. Try accenting the *backbeats*—the second and fourth beats in a measure of 4/4—which are usually the weaker beats. You can hear the backbeats accented in much popular music.

The first measure below is the Pattern with the backbeat accented. The second measure is the Pattern Variation with its backbeats accented, and the third measure is a Variation on the Pattern Variation that also features accented backbeats. Play slowly and keep your wrist loose when playing the last one, or you will soon discover why I bothered to tell you this.

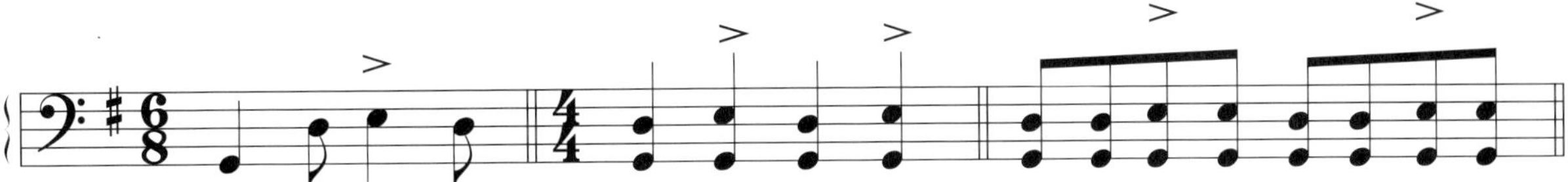

To do great work, a person must be very idle as well as very industrious. —Samuel Butler

Blues on Black

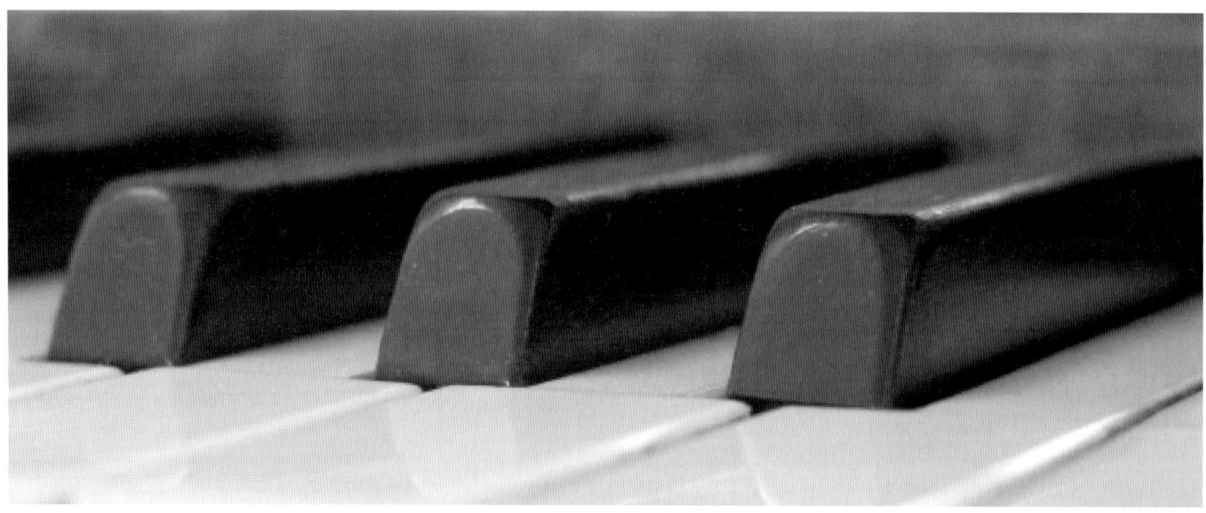

Pattern (Bass Player)

Here again we have a Pattern that is a variation of the twelve-bar Blues Progression. Just as in *Lazy Days* and *I'm Confused Blues*, a one-measure Pattern is played in three locations over twelve bars. This time, we are creating in the Key of E-Flat Minor Blues and the Pattern is a bass line—no chords in sight. At least for now.

As usual, first memorize the Pattern. Be able to play it without thinking about it, just *feeling* it. Create melodies above this using the notes of the E-Flat Minor Blues Scale (see the next few pages for ideas). If it sounds good on your piano, play every one of these notes down an octave.

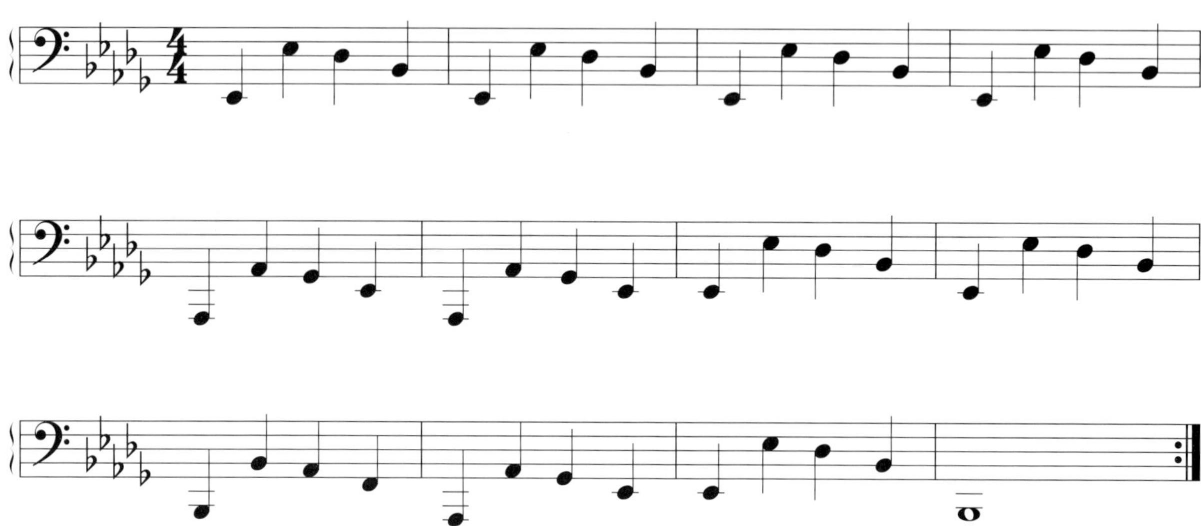

Though you may want to change the rhythm of these notes, it's a good idea to start creating with them as written in order to get a strong feeling for the beat. This type of bass is called a *walking bass* because it keeps walking steadily through its notes. No pedal here, so the rhythm is clear.

Right Side: The E-Flat Minor Blues Scale

Here are the notes of the *E-Flat Minor Blues Scale*—all the black keys with one lonely white key (*a natural*) to make all the black keys feel blue. This scale has so many moods, all mixed and marbled together. Perfect for times that have strong feelings.

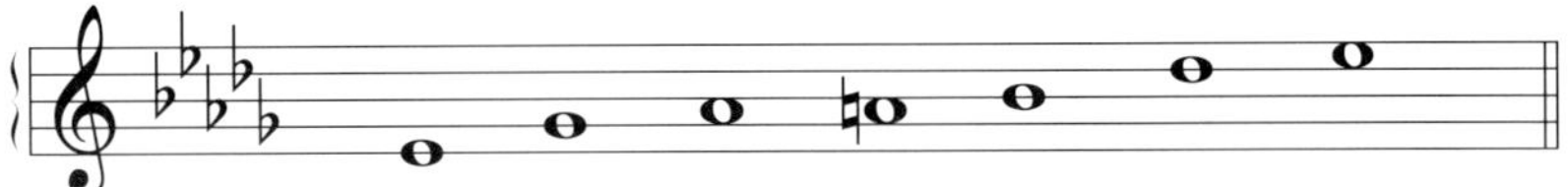

If you want to make these notes into a scale that you can play quickly, you may as well know the truth: there is no easy way to finger this scale because there is only one white key. Knowing this might help you get in the mood to play the blues. Or, add an *f natural* to make fingering a lot easier.

As for creating melodies, keep it simple at first, playing melodies with short Rhythm Patterns over and over. The next page explores a number of ways of creating melodies in a blues style. Just now, however, that bass player is getting bored with playing only quarter notes in the same sequence, and wants something different.

The Bass Player Gets Creative

Though the Pattern gives your left hand just four notes to play at a time, there's no limit to the different ways to play them. Here are fifteen other options—change between them as often as you like during the twelve-bar Pattern. *Swing* the eighth notes for a blues-style sound. For a rock sound, play them *straight*, as written. I'll explain this concept again on the next page because it is so essential.

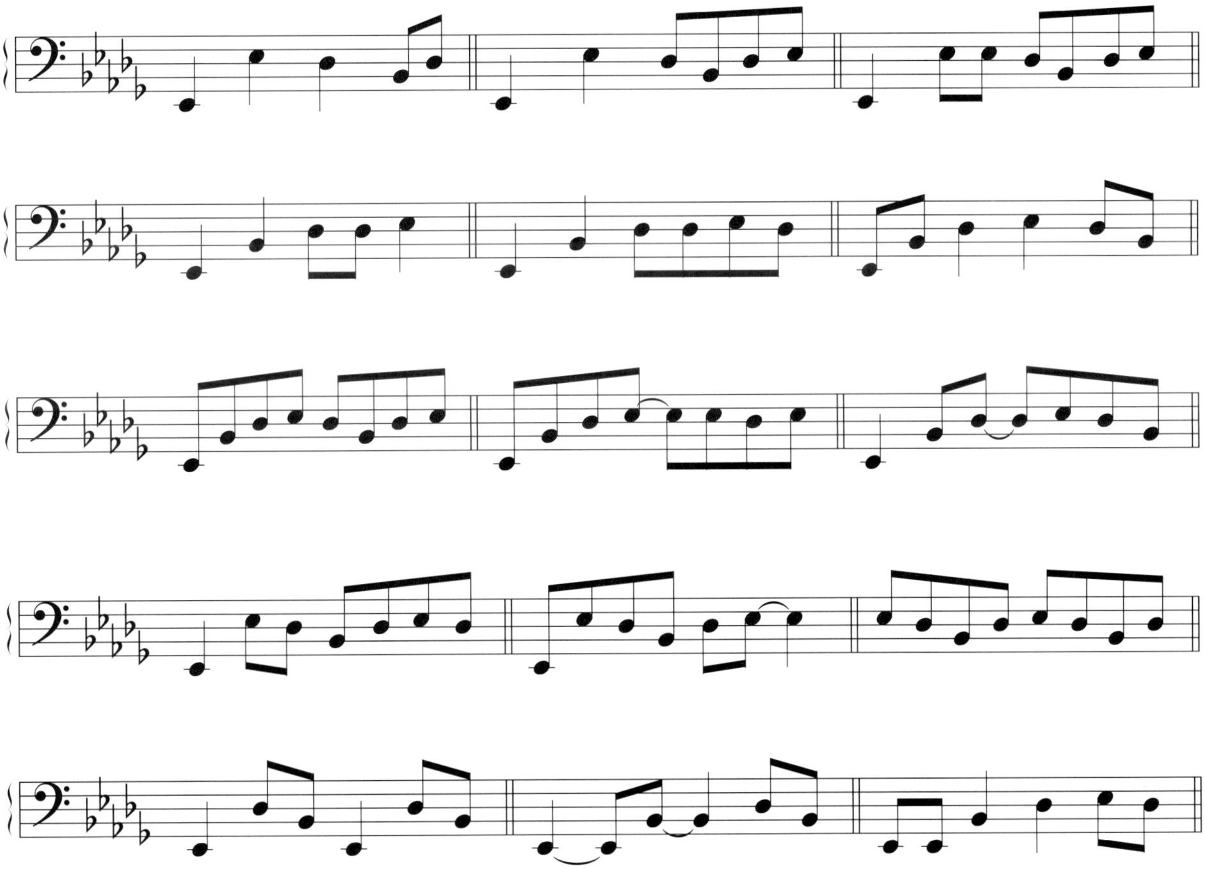

Getting the Blues in the Melodies

To help you feel the rhythm of the blues, repeat triplets over and over while you walk along with quarter notes in the bass. The traditional blues feeling grows out of this triplet feeling.

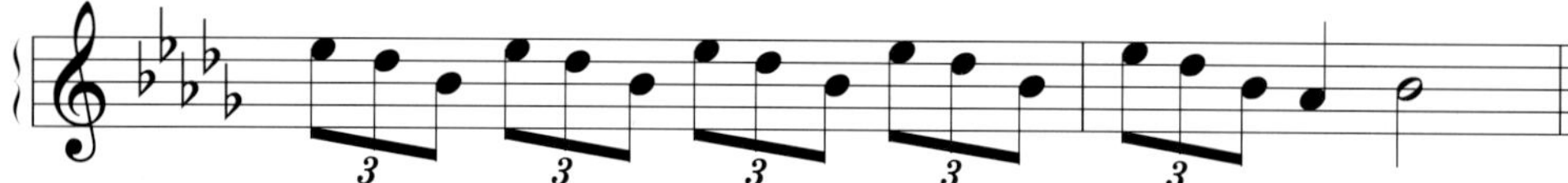

To expand on what I said earlier, in traditional blues style, you play eighth notes with a *swing rhythm*. This means that when you play a pair of eighth notes, you play the first one much longer than the second—about twice as long. This means that the first eighth note lands where the first note of a triplet would be, and the second note lands where the third note of a triplet would be.

Play the first measure below in straight rhythm and then in swing rhythm. When you play it with a swing feel, it should sound as if you're playing the second measure below, the one in 12/8 time. Swing rhythm is usually not written out exactly—it is just understood that eighth notes are played that way. So the first measure below would sound like the second when played by blues musicians. (Of course, this is just an approximation of what is done. Listen to the CD to *hear* the difference.) The straight feeling is used in classical and rock music while the swing feeling is used in jazz and blues. If you want a rock sound, play it straight. If you want blues, swing it.

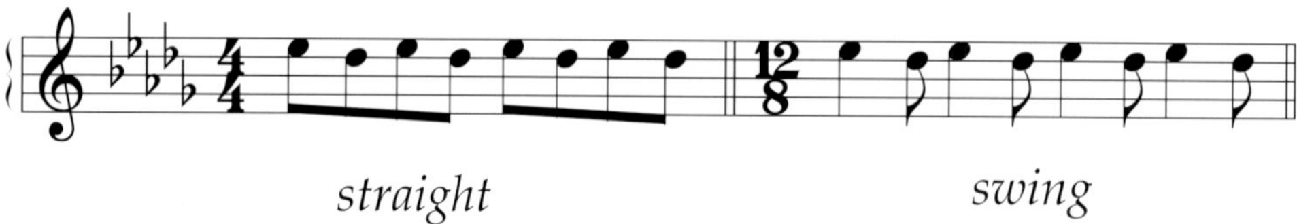

In the blues, melodic phrases are usually just one or two measures long. These phrases often repeat at least once, often many times. It's a very simple, straightforward way of making melodies. In the example below, the melody is a two-measure phrase, repeated with a slight variation. Play this example three times to fill the twelve-bar Pattern, varying it a bit with each repeat.

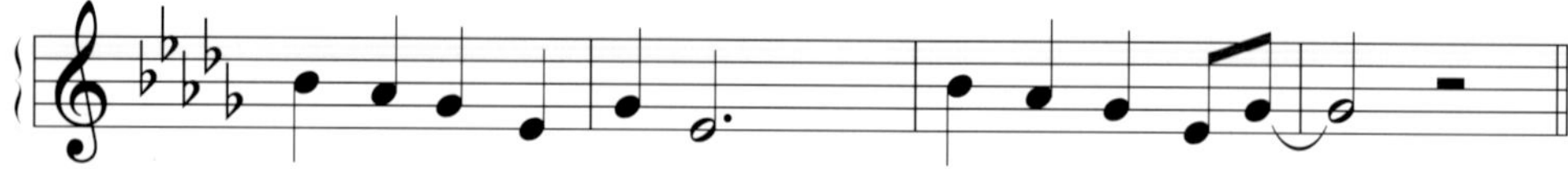

Try getting stuck on one key while you play others with it. *E flat* works especially well as a "stuck note," though other notes of the blues scale work well, too.

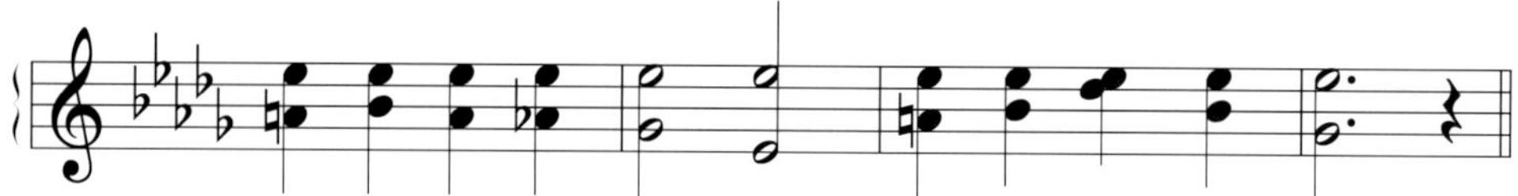

Below, I used the same notes as in the example above but played some of the notes as crushed notes. This sound is a major ingredient in the blues.

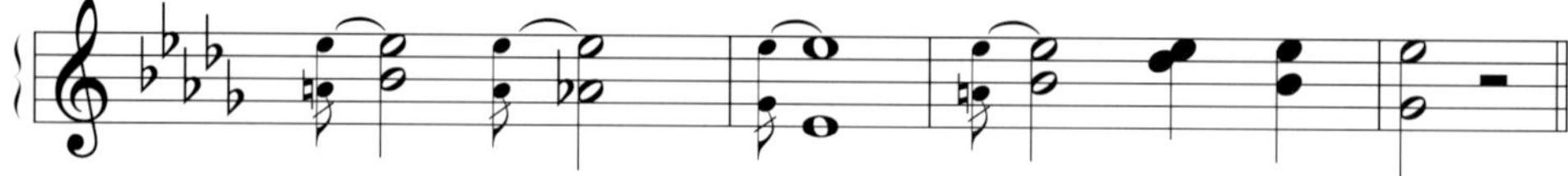

Welcome to Three-Hand Land: Add a "Guitar Part"

Until now, you have been creating bass lines with your left hand and melodies with your right. Two parts with two hands. It's time to call on a friend to add a third part. Or you can stretch your mind and play three parts with just two hands.

If you are accompanying a friend who is making melodies on the piano or some other instrument, play what sounds like a "guitar part" above the bass line. Below is an example of what your accompaniment might sound like. Notice how I played the three chords in different rhythms. Those whole notes get dull in a hurry! The exact rhythms you play will depend on where your friend is going with the melody.

If you want to play all three parts by yourself, keep playing the bass part with your left hand while you play *both* the guitar part and a melody with your right. Turn the page to see how this might look.

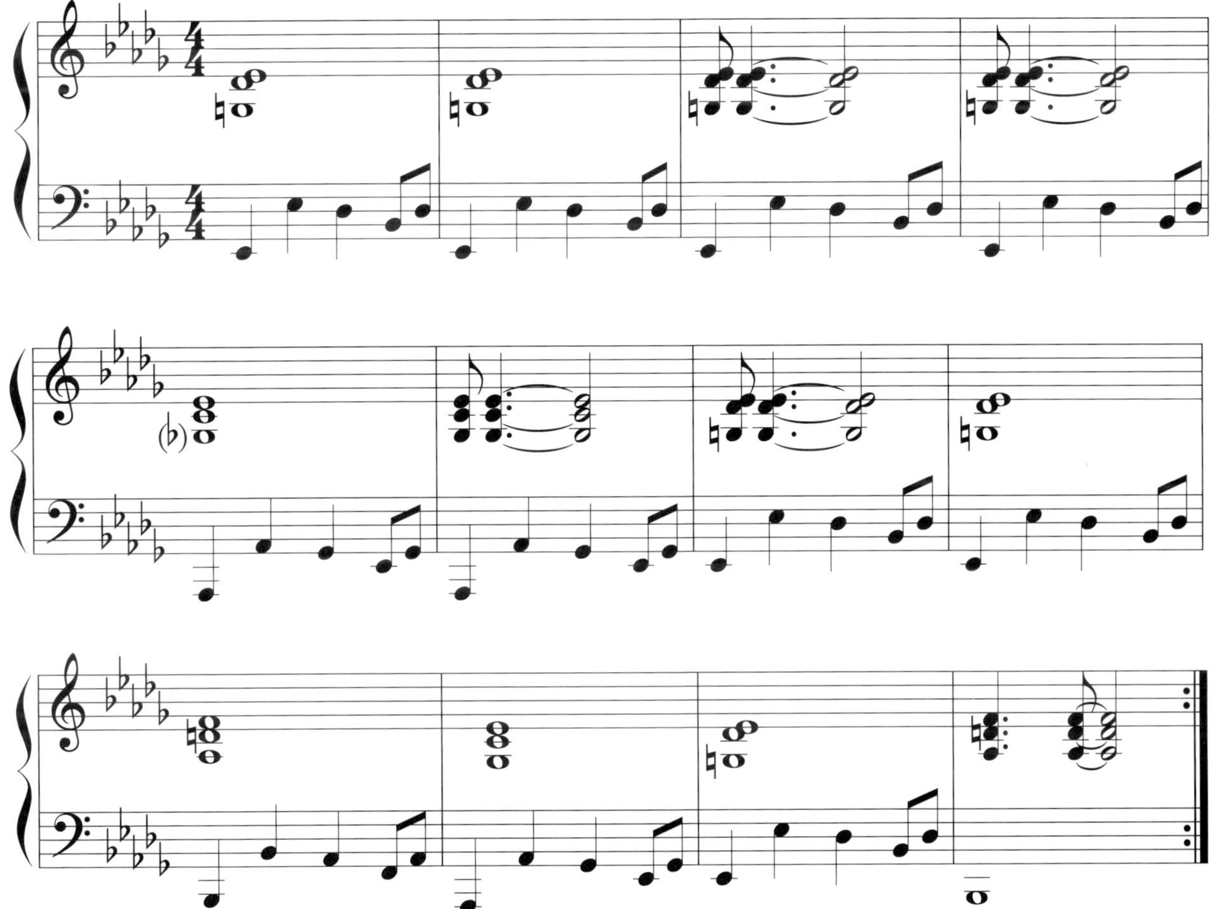

Real Guitar Players

Though it's easy for us pianists to create on black keys, guitarists find this Key quite challenging. They prefer E Minor Blues. This is because the guitar is tuned to the pitches of *e, a, d, g, b,* and high *e*, all the notes in the E Minor Blues Scale except *b flat*. Playing in E Minor Blues, they don't have to "fret" about a lot of flats. So, to create music with real guitar players, move the bass line on the last page up a half step and create melodies in E Minor Blues while they play the chords. When they play the lead (the melody), play both the bass line and the chords up a half step so you are in E Minor Blues.

Three Parts with Two Hands

When you have enough experience and confidence (and patience!), you can comfortably be a bass player, guitarist, and soloist, all at the same time. Three parts with two hands. It's a challenge, but it's worth the effort. I'm reminded here of what Gershwin wrote about holding hands at midnight: "Nice work, if you can get it!"

Below, I played through the twelve-bar Pattern twice in three-handed style. In this example, I played bass throughout with my left hand. My right hand was kept busy being both a soloist making melodies and a guitarist adding harmony and rhythm. You can also try it another way: Jump between bass and guitar parts with your left hand while your right hand just plays melodies. Or, move between both these ways of playing as you create.

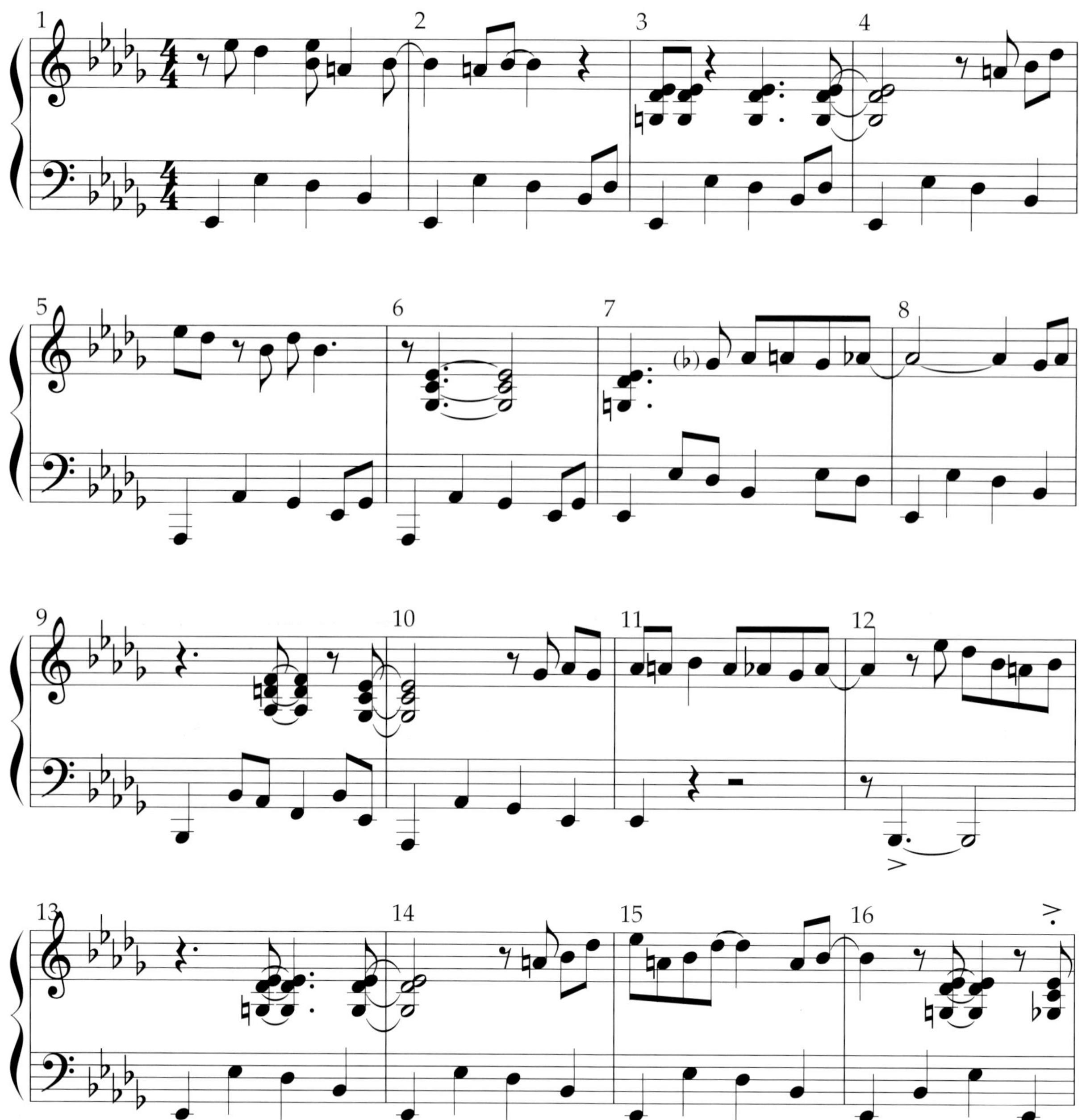

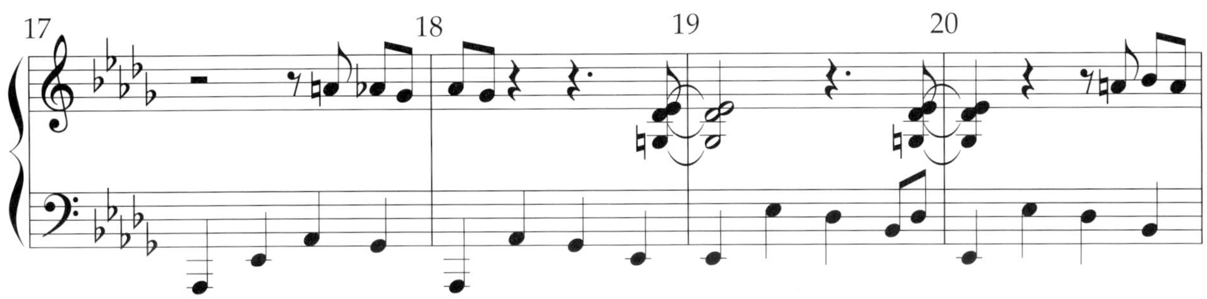

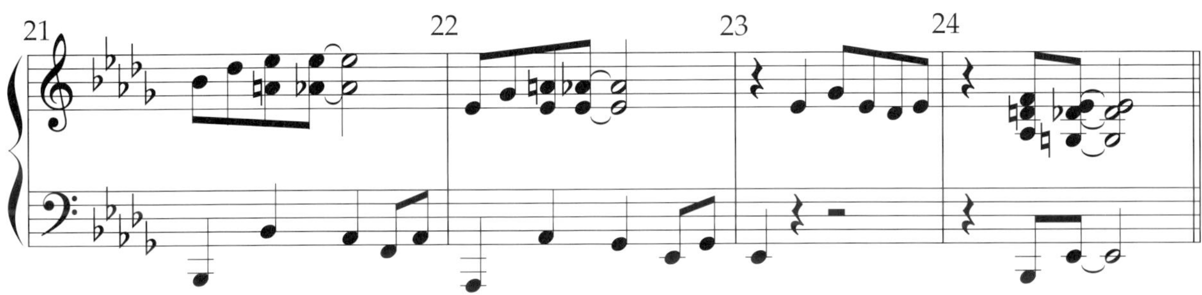

Some Notes on These Notes

Notice the many rests and sustained notes on the right-side part. There's lots of time to move between the melody and the guitar part. No hurry.

These melodies are made entirely of members of the E-Flat (Minor) Blues Scale. The guitar part is made entirely of the three chords given two pages back. There's no end to the music that can be made with this one scale and these three chords. Most blues songs are made from just these few materials, though the blues are more often played in C Minor Blues or E Minor Blues.

Notice how the "guitar player" plays the chords differently to fit the changing melodies and moods. These chords usually come before or after the beat, rather than on it. This gives the rhythm more life. Jazz players call this *comping*. The bass player is also responsive to the melody and mood, not getting stuck in a rut.

In Measures 11 and 12, and also Measure 23: The bass and guitar player both take a break during the "turnaround measures." This is commonly done. After this break, then it is nice to come back to the steady beat of the bass.

Measure 16: The left side plays just three of its usual four bass notes. You don't have to play all four notes in every measure.

Measure 24: This is one way to end it. The *b-flat* chord with *b flat* in the bass goes to the *e-flat* chord with *e flat* in the bass. Blues players will often play the last chord with jittery fingers (*tremolos*). To do this, press the pedal down and then play the individual notes of the last chord as fast as you can. Another good sound: Play the jittery fingers, then play the same notes up an octave, then up another octave. Get louder as you go. Shake the house, rattle the windows.

What we play is life. —Louis Armstrong

Many Ways Home

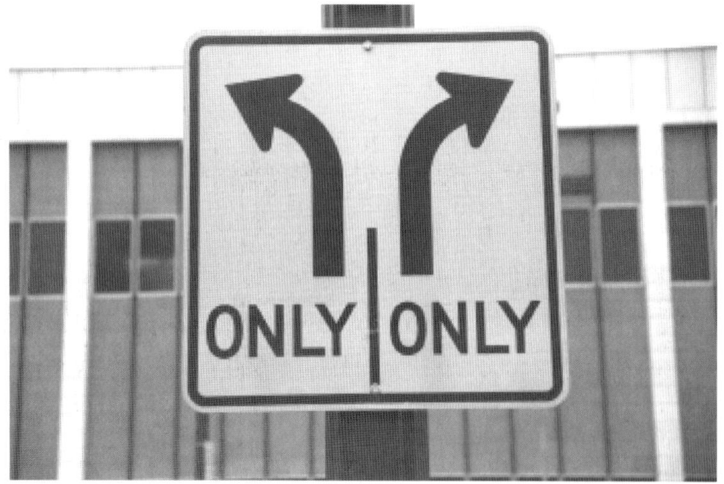

Go left *or* go right. ONLY! This sign vividly illustrates our normal way of thinking. Yes or no, right or wrong, this or that.

As we continue traveling down the *Creator's Road*, discovering our way as we go, we see very different road signs. This is because there are always more than two ways to go, always a number of possibilities yet to be recognized. We can go left or right, forward or backward, turn around, make a tunnel, or fly into the sky!

Pattern

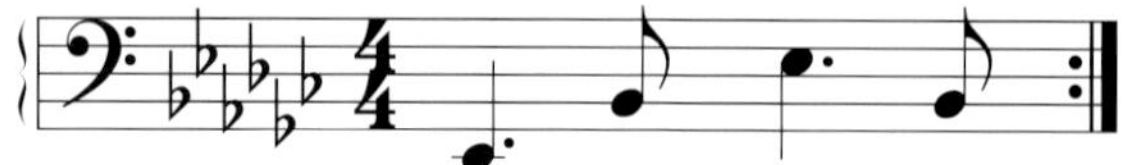

If you find this difficult to play when adding melodies, leave out the *b flats* for a while. Add them in once you feel a strong, steady beat.

Ideas for the Right Side

While keeping your right hand in a five-key Hand Shape on black keys, play any pairs of keys that leave one unplayed key between them. Create melodies using these shapes and sounds, mostly fourths.

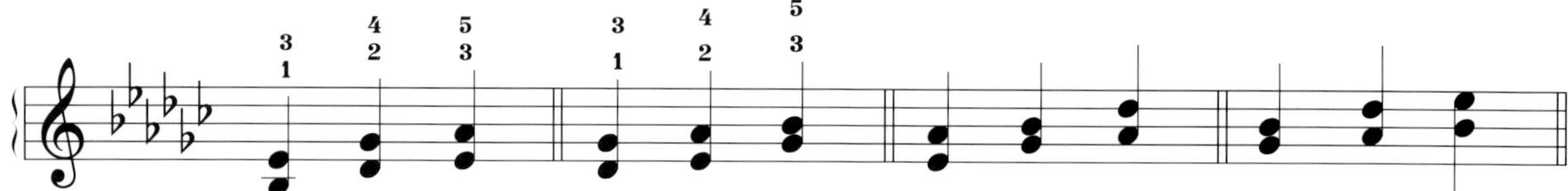

Also create with any notes of the E-Flat Blues Scale—all the black keys plus an *a natural* to jangle your nerves. I've written this scale in the first measure below. Then there is a typical *lick* or *riff* ("short, melodic phrase" in jazz terms) that features the sound of fourths, using notes in this scale.

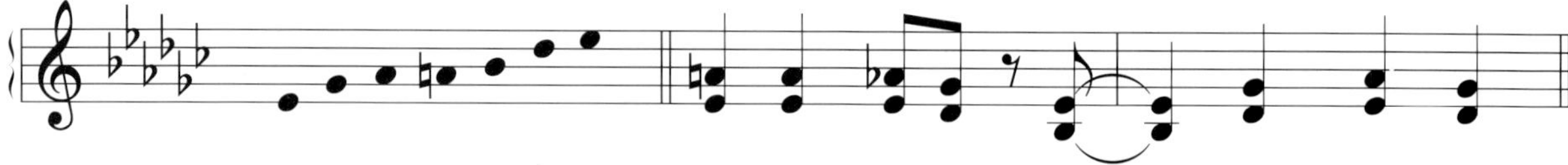

This is how that sign might look on the *Creator's Road*. So many choices! So many new ways to go! It's no wonder many people prefer a simpler sign!

The Vacations below are made out of fifths in the Key of E-Flat Minor. They are all ways of leaving the Pattern and then returning to it. So many ways to roam, and then so many ways to come back home.

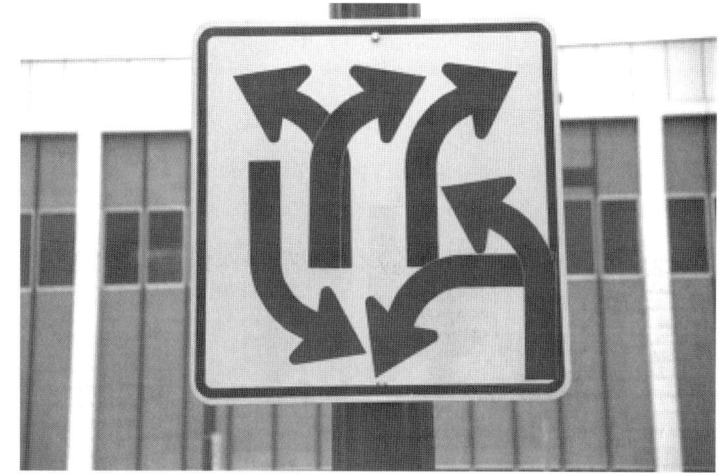

Vacation One

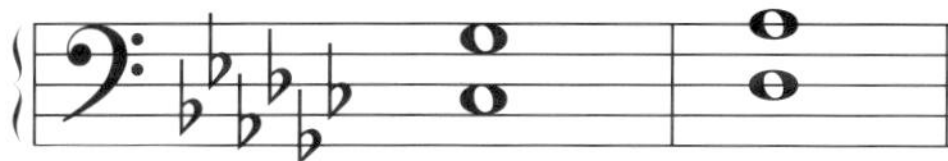

In all these Vacations, you can make your own rhythms rather than just play whole notes. Or hold these notes as long as you want (longer than the four beats written here) without keeping any feeling of a beat whatsoever.

Vacation Two

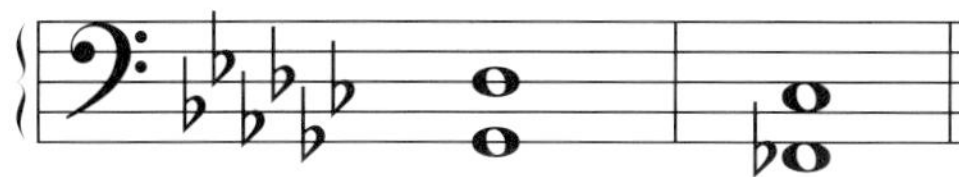

Repeat each Vacation as many times as you like before returning to the Pattern. Or play them just once.

Vacation Three

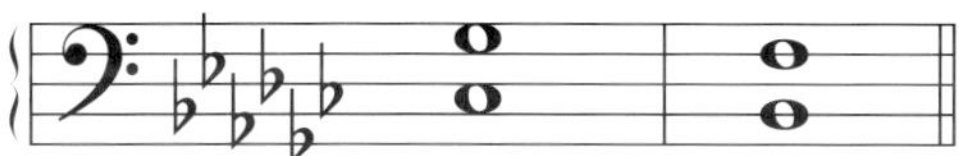

Try putting two Vacations together to make a longer Vacation. (I especially like playing Vacation Three, then Five.) Put three Vacations together, or even four.

Vacation Four

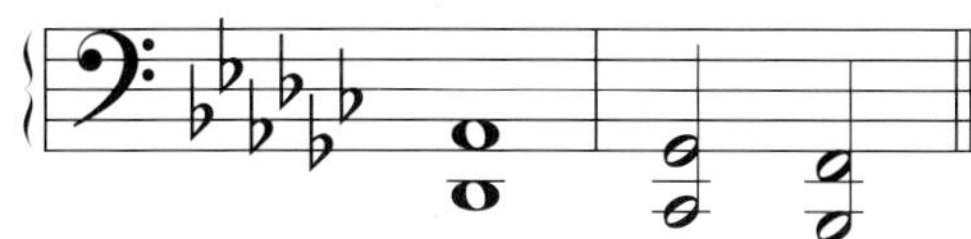

Each time you play this piece, you can make it quite different. One day, you may simply play the Pattern, go to Vacation One, and then return to the Pattern.

Vacation Five

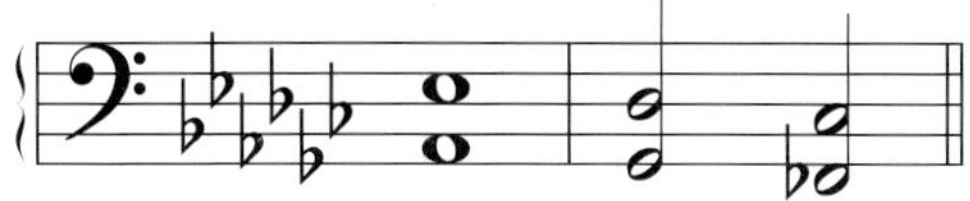

Another day, your trip may be complex. You may play the Pattern, then Vacations One and Two, the Pattern, Vacation Five, the Pattern, Vacations One, Five, Three, and Five, and then back to the Pattern. Which way today?

Adding Melodies

The Pattern of this piece is hard to create with until you get its rhythmic feeling pulsing through your body. A good way to establish this feeling is to play patterns of eighth notes over and over with the Pattern. Repeat these eighth notes until they really flow. Here are two such patterns to get you started. Make up more patterns of your own.

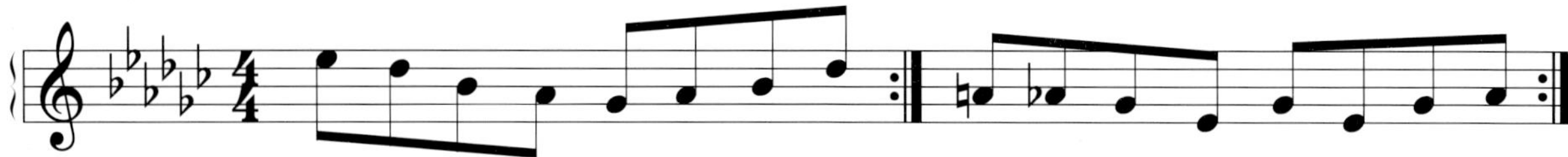

After a while, you'll find that these short patterns naturally grow into melodies. Here's one melody that grew from the example above.

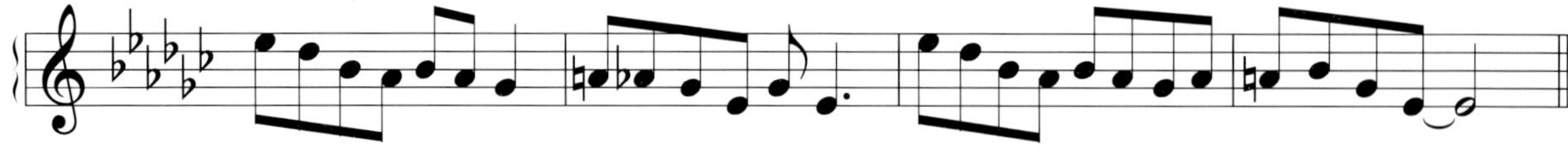

While keeping that same flowing eighth-note feeling, add a rest on the first beat of the first measure. This one small rest makes a big change in the rhythm. Here's a melody to try.

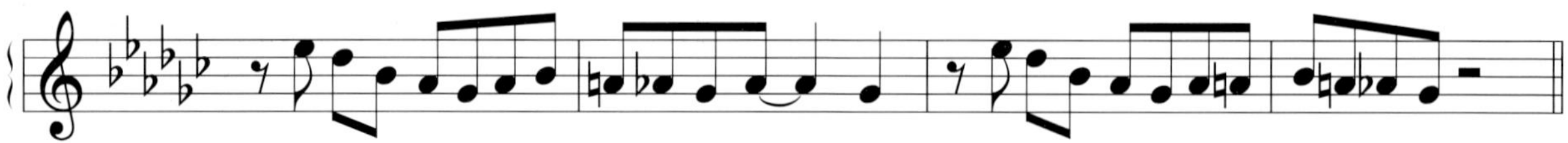

Here's a melody that has the same rhythm as the melody above. I used *e flat* as a "stuck note" while creating a melody below it using only notes from the E-Flat Blues Scale.

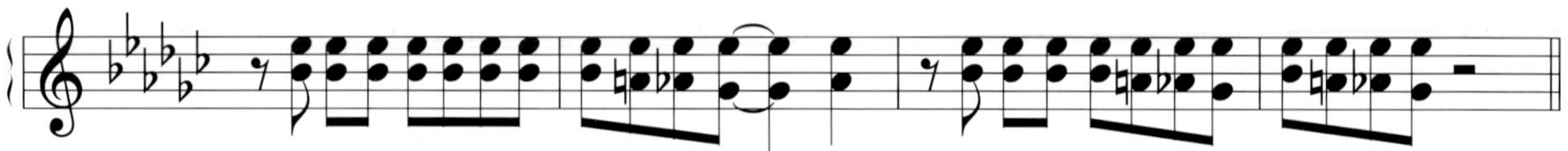

Now and then, play up in the rafters of the piano. The higher register can startle the staleness right out of the air. The second example below looks like another harmless pattern of flowing eighth notes until you try it. The repeated three-note pattern creates a syncopated rhythm against the bass.

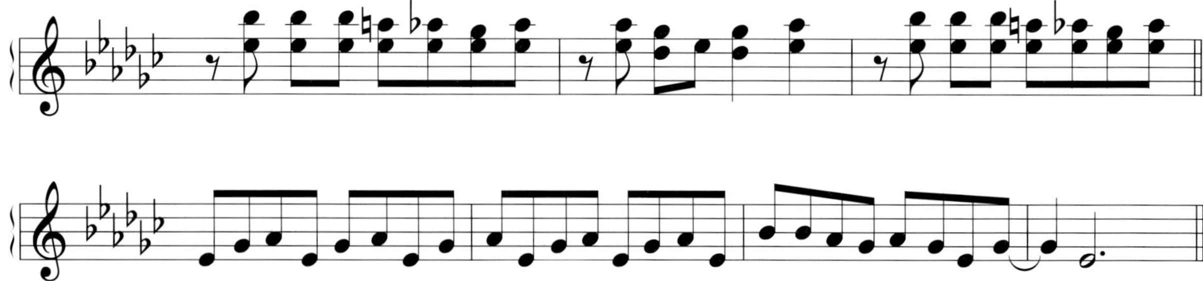

More Ideas for Creating Melodies

Now it's time to get a feeling for quarter notes. With this particular Pattern, quarter notes are more of a challenge than eighth notes. To make it easier, play the example below until you don't have to think about it at all, until all these notes are just a rhythmic feeling.

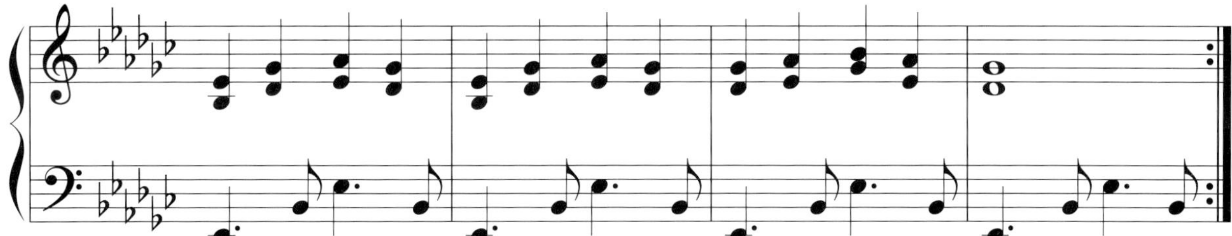

Now play the first melody below with the Pattern in order to feel quarter notes and eighth notes moving together. This will also help mold your hand to these good-sounding Hand Shapes. The second example uses different rhythms and two Hand Shapes instead of just one.

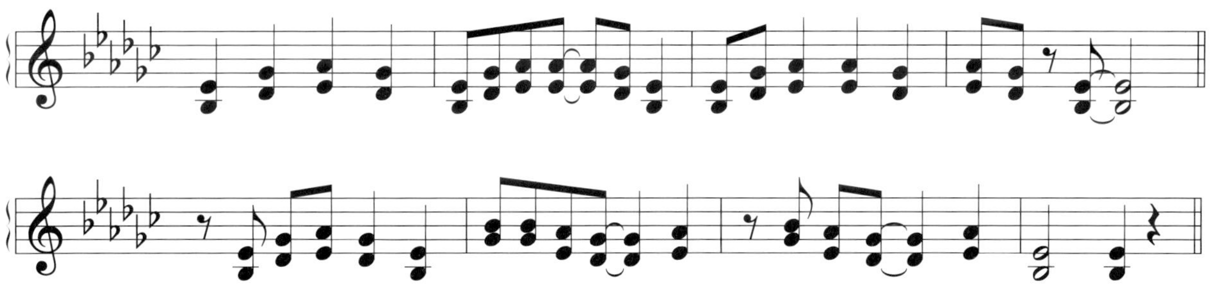

In this example, some of the right-side ideas from above are played with Vacation One. Try playing this same melody with other Vacations.

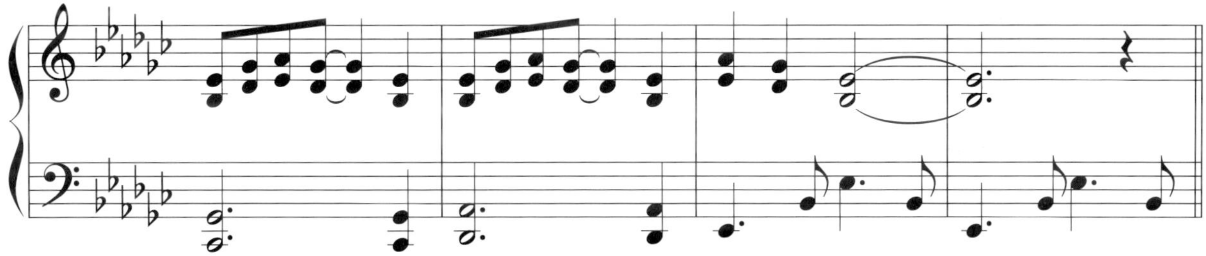

In this example, the left hand moves from Vacation Three to a slight variation on Vacation Five. Though I ran out of room to show it, at this point the music traveled back home to the Pattern.

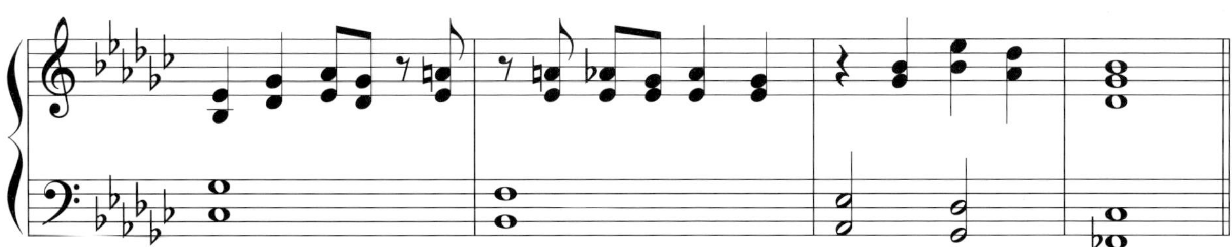

Free Play

It is something to be able to paint a particular picture,
or to carve a statue, and so to make a few objects beautiful;
but it is far more glorious to carve and paint the very atmosphere
and medium through which we look.
To affect the quality of the day—that is the highest of arts.

—Henry David Thoreau

At the end of each section, there has been a *Free Play* piece. First, you played freely on black keys, then on white keys, and then all on keys. What's left now?

Why not take what you have discovered at the piano out into the world? Just as we learn to relate to the piano in an honest, playful way rather than a habitual and mechanical way, so we can also learn to relate to all the circumstances of our life in the same way. We can do anything creatively—whether it be driving to work, brushing our teeth, or taking exams—by allowing new responses to emerge from a state of playful openness.

For this piece, make music in some other part of your day, using anything as your instrument. If we live our lives in the same way we create at the piano—with confidence, openness, and playfulness—we can bring more joy and harmony into a world that always needs more. We can inspire others to live creatively, too.

Henry Miller wrote, "Art is only a means to life, to the life more abundant. It merely points the way." By playing music, we develop new sensitivities and abilities, and these gently seep into the rest of our life. This new awareness spreads out into everything we do, and we begin to feel the music in everything, everywhere.

Looking Ahead

I included these two final pieces to give you a taste of what the future may hold. Also, I wanted to include a few more jazz pieces in this book. These pieces are challenging, so their time might be another day.

The first piece, *Fourth Dimension,* introduces you to Volume 3-A of *Pattern Play* which is all about creating with scales known as *modes.* This piece, though it is played on white keys, is not in the Key of C Major or A Minor. It is in *D Dorian,* one of the many modes. It amazes me how expressive modes are, and yet how few people know about them. This piece also features a different brand of harmony, using chords made out of fourths instead of the usual thirds.

The last piece, *Three-Hand Jazz,* introduces you to sounds explored in Volumes 2-A, Four, and Five of *Pattern Play.* These volumes explore ways to create your own Patterns out of chords made with four or more notes. These chords are called 7th chords, 9th chords, 11th chords, and 13th chords. As a group, I call them "color chords" because they shimmer with so many colorful tones.

There's No End

Though every book must have an end, there is no end to the Patterns that can be discovered and played. Hidden within the silence around us is an endless amount of music, just waiting to be sounded out! How fortunate we are to be creators of music, walking down a road with such beautiful scenery, a road that has no end.

Fourth Dimension

M*odes* have been around for thousands of years, and were once much more popular than their cousins, the Major and Minor Scales. Their expressive powers are now being rediscovered. This piece is in the Key of *D Dorian*. *D* is prominent in the bass, and this makes the white keys sound quite different.

Nearly all our harmony is made by stacking thirds on top of each other to make chords. In this piece, chords are made by stacking fourths. These are known as *fourth stacks*. This is a popular sound in modern music, especially jazz. As usual, there are countless ways to play these Hand Shapes. Consider a basic design made out of four circles. The ways we can vary these four circles to make different designs are without end. Likewise, the ways we can vary the notes of any fourth stack are just as endless. Welcome to the Fourth Dimension. *May the fourths be with you.*

The fifth in the bass clearly establishes that you are in the Key of D Dorian rather than C Major. Play these notes in any other rhythm you like, as long as you keep a strong, solid beat.

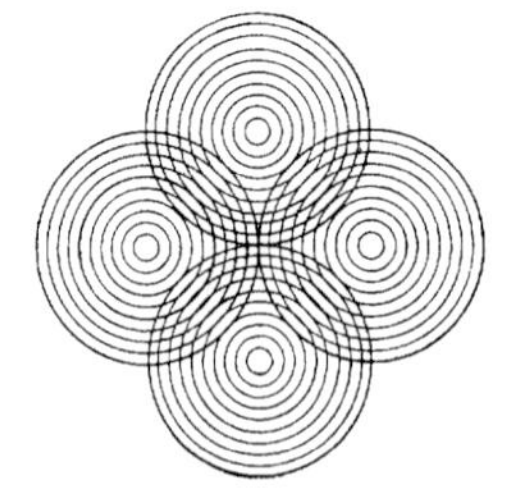

Pattern

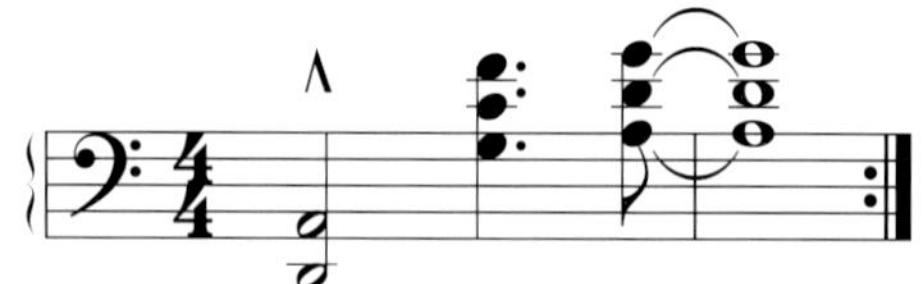

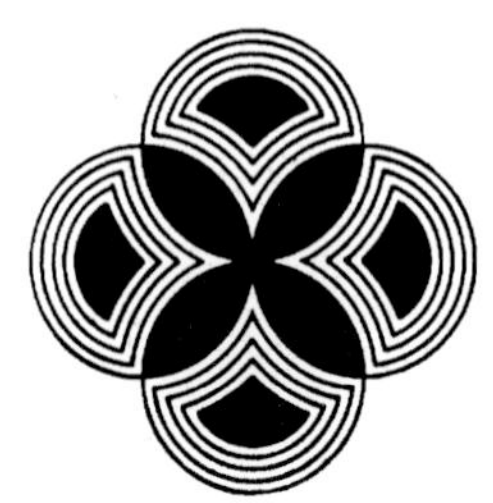

This Vacation is merely the Pattern transposed up a half step to the Key of E-Flat Dorian, shifting from white keys to black. Create melodies with black keys, along with *f* and *c natural*.

Vacation

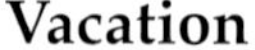

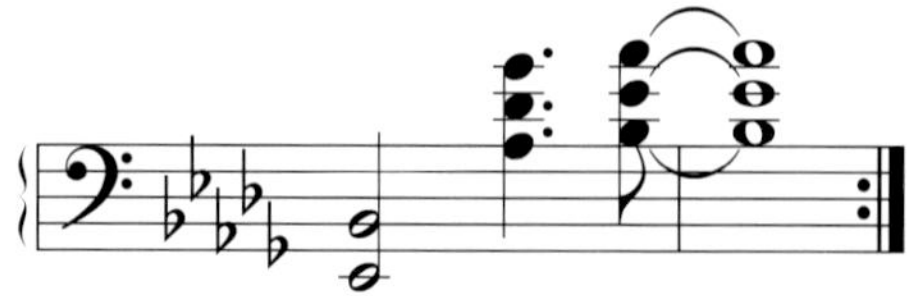

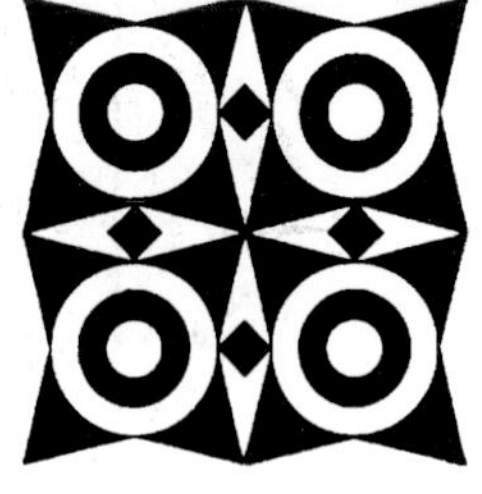

Each design on this page is a variation on the theme of "four similar circles." Here, diamond shapes have been inserted between the circles. Likewise, in this Variation, I inserted another chord in the Pattern.

Pattern Variation One

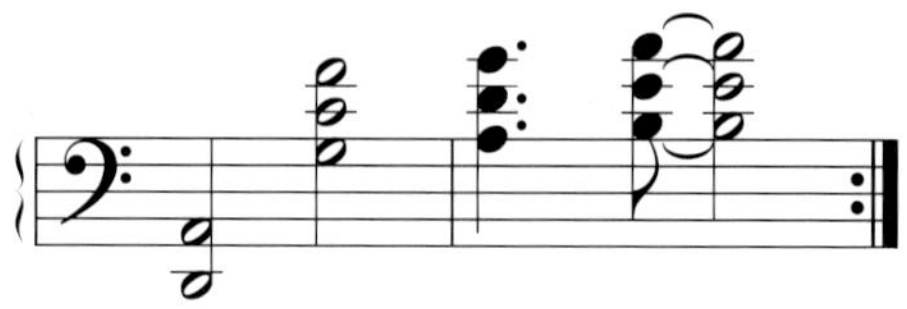

Here, the diamond shapes are enlarged and moved. In this Variation, the sounds of the last Variation are also moved around. Make your own Variations using these same notes in other ways.

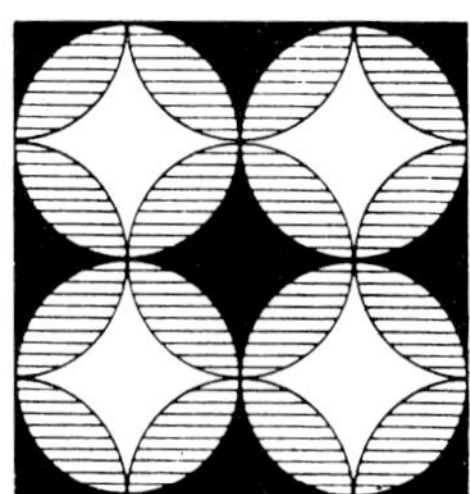

Pattern Variation Two

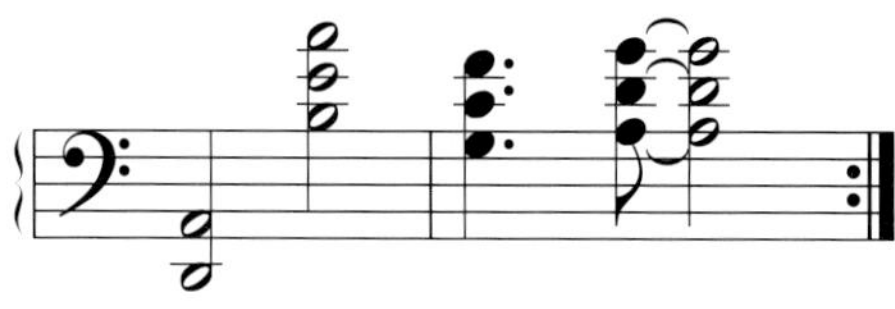

More Variations

So far, you have created Pattern Variations using just a couple of fourth stacks. Now create new Variations using the fourth stacks shown here.

You could use fourth stacks that are higher and lower than these but, generally speaking, jazz players play chords in the neighborhood of *middle c*. If we get too low with chords, we sink into the mud. If we get too high, we not only encroach on the melody's territory, we start sounding rather brittle and tinny.

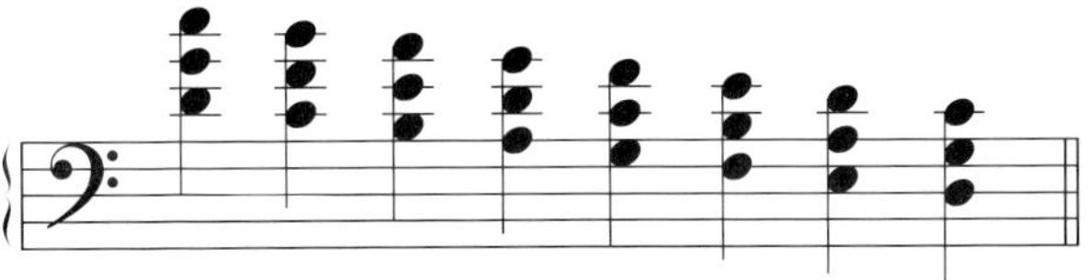

Pattern Variation Three

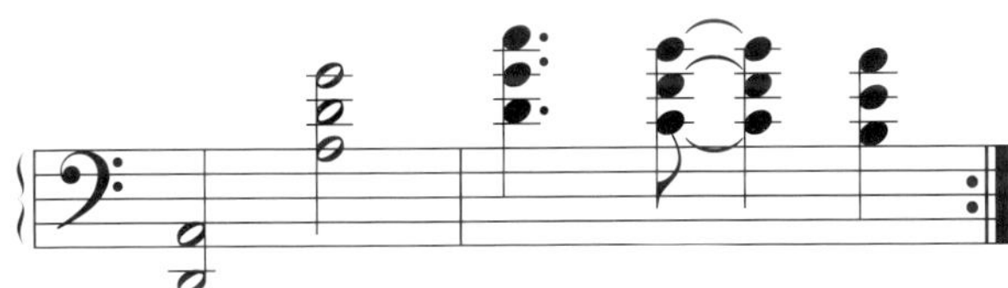

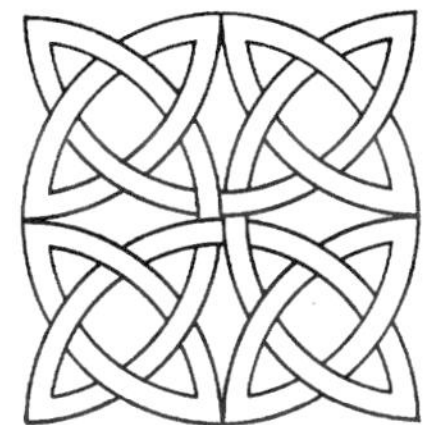

This design features complex variations on the theme of "four circles." Likewise, the rhythms in these next two Variations are also more complex.

Pattern Variation Four

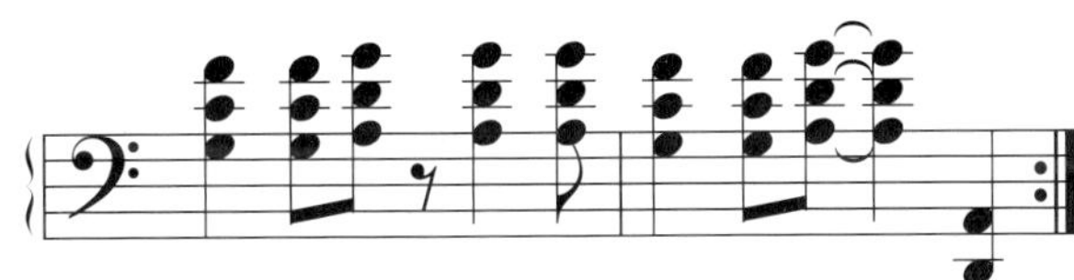

The fifth in the bass doesn't always have to come on the first beat. In fact, the music has much more life when the bass notes make surprise entrances.

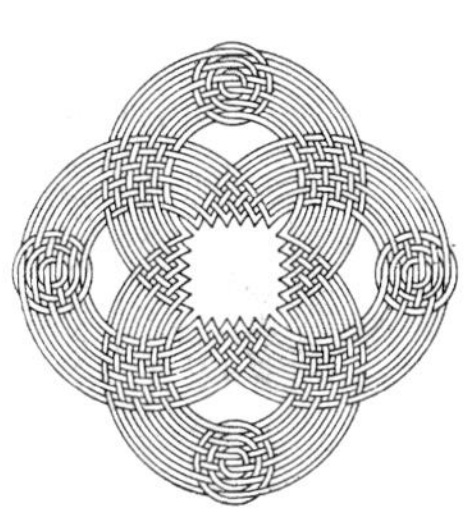

Pattern Variation Five

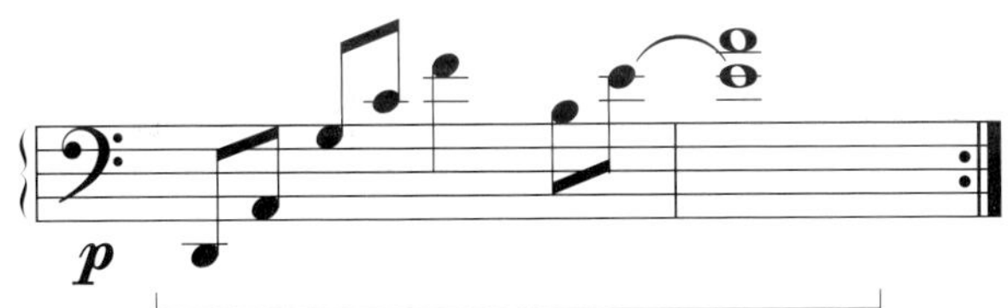

Here the notes of the original Pattern are broken up and played softly. To create an even more dramatic change of mood, play these notes slowly without a beat.

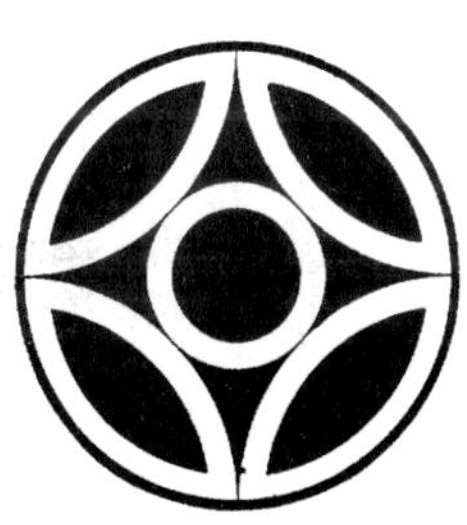

Pattern Variation Six

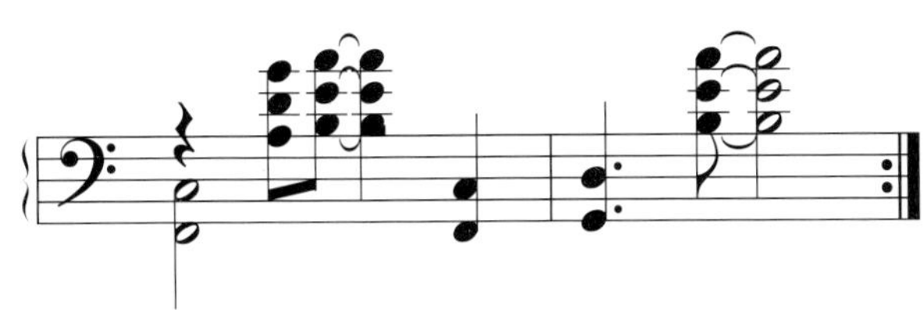

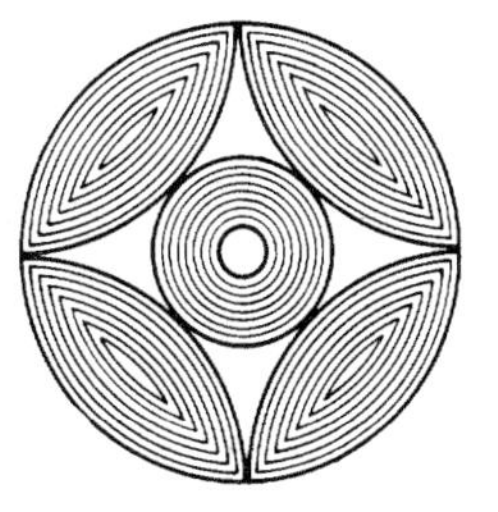

The design becomes even more intricate. In this Pattern Variation, other fifths are used in the bass. Vary their placement to create intricate rhythms.

The One Finger, One Note, One Rhythm Approach

Since this Pattern is one of the most difficult in this book, you may either need to start creating with simple ideas, or quickly develop the patience of a saint. If you choose the first way (much easier), here is a simple and effective approach for creating new rhythms. This approach also works for any other Pattern that has a strong beat.

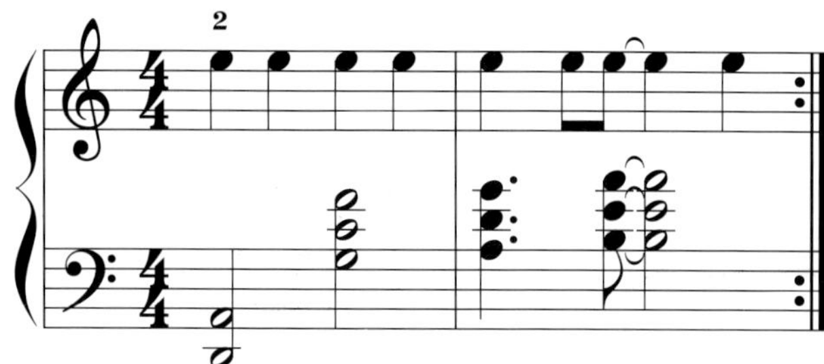

Start creating with just one finger and play on just one key. Find a rhythm you like and play it over and over again. From these humble beginnings, powerful rhythmic ideas will grow. We have to get *into* the rhythm first, and then melodies will come *out*.

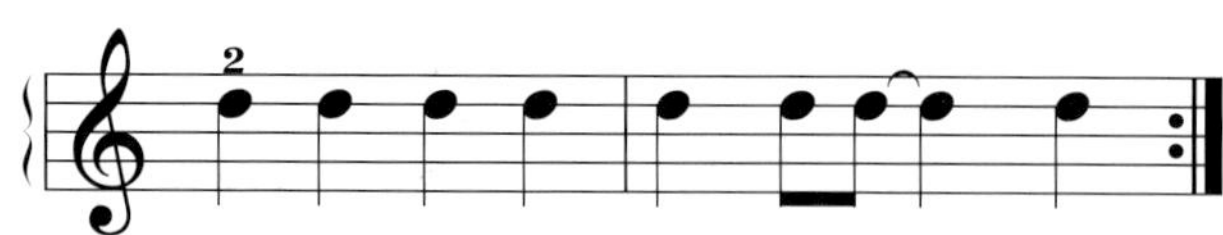

Keep playing the same rhythm with the same finger, but move to another key for a while. Then another. Get your ears acquainted with the different sound that each key makes when played with the Pattern.

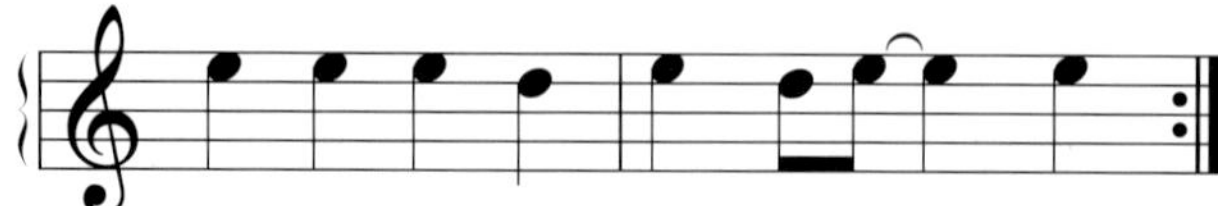

Start to move between a couple of the keys to make melodies, still playing in the same Rhythm Pattern, and still using one finger.

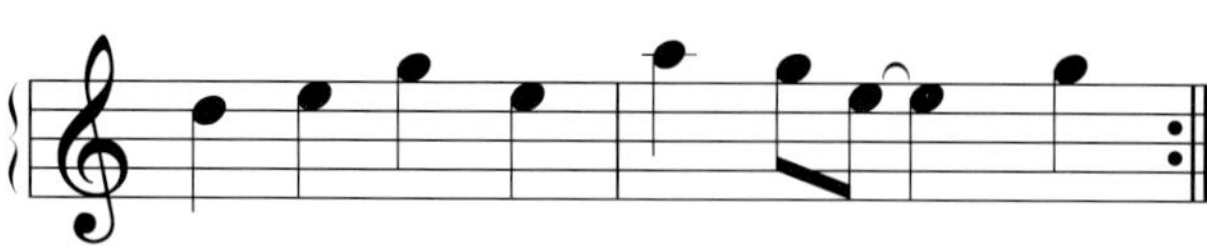

Once you have a solid rhythmic feeling and you don't have to think about what you're doing, bring the rest of your fingers into play. Start creating on just three or four keys, so you don't have to move your arm. Stay with that same Rhythm Pattern.

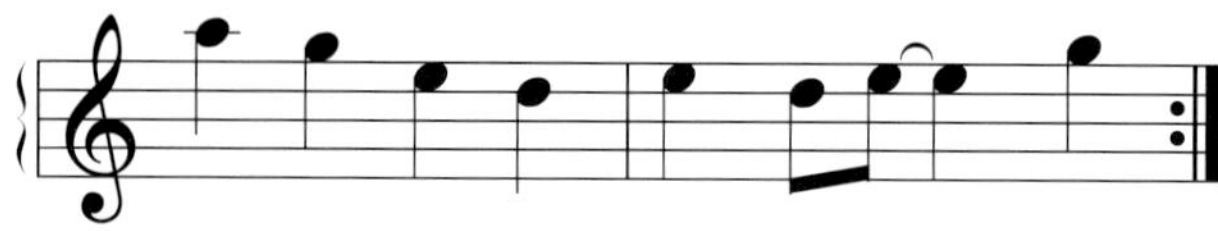

Here's another melodic pattern made from the same group of four notes used in the last example. Create other melodies using these four notes and the same Rhythm Pattern.

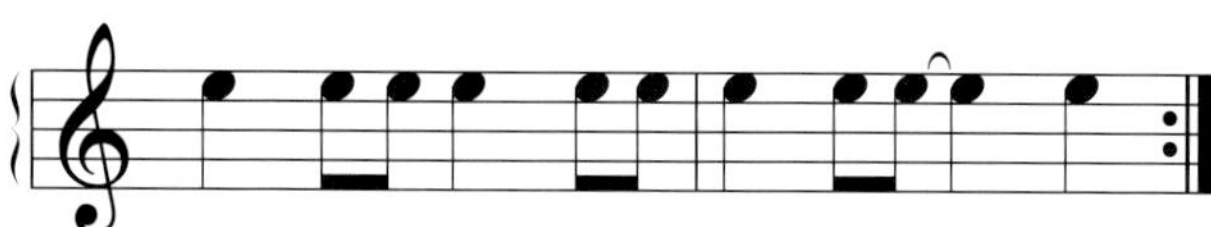

Then start over again with a new rhythm that you like. Go through the same approach. Here's another rhythm to try.

If you take this approach a number of times with a number of different rhythms, soon you will have many interesting Rhythm Patterns in your hands. You will end up with many more rhythms than if you had just played in a habitual way. Best of all, you will discover that, as you improvise, your collection of Rhythm Patterns will begin to combine with each other to make new and unusual Patterns. This creates a constant source of surprise and delight. It all starts with simple rhythms.

Advanced Ideas

Try creating with fourth stacks on your right side, too.

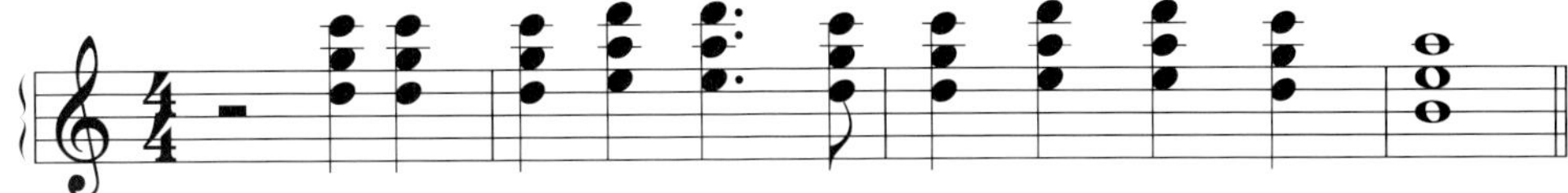

Try breaking up these fourth stacks in various ways.

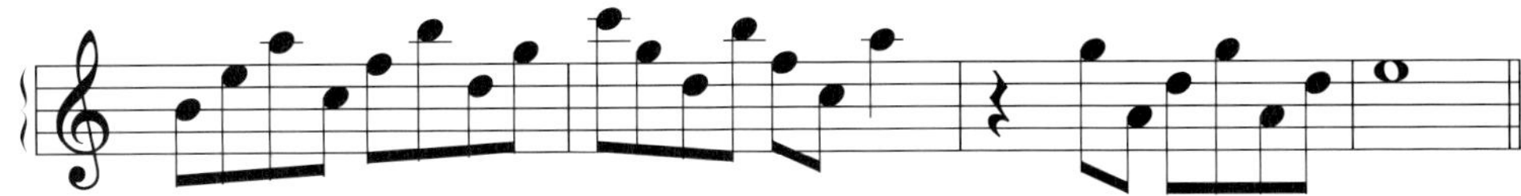

This melody leaps around while the hand stays in the Hand Shape of a fourth stack.

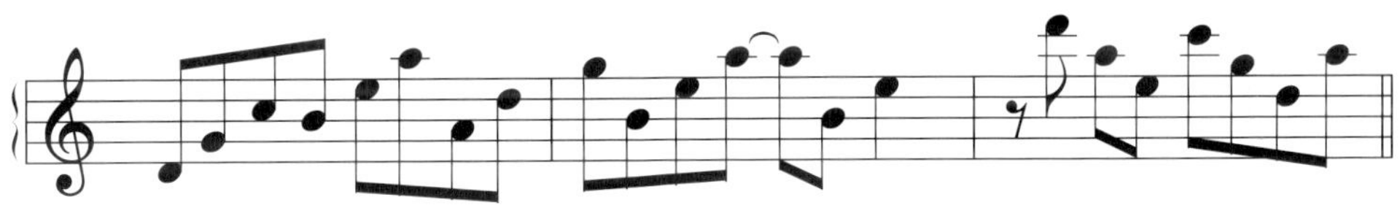

Octaves can cut through the roar of the bass notes. Repeated tones can build intensity.

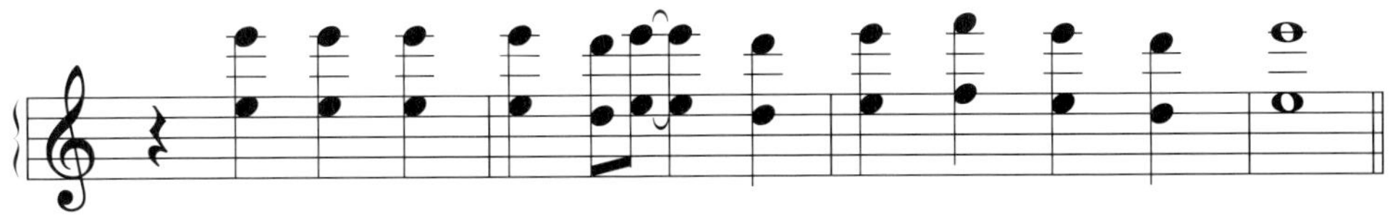

Add a fourth dimension to octaves by adding a fourth above the bottom note and a fourth below the top.

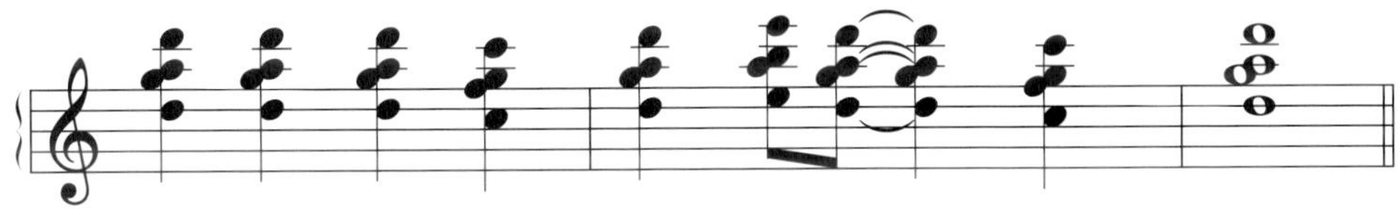

Here are three ways that the last Hand Shape might move around.

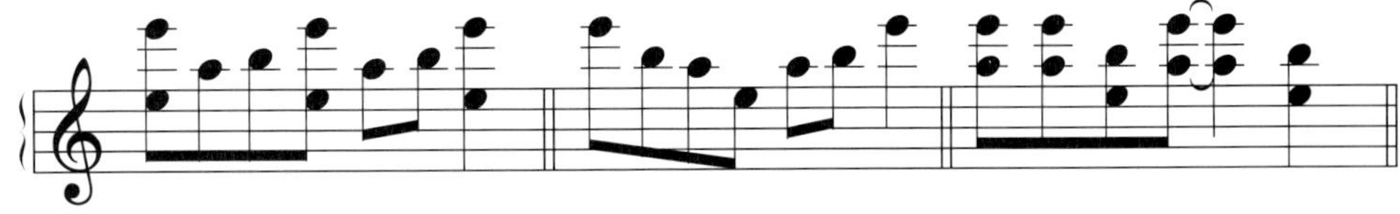

Try playing your two sides together to make a powerful, driving sound.

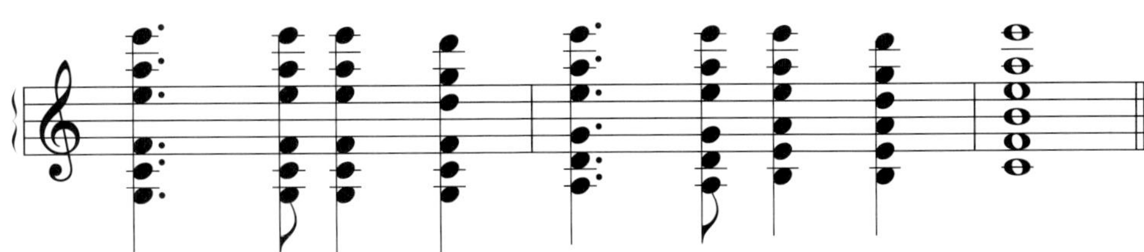

Three-Hand Jazz (Solo or Duet)

Volume 2-A and **Volume Four** of *Pattern Play* explore how you can create your own Patterns in many musical styles using seventh chords. These chords feature the sound of a seventh between the root and the top note. Pattern One of this piece features the sound of seventh chords, though these chords will soon be transformed into more complex chords (9th and 13th chords) in Pattern Two.

Volume 2-A and **Volume Five** explore how to create in many styles of music with fuller-sounding harmonies—9th, 11th, and 13th chords—"color chords." For now, this piece introduces the sound and feel of the most essential color chords to know for playing jazz, the chords I often refer to as "the alphabet of jazz." For now, it is enough to play with them, explore them, and prepare your hands and ears for creating your own Patterns with them another day.

Pattern One

Begin by playing this Pattern made of seventh chords until you can do it by memory. While keeping a beat, create various Rhythm Patterns with these three chords. Later, when you add some bass tones to these chords, this humble Pattern will become the most important Pattern in all of piano jazz.

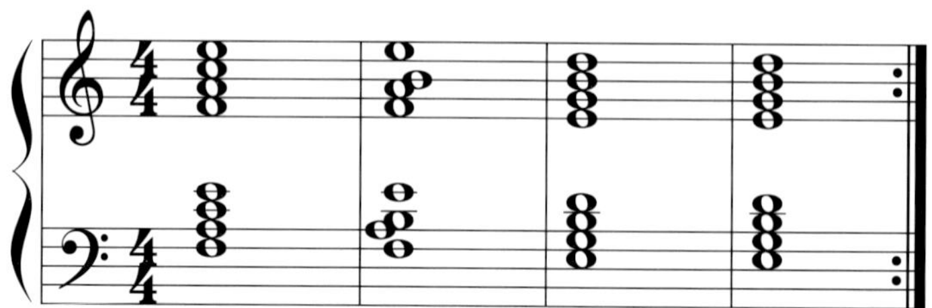

Creating with Chord Tones

Now break up the right-hand chords to make melodies while playing the left hand as written. Keep your right hand in the shape of the chord for a while, as in the three examples below. Move the same Hand Shapes up an octave or two and create melodies there. Creating this way will prepare your ears and hands for what is to come. Remember to *swing the eighth notes*, as in the blues pieces.

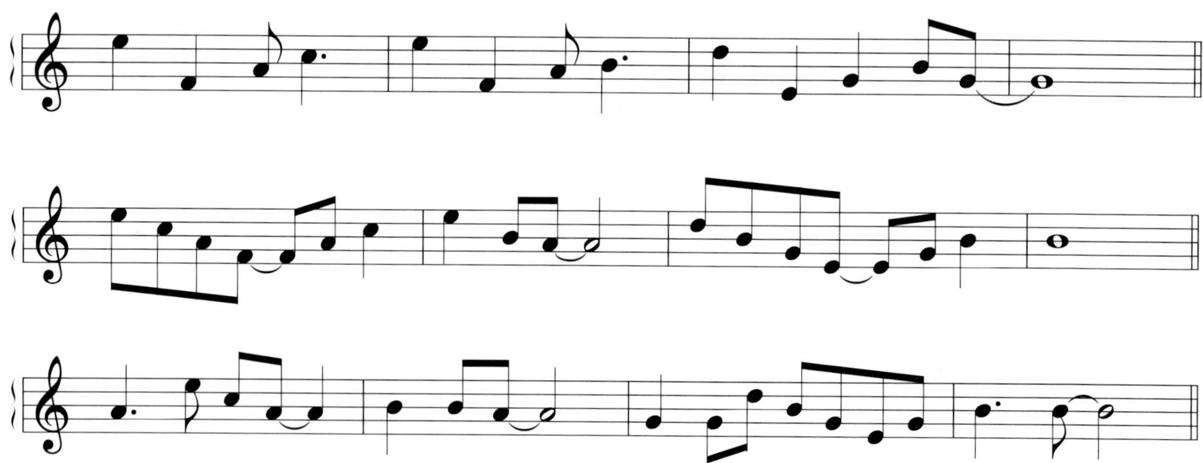

Comping

In jazz piano playing, the left hand doesn't just play a chord at the beginning of a measure and then sit around doing nothing for four beats. It's usually quite active, especially when the melody is pausing. I wrote earlier that this rhythmic way of playing chords is called comping. In the first example below, the left side keeps the music going. The second example features a common comping Pattern.

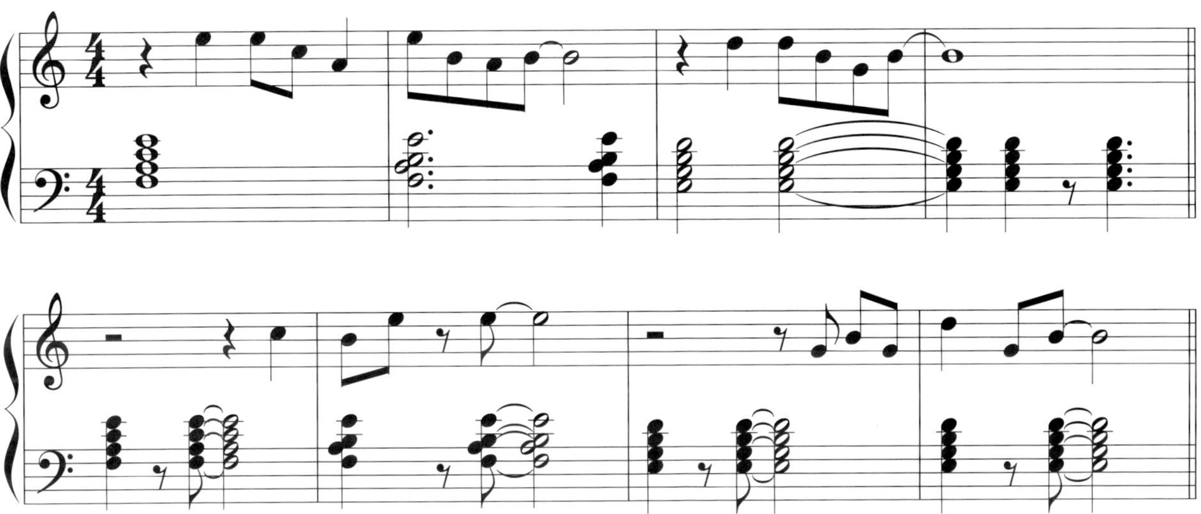

The left hand functions like a good friend. Just as a friend supports us, so the left hand in the first example plays right along with the right. Just as a friend will challenge us to keep going when we are losing our desire, so the left hand challenges the right in the second example. In the third example, the left hand does some of both while the right hand (staying within Hand Shapes) flies around the piano.

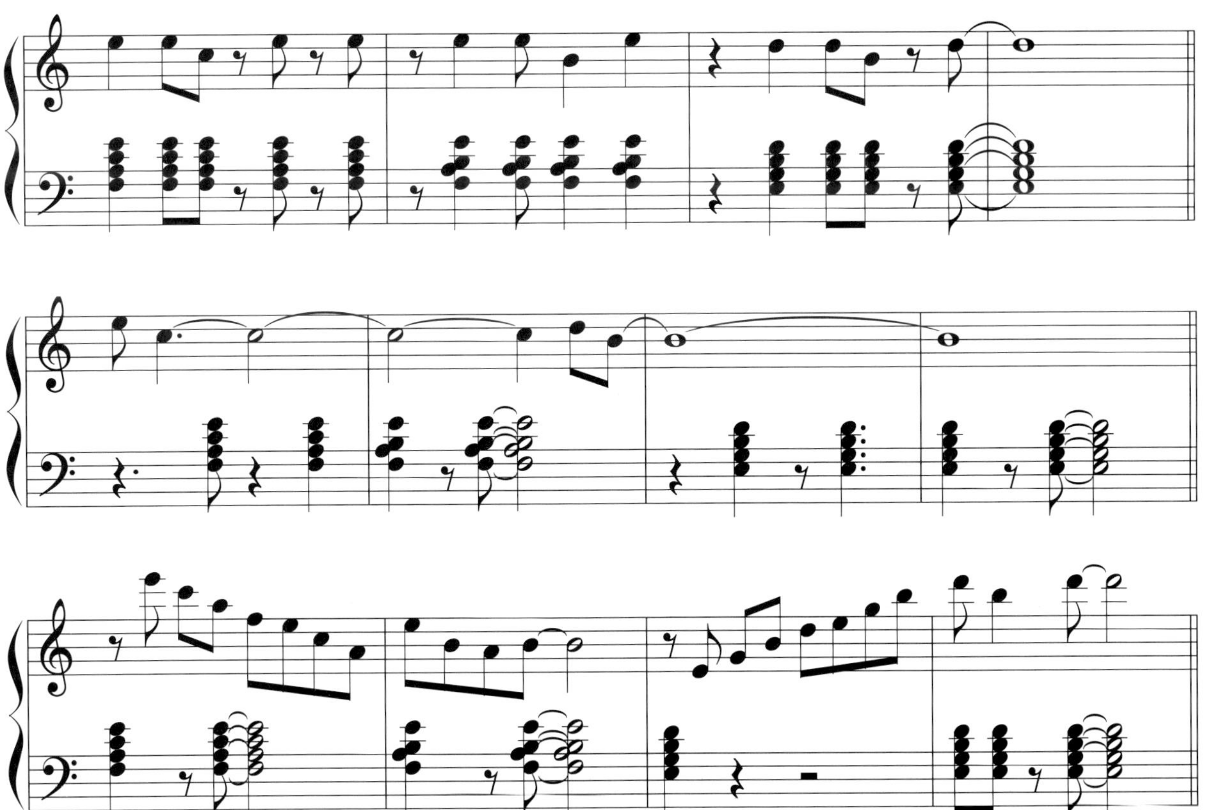

Melody Ideas

After creating melodies using only notes of the chords, it's time to create with other tones. Create with *any* white keys now. Listen to the ways the non-chord tones create new tensions.

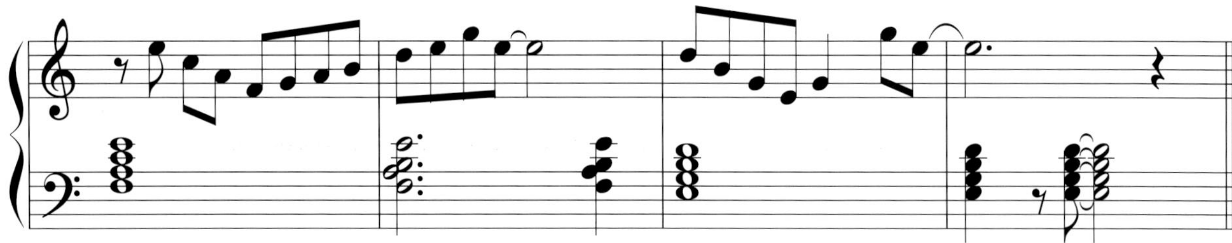

To prepare yourself for playing runs of eighth notes, play the example below a number of times with the Pattern (in swing rhythm, of course). Then, while keeping in the same rhythm, change these notes to make your own melodies. After you do this for a while, change the rhythms of your left-side chords to make more interesting comping patterns.

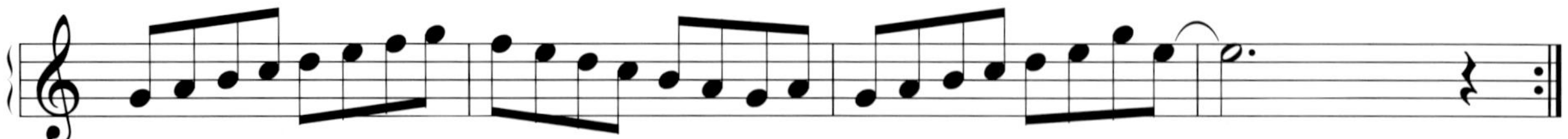

After playing with these chord tones and non-chord tones, your hands and ears have a good sense of where the consonant tones are. Now it is time to start going further "outside." Beneath each of the four chord tones is a lower neighbor a half step away. As you explore the sounds of these lower neighbors, keep bringing your hand back to the original chord shapes. Now you're playing jazz!

The fingerings are strange in the example below, but they allow your hand to keep returning to the original chords. In jazz, since you are creating as you go, it helps to actually practice awkward fingerings to prepare yourself for any situation. This is different from classical pieces where you know exactly what notes you will be playing, and it is wise to practice only the best fingerings.

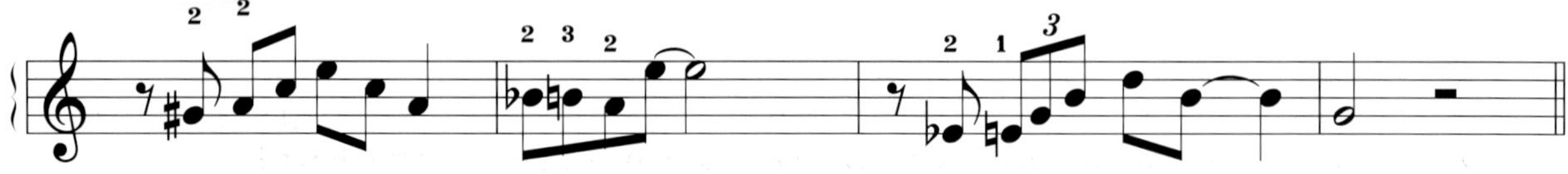

Now do everything at once. Move freely around the top half of your piano using the chord tones (the notes in the original Pattern), plus all the white keys in the Key of C (non-chord tones), and all the lower neighbors of the chord tones. Every single key on the piano becomes playable! Every key is either a chord tone, a lower neighbor to a chord tone, or a tone in the Key of C Major. Now you've got every key "on hand."

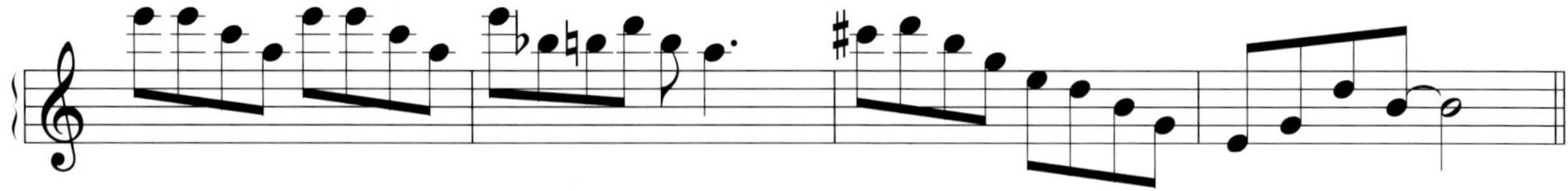

Entering Three-Hand Land

How did this piece get its name? In jazz piano, and in most piano styles, there are three parts: a melody that usually lives in the upper half of the piano, a bass part that always lives in the lower ranges, and a harmonic accompaniment that usually lives in the mid-range of the piano. So far, in this piece, we have the melody and harmonic accompaniment, so now it's time to add the bass.

With three parts to play (bass, chords, and melody) and only two hands, what's a person to do? As long as you play solo jazz piano (in other words, as long as you are not working with a bass player), you will have to solve this problem. This page and the next explore some solutions.

Pattern Two

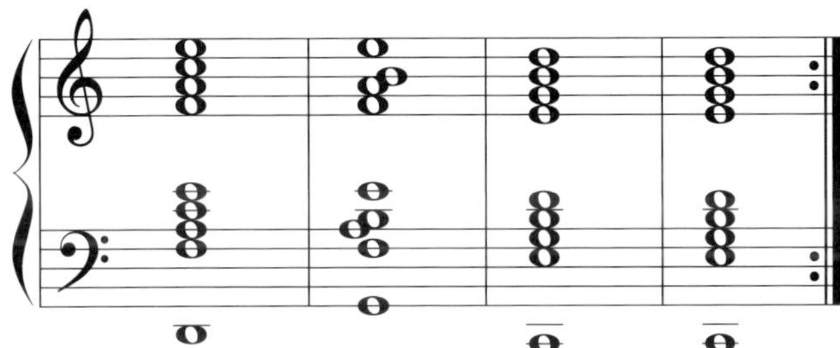

This Pattern is the same as Pattern One but bass tones are now added. The seventh chords in Pattern One turn out to be the top notes of more complex chords. In case you know or want to know, these chords are *Dm9, G13,* and *Cmaj9.* I'll explore these in Volume 2-A and beyond.

Below, the left hand plays the bottom two parts while the right hand plays the melody. This three-hand style works well with ballads and other pieces that have a mild beat and don't need a rhythmic bass to propel the music forward. Notice how, in this example, there are no bass notes in the second and third measures, and the bass tones comes after the chord in the fourth.

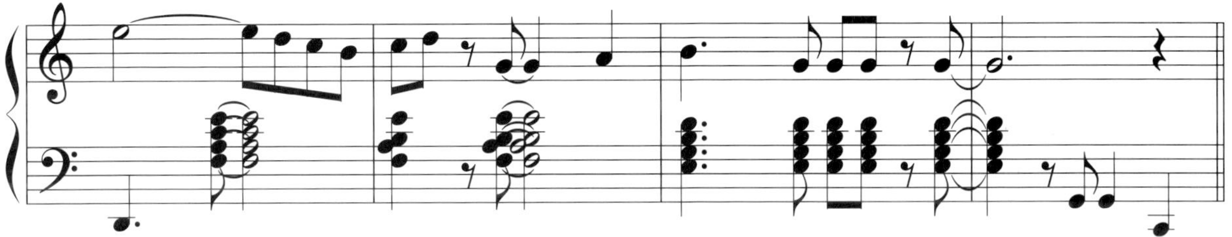

Vacation (Pattern Two in D-Flat Major)

For a Vacation, why not move every note of Pattern Two up a half step and create melodies in the Key of D-Flat Major? This rich Key features all five black keys plus *c* and *f*. Notice how, in the example below, I also included a half-step lower neighbor (*f flat*) below the *f* simply because it sounded good.

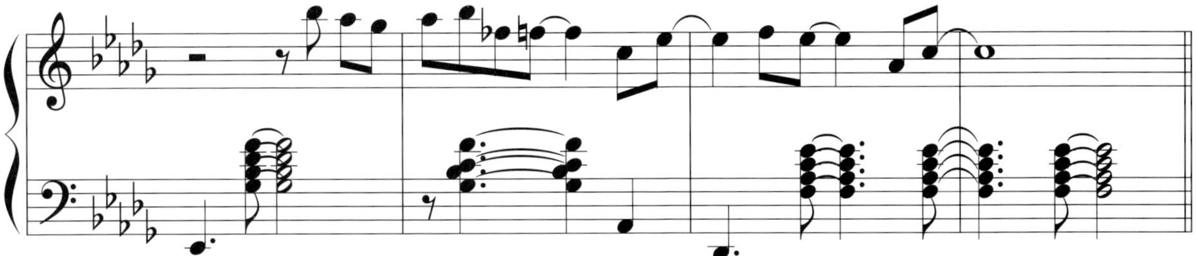

For another Vacation, move up another half step to the Key of D Major. Then to E-Flat and E. At this point, the left-hand chords are starting to crowd the right hand's domain. What to do? See page 143.

Walking Bass

There are other ways to play the three parts (melody, chords, and bass) with two hands. This page explores two popular styles, both of which feature a stronger, more rhythmic sound in the bass. In these styles, the left hand is employed full-time as a bass player. The first example features a walking bass, great for up-tempo pieces because of the steady, driving rhythm. Learn the bass line first by memory, and then break up the chords of the Pattern to make melodies, as in this first example.

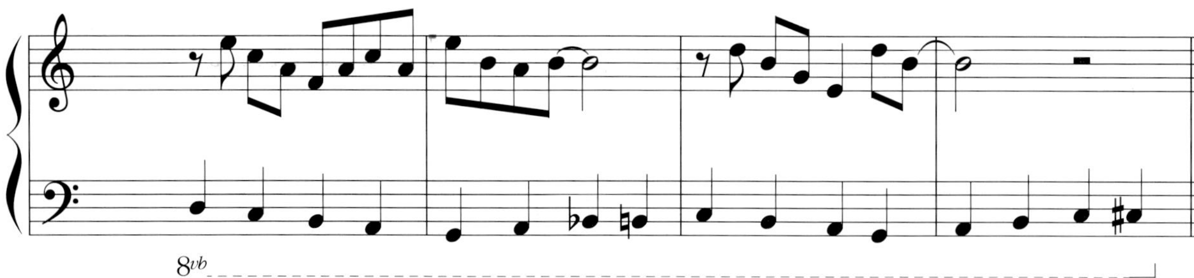

Now let's return to three-hand land. Below, your right hand alternates between playing chords and melodies while your left hand just keeps walking step-by-step between the bass notes. You could also play just the bass and chords and leave the melody to a friend who plays saxophone, trumpet, flute, kazoo, whatever! Or you could sing a melody if you feel so inspired, even singing nonsense syllables. Jazz singers do this all the time. It's called *scat singing.*

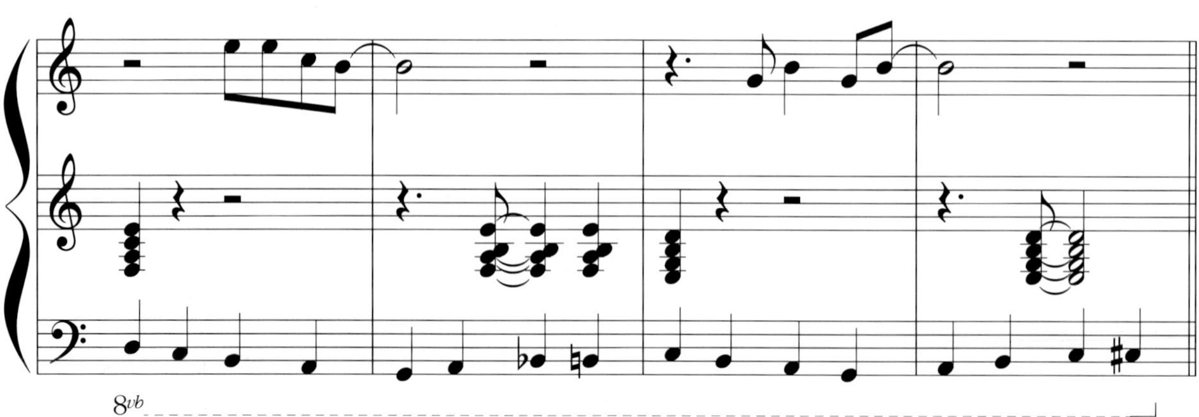

Bossa Nova

Here, Pattern Two is played in *Bossa Nova* style. Your left hand plays a rhythmic bass line made of the root of the chord and the note a fourth below. Your right hand plays the jazz chords. Either add a melody with your right hand as you did above, alternating between playing melody and chords, or have someone else add the melody—another pianist, a singer, perhaps a sax player.

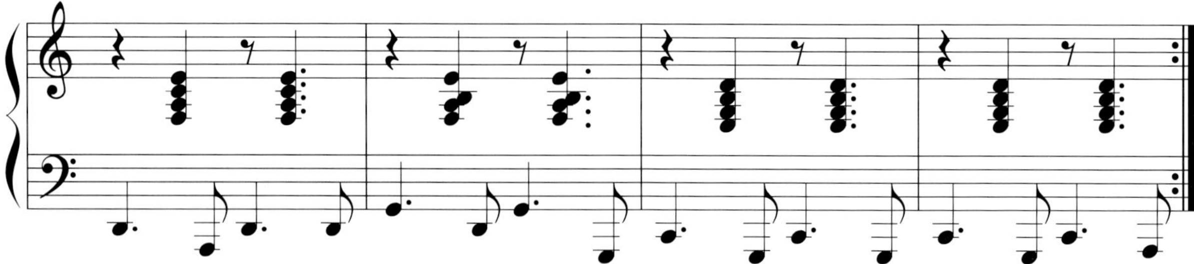

The Alphabet of Jazz

Just as the colors on a color wheel are derived from three basic colors (blue, red, and yellow), most of the chords used in jazz can be derived from the three flavors of chords in Pattern Two—the first is a minor 9th, the second is a dominant 13th, and the third is a major 9th. If you want to prepare yourself for playing jazz, you can do no better than to learn to play Pattern Two in all twelve Keys. If you can play these thirty-six chords (three chords in twelve Keys), then you have a very solid foundation for all further chord study. Again, I'll go into this in depth in Volume Five. Below, I've written the left side of Pattern Two in D Major. Create as before, first with chord tones, then non-chord tones in D Major, then adding lower neighbors, and finally playing it in ballad style, walking bass style, and Bossa Nova style. The chords in this Key are named E minor 9, A13, and D major 9.

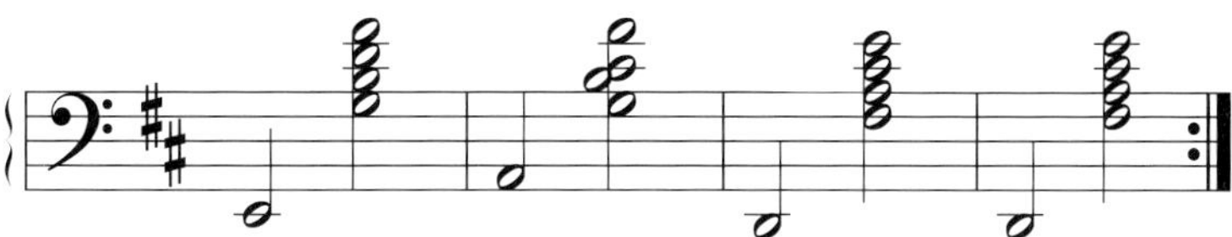

Now move Pattern Two down a half step from C to play the Pattern in the Key of B Major. You played in D-Flat Major on the page before last, and perhaps D, E-Flat, and E. By the Key of E Major, the chords are getting a bit too high, so for the remaining Keys (F Major, G-Flat, G, A-Flat, A, and B-Flat), the top two notes of each chord are played an octave lower, keeping the chord in the neighborhood of *middle c*. The Patterns in F Major and G Major would then look like this.

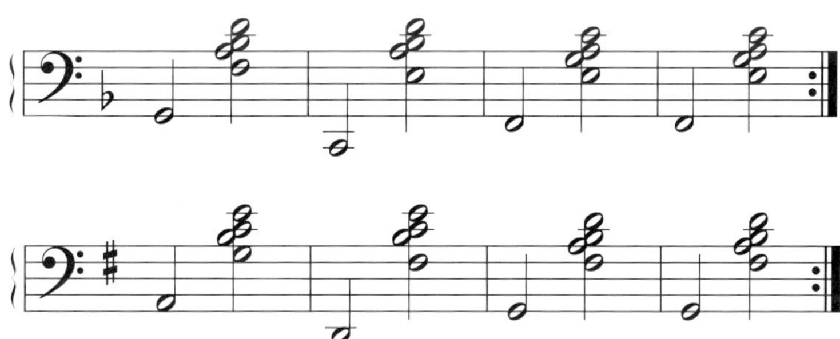

This Pattern is known as a *two-five-one progression* (written in Roman numerals as II, V, and I) because the chords are the second, fifth, and first chords in a Major Key. As you learn to play this in all twelve Keys, keep a strong feeling for the beat, and a strong feeling for the music. This Pattern is not to be reduced to a mechanical exercise, but played as another doorway into creativity and joy.

Thank You!

Thank you for taking this journey with me. Thanks to everyone who has helped me create the *Pattern Play* books. I would especially like to thank my first piano teacher and dear friend, Donald Denegar, for awakening my love of both piano literature and music teaching. My deep gratitude also to Aadil Palkhivala, whose inspiring classes gave me the energy and clarity to create for over a decade.

I am grateful to all those who have given me invaluable help with these books: Akiko was the mighty force that finally pushed this book (and its author) out into the world. Alfred Rordame, with humor and quirky wisdom, helped me make visible whatever I imagined. Jerome Grey, jazz teacher, widened my path with his approach. Special thanks to Anne Reese, Susan Smith, Steve Burgess, Phil Jensen, Chris Trivelas, Sydney Wallace, Karen Gale, Amy Yokoyama, Mike Pierson, Andrew Peate, Darden Burns, and Gina Mikkelsen. Thanks to Kevin Helppie and Jaclyn Weber for helping me realize the profound joy in co-creating music. Thanks to my family members, students, friends, and colleagues for inspiring me to keep creating and refining. There is not enough time or space to thank you all.

Index of Pieces